Unruly Waters

Unruly Waters

A SOCIAL AND ENVIRONMENTAL HISTORY
OF THE BRAZOS RIVER

KENNA LANG ARCHER

University of New Mexico Press | Albuquerque

© 2015 by the University of New Mexico Press
All rights reserved. Published 2015
Printed in the United States of America
20 19 18 17 16 15   1 2 3 4 5 6

Library of Congress Cataloging-in-Publication Data
Archer, Kenna Lang, 1982–
  Unruly waters : a social and environmental history of the Brazos River / Kenna
Lang Archer. — First edition.
     pages cm
  Includes bibliographical references and index.
  ISBN 978-0-8263-5587-4 (hardback) — ISBN 978-0-8263-5588-1 (electronic)
   1. Brazos River (Tex.)—History. 2. Brazos River Valley (Tex.)—Environmental
conditions—History. 3. Brazos River Valley (Tex.)—Social conditions—History.
I. Title. II. Title: Social and environmental history of the Brazos River.
  F392.B842A75 2015
  976.4—dc23
                                    2014031881

Cover photo courtesy the Texas Collection, Baylor University, Waco, Texas
Cover design and text composition by Catherine Leonardo
Composed in Sabon LT Std Roman 10/13   ·
Display type is Minion Pro and Syntax LT Std

This work is dedicated to Charles Turnbo, the author and uncle and vibrant personality who inspired my first history paper and inspired all of those around him. Though cut short far too soon, his was a life well lived.

Contents

Illustrations

Maps

Acknowledgments

Archivists, curators, poets, painters, family members, nonprofits, and colleagues have contributed to my work, making this a collaborative effort in the truest sense of the word. Most obviously, numerous institutions and organizations provided funding for my research, and since my work began with that tangible support, it seems only fitting that I begin my acknowledgments there. The Texas Collection and the Poage Legislative Library at Baylor University granted me travel fellowships that allowed me to spend several months poring over their respective archives, and the Dolph Briscoe Center for American History at the University of Texas at Austin, likewise, gave me funding for research that allowed me to spend an entire summer in the well-endowed stacks of that institution. This project grew from work that I began at Texas Tech University, which provided me generous funding through the Department of History, the University Women's Club, and the Helen Jones Foundation. I am profoundly grateful for the travel grants and other awards, as my ideas on the Brazos River would have been meaningless without an ability to expand on them through archival work that is always time-consuming and often costly.

Along those lines, I owe much to the staff of the libraries, archives, and agencies that I visited. The following individuals, in particular, gave of their time generously and abundantly: Sister Maria Flores, CDP, and Joseph De Leon at Our Lady of the Lake University's Center for Mexican American Studies and Research; Dara Flinn at Rice University's Woodson Research Center; Nikki Thomas at the University of San Antonio's Special Collections; Barbara Rust at the National Archives and Records Administration, Fort Worth Division; Samuel Duncan at the Amon Carter Museum; Michael Danella at the Army

Corps of Engineers, Fort Worth; Lea Worcester and Ben Huseman at the University of Texas at Arlington's Special Collections; Sandy Rogers at the Texas Prison Museum; Geoff Hunt, Amie Oliver, and Tiffany Sowell at Baylor University's Texas Collection; Ben Rogers at Baylor University's Poage Legislative Library; Amanda Cagle and Catherine Hastedt at Texas A&M University's J. Wayne Stark Galleries; Bill Page at Texas A&M University's Cushing Library; Nancy Ross at the Carnegie History Center in Bryan, Texas; Velma Spivey at the Brazos Valley African American Museum; Jamie Murray at the Brazoria County Historical Museum; Michael Grauer at the Panhandle-Plains Historical Museum; Claire Howard at the University of Texas's Blanton Museum of Art; Janet Neugebauer and Monte Monroe at Texas Tech University's Southwest Collection; Catherine Best at the University of Texas's Center for American History; and Shawn Carlson at the Star of the Republic Museum. It hardly seems adequate merely to list these individuals, but for now, it must suffice for me to say thank you one more time.

I also owe a debt of gratitude to the individuals who have guided this research. Dr. Mark Stoll read through multiple drafts of my chapters and talked through countless iterations of my ideas, giving of his time, skill, and intellectual energy in a way that was both gracious and generous. He embodied, in every way, the characteristics that we all seek in a mentor and guide: I asked more of him than I probably should have, and he gave still more than I asked. Drs. D. C. Jackson and Char Miller, likewise, offered guidance and support as they read through early drafts of this work or acted as a sounding board for my shifting ideas about development. To have received this assistance from scholars in my field (men whom I admire greatly) is something for which I am intensely grateful.

Individuals outside of the field of environmental history also gave of their time, critiquing my work and generally helping me to make this riparian history both relevant and engaging. Mrs. Maggie Elmore and Drs. Miguel Levario, Ethan Schmidt, Sean Cunningham, Aliza Wong, and Philip Pope shared their time as well as their intellectual energy with me. Their input—given generously and abundantly—shaped my project in ways that I never anticipated but for which I am profoundly grateful. Dr. Luis Crotte read through my Spanish translations and helped me to ensure that I maintained a certain level of accuracy, and to him I also say a very heartfelt (but not at all sufficient) thank-you. Without that assistance, I almost certainly would still be working to untangle the meaning behind the seventeenth- and eighteenth-century ecclesiastical writings that I used.

Finally, my husband gave of his time and mental energy in such a way that I shortchange him by calling it "generous." He supported me financially, emotionally, and verbally as I worked toward my doctoral degree as a long-distance and commuting student, giving up much so that I might pursue my work as a student. That support continued after my graduation as I began work on this book project. No thank-you could ever suffice, but I say it again anyway. To my husband and my complement: thank you, my love, for your support, guidance, and patience . . . you are a good man and an encouraging spirit.

One final note—all that is good in this book is a reflection of the support that I have received along the way, and what mistakes, inconsistencies, or simplifications might exist are a reflection only on myself.

Introduction

The Brazos is an unpleasant stream. Its waters are at all times muddy; its banks are generally low and present a raw edge to the eye as you pass along; and in many places the navigation is rendered difficult, by reason of the many snags. At its mouth, there is a bar, generally having not more than five or six feet of water; and the channel so narrow that a vessel can only pass through with a fair wind. Three vessels had been wrecked on the coast the past season. The remains of two of them, lay in sight partly buried in the sand.
—ANDREW AMOS PARKER, *Trip to the West and Texas*, 1835

Since the days of the first settlement on the river, the Arms of God have alternately been raised in wrath or extended in a benediction. They have lashed the river bottom farmers in times of flood and have blessed them with the best crops in all Texas in years of moderate water flow. In the 28,000,000 acres of land in the Brazos Valley is the most fertile land in the United States, land richer than that of the Valley of the Nile, according to agriculture experts.
—DICK VAUGHAN, "Federal Government Funds," 1934

In water-thirsty Texas, engineers try to make every drop of water do its duty. In the Brazos River projects, they seek to make each drop do its duty several times over.
—BRAZOS RIVER AUTHORITY, *The River*, ca. 1950

IN 1957, TWO MEN—each a politician in his own way—began exchanging letters on the subject of Brazos River improvement. Both of the writers expressed some amount of frustration with the prospect of developing what a 1934 newspaper article had dubbed the "wild and wooly Brazos."[1] But one man found the outlook to be particularly bleak. Writing of the floods and droughts that seemed so often to darken any possibility of capital accumulation or urban growth, this man eventually made known what must have been both a deeply personal and an unexpectedly difficult confession: "It will surely be fine if I can just wake up some morning and find there 'ain't any Brazos River problem.' Maybe if I don't look real close, this problem will go away. But I am not quite as hopeful as you are."[2] The river of 1957 looked rather like the river of 1857, so any number of improvement-minded individuals might have penned these words. The identity of the author, however, was both unexpected and notable. These words about the unruly waters of the Brazos River were penned not by an insolvent businessman, thwarted farmer, or rattled mother but by the river's champion, Democratic congressman William Robert (W. R.) Poage, in a private letter to John D. McCall, general counsel for the Brazos River Conservation and Reclamation District.

W. R. Poage served in the halls of Washington, D.C., and Austin, Texas, during the early and mid-twentieth century, and he worked throughout his congressional career on behalf of the Brazos River. He defended the river's virtues and drew attention to its limitations, seeking to transform the waterway into a space that captured the ideals that generations of Texans had bestowed upon it. Though better known nationally for his work on behalf of agricultural interests, many Texans came to view Congressman Poage as the iconic figure, the patriarch, the symbol for Brazos development. The Brazos River Conservation and Reclamation District (known regionally as the Reclamation District and renamed the Brazos River Authority in 1953) also strove throughout the twentieth century to tame this impetuous river. Representatives for the Reclamation District proposed dam projects and built dams; they supported lawmakers and pushed legislation; and they managed (or attempted to manage) the development of a watershed that encompassed close to 43,000 square miles of the Texas landscape.

Both Congressman Poage and the employees of the Reclamation District worked tirelessly and zealously for improvement of the Brazos River and seemed never to waver, at least in public, from their stated goal of full control over the basin. Yet, even these stalwart advocates grew somewhat frustrated with the task set before developers. Bankers, farmers, merchants, and laborers from across the state and from different political groups would have empathized with the almost-despairing thoughts expressed in Congressman Poage's letter. Indeed, the men and women who lived within the confines of the Brazos River watershed during the nineteenth and twentieth centuries regularly voiced their frustration with the pace of Brazos development and the regularity of Brazos outbursts. They submitted a flurry of letters to regional politicians, produced countless editorials for local newspapers, and formed local associations that advocated passionately for a greater measure of riparian control.

The sheer volume of complaints suggests that this was not simply a series of overreactions from Brazos dwellers: many people seem truly to have understood the frustration that prompted W. R. Poage's 1957 dispatch. The annoyance both of Brazos politicians and of their constituents was to be expected. As much as men like Poage might hope one day to find that there "ain't any Brazos River problem," the history of this river suggested instead that control had long been (and might long be) exceedingly difficult to realize in any form. Civic groups and individual cities had succeeded in completing a number of small-scale improvement projects by 1957, and a handful of larger dam structures stood within the watershed as well. However, there was relatively little to show for the collective efforts at broader control of the Brazos River: floodwaters continued to surge through the river corridor every few years, and droughts continued to punctuate the intervening years with moments of extreme low flow. Still, the relative dearth of successful projects did not halt developmental efforts along this corridor (nor did Congressman Poage's moment of despair interrupt his work on behalf of an improved river), and from that commitment to riparian control emerges both the significance and the story of the Brazos River.

This waterway has not shaped empires outside of the short-lived Republic of Texas or earned a definite space within the national imagination. The Brazos is no Mississippi. The river, moreover, defies easy categorization as being either West or South, as does the state through which it flows. Yet the Brazos River is nevertheless a well-suited subject for study because it tells a unique story about the meaning, purpose, and potential of riparian development projects. The men and women who advocated improvement of this waterway erected lock-and-dam structures and then watched as the river shifted course, built large-scale dams and then sat by helplessly as floodwaters surged over the concrete rims of these colossal structures, and constructed levees and then looked on as unstable soils collapsed beneath the burden of expectation as well as the physical weight of the improvements. The vast majority of improvement projects proposed or constructed for this river were cast aside as unequivocal failures, abandoned (in many cases) even before their completion. Yet lawmakers and laypeople, boosters and

Untitled photograph of the 1902 Waco flood. Courtesy the Texas Collection, Baylor University, Waco, Texas.

engineers continued to embrace the possibilities inherent in riparian development.

The story that emerges from their commitment is necessarily unique to the Brazos, but the frequent inability of engineers to tame this river (and their persistent efforts toward that end) offers a subtle but suggestive commentary on the broader effort to regulate or manipulate this nation's rivers. More specifically, the developers who struggled to temper the destructive whims of the Brazos River engaged an attitude of technological faith that has long been a central feature of our national identity. People living within the watershed or otherwise working on behalf of regional interests consistently turned to technological solutions for their riparian problems, embracing locks and dams and diversion schemes as a means of attaining their culturally defined ideals of improvement. Control over the river proved elusive, however, undone by the geology of the river as much as the financial cost of improvement. A drawn-out story of developmental inertia is not always apparent in the study of this nation's rivers—where the visual terrain of dams and channels can obscure the subtleties and complexities of improvement,

Photograph of the 1909 flood in Waco that shows "the Brazos on a Rampage."
Courtesy the Texas Collection, Baylor University, Waco, Texas.

but the battle between human persistence and riparian defiance is well
defined within the Brazos narrative. As a result, the string of projects
proposed along the Lower, Middle, and Upper Brazos Rivers between
1821 and 1980 speaks not only to the determination of a people committed to the broad idea of development but also to shifting ideas about
the shape, form, and purpose of improvement.

Nestled within this analysis of riparian development are three key
points. First, Brazos dwellers are not alone in their fixation with improvement. A technocratic conviction—the belief that scientific knowledge and industrial forces could address practical concerns and issues
of efficiency—has distinguished the American character from the earliest days of our nation. From the capture of waterpower at early textile
mills to the construction of a transcontinental railroad, Americans have
consistently sought technological tools with which to tame a landscape
alternately described as wilderness or frontier or Eden. Although the
focus has not been with water alone, a lasting faith in technology has
shaped riparian projects as geographically and chronologically dispersed as the construction of New York's Erie Canal during the early

republic, the creation of a regional water system in Southern California during the late nineteenth century, and the erection of multiple dams by the Tennessee Valley Authority during the interwar and postwar years.

The expectations that Americans attach to their requests for improvement have not always been realized, but there is no denying the general optimism with which the public has approached the ideal of environmental control. Technocratic faith influenced the broader trajectory of American history in especially obvious ways throughout the nineteenth and twentieth centuries, dramatically shaping the nation's economic and social frameworks and also creating an ideological base onto which such ideas as imperialism and manifest destiny would be built. American citizens and newly arrived immigrants created a new nation, in a very literal sense, as they expanded southward and journeyed westward, underwent an Industrial Revolution and applied new tools to new businesses, and experienced war and peace and then took to war again.

The technocracy that so often defines the American character has effectively created a national narrative of progress—as in the maxim to move west and conquer—but that narrative has been built upon an assumption of success. Americans have indeed constructed dams, canals, mines, and even towns with little more than government assistance, enabling legislation, and a sheer determination to mold the landscape to their own designs. But such moments of technological achievement reveal only part of our history. Though dams now litter American rivers and bear witness to technical might, developers have struggled to define the proper use of natural resources and to construct projects that they had hoped could realize those uses. Rivers have broken through dams, mountains have slid into the plains below, and the very air of our larger cities has become toxic. Improvement of the Brazos River highlights in a particularly vibrant way both the aforementioned commitment to technical solutions and the frequent inability to realize developmental expectations for the landscape.

Second, although Americans at different times and in distinctive geographies have demonstrated a general commitment to technocracy, the focus of their attention has shifted as national needs have changed. For example, advocates of riparian improvement have promoted models of development that alternately privileged navigation, reclamation, flood control, recreation, industrial development, and a mass of other ideals. In the West, concerns over aridity and reclamation since the mid-nineteenth century have commonly pushed dams, reservoirs, and irrigation canals to the forefront of the public mind. Living in proximity to small but fast-moving streams and rivers historically prompted people living along the East Coast of the United States to adapt industrial uses for waterpower. Along the much larger and slower-moving streams of the southern states, navigation became a central concern and so locks, levees, and canals absorbed the developmental focus. Obviously, canals for navigation have been constructed or discussed in states lying west of the Mississippi River just as dams have been erected in southern regions. These models of development are necessarily simplifications. Still, they generalize from what has historically held true in the diverse regions of the United States.

Many rivers provide clear examples of these different models for riparian development. The Colorado and Columbia Rivers, for example, have been dammed almost to the point of ecological collapse; navigation has flourished along the Mississippi and Arkansas Rivers due to the construction of locks and levees; and New England rivers such as the Merrimack have been commoditized since the colonial period for proto-industrial and industrial purposes. These and other rivers undoubtedly speak to a more orthodox story of navigation or dam building, but they rarely speak clearly and meaningfully to multiple models of development, to a story of navigation *and* dam building.

Improvement of the Brazos River, in the span of fewer than two hundred years, gave almost equal weight to navigation, flood control, agricultural use, and reclamation. Development of the river privileged a Southern model of navigation and economic growth during the mid- and late nineteenth century as settlers along the Lower and Middle Brazos built their lives and their dreams on a foundation of agriculture. Along the Upper Brazos River, a Western model of development that emphasized flood control, reclamation, and irrigation became the focus during the mid-twentieth century as Brazos dwellers engaged the realities of low flows and frequent drought. The lower two-thirds of the Brazos resembled a southern river suitable for extensive cultivation, and the development projects in this region reflected as much. Likewise, the upper third of the Brazos resembled a western river prone to drought, and the development projects engaged that reality as well.

Because Brazos River development projects have incorporated multiple ideals and perspectives, this waterway serves as a historiographical bridge between a South and Northeast that historically allocated water resources to industry or to navigation and a West that commonly allocated water resources to reclamation or to irrigation. In terms of its culture and geography and history, the Brazos is a western river with a southern ending, a river whose headwaters punctuate the semiarid and arid lands of the Texas Panhandle and whose endwaters flow through abandoned plantations en route to the famously fertile plains of the Gulf Coast. The narrative of Brazos development reflects this natural variation and, consequently, plays out within that space between historiographies, engaging the Bureau of Reclamation and the Army Corps of Engineers, emphasizing irrigation and navigation, and involving civic groups and federal funds.

Third, though not immune from the effects of development and an expanding population, the Brazos has retained a greater measure of ecological integrity compared to many other American waterways. This waterway stands somewhat apart in its story of improvement. Despite long-standing efforts to tame, bind, or otherwise rein in the waters of the Brazos, the river has not been transformed into an organic machine, and there is no hydraulic empire. This is no Columbia, dotted with massive dam structures and commonly characterized by ecological problems; nor is this a Colorado or Tennessee, rivers divided between state and regional bureaucracies. The Brazos has been the center of intense development activity since 1821 and yet no organizations, agencies, or governments have ever exerted complete control over it, or even close-to-complete control. Command over its waters has been elusive, projects have proven ineffective, and the well-intentioned plans of pro-development groups have not overcome the geological realities of a defiant river.

As such, despite the many ways in which it echoes the characteristics of other waterways, the Brazos is not simply one of many American rivers. It is not one of many places where forces such as technocracy, persistence, and resistance have been felt, and is not a simple copy of such rivers as the Tennessee, the Rio Grande, or the Mississippi. The Brazos is a singular waterway for, despite any hopes that the river might lend itself easily to development, its failure to be harnessed is particularly evident, and the determination of its boosters is especially long lived. Thus, the process by which developers have approached this waterway—seeking to erase its outbursts and to harness its energies—offers a subtle but no less significant commentary on the needs of the Brazos populace and the ideals of a technology-centric American public.

This study fashions the narrative of resistance and persistence that has marked the Brazos River by examining the evolution of physical improvements from 1821 to 1980. The story of development begins along the Lower Brazos River in 1821, a significant and tumultuous year within the area that would shortly join the Union as the State of Texas. In August of that year, representatives for the Armies of Spain and for the Imperial Mexican Army signed the Treaty of Córdoba. That treaty effected a number of changes in the relationship between the Spanish Crown and the area known as New Spain, but the most important of those changes was the recognition of Mexican independence. Although political stability would not be captured quickly or easily within the area subsequently known as the Mexican Empire, its central government began working immediately to define the political, economic, and social characteristics of the new nation.

The Mexican government also sought to secure the physical boundaries of the state. Security, however, did not simply mean arms and armies. It could also be found in a civilian population that created a cushion between the Mexican State and the surrounding imperial powers, most notably, the expansive and expanding United States. Indian Wars and local rebellions that periodically broke out within the northern tier of Mexican states throughout the 1820s and 1830s made the progressive march of the American people to the southwest and the demographic disadvantage in Texas still more pressing. This fear of American expansion and this need to populate the peripheral territories led the Mexican government to honor colonization agreements that the Spanish Crown had made with various individuals. These impresarios, men such as Martin de Leon and Stephen F. Austin, vigorously acted out the meaning of their title—"entrepreneur." They created colonies on the lands awarded to them, advertised grants, wooed immigrants, and very gradually expanded the population of this frontier land.

These colonists had no sooner planted themselves along the Brazos River, an early focal point for many impresarios, than they began to devise projects to transform the landscape. In other words, the year 1821 also marked the formal beginning of American immigration into what would become the state of Texas. Development of the river, however, did not begin at this time. For centuries, indigenous groups of American Indians had manipulated the land for their use, building irrigation structures and practicing agriculture. Spanish missionaries, soldiers, and townspeople during the colonial period not only built canals but also small-scale embankment dams. Still, the year of Mexican independence witnessed an important break. The development projects that were proposed and/or implemented after 1821 might have mirrored those projects put in place centuries earlier, but they were accomplished and envisioned on a scale that Spanish friars and Indian villagers surely did not foresee. As a result, links that would only grow stronger through the years of the Texas Republic and early statehood were subtly but lastingly established between American technocracy and Texas lands in the year of Mexican independence.

The year 1821 serves as a satisfactory, if imperfect, starting point for this project; in a similar manner, 1980 serves as an appropriate end point for a study of Brazos River development. Improvement of this river continues today as a point of discussion for lawmakers, engineers, and people living within the confines of the Brazos Basin. Groups such as the Friends of the Navasota River have continued working actively to debate the location and justification of proposed dams, students at Baylor University have dedicated several decades to the study of algae in the Brazos reservoirs, and Texas cities such as Waco and College Station have debated and planned for an expansion of the river's economic uses. Baylor University recently completed construction on a $260 million football stadium that sits prominently (and very intentionally) on the banks of the Brazos River. Without question, development has not ended, but the pace has slowed and its purpose shifted.

In the years since 1980, improvement projects along the Brazos River have generally been limited to small-scale municipal projects or have remained entirely theoretical. No large-scale projects have been both proposed and completed since that year. This shift reflects a number of changes to the national landscape. For one thing, the burgeoning growth of ecology during the 1960s and 1970s—as well as a growing awareness of that scientific field among the American public—has prompted greater scrutiny of large-scale development projects. The building of dams slowed to an almost-imperceptible crawl after those decades, as scientists pointed to the detrimental effect of riparian manipulation on aquatic populations. This was true not only within the Brazos Basin but also within the nation at large. In addition, the emergence and growth of a formal environmental movement during the 1970s made it that much more difficult to advocate for diversions, dams, and other extensive manipulations. Contemporary lawmakers felt increasingly pressured to justify their projects not only from an economic perspective (a task, always difficult, that was made still more difficult by an economic downturn) but also from an environmental one. Consequently, it seems fitting to end this study at the moment when the developmental impulse itself changed course.

The improvement projects that were proposed for the Brazos River between 1821 and 1980 serve as a tool with which to unmask the human experience and to trace the changes in thought about the purpose of development. As a result, the chapters in this book generally proceed chronologically, following settlement away from the coast and toward the source of the Brazos River. The first chapter traces the ecology of the river from the prehistoric origins of the watershed. This ecological review, which focuses on quantitative data, examines the geology, geography, hydrology, flora, fauna, and climate of the watershed. It provides readers with some understanding of the natural forces that have operated on the riverscape and also describes the landscape as it might have appeared on the eve of settlement. More important, the chapter gives readers an opportunity to learn something of the geological realities that both shaped and shadowed improvement of the Brazos River.

The cultural review in chapter 2 examines cultural production (e.g., songs, paintings, folktales, poems, and books) along the river in the years since 1821. The text also attaches these artifacts to a temporal and geographic space, providing readers with an opportunity to understand the parallel ways in which Brazos settlers have reimagined or remade the river. Most notably, people living within this watershed have fixated on two images in particular—that of Brazos as South and Brazos as West. These cultural ideals reflect broader questions about the place of Texas next to other regions but also anticipate the models of development that would persist along the river. Thus, even while they have immortalized the river through ink and paint and song by referencing the tropes of cowboys or cotton, the people living within this watershed have used their artistic expressions to conform the waters to their expectations. Cultural production along this river, in other words, speaks to the priorities that shaped the process of development and to the ties that bound a frustrated people to a destructive land.

Chapter 3 introduces the story of riparian improvement along the Lower Brazos River with a discussion of early reactions to the river by incoming emigrants. For that reason, this chapter begins with Stephen F. Austin's incursions into Texas (1821), opening with an examination of Brazos boosterism and then highlighting the intellectual maneuverings that connected boosterism with developmental activity. Most notably, along this section of the river, Texans sought a reliable transportation network that would provide cultural links to southern landscapes and would bring their agricultural commodities into national and, perhaps, international markets. This desire to make the Brazos into a riparian highway ultimately led to the construction of a regional canal, a port, and a pair of jetties.

Chapter 4 studies the lock-and-dam projects that Progressive Era Texans proposed for the Middle Brazos River. The chapter begins in 1890, describing the same impulses toward navigation that had propelled development along the Lower Brazos River, and it ends in the early twentieth century, with the conclusive failure of the lock-and-dam project. During this period along the Middle Brazos, Texans continued to emphasize navigation as the foremost developmental ideal. The projects that were proposed along this stretch of the river, however, were much larger and technologically complex than what had been envisioned farther downstream, a reality that reflected both national advances in technology and also an increasing recognition of the river's unwillingness to be tamed.

Chapter 5 addresses what is arguably the most successful period for improvement along the Brazos River: dam building along the Upper Brazos River during the mid-twentieth century. Developers and engineers, working within what Marc Reisner famously called the "Go-Go Years" of dam building, proposed during the interwar and postwar years a succession of dam projects for the riverscape.[3] Through these projects, they hoped to obtain economic relief as well as hydroelectric development and flood control. Chapter 5, as a result, picks up with the formation of the Brazos River Conservation and Reclamation District in 1929 and the regional turn away from navigation. Although flood-control projects initially dictated the direction of improvement, developers soon began to emphasize multiuse projects that might be incorporated into regional plans for improvement.

Chapter 6 analyzes the importation and diversion schemes that garnered attention during the second half of the twentieth century and targeted improvement of the river as a whole. The chapter begins its analysis with the formation of the U.S. Study Commission in 1958 and concludes its analysis with the year 1980. Chapter 6 examines projects proposed not only by the federal commission but also by state agencies and individuals concerned with water issues. Though entirely theoretical, these projects echoed the needs and frustrations that had driven the earliest improvement projects, doing so on a much grander and more ambitious scale. Chapter 7 offers concluding thoughts on the narrative of Brazos River improvement, highlighting the ways in which models of development shifted with time and searching out skeins of developmental continuity within changing ideas of riparian improvement.

Ultimately, these analyses of dams and levees, immigrants and promotional pamphlets point to the same conclusion. This is the tale of a river that has defied what people define as progress. This is a story about individuals who put their faith in what often proved to be unfettered expectations for riparian control. The engineers, developers, and laypeople who lived along the Brazos struggled to conform this river to their expectations, and yet these same individuals stuck doggedly, perhaps even dogmatically, to the ideal of an improved river. The narrative of this river begins and ends in that place of contradiction—that space where hope and despair comingle with expectation and reality— because advocates for improvement have worked within that arena, seeking to undo the natural limitations of the landscape and trusting consistently (though not unceasingly) in their ability to find technological solutions to daunting riparian concerns.

In the end, this is not a techno-engineering history. Although this account depends heavily on the progression of improvement projects, steel and cement have relatively little to do with the ensuing text. Nor is this an economic study, though capitalist impulses play a crucial role in the story of Brazos development. Rather, this study most closely resembles a sociopolitical history of development: it investigates and articulates the hopes, needs, and frustrations that have both propelled improvement of the Brazos River and paralleled broader changes to this nation's economic, political, and geographical landscape. Dams have crumbled, levees have failed, and locks have washed away, but boosters and laypeople and politicians have maintained, and at times clung to, a steadfast faith in their ability to apply technological solutions to the Brazos River. The story that can be teased from that disconnect sheds light on narratives of development that, though subtle, have shaped improvement not only along the Brazos River but along this nation's many rivers. And that story begins with the geology of an inflexible river and the ecology of an oversized watershed . . .

CHAPTER ONE

Ecology and Geology along the Mighty Brazos River

[The Brazos] rushes suddenly into the sea; challenges it proudly with high banks; officiously invites these banks to build up a bulwark that may protect its entrance; and offers shelter to navigators, and opportunity for them to examine the vast and uninhabited regions that it waters.

—ATHANASE DE MÉZIÈRES, *The Explorers' Texas*, 1779

How many attractions does this splendid country appear at first sight to offer to a settler from our cold and Northern States! No rocky and barren edges to lie waste forever; no steep acclivities to be tilled or to be climbed over; no provision to be made for the housing of cattle; no raising, cutting, curing, removing, stowing or feeding out of winter fodder; not even the construction of hay stacks; much less the erection of barns or stables for crops and stock. . . . The whole business of raising cattle is of course reduced, as it was in the land of Canaan, to the simple operation of letting them take care of themselves, eat, drink, and fatten on the rich pastures and under the genial climate, until the owner chooses to claim tribute of their flesh, hide and horns.

—FISK, *A Visit To Texas*, 1834

The Brazos does not come from haunts of coot and hern, or even from mountains. It comes from West Texas, and in part from an equally stark stretch of New Mexico, and it runs for something over 800 miles down to the Gulf. On the high plains it is a gypsum-salty intermittent creek; down toward the coast it is a rolling Southern river, with levees and cotton fields and ancient hardwood bottoms.

—JOHN GRAVES, *Goodbye To A River*, 1960

IN THE MIDST OF that great internal struggle known as the Civil War, a small group of men journeyed to Texas to undertake a task that was formidable in its own right. These men, armed with basic scientific

1

instruments and in need of tremendous patience, hoped to construct a map of the state that traced the creeks, highlighted the hills, exposed the terrain, and uncovered the trails. Legends have suggested both that these men were Union spies working through the Confederacy and that they were Confederate spies working through the Union forces—in short, their identity and backstory remain shrouded in a healthy amount of mystery. Whatever their loyalties, these men ultimately produced a map for the Army Corps of Engineers that was published in 1865. In their endeavor to give the Texas landscape a more complete identity, they succeeded in not only crafting a tremendously accurate map but, equally important, in creating a document that would serve as a reminder to later generations that the "lordly Brazos" and its adjoining landscape had long been places of spectacular diversity.[1]

In the case of the Brazos River, this map labeled that waterway with phrases that spoke to the natural shifts of the landscape: "prairie streams heavily timbered," "supplies plenty red sandy soil," "corn cotton beef abundant," "undulating country timbered with oak," "cattle plenty," "country hilly—prairie and timber well divided," "high Rolling Plains—supplies scarce," "true coal measures."[2] These nineteenth-century engineers recognized and essentially paid homage to the variation of the landscape, and in truth they could not have overstated how rapidly and completely the lands and waters of this basin remade themselves. Refusing to bend to any single interpretation of itself, the Brazos is a river that becomes swollen then waterless, hostile then motionless, docile then boundless. This is a river of many faces, one that enjoys a gluttonous feast of water or no water at all. The vegetation, geology, and hydrology of the river are similarly indecisive, alternately springing forth as treeless mesas, flowered hills, and swampy lowlands.

Such inconstancy would prove to be a near-constant annoyance for the individuals and families who lived along the river, envisioned its ideal form, and dealt—both begrudgingly and belatedly—with its realities. They devised projects intended to address the persistent flooding and then watched as high flows coursed over, around, and sometimes through those same improvements (often in dramatic and damaging style); they wrought projects of steel and cement and wood and then lamented the destructive power of moving water over these same materials. The bare science behind the river's variability, in short, casts a light on the purpose as well as the fate of the many projects that sought to temper the Brazos River. The geological character of the river—the floods, the droughts, and the porous soils—did little to constrain the

A. R. Roessler's *Map No. 59: Texas* (Washington, D.C.: Engineer's Office, Department of the Gulf, 1865). Courtesy Special Collections, University of Texas at Arlington Library, Arlington, Texas.

hopes and expectations of people living within the watershed, but it did much to shape the models of development that could be successfully applied to the Brazos Basin.

The diversity of the Brazos River landscape, the frenzied variation that would both frustrate development and undermine expectation, is most easily explained in the context of what John McPhee has called "deep time."[3] The Brazos River emerges in a region of the Great Plains known as the High Plains, an area that includes most of the Texas Panhandle and portions of several midwestern states.[4] The High Plains began to form 175 million years ago when the Pacific and North American plates collided. This impact gradually thrust the western half of the United States upward, causing tremendous upheaval as it slowly created a series of mountain chains. However, erosive forces began tearing down these mountains even as the west coast continued its climb. Rain and, to a lesser extent, wind wrought a subtle but significant change as they carried minute pieces of mountain debris toward the east, onto the eastern-lying lands and seas that would come together as the Great Plains.[5]

These conjoined processes of construction and destruction also created a durable, almost cement-like, layer within the High Plains known regionally as the Caprock. Calcium carbonate, carried east by various rivers in their journey from the Rocky Mountains, gradually built up in the rock layers of the Great Plains. River water laden with minerals drew upward when the surface soils dried, and the evaporation that followed this capillary action concentrated the calcium carbonate. The durable surface layers of the Caprock acted as something of a protective barrier for the loosely packed sedimentary soils below, but erosive forces nevertheless continued their work. Gradually, the combined effects of wind and rain carved into the newly formed lands of the High Plains the rivers currently known as the Brazos, Red, Canadian, and Colorado.

The weathering of the High Plains and the creation of new river systems, in turn, helped to create the Rolling Plains and the prairies of North and Central Texas. As the western half of the state uplifted and the surface layers of the High Plains fractured during the Cenozoic Era, erosive forces began to carry away the geological rubble.[6] Wind and, even more so, water swept away the debris at the same time that new landforms emerged from a sea that still covered lands to the east and southeast. As a result, during the Cenozoic Era, the High Plains began contributing to the formation of the Rolling Plains, the Blackland and Grand Prairies, and the Cross Timbers. The Coastal Plains boasts a somewhat different story. These plains emerged from a waterway known as the Gulf of Mexico Basin, which formed during the Mesozoic Era as the Northern Atlantic Ocean was gradually isolated.[7] The Gulf of Mexico Basin came together at the same time that the western half of the state continued to uplift and the plains of the state's center continued to erode. The result was that the seas covering the future state of Texas receded very gradually and, as they did so, exposed what would become a new landform—the Coastal Plains.

These processes of folding, uplifting, eroding, and compressing may have little obvious relevance to the study of history, but they explain the variation of the Brazos River Basin: indeed, the external features of the watershed shift in ways that reflect the basin's geologic history. Though the river itself does not breach the boundaries of Texas, the Brazos nevertheless crosses more of its landscape than any other waterway, save the Rio Grande. The main stem is, by most accounts, roughly 850 to 950 river miles in length, and the length of the Brazos increases to roughly 1,250 river miles when the size of any one of its formative tributaries is considered. As a result, it is the eleventh-longest river in the United States and longer than such rivers as the Columbia, Platte, Snake, and Tennessee.[8] In contrast to the (self-contained) river, the watershed begins in eastern New Mexico. The Brazos, however, is primarily a product of Texas.[9] In its journey to the Gulf, the river drains roughly 45,000 square miles (an area that is around the same size as Pennsylvania or Ohio), and only 2,000 of those miles lie in New Mexico.[10]

Within the expanse of that watershed, the topography and appearance of the Brazos River corridor shifts dramatically. From canyonlands and plains to swamps and coastal prairies, the Brazos River touches most of the major ecological zones in the state of Texas en route to its mouth at the Gulf of Mexico. The river rises within the Staked Plains, skirts the Llano Uplift and the Edward Plateau, drives through the Rolling Plains, meanders through the Black and Grand Prairies, brushes against the Lower Cross Timbers, then coils its way across the Coastal Plains.[11] To phrase it another way, the Brazos flows in a southeasterly and serpentine manner through the semiaridity of the canyonlands, the luxuriant grasses and forests of Central Texas, and the occasionally swampy lowlands of the Gulf Coast.

Nineteenth-century emigrants both commented on and made use of the resources endemic to these different regions, and a figurative walk along the Brazos River unmasks the riverscape as it might have appeared to them on the eve of settlement. That journey begins at the river's endpoint, where settlement by European and American emigrants commenced. At its mouth, this river flows not into any bay but instead empties directly into the Gulf.[12] The nature of this coastline exit distinguishes the Brazos from other Texas rivers. The Rio Grande, for example, ends its journey in the hypersaline bay known as Laguna Madre. The Nueces River pours into Corpus Christi Bay; the San Antonio and Guadalupe Rivers feed San Antonio Bay; and the Lavaca and Colorado Rivers flow into the oversized Matagorda Bay. The San Jacinto and Trinity Rivers, Neches and Sabine Rivers plunge, respectively, into Galveston Bay and a bay-complex known as Sabine Lake.

The singularity of the river's abrupt end at the Gulf of Mexico was not lost on Spanish explorers, who commented on the distinctiveness of the Brazos mouth during their earliest excursions within the region. For example, Athanase de Mézières, who visited the Texas-Louisiana frontier during the 1760s and 1770s, wrote of the river's bold exit into the Gulf: "The Brazos does not disembogue into a lagoon, like those on the coast. It rushes suddenly into the sea; challenges it proudly with high banks; officiously invites these banks to build up a bulwark that may protect its entrance; and offers shelter to navigators."[13]

The absence of a proper bay not only intrigued Spanish visitors but also captured the attention of early American settlers hoping to construct the next great port, the "Liverpool of the Trans-Mississippi."[14] To nineteenth-century minds dreaming of harbors and shipyards, this unobstructed coastline was beneficial, rather than problematic, as there seemed to be no visible breakers to hinder entry into the river corridor.

Upon crossing the threshold that separates land from sea, visitors to this watershed first came upon the Lower Brazos River. The Lower Brazos flows almost entirely through the Coastal Plains and Coastal Lowlands and so the landscape is wetter and the Brazos wider than on any other reach of the river.[15] This portion of the watershed, which begins near the cities of Bryan and College Station and ends in the murky waters of the Gulf of Mexico, grades from a "gently rolling-hilly topography . . . to the low, relatively featureless plains along the coast."[16] The land is generally flat and somewhat unstable along the Lower Brazos River with the result that oxbow lakes, river bends, and saltwater marshes occur with some frequency.[17] This stretch of river also includes Hidalgo Falls, located near Navasota, Texas. The Hidalgo Falls, as well as the Falls-of-the-Brazos along the Middle Brazos River, are created as the river rushes over a ledge of submerged limestone.[18] Despite what the names suggest, however, these "falls" are more akin to rapids. The rippling waters simply pay homage to the regional flatness of the watershed and to the limestone shoals that populate the streambed in this region.

The banks of the Lower Brazos are relatively low, so floods have proven to be a constant problem along this stretch of river. Indeed, small-scale floods historically hit the southernmost stretches of the Brazos on a near-yearly basis. The earliest European and American emigrants to this region commented on the destructive power of frequent floods, and such overflows continued to frustrate later generations of Brazos dwellers. An Army Corps of Engineers report lamented in 1937, for example, that "a large amount of fertile bottom land must be withheld from possible or reasonably continuous cultivation, because of the likelihood of disastrous inundation resulting from even relatively small rises."[19] In consequence, flood events quickly became the target of development projects as Brazos dwellers sought to undo those aspects of the riverscape that hindered productive use of the land.

Complementing the marshes and oxbows and low stream banks were soils that, likewise, reflected the natural variation of this section of the river. The soils of the Lower Brazos could be loosely divided into four categories—bottomland soils, alluvial soils, upland soils, and prairie soils. Bottomland soils populated the low-lying areas of the floodplain while alluvial plains and terraces were formed through a continual, if unhurried, process of deposition. Both soil groups tended to be nearly level to gently sloping, moderately well drained to well drained, and moderately deep to very deep.[20] Because bottomland and alluvial soils were frequently deep and fertile, they supported extensive agricultural production within the Lower Brazos River region. However, bottomlands and alluvial soils also possessed a "high shrink-swell potential and restricted permeability," which means that they were relatively unstable.[21]

In contrast, soils associated with the Brazos uplands tended to be gently sloping to sloping, poorly drained to moderately well drained, and shallow to very deep.[22] These soils were generally more stable than those associated with the bottomlands and alluvial plains and, depending on the location, were even underlain by sandstone, mudstone, claypans, shale, or Pleistocene terraces that provided an additional level of stability.[23] The soils of the inland Coastal Prairie were often nearly level to gently sloping, poorly drained to moderately well drained, and moderately deep to very deep.[24] Developers found, as a result, that improvement of the uplands was fairly easy while improvement of the Lower Brazos River along the corridor itself was a difficult endeavor: soils frequently washed away, riverbanks occasionally collapsed, and the river itself periodically changed course.

In the earliest days of settlement, the grassy species of the Lower Brazos River nearly dominated the landscape, springing forth in a multitude of plants that included bushy bluestem, brownseed paspalum, and rattail smutgrass.[25] Flowering plants were, however, almost as plentiful along the Lower Brazos River and included well-known species such as the huisache daisy, common sunflower, brown-eyed Susan, and pinkscale blazing star.[26] A variety of tree species were also common along the river, and they endowed the entire Lower Brazos with a riparian corridor (or river-based community of species) that manifested as Post Oak Savannah along the uppermost reaches of the river. The best known of these tree species included cherry laurel, bald cypress, water hickory, red mulberry, and black walnut.[27]

Countless birds, reptiles, amphibians, and mammals, likewise, inhabited the lower stretch of the Brazos River. Historic and scientific sources revealed, for example, that early settlers encountered swamp rabbits, black bears, bison, coyotes, and wild horses (mustangs) with some frequency.[28] Avian species also abounded, most commonly as gaggles and swarms and flocks of bobwhites, mourning doves, wild geese, and swans as well as various species of songbirds, herons, egrets, raptors, and ducks.[29] The roof rat, Norway rat, and house mouse (all non-native) were present along the Lower Brazos River soon after American settlement began, and the increase in their numbers paralleled the local extinction of species such as the gray wolf, mountain lion, collared peccary, jaguar, and ocelot.[30]

Pulling all these characteristics together, the Lower Brazos River took on a very particular appearance for early and mid-nineteenth-century emigrants. Personal descriptions of the Lower Brazos River varied tremendously from one decade to the next, but they generally emphasized the seemingly unrivaled beauty of the land.[31] Dr. John Leonard Riddell made use of words such as "pleasant" and "beautiful" to describe his impressions of the land during an 1839 tour of the state, as did Stephen F. Austin upon his visit to Texas in 1821.[32] Other accounts complemented this attention to aesthetics with comments on the productiveness of the land.[33] William Kennedy, for example, went so far as to suggest that along the Brazos, "an abundance of timber may always be procured," and Andrew Forest Muir prophesized in 1837 that "the Texian in all future ages will fix his habitation and as he gazes upon his almost countless herd of cattle which feed upon the plain will see himself grow rich almost without any exertion."[34]

While the lower third of the Brazos River flows entirely through a land of coastal prairies and plains, the middle third of the river cuts through the Blackland Prairie, the Grand Prairie, and the Post Oak Savannah.[35] The Middle Brazos, which reaches from just north of Waco to the Bryan/College Station area, boasts quite a few areas of flat terrain but was generally more rolling than the land of the Lower Brazos River, with "eroded, rolling plains, canyons of moderate relief, and isolated mesas or buttes."[36] The banks of the river were shorter, less steep, and less clearly defined than along the upper third of the river but higher, steeper, and more clearly defined than along the lower third of the river. Moreover, fewer alluvial terraces flanked the Middle Brazos, replaced by staggered limestone cliffs.

The Brazos River watershed inclines slightly toward the Gulf of Mexico and also toward the east. As a result, the valleys, the hills, the canyonlands, and the plains all slope to the southeast in what resembles an elongated and reversed S-shape. The geography of the entire state follows this basic pattern. However, the topographic characteristic is particularly noticeable along the midsection of the river because here the land flattens out near the Panhandle and coastline, leaving the Middle Brazos to follow the state's natural curvature to the coast. The tangible significance of this geological nuance is that the river's drainage lies largely to the south and west of the river's main stem; nearly all of the major tributaries flow to the east.[37] The only tributary to depart from that rule is the Navasota River, which lies to the east of the Brazos River and flows, consequently, to the west.

The volume of the streamflow also changes within the Middle Brazos. With the exception of the three formative streams, all of the major tributaries join the Brazos along its midsection.[38] Consequently, the volume of the Brazos River increases noticeably as one moves away from the source and toward the coast.[39] The watershed also intersects the Balcones Fault Zone along the Middle Brazos River.[40] The Balcones Fault Zone—thousands of small breaks or fault lines that run across Texas from the southwest to the northeast in a broadly curving line—is arguably one of the most determinative factors in shaping the hydrology, geology, and flood potential of the Brazos

River.[41] It influences rainfall patterns and soil types as well as stream-flows and, therefore, greatly influences the susceptibility of the Brazos River to improvement.

The soils of the Middle Brazos River were similarly diverse. The soils of the floodplains were often nearly level to gently sloping, deep to very deep, and poorly drained to well drained.[42] The alluvial soils were, for the most part, nearly level to gently sloping (and occasionally hilly), moderately deep to very deep, and moderately well drained to well drained.[43] Several different groupings of upland soils also populated the middle stretch of river.[44] Those soil combinations that were associated with the Prairies or the Post Oak Savannah tended to be nearly level to hilly, shallow to moderately deep, and poorly drained to well drained.[45] Other soil groupings, associated broadly with the uplands of the Middle Brazos River, could be shallow or deep, poorly drained or moderately well drained, and nearly level or steep.[46]

The patchwork of soil groupings was reflected in an exterior of vegetation that was equally diverse. Early settlers frequently remarked that the midsection of the river flowed through a landscape striped with alternating bands of prairie and forest.[47] Here, the prairies and forests of Central Texas met, draping the Middle Brazos River watershed in a pattern of shrubby grasslands and oak-ash-pecan forests. In 1939, Benjamin Tharp noted the patchwork of vegetative zones and aptly labeled these junctions the "sinuous line of contact between woodland and prairie."[48] These sites of vegetative union marked the spots where the available resources—both riparian and land based—could be maximized and so these sites were often prioritized for settlement.[49]

The grasses of the Grand Prairie, Blackland Prairie, and Rolling Plains included well-known species such as big and little bluestem, sideoats grama, and Texas wintergrass; though trees were relatively rare in the grassy prairies, settlers noted the presence of live oak, cedar elm, pecan, or ashe juniper.[50] Trees were far more common along the lower stretch of the Middle Brazos, where the Post Oak Savannah flourished, and immediately along the riparian corridor itself.[51] Flowers—such as Texas thistle, butterfly weed, Queen Anne's lace, and plains blackfoot—also broke up any monotony that might have characterized the landscape.[52] Birds, reptiles, amphibians, and mammals also thrived along the Middle Brazos River. Emigrants encountered animals (now unknown to the region) like the black bear and bobcat but also saw better-known species like the American beaver, coyote, red fox, river otter, and white-tailed deer.[53] As with the Lower Brazos River, the roof rat, Norway rat, and house mouse were ubiquitous along the Middle Brazos River shortly after settlement, while the gray wolf, black bear, mountain lion, red wolf, jaguar, ocelot, and bison gradually declined in number after 1821.[54]

Again pulling these geological and geographical characteristics together, the Middle Brazos River would have taken on a certain appearance for mid- and late nineteenth-century emigrants. Letters, memoirs, diaries, and other historic sources from the time mentioned trees and flowers and birds with some frequency, but they most commonly talked about the disarming beauty of the landscape. In 1844, George Wilkins Kendall described his initial impressions of the Bosque River, writing at length about the plant and animal life.[55] In 1852, W. B. Dewees offered a more general, but more effusive, description of the Middle Brazos River, which he described as a place of "almost fairy-like beauty": "Imagine for yourself a vast plain extending as far as the eye can reach, with nothing but the deep blue sky to bound the prospect, excepting on the east side where runs a broad red stream, with lofty trees rearing themselves upon its banks, and you have our prairie. This is covered with a carpet of the richest verdure, from the midst of which spring up wild flowers of every hue and shade."[56] So common were protestations of beauty that multiple sources referred to the Middle Brazos River as the "garden of Texas."[57]

In contrast to the Lower and Middle Rivers, the upper third of the Brazos coils through an area that grades from leveling plains to elevated canyonlands. The Upper Brazos River forms in the southeast corner of the Llano Estacado near Lubbock, but moves quickly into the less arid landscape of north-central Texas's Rolling Plains and subsequently ends near Waco.[58] That transition from the Llano Estacado to the Rolling Plains is conspicuously marked. The Caprock Escarpment, a series of outcrops that manifest (depending on one's perspective) as a daunting wall of sedimentary rock or a series of rough drop-offs, divides the two regions topographically. Elevations can top 5,000 feet above sea level in the northwest regions of the Llano Estacado, but the Brazos rises in a section of the plateau that boasts an elevation closer to 3,000 feet.[59] Along this length, the river is "well confined within steep banks which are not subject to appreciable overflow from even the highest floods."[60] In other words, even when rains are excessive, the stream banks contain most of the flood flows.

Along the Upper Brazos, the soils of the bottomlands were historically and are now deep to very deep, nearly level to gently sloping, and moderately well drained to well drained.[61] The soils of the alluvial terraces and plains are, similarly, deep to very deep, nearly level to sloping, and well drained.[62] Bottomlands and alluvial terraces occur infrequently along the Upper Brazos River in comparison to the lower two-thirds of the river, but when present, they still prove remarkably fertile. As a general rule, the surface layers of the uplands boast deep, moderately well drained to well drained, and nearly level to sloping soils.[63] Some upland soils are associated expressly with the plains, and these soils range from shallow to deep, nearly level to steep, and poorly drained to well drained.[64] The soils of the North-Central and Central Texas prairies were shallow to deep, nearly level to rolling, and moderately well drained to well drained.[65]

The soils of the Upper Brazos River shared a number of characteristics. First, these soil types generally included a large amount of clay so developers endured fewer problems with unstable soils. Additionally, many of these soils were red in color. The driving rains that periodically visited the Upper Brazos washed these red soils into the river and subsequently carried them downstream, a process that in turn stained the Brazos a rich crimson hue. Early settlers of the Lower and Middle Brazos often noted these "red rises," which added an element of mystery to the visual landscape and foretold of high waters further upstream.[66] Finally, the soils on this stretch of river were generally irrigable, often concealing vast supplies of subsurface water (such as the Ogallala Aquifer). The lands of the Upper Brazos enjoyed a much lower rainfall compared to downstream sites, so this characteristic ultimately played a leading role in the river's economic narrative, drawing ranchers and farmers into the region and creating an agricultural market that defied the low streamflow of the river itself.

As early visitors knew all too well, grassy species—such as big and little bluestem, Texas bluegrass, and sideoats grama—consumed much of the Upper Brazos River landscape, but trees interrupted the horizon periodically.[67] These trees were generally associated either with riparian corridors or with the Cross Timbers—long, thin fingers of forest that reached from Texas, through Oklahoma, and into Kansas. The Rolling Plains boasted species such as green ash, plains cottonwood, American elm, pecan, and black willow.[68] The Cross Timbers and, to a lesser extent, the prairies, included species such as cedar elm, Texas red oak, eastern redbud, and wafer ash.[69] The most common flowers included wild blue indigo, yellow thistle, upright prairie coneflower, and Arkansas dozedaisy.[70] For the early settlers, animals supplied additional variety within this landscape and commonly included the big brown bat, black-tailed prairie dog, common gray fox, antelope, and white-tailed deer.[71] The roof rat, Norway rat, and house mouse were also present in regrettably large numbers, while the gray wolf, black bear, mountain lion, jaguar, pronghorn, and bison were involved in an accelerated decline that paralleled the expansion of white settlement.[72]

The Upper Brazos River would thus have taken on a very particular appearance for late nineteenth-century and early twentieth-century emigrants—that of a surging, undulating landscape that offered not only grasses but also an array of tree species.[73] Historic sources reinforced this view of an arid but lively Upper Brazos River, speaking to beauty and fertility more often than sterility and emptiness.[74] George Wilkins Kendall published an account of his journeys along the Upper Brazos River, commenting on the desolate prairies, the fertile bottoms, and the grandeur of Comanche Peak.[75] Despite any seeming aridity, Kendall noted that even in the plains, "The valley of the Brazos . . . abounded with every species of timber known in Texas."[76] Obviously, it was to the advantage of boosters and early settlers to paint this region as one of opportunity rather than difficulty, but the sheer number of accolades (as well as the scientific accuracies hidden behind those descriptions) suggests that there was some truth to the idea that the Upper Brazos River crossed through more than a barren desert.

Complementing the three segments of the river's main stem are the formative tributaries of the Brazos River. Emerging in a section of the High Plains known as the Llano Estacado, the Salt Fork, Clear Fork, and Double Mountain Fork of the Brazos River flow briefly but dramatically through a semiarid landscape.[77] John Miller Morris captures the essence of the region in his book *El Llano Estacado*: "Renowned for its flatness and the disorientation it can cause, the historical geography of the Llano Estacado from 1536 to 1860 is the story of human learning: of discovery, exploration, and imagination in one of North America's stranger bioregions."[78] This land, called lo Llano by the first Spanish explorers, is often characterized as featureless. Indeed, the first maps labeled the area terra incognita. Early American visitors, in a similar manner, dubbed it expansive, monotone, disorienting—the "Great American Desert"—and characterized it as an "endless waste."[79] In 1885, the Reverend Homer Thrall went so far as to dub the area "a desolate and sterile plain," and geologists of the early twentieth century (with perhaps a bit of wit) dubbed it the "Central Denuded Region."[80]

Despite a somewhat prevalent belief that the Llano Estacado was little more than a "vast desert . . . a dreary, barren waste of solitude, without tree, shrub, spring, or stream," this was also a land of striking, if restrained, splendor.[81] The Caprock (composed of marl, chalk, gravel, and various sedimentary rocks) topped layers of sandstone, clay, and shale that were far more erodible.[82] Consequently, once the Caprock began its inevitable crumbling, it did so in colorful and arresting ways. Streams and creeks, for example, cut through the Caprock to form deep canyons, the best known of which were Double Mountain Canyon, Blanco Canyon, and Yellow House Canyon.[83] These canyonlands remain largely unpopulated so they feel very much like a space out of time. With occasional trees, sharply eroded riverbeds, and elevated tablelands, these canyonlands feel ancient or antiquated, depending on whether the landscape wearies or engages the viewer.

In a slight departure from the soils of the main stem of the Brazos River, the soils of these tributaries primarily reflected a combination of alluvial and upland soils. The soils of the alluvial plains were moderately deep to very deep, well drained, and found on nearly level to gently sloping terrain.[84] The upland soils ranged from shallow to deep, were moderately well drained to well drained, and populated land that was nearly level to steep.[85] Most of these surface soils were underlain by sandstone, claystone, or by limestone bedrock.[86] Consequently, boulders, fragments, and outcroppings became a fairly common feature. The broken lands—escarpments, canyons, and any lands too eroded for use—possessed any number of characteristics, ranging from shallow to moderately deep, poorly drained to moderately well drained, and nearly level to steep.[87]

The headwaters of the Brazos flowed through a semiarid region that inherently restricted the "vertical architecture common elsewhere of trees, vines, and shrubs."[88] As a result, a sparsely timbered, grassy ecosystem met incoming emigrants. Grasses dominated the visual landscape while flowers provided a constant break within the scene, and trees, an occasional one. Nineteenth- and early twentieth-century settlers found grassy species like black grama, sideoats grama, and yellow Indian grass, and flowering species such as tansyaster, firewheel, common sunflower, and plains blackfoot augmented those grassy shades of green, yellow, and brown.[89] The most common trees historically included those species that populated riparian corridors—like ashe juniper, cedar elm, American hackberry, and pecan—as well as plains species like escarpment live oak, honey mesquite, live oak, and Texas ash.[90]

In the end, early visitors, if willing to face their assumptions about an empty landscape, found that the land of the Brazos tributaries was anything but lifeless. The river flowed through a land of canyons and prairies marked by colorful interludes, particularly yellow, purple, and orange flowers. Reptiles, birds, amphibians, and mammals also flourished. Depending on the location, black-tailed prairie dogs, red foxes, bobcats, pronghorn, and white-tailed deer were found in great number along the length of these Brazos tributaries.[91] Visitors also found various species of turkey, quail, dove, and songbird, as well as the invasive rodents—the roof rat, Norway rat, and house mouse. As with the entire main stem, some species were declining in numbers by the time that settlement picked up, most notably the gray wolf, black bear, mountain lion, collared peccary, red wolf, jaguar, and bison.[92]

Visitors to the Brazos River in the early years, and even after decades of settlement, found a land of immense variety, a river of many faces. The Upper Brazos River and its tributaries—a landscape of mesquite and thirst—was "deeply entrenched and confined in a narrow valley having steeply sloped sides or bluffs."[93] Here, limestone hid just beneath a thin veneer of soil, the land where cattle tread. Along the Middle Brazos River, the terrain graded from the rugged slopes of the Rolling Plains to the gentle valleys of Central Texas. The floodplain was wide and the land, fertile. The Lower Brazos River, in contrast, boasted a rolling topography only briefly before moving into the flatter, wetter coastal areas. The river was wider here and the floodplain, narrower than along the stretches of river that preceded it. This land, marked by rich soils and deep alluvial terraces, saw the earliest visitations, and its fertility spawned an immediate desire for agricultural markets.

These geological facts very clearly pointed to a natural variation within the Brazos River watershed, but what did they mean more tangibly for the farmers and lawyers, housewives and doctors who ultimately settled in the region? First, the river was historically susceptible both to droughts and to floods. In the century that followed the beginnings of Brazos settlement by American immigrants, severe floods occurred along the Brazos River on at least eighteen occasions; small-scale floods occurred far more frequently, on an almost-yearly basis.[94] Frustrated with the reality of frequent outbursts, residents of the watershed regularly voiced their irritation in letters and editorials, and they were joined in that refrain by journalists from across the nation. The *New York Herald*, for example, noted after the 1869 flood that "those who yesterday rejoiced in the possession of a competency to-day find themselves and their families in absolute want of the common necessaries of life." [95] An Eldora, Iowa, newspaper commented more specifically on the issue of property, noting that the 1899 flood tossed "scores of houses" into the Brazos River.[96] In a particularly poetic commentary, a Wisconsin article from 1899 noted that the "rain is descending as if the heavens were dissolving." [97]

The history of the Brazos was, for many early residents, a story of flood concerns, flood events, and flood controls, but droughts proved to be an equally pressing, if less dramatic, concern. John Washington Lockhart, who lived in Washington-on-the-Brazos during the mid- and late nineteenth century, described the drought of the 1830s in an 1893 newspaper article, noting that "many times, when a boy, I have pulled off my shoes, rolled up my pants to my knees and waded across the river at Washington, and the water would not come up half way to my knees." [98] Waco families such as the Eichelbergers had elevated their homes upon stilts only a few years before that drought, and here, Lockhart talked of walking quite literally on the waters of the Brazos River.[99] Dr. Riddell provided an equally compelling description of a parched landscape in his 1839 travelogues: "The grass and herbage are rather sparse, and in tracts many ten thousand acres have been scathed and blackened by fire." [100]

As a result of such flood and drought events, the idea of moderating the inconstant flow of their regional watershed became a fixation for Brazos developers. The individuals who called for bills, built projects, or celebrated the completion of proposed schemes would ultimately find that the introduction of cement and steel, the channelization of the riverbed, or the dredging of the coast could not entirely prevent the effects of such climatic events from being felt. However, there was no denying the immediate enthusiasm with which Brazos dwellers approached the topic of moderating floods and droughts.

Second, the Brazos was historically most flood prone along the lower and middle reaches of the river, where the population was greatest. The steep slopes and elevated banks of the Upper Brazos provided some amount of flood protection for people living along this stretch of the river; the individuals living along the Middle and Lower Brazos River were not quite so fortunate. They lived alongside a riparian corridor with lower banks and less stable soils, a river whose waters had increased in quantity and velocity within the streambeds of the upper reaches. In other words, people living within the lower two-thirds of the river endured "quick runoff, flashy rises and sharp flood crests." [101] Well into the mid-twentieth century, the Lower and Middle Brazos

Rivers experienced moderate floods once every three years and minor floods every year.[102]

To the consternation of people living along those lower stretches of the river, this also meant that the Brazos was most easily developed (and the waters, controlled) along the upper reaches of the river, where floods were less common and less devastating. The limestone cliffs and deep canyons of the Upper Brazos River facilitated development because they provided a solid geological foundation into which dams and locks could be anchored. For example, a picture entitled "Bluff overlooking Brazos River where it is proposed to build the dam" (taken in 1936 near the Possum Kingdom dam site) revealed tall limestone cliffs flanking a river of moderate size.[103] These geological formations were effectively absent downstream, and the bedrock of the Lower Brazos River rarely proved stable enough to support the structures that boosters, developers, and lawmakers hoped to put into place. The locks and levees constructed along the lower third of the river, consequently, endured soils that collapsed, eroded, and shifted, a problem that was comparatively unknown at sites like Possum Kingdom.

Third, the individuals who settled the Brazos River after 1821 engaged the river and its geological realities in ways that simultaneously echoed and broke from earlier uses of the river. For the Brazos dwellers who hoped to reconcile the realities of the landscape with flights of their imagination, riparian-improvement projects presented an obvious solution to the twin problems of flood and drought. The American and European emigrants who first proposed and then built these projects, however, did not initiate change. Instead, they continued the riparian transformation begun by earlier groups, most notably American Indians and Spanish settlers. American and European emigrants often overlooked these groups and disregarded any changes they might have wrought on the landscape, a perspective that transformed this bountiful land into a canvas onto which the new settlers could carve their own changes and visions. Still, there was no doubt that these later arrivals actively participated in a process of change that predated, in most cases, the existence of the United States itself.

A lack of extant sources makes it difficult, if not impossible, to analyze pre-1821 uses of the river in a satisfactory manner. However, even a few examples of these early engagements with the Brazos suffice to indicate developmental continuity and to unveil developmental hegemony. Most obviously, the improvements that were proposed before 1821 addressed the same general issues—agricultural production and

Photograph of the Possum Kingdom dam site along the Brazos River; taken in 1936, this photograph shows the sheer cliffs that made this site attractive to developers. Courtesy Basil Clemens Photograph Collection, Special Collections, University of Texas at Arlington Library, Arlington, Texas.

flood control—that would prompt the locks, levees, and dams of later decades. They even incorporated similar, though much simpler, applications of technology. European explorers commented often, for example, on American Indian groups that irrigated and cultivated crops along the Lower Brazos River, one of the more obvious ways in which Native interactions with the river anticipated later uses of the river by white settlers. In the 1680s, for example, an unnamed Palaquechare Indian told a French explorer named Henri Joutel that they practiced agriculture, planting both corn and beans.[104] Archeological reports from the late twentieth century noted, likewise, the presence of "Indian farmlands just across the Navasota River" in 1716 and even noted the use of slave labor.[105]

Indigenous groups also practiced some amount of agriculture along the Middle Brazos River. François Simars de Bellisle indicated in the 1720s that local Biday Indians practiced agriculture, and Manuel de Mier y Terán reported in 1828 on the Hueco (or Waco) Indians, noting that "El terreno cultivado es de 240 o 250 acres que esta sembrado de maiz, frijole, calabaras, sandias" (The cultivated land is of 240 or 250 acres and is sown with corn, beans, pumpkins, watermelons).[106] There are far fewer references to agriculture along the Middle Brazos River compared to the Lower Brazos River, but this does not inherently mean that agriculture was less common. Instead, the lack of references is more likely due to the difficulty of finding sources about the indigenous groups that populated the watershed before the 1820s. The geologies of the Lower and Middle Brazos share enough commonalities that nineteenth-century developers along both stretches of the river emphasized agriculture and prioritized navigation. A similar, if imperfect, correlation seems to have characterized American Indian groups as well.

Spanish officials and settlers also manipulated the river. Most notably, Spanish priests constructed three missions—Missions San Francisco Xavier de Horcasitas, San Ildefonso, and Nuestra Señora de la Candelaria—along the San Xavier River, a tributary near the boundary between the Middle and Upper Brazos Rivers.[107] The institutional structure of these missions reflected several commonalities with later development projects. For example, the Franciscans at these missions tended croplands both alongside and removed from the river, working diligently to weed fields and to erect fences.[108] These missionaries also incorporated groundwater into their water policies, constructed irrigation canals, and oversaw the construction of a small rock dam by gentile (i.e., indigenous) converts.[109]

In yet another statement of continuity, Franciscan friars noted (and complained about) flood and drought events.[110] A 1752 document, speaking specifically to the effects of streamflow on the missions, noted "el corto caudal del Rio de S. Xav.ʳ imposibilidad de las sacas" (the reduced flow of water in the River of San Xavier, and the impossibility of withdrawals), and a 1756 letter to Diego Ramón indicated that the missions were ultimately relocated from the San Gabriel River because of "drying up of the water due to well known reasons."[111] Fray Mariano de los Dolores, who proved to be the missions' greatest advocate, spoke specifically to the missionaries' efforts to tame this small slice of the Brazos River watershed. For example, he noted in a 1750 letter that "la dificultad puede ofrezerse en la permanencia de las presas por sus desmedidas Crecientes.ᵒⁿ" (the only difficulty that offers itself is the permanence of the dams needed to control the excessive floods).[112]

Evidence of those Spanish buildings, abandoned not even a century earlier, still existed along the San Gabriel River during the nineteenth century, and the earliest emigrants in Texas took note of the structures. J. H. Fulcher, descendent of one of the many immigrant families who populated the Brazos Basin in the 1820s and 1830s, lived out his formative years in a region that was still along the fringe of Texas settlement in the 1860s and 1870s.[113] Fulcher reported in his memoirs that he would walk the San Gabriel River as a child and marvel at the evidence of long-defunct missions, sometimes questioning the meaning of the random foundations and at other times taking note as neighbors borrowed from the rubble for their own purposes.[114] Although the emigrants who moved into the area after the 1820s did not phrase it in this way (and almost surely did not conceptualize such an idea), the actions that they undertook in the figurative shadows of the Spanish missions offered an extraordinary word picture for the continuity in development that quietly persisted along the river.

White settlers built their homes from the literal wreckage of Spanish dams, and their ideas on development, likewise, hearkened back to earlier narratives of improvement for the Brazos Basin. The development projects that were proposed and/or implemented after 1821 were accomplished and envisioned on a scale that Spanish friars and Indian villagers surely did not anticipate, but they nevertheless mirrored those projects put in place centuries earlier. American Indian and Spanish groups interacted with the river before the arrival of American settlers in the 1820s, manipulating the river and its adjoining landscape to better meet their needs, and later inhabitants of the Brazos River watershed did likewise. There is a subtle continuity in water use between the embankment dams of the eighteenth-century Spanish missions and the concrete dams of the twentieth-century American river, and between the irrigation ditches of the American Indian villages and the irrigation canals of the American towns and Spanish presidios.

In addition to these threads of developmental continuity, the interactions of American Indian and Spanish groups with the Brazos River became the foundation upon which a structure of developmental hegemony would be constructed.[115] In the case of the Brazos, a single class gradually came to administer a strictly defined definition of improvement along the river. White Americans disproportionately dominated conversations of improvement after 1821: as landowners, legislators, and engineers, they dictated the dialogue on improvement and wove into those discussions increasingly grand schemes for riparian control. The lock-and-dam structures, the levees, the jetties, the canals, and the dams generally sought to reduce the impact of floods along the Brazos and to increase the flow of the river during times of drought. Earlier manipulations of the river had sought comparable goals for the river, but the increasing scale of the improvement projects and the growing dependence of these particular ideas of water use on private landownership gradually obscured any similarities.

The result was that the individuals who had once shaped the watershed and even anticipated future manipulations gradually found themselves on the wrong side of the hierarchical structure. Though the Comanche Wars would continue through the Red River Battle of 1874, most American Indian groups in Texas had been confined to reservations along the Brazos River by the 1850s. These same groups were ultimately moved to reservations in Oklahoma. Spanish and, later, Mexican individuals became excluded from enjoying the benefits of Brazos improvement in a more subtle but equally insidious way. Where Spanish friars and soldiers and settlers had benefited from and had even overseen the construction of dams and irrigation ditches along the San Xavier River, Mexican laborers later participated in these improvements as they worked in agricultural fields or on dam projects.[116] Although some individuals escaped disfranchisement through landownership, Hispanics often became relegated to the role of laborer and found themselves excluded from the reservoirs, parks, and social clubs that rose up around an improved Brazos.

Despite the rather tragic repercussions of this hegemonic shift (which shaped the lives of other minority groups as well), it would not be reasonable to assume that white settlers were intentionally acting out such an ideology. It is certainly possible that some developers and boosters recognized the race- and class-based shift in power, but the structure of strictly defined development came into play gradually and, at least in part, stemmed from the need of immigrants to create (and to reinforce) imagined communities of kinship.[117] The American population in Texas was composed almost exclusively of immigrants during the nineteenth century. Isolated from family and friends in an often-harsh land, these early settlers worked toward re-creating a known landscape—constructing familiar homes, cultivating familiar crops, and making the Brazos into a familiar riverscape. Manipulating the river in familiar ways became a tool of dispossession, but it also allowed these immigrants to maintain cultural ties with distanced groups.

Banks that eroded, floodwaters that surged, soils that colored the river itself—this was the face that the Brazos presented to those who dared to engage and, ultimately, to challenge its unruly waters. From 1821 onward, newspapers and memoirs, letters and reports spoke of the need to temper the unwieldy Brazos, to regulate its flashy waters and to rectify the riparian problems that shadowed daily life. Development to those ends would become something of an obsession for people struggling to make sense of this river and its potential. They proposed dam-building projects that called for everything from a single well-placed dam to a string of twenty-three dams, and they envisioned diversion schemes, intercoastal canals, and harbor projects that rewrote the economic and social landscapes of entire regions. Most of these projects would be cast aside as undeniable failures, undone less by economic considerations and more by geological ones. The progress that developers sought, in other words, could not always be realized within the reality that was the Brazos riverscape, undone by a geological narrative of floods, soils, plants, animals, and faults. Still, the impetus for development remained strong and proved to be as potent as the riparian forces that defied that same quest for control.

CHAPTER TWO

Culture, Continuity, and a Brazos River Reimagined

I may wander the rivers
And many a shore,
But down by the Brazos
I'll wander no more.
—BUCK RAMSEY, "The Brazos River Song," 2003

The Brazos seems secretive now, but still she offers resonances with a spirit
beyond my senses, and mysteries, too, cumulative and particular.
—"EPILOGUE," Scott Lennox Art

All dey knowed was haa'd work, mean obuhssers, chu'ch oncet a mont', big
dinnuhs on a Sunday, Saddy night chu'ch suppuhs an' string ban' flang-dangs.
—"THE SINNER MAN'S SON AND THE PREACHER," in John Mason
Brewer, The Word on The Brazos, 1953

IN 1831, MARY AUSTIN Holley toured the colony that her cousin
Stephen F. Austin had recently planted alongside the Lower Brazos
River in Texas. As a result of her journey, Holley penned what is now
a well-known, often-used diary of her trip.[1] She also penned the less
well-known "Brazos Boat Glee," largely considered the first English-
language song written in or about the future state of Texas.[2] Allegedly,
a steam voyage up the Brazos River inspired the tune, but only one line,
buried in the second verse, referenced the Brazos in any capacity:

Swift o'er thy silent tide,
Brazos our bark shall glide,
And rest in our forest home,
Far o'er the wave.

Although the tune afforded only nominal attention to the Brazos, Holley nonetheless managed to link this largely unknown river with the center of established settlements in Nueva España and the beginnings of steam travel in the Mexican state of Coahuila and Texas.

Mary Austin Holley also participated substantively if unknowingly in the construction of a Brazos culture. A general, prolonged failure to transform the Brazos into a mechanized, industrialized, commoditized, or controlled space in the years between 1821 and 1980 allowed this body of water to act as a unifying force for groups otherwise distanced by time or place. These interpersonal connections with the river have resulted in cultural artifacts such as paintings, songs, and photographs that have reflected the perspectives with which different individuals have approached the Brazos and its potential uses. Furthermore, this process of cultural creation has occurred among immigrant groups and indigenous villagers, enslaved populations and free communities, and it has birthed, from the experiences and ideals of those groups, a series of communally created, place-specific symbols for the Brazos River.

Brazos settlers—from the Lower to the Upper River, from the 1820s to the 1980s—used cultural products to create parallel representations of the river, depicting the watershed as a place of prison culture, plantation culture, Western culture, and so forth. The significance of that cultural production is in those very parallels. Just as scholars today debate the regional identity of Texas—struggling to define the state as wholly South or West—the improvement projects constructed and/or proposed along the Brazos River have reinforced both Western and Southern characteristics. The Brazos River, consequently, serves as something of a link between the cultural symbols of the South and West, incorporating the economic, social, and political structures of individualistic cowboys and arid lands but also the ideals of plantation lifestyles and cotton fields. Because these tropes craft a somewhat consistent message from a multiplicity of perspectives, cultural production along the Brazos River speaks faintly but unmistakably to the priorities that have shaped the process of development, to the ideological ties that have bound a frustrated people to a destructive land, and to the regional identities that have supported and shaped a long line of development projects.[3]

The perception of Brazos as South developed before that of Brazos as West, so this story of cultural production begins there, in 1821 with a plantation culture crafted by Stephen F. Austin, the emigrants who responded to his efforts as impresario, and their expectations that survived the long journey to this watershed. Cultural production among the earliest American and European emigrants lent itself snugly if not quite perfectly to the well-known ideals of an antebellum plantation culture; indeed, the Brazos River ultimately came to mark the westernmost boundary for an antebellum cotton culture in Texas. That form of Southern identity did not, however, become established in the region until the 1840s. Instead, newly arrived emigrants focused initially on the practicalities of moving to, settling in, and making over a land perceived as both wilderness and threatening. Their physical attention, if not always their abstract dreams, turned more often to sturdy homes, subsistence crops, and protective measures than to cotton-borne estates. In the first decades, Texas emigrants farmed potatoes, corn, and sorghum, they grew figs and oranges, and they cultivated rice. As families became more settled during the 1840s and communities grew more populous, cotton became a more common crop.

These farmers and landowners did not, however, delay their transition into a slave-based economy. Many of the individuals who settled within the Lower and Middle Brazos River watershed hailed from southern states, and they looked immediately to slavery as a convenient form of agricultural labor, privileging it (when possible) over wage labor or indentured servitude. As the 1830s progressed, an increasing number of white settlers began to accumulate wealth through the production of crops while an increasing number of African American slaves worked the fields that bore such wealth. Multiroom cabins replaced one-room log cabins, and manorial brick homes promptly replaced those once grand multiroom cabins. Some amount of illicit slave trading even flourished along the Brazos during the 1820s and 1830s.[4]

Brazos farmers of this era, whether engaged in slave-based monoculture or family-centric subsistence farming, depended on the Brazos watershed as their best and, in some cases, only form of transportation. Railways had not yet overcome the size of this expansive state, and the relatively few roads in existence were generally not dependable as an avenue of transportation. Extensive agricultural production meant little if the crops could not be transferred to an urban market, so early Brazos settlers quickly began to call for canals, levees, and channels that would be built on the model provided by such rivers as the Chattahoochee and the Mississippi.[5] An expanded transportation network and the trappings that came with it became the foundation upon which these early Texans built their expectations and the catalyst for what they hoped would be economic growth.[6]

The end result was that people living along the lower half of the river gradually wrought a Brazos of cotton and slaves, small farms and manorial homes. The enslaved man working the fields near Eagle's Landing, the emigrant mother in Marlin imagining a new life for her children, the small- and large-scale farmers at Groce's Landing who were floating goods down the river—these were the figures that contributed to a plantation lifestyle along the Brazos River. Numerous cultural forms played to this symbolism, but folktales were among the earliest type of artifact to portray the Brazos River in terms of a plantation culture. Emerging during the mid- to late nineteenth century and persisting into the early twentieth century, these tales usually took place in the Brazos bottoms and emphasized both the realities and the tropes associated with the plantation image. In some cases, such folktales were similar or even identical to tales told in other regions. Polly Redford, in her book *Raccoons and Eagles*, recorded a tale from the Brazos Basin in which Br'er Rabbit and Br'er Coon attempt to trap the wily Br'er Frogs; J. Frank Dobie, likewise, reported a number of tales from the Brazos River that resembled the more familiar stories of Uncle Remus.[7] The folktales that Redford and Dobie relayed are moralistic in nature, emphasizing triumph over circumstance and wit over brawn, and the largely enslaved populations who recounted the tales surely found meaning in these stories that flipped the narrative of dominance.

Other folktales were born along the Brazos River and spoke very specifically to life in this region. Many of these folktales rely on humor and wit to communicate the harsh realities of slavery, agriculture, and disfranchisement—for example, "Uncle Israel Changes his Mind" tells the story of a slave who prays every night for the Lord to carry him home.[8] Israel's owner overhears these prayers and, disguised as God, knocks on his slave's door three nights in a row. Each night, he invites Israel to leave for heaven, to make good on a desperate cry. The first two nights, Israel hides. The third night, an incensed Israel responds to the repeated invitation by refusing the offer and insisting, "Ah see now why de Jews kilt you; youse so damn haa'dhaided!"[9] This folktale acknowledges the realities of slave life throughout the text and even reinforces the tropes associated with a Southern antebellum culture, but the text is less about pity and more about agency. It humanizes the slave Israel, granting him a story line within which he cracks jokes, keeps house, and holds meaningful, if illusory, power over his fate.

In something of a departure from those tales that focus on adversity, many folktales speak, instead, of family, religion, good times, and boyhood pranks. Tales about religion commonly address one of three struggles: the struggle for all to lead a good Christian life, the struggle for wives to convert wayward husbands, and the struggle of men to understand religion.[10] These tales also remind their listeners (or readers, as the case may have been) that preachers suffer their own vanities and failures—from false teeth and balding heads to financial losses and illegitimate children.[11] The tales that speak directly to family life offer still more insights into the humanity that could and indeed did thrive along the Brazos River. These folk stories, for instance, tell of poverty and racial dissension, educational deprivation and "devulmint," but also stress the realities of flu scares, the joys of courtship, and the fears of "going' to hell head fo'mos."[12]

Paintings also contribute to the idea of the Brazos as a place of plantation culture. Though they often create a visual landscape that incorporated an antebellum hierarchy of race, these paintings nevertheless downplay any scenes that would have pointed clearly to slave labor and instead emphasize the context in which that plantation culture was imbedded. As a result, paintings of the Lower and Middle Brazos Rivers often focus on the landscape that both shrouded and bred the antebellum culture of cotton and slaves.[13] This is true of paintings that incorporate the built environment of mansions and carriages and steamboats but also of paintings that focus exclusively on what might be called the natural, physical landscape of the Brazos River.

For example, many paintings construct an image that focuses on the agricultural infrastructure. An undated drawing titled *Bernardo, Groce Plantation* and an 1834 painting by J. T. Hammond, McNeil's Estate near Brazoria, framed towering trees, rustling grasses, and log cabins in a pastoral image that ignores the human participants entirely.[14] Don Hutson also prepared a series of paintings on Brazos plantations in the late twentieth century, some of which speak more overtly to the racial implications of this plantation ideal. These paintings—which depict Jackson Plantation, Ellersley Plantation, Patton Plantation, and Eagle Island Plantation—share common elements: manorial brick homes (often with Corinthian columns), finely dressed families of polished white skin, and plainly dressed individuals of darker skin tending to the horses and the fields.[15] Despite the fact that more than a century has passed between the paintings of Hammond and Hutson, the general ideals on display remain the same. What Hammond painted as a visual record of agriculture as it existed in the minds and/or lands of contemporaries, Hutson painted as a graphic prompt that speaks to how people within the Brazos River watershed remembered that earlier period.

Other paintings focus still more exclusively on the physical environment that supported the Southern antebellum culture. In these representations, the river is hardly distinguishable from any other riparian forest scene, and few crops or homes or workers are present.[16] Paintings such as Sylvia Morgan's *Brazos Palmettos* and Sheri Jones's *The Brazos River, Brazos River, The River at Pecan*, and *Brazos River Beach* depict placid streams with leaves reflecting off still waters and boughs dipping to the earth.[17] This representation is especially common during the twentieth century. The reasons for this emergent focus on the land itself are not entirely clear, but there is no doubt that the river in these paintings is one that Brazos dwellers had long sought through the construction of canals and levees, the river that they had deemed necessary for the realization of the land's agricultural potential.

On rare occasions, artists used the Brazos River as a backdrop for immortalizing not the plantations and farms but the boats that carried the agricultural bounty to waiting harbors. These paintings contribute overtly to a narrative of Texas nationalism that is rooted in that early economy of crops and slaves. During the mid-nineteenth century, Karl Bodmer and George Catlin painted the steamship *Yellowstone* as it carried frightened civilians away from an advancing Mexican Army. Lee Jamison painted two pieces in the twenty-first century (*Austin's Last Journey* and *The Runaway Scrape: Loading the Yellow Stone at Groce's Plantation*) that features the river and, likewise, centers on a geography associated with slavery.[18] Don Hutson's painting of the steamboat *Hiawatha*, in something of a departure, focuses on an imagined journey of the gloriously outfitted, self-named steamboat that would have carried Brazos goods along the river.[19] The passage of time did little to change how these artists portrayed the steamboats and their role in creating (or protecting) a Brazos economy. The river in all these paintings is deep enough and wide enough to include the steamboats that did frequent these spots from time to time, again speaking to the river that people envisioned as well as the river that they actually engaged.[20]

On still rarer occasions, artists explicitly addressed the issue of race and labor, using their canvas or linen or paper to highlight the slave system on which the plantation culture depended. A 1959 painting of Orozimbo Plantation by Don Hutson reveals that same style of manorial home with fence and carriage and finely dressed family, but it

Undated painting of Ellersley Plantation by Don Hutson. Courtesy Brazoria County Historical Museum, Angleton, Texas.

includes a small cabin and dark-skinned, shadowed figures working the field between the respective living quarters. Russell Cushman's *Planters in the Field* and [*Pickers in the Cotton Field*] were painted still later in the twentieth century, but they, likewise, focus on the men and women who worked those agricultural fields. In this case, Cushman focused, respectively, on two young slaves and a slave owner's daughter in a field (dividing seed) and then two slaves picking cotton.[21]

Although they do not contribute explicitly to an ideal of Brazos plantation culture, artists have also begun in recent decades to paint the sharecropping culture that replaced the slavery infrastructure. Oftentimes the paintings that result from their efforts overtly incorporate, manipulate, and reflect the themes that originally contributed to the image of Brazos plantations conjured by earlier artists. For example, Leon Collins has created several untitled pieces in the twenty-first century (in the style of what he calls contemporary folk art) that portray black men and women in the cotton fields.[22] [*Sharecroppers in a Brazos River Cotton Field*], [*Sharecroppers in a Brazos River Cotton Field 2*], and [*Musician with Crops in Background*] by David Woods likewise integrate some combination of live oak trees, cotton fields, and black workers into contemporary analyses of the sharecropping culture.[23]

Whatever the intended purpose of paintings that showcase solitary rivers, triumphant steamers, and workers in a field, all of these works reinforce a linkage between agricultural labor, dispossession, and racial hierarchies along the Brazos River.[24] For the early settlers and also for later inhabitants of the Brazos River watershed, paintings unveiled the plantation-era power structures but also reinforced them. In a similar but perhaps more visible manner, people living within the watershed continued to examine, to negotiate, and to recover the tropes of the plantation era as they celebrated cotton throughout the twentieth century.[25] That focus on cotton reflected not only a continuation of what might be called a Southern culture but also the economic, social, and political realities of the watershed. The economy of the Lower and Middle Brazos Rivers depended heavily on agriculture and on the processing of agricultural goods in the nineteenth century, and that dependence receded little in the twentieth century.[26]

Accordingly, Texans began celebrating the economic and social importance of cotton around the turn of the nineteenth century with pageants, parades, museums, and other cultural tokens.[27] The City of Waco built the Texas Cotton Palace in 1894 to honor the year's success in cotton growing and then hosted annual pageants into the 1930s. As part of the yearly Cotton Palace celebration, Wacoans cheered the "first bale," crowned a cotton queen, and hosted arenas filled with musicians as well as agricultural tools.[28] A flyer that the city sent out for their inaugural Cotton Palace embodied the prevailing rhetoric of agricultural appreciation: "See Waco, The Greatest Inland Cotton Market in the World, and Central Texas, the Greatest Cotton Growing Region on Earth."[29] The pamphlet extolled almost endlessly the regional importance of cotton, dubbing Texas "the greatest of cotton producing States" and exciting public interest with a promise that the celebration would conclude with fireworks and illuminations at night.[30] These local celebrations drew vast public attention and pointed to the continuing significance of agricultural production along the Brazos—serving as a rather extravagant reminder that, in many ways, the cultural importance of cotton had only expanded with the decline of an antebellum economy.[31]

Along the Lower and Middle Brazos, people also came to imagine the river as a place of prison farms and convict labor from the mid-nineteenth century onward. This particular depiction, like the previous

Photograph of cotton in the Waco Town Square, taken in 1911 by local photographer Fred Gildersleeve. Gildersleeve very clearly captured the continuing, and at times increasing, importance of cotton to the regional population. Courtesy the Texas Collection, Baylor University, Waco, Texas.

cultural ideal, circles back to the idea of Brazos as South. More specifically, the focus on prison farms and prison labor underlines the continuing importance of agriculture for the regional economy and speaks to a continuing desire to take advantage of the watershed's natural fertility through unfree labor. People living along the river would likely have downplayed such connections, but suggestions of hegemonic continuity tie together the work of African American convicts in Brazos fields and African or African American slaves on Brazos plantations. This representation, in other words, reflects occasionally uncomfortable (but no less real) truths about the organization of labor along the river during the late nineteenth and early twentieth centuries.

The first state prison was located near the Brazos River in Huntsville. Moreover, the earliest prison farms in the state were sited along former Brazos plantations. These prison farms connected convict labor to agricultural production and made use of the region's natural fertility; the system of prison farms in Texas also reflected a broader pattern that

Cotton Palace parade forming on Square, 1912

Fred Gildersleeve photograph of the Cotton Palace Parade forming in the Waco Town Square in 1912. Courtesy the Texas Collection, Baylor University, Waco, Texas.

existed along other southern rivers (most notably, the Mississippi and its vast network of prison farms). Texas lawmakers used these prison farms as part of their convict-leasing program, which engaged inmates in various forms of manual labor. Not all convicts were relegated to cotton and cane fields, but lawmakers and prison officials genuinely believed that fieldwork offered an appropriate (and profitable) tool with which to save those convicts who could be redeemed and to control those convicts who could not. As a result, a rather startling number of Texas inmates spent some amount of time as agricultural laborers during the first half of the twentieth century.[32]

The convict-leasing program that developed at these farms persisted into the mid-twentieth century and ultimately involved individuals of many ethnicities. However, prison farms initially relied heavily on the labor of African Americans. Many of these convicts found themselves engaged in the sugarcane fields, a particularly taxing and brutal type of agricultural work, and the labor that they performed necessarily became entangled with the echoing memories of enslaved workers, sharecroppers, and tenant farmers.[33] The inmates tended long rows of crops under a burning sun and worked within eyesight of mounted, armed white guards. Inmates fell sick from exhaustion, and they were often judged by a quantification of their daily production.

These convicts spoke of what they called their hell in songs that, like the call-and-response melodies associated with slaves and freed blacks, became co-opted by faraway groups. Such work songs, accordingly, became the most common vehicle for highlighting the realities and tropes of a Brazos prison culture. The narrative of race that connected farmhand and prison hand with cotton, cane, and dispossession was not lost on Bruce Jackson, who edited a collection of prison songs called *Wake Up Dead Man.* In the introduction, Jackson describes his interviews with the wardens and guards who had been involved in crafting this labor system: "The field guards and officers and wardens who made these statements were not apologizing or justifying the system; they were just explaining it. . . . I never doubted that anyone who echoed the rationale believed every word of it; nor did I have a doubt that the structure of the southern prison was wholly grounded in the model of forced labor developed in the antebellum agricultural South."[34]

These convicts, as well as the men who hired and guarded them, became the purveyors of a prison culture that revolved around the Brazos River. Indeed, Jackson reports that the convicts often called their tunes "river songs" rather than "work songs" because the Brazos played such an integral role in shaping the culture, as well as the livelihood, of prison inmates.[35]

The best known of the prison songs, *Ain't No More Cane on the Brazos*, was first attributed to Huddie Ledbetter but was remade by the likes of Lightnin' Hopkins, Bob Dylan, and Lyle Lovett.[36] The chorus is simple: "Ain't no more cane on the Brazos. It's all been ground down to molasses," but the underlying message is one that speaks to the realities of injustice and suffering. *Ain't No More Cane on the Brazos*, told from the perspective of Jim Crow–era prisoners, speaks expressively and graphically about the hardships of life on Brazos farms. Prison farms transformed the Brazos into a place of death: "You ought to come on the river nineteen-fo', You could find a dead man on ever' turn row."[37] Prison farms shaped the Brazos into a place of oppression: "You ought to been on the river in nineteen-ten, They's rollin' the women like they drive the men." Prison farms created a space in which the hardships of agricultural labor were laid bare: "Captain, don't you

Undated photograph of convicts from the Brazos River prison farms working a line in the cane fields. Courtesy the Texas Department of Criminal Justice, Austin, Texas.

do me like you done poor old Shine. Well, ya drove that bully 'til he went stone blind."

Sugarcane Collins released an album that, likewise, drew attention to the difficulty of life as a Texas inmate relegated to these fields. Indeed, the Brazos holds a unique, if unwanted, place on his album of riparian tunes. Only two of Collins's songs mention a river by name, and one of those tells of a creek on which a local Indian tribe lived. The other song, *One Wing Frank*, is the story of a man who chopped off his hand to avoid the hard labor of the Brazos River prisons:

> I was taken back down to Sugarland and they whipped me till I
> was raw

And right there and then I made my mind up
I ain't going to work no more
Next day out in the bottom I knocked this Joe a permanent one
And with one neat swing I took off a wing
And my hard working days were done
If ever I get back home from Sugarland I sure am going to tell
That the state penitentiary down on the Brazos River
It's a doggone burning hell![38]

In the folk song "Old Rattler," a prisoner named Riley makes a less dramatic, but equally dangerous, decision to escape prison life by fleeing through the swamps.[39] "No More Good Time in the World for Me" also speaks candidly of the conditions, even incorporating a similar rhetoric: "If I ever go free, buddy, just goin' walk and tell, / 'Bout this lowland Brazos, it's a burnin' hell, / Well this lowland Brazos, partner, sure a burnin' hell."[40]

Still, prison work songs do not always discuss brutality and oppression in such exposed language. A small number of songs employ a deeply ironic tone to highlight the hardships of prison life or the brutalities of the prison system. Most notable of those tunes is the "Moore Brothers' Blues."[41] The Moore Brothers owned a plantation on the Brazos River near its confluence with the Navasota. Despite a reputation for being "hard on their niggers" (the Moore Brothers would later come under investigation by the state for mistreatment of prisoners), the song does not directly mention mistreatment but instead speaks more tangentially and dryly about the difficulty of life on the Moore Brothers' place:

I likes to work for the Mo' brothuhs—I tell you it's a fack—When
    yo' black gal runs away
They sho' nuff brings her back.[42]

Prison songs, in other words, focus on the realities of daily life for these prisoners—"Wake up on a lifetime, hold up your own head. Well you may get a pardon and then you might drop dead"—but point also to the forces, both well intentioned and not, creating the sociopolitical context within which they labored.[43]

Work songs, arguably, became the best known of the prison artifacts, but photographs reinforce this cultural ideal as well. Many of these photographs were not intended for vast, public consumption. Still, whatever the motivations of the guards and lawmakers and wardens

Photograph from 1911 of convict laborers and prison officials along the Brazos
River. Courtesy the Texas Prison Museum, Wm. Terrell IV Collection,
Huntsville, Texas.

who constructed these institutions, the photographs clearly tied prisoners to the river, to agriculture, and to a system that often grew from the
structures of a plantation culture. These images reveal black men working cornfields, cotton fields, and sugarcane fields.[44] They portray convicts bent over to fill long sacks with white gold or perched on machinery
to participate in the mechanized version of that cotton-growing process.[45] The photographs also indicate that the structure of armed white
guard and laboring black convict is too simplistic. Though fewer in
number, photographs at times reveal a convict band, a convict athletic
team, or convicts napping in the sun, and photographs that dated to the
second half of the twentieth century even included African American
guards.[46]

   In the same way that the realities of life along the Lower and Middle
Brazos Rivers lent themselves to the tropes of a Southern antebellum
culture, people living along the Upper Brazos saw in their daily lives
aspects of the riverscape that reflected a Western culture. Geography
alone would have pulled the Upper Brazos River watershed into the late
nineteenth-century process of expansion that shaped such rivers as the
Columbia and the Colorado, but the upper third of the river also engaged the demographic, social, and economic shifts attributed to the
so-called American West.[47] Many of the long-studied characteristics of

Undated photograph of convicts from the Brazos River prison farms picking cotton. Courtesy the Texas Department of Criminal Justice, Austin, Texas.

Western development—urbanization, industrialization, agricultural expansion, and the building of railroads—were present in the Brazos watershed as early as the 1840s and 1850s.[48] Additionally, many Brazos settlements grew up around a line of forts that incrementally moved west through the state of Texas after the Civil War, protecting an expanding population from the threat of attack—real or imagined—by American Indians, Mexican bandits, and Texas outlaws.

This representation, then, emerges from the actual histories of young men guarding the lonely plains around Fort Griffin, pioneer families living in scattered cabins, Comanche warriors roaming the plains, and Spanish friars toiling faithfully in missions.[49] However, the ideal of an American West often privileges some elements of Brazos history over others. The reality of conquest and invasion, for example, rarely featured in cultural artifacts, was replaced by references to mounted cowboys and empty landscapes. American Indians usually played the role of angry warriors, and Spanish or Mexican individuals, the role of friar or bandit. In short, the cultural West that flourished along the Brazos River said as much through what it excluded as what it included.

Most of the cultural artifacts that contribute to the representation of Brazos as West tell their stories from the perspective of white emigrants. Fortunately, a small amount of American Indian rock art, folktales, and music survived the passage of years, offering a richer and more complete study of this representation. Perhaps most intriguingly, the Brazos River found its way onto an album of American Indian flute music. The tune, titled "Brazos River Song," featured no other instruments: the sound of rain provided the only background for the flautist.[50] Other songs on this album boast titles like "Zuni Sunrise," "Yah-Vey-Tsee-Kee-Nah," "Belo Tay-Daw-Gyah-Daw," "Kiowa Eagle Spirit," and "Corn Harvest Prayer." That an individual of Kiowa and Comanche descent would record a song memorializing the Brazos is significant, for neither group had a permanent, extensive presence along the Brazos. Indeed, the Brazos River sat on the fringe of their historic territories. The album, then, helps to insert the Brazos River into a certain manifestation of Western culture that was relatively uncommon within the watershed.

Literary efforts also speak to the activities of indigenous groups in the watershed. Unfortunately, these pieces did not completely escape the Westernized view of American Indians, but they do offer a step toward a more authentic understanding of Native culture along the Brazos. For example, the *Poetry Journal* published a piece in 1913, "The Wild Bees," that discusses how American Indian groups might have interpreted white settlement along the Brazos and Colorado Rivers. In this poem, the humming of bees alerts the indigenous peoples of the river valleys to the coming of white settlers. These new settlers—not the "fiery filibusters passing wildly in a moment" or the "Mexicans and Spaniards, indolent and proud hidalgos"—necessitate a warning from the wild bees, who might bear witness to the effects of American migrants on lands further east.[51] Although the stanzas incorporate racist ideologies, the poem was nevertheless written from the perspective of Brazos Indians, and it speaks to the very real concerns of Native groups in the earliest days of settlement by white Americans.

Far more common are artifacts that explicitly construct a Western ideal from the experiences of white Americans. The representations that emerge from these cultural efforts portray the Brazos River as a romanticized space that had been saved from overdevelopment and that had escaped the less pleasant realities of water scarcity. Such artifacts include overt, if simplified, references to Western ideals—cowboys and Indians and aridity—and also more subtle descriptions of the landscape associated with those tropes. Poems, stories, and novels emphasize these themes throughout the nineteenth and twentieth centuries. For example, Edgar Rice Burroughs wrote a Western tale in 1922 that includes a pony named Brazos, and Zane Grey wrote a series of short stories during the 1940s that features a character named Brazos.[52] Long before that, Captain Mayne Reid and General Albert Pike published a series of books and poems that set their stories of adventure and murder in the West, using the Brazos River landscape to help define the image of a western land.[53]

The literary efforts of late twentieth-century authors focus on similar themes—tenacious lawmen, desperate bandits, dangerous adventures, and new lands. Larry McMurtry authored several books in the mid-twentieth century that feature the Brazos River, including the award-winning *Lonesome Dove* series, and contemporary authors such as E. Roy Hector, Cormac McCarthy, Lucia St. Clair Robson, and Caroline Clemmons also incorporate the Brazos into their Western series.[54] These books clearly play with the Western themes, incorporating them while also reinventing them. What attracted writers to the subject and the place of the Brazos River undoubtedly changed with time, but that attraction proved remarkably stable. Whether remembered as a reflection on the past or recorded as a sentimentalizing of the present, these works emphasize a similar landscape with familiar characters.

These literary productions collectively reveal the continuing, and perhaps escalating, attraction of the Brazos River landscape, but paintings also link the tropes of a Western culture to the Brazos. Unlike other cultural forms (whose subjects and messages shifted somewhat with the passage of time), paintings of the nineteenth century almost universally represent the Brazos in the same manner as twentieth- and twenty-first-century paintings. For example, Frank Reaugh, L. O. Griffith, and Jim Clements captured cultural moments in their paintings during the late 1800s, playing with the iconography intentionally and frequently. Reaugh's *Crossing the Brazos* (1880s), *Cattle in the Brazos* (no date), and *Scene on the Brazos* (1893) make use of cattle and cacti, mesas and mustangs to symbolize the culture of the Brazos and, more specifically, to insert the canyonlands of the northern reaches of the river into that context of cattle and cowboys.[55] A mural (ca. 2007) painted by the artists of Rotan, Texas, and Jim Clements's *Break at the Brazos* (ca. 2010) similarly feature a cowboy, his mount, and the Texas canyonlands.[56] The style of painting changed as decades and even centuries folded one into the other, but the subject generally resisted what changes the passing years had wrought on the physical landscape of the Upper Brazos River.

Despite the enduring interest in cowboys and Indians, Brazos paintings do not always play up the Western themes so explicitly. Some artists reinforced the idea of Brazos as West by fixating instead on the landscape that made possible the cultural tropes—the stark, somewhat nostalgic beauty of the river's semiarid landscapes. Paintings of the canyonlands emphasize the ephemeral nature of the river, the scattered pockets of rugged cliffs rising from shrub and mesquite, the rich red of boulders and sands, and the strands of wispy cirrocumulus clouds. Artists such as Laura Lewis and Scott Lennox painted entire series along the forks of the Brazos. Paintings such as L. O. Griffith's *Whitetop Field, West Texas* (1900), *Seymour, Texas* (1901), and *Valley View* (1909) and Josephine Oliver's *Untitled* (1932) use vivid colors and soft strokes but still focus on the aridity of this landscape, while other paintings—such as Griffith's *Untitled* (1900), Amy Winton's *Sunflower Sea* (2007), and most of Laura Lewis's works—use more muted colors.[57]

Much like Brazos paintings, photographs also preferentially highlight the canyonlands of the river's northern reaches. Photographers such as Scott Bourland, Wyman Meinzer (the state photographer for Texas in 1997), and Ray Rector (a turn-of-the-century photographer) captured the Brazos in photographs that effectively minimize any effect that the passage of time might have had on the land.[58] The reaches of the Brazos River that they photographed—fleeting trickles of shallow water tucked away into steeply cut banks—often include as much sand as water.[59] The coloring, as well as the subject, of these images tends to reinforce the idea of aridity and provides visual confirmation that pro-development individuals may not have overstated their concerns over the availability of water.[60] An image of Yellow House Canyon, for example, shows Turkey Mesa colored yellow by the sun, silhouetted by the deep black of threatening storm clouds, and otherwise lacking the cobalt or gray-blue shades of water.[61]

Photographers tended to be drawn particularly to the mesas along this section of the Brazos. Whether photographs were taken from an aerial or on-ground perspective, only the occasional rock grouping or sunken streambed breaks the stark flatness of these plateau lands. These mesas reflect rather succinctly the image of the canyonlands and embody quite perfectly the feel of the space.[62] Dan Flores describes the singular beauty of the mesas—the attraction of a "sudden interruption of the restful horizontal plane by a detached, hemispheric mound"—in his book *Canyon Visions*.[63] According to Flores, humans were prompted to pause "and let sight outrun the other senses" when confronted with a towering plateau butte, or hill.[64]

In the wide open spaces photographers captured in their work, people are reminded of a Brazos still largely free from development. Blue sky, red dirt, and gray-green scrub: photographs of the Brazos headwaters and canyonlands tend to emphasize the rugged nature of the landscape and, more often than not, suggest the reality of water famine rather than water feast.[65] The images reveal a river not yet begun to coalesce as a permanent source of water. Photographs also capture the flora and fauna of this river, particularly along the northern third of the river where the land was less settled and the nonhuman life, seemingly more exotic.[66] These photographs show a gnarled Juniper tree in Yellow House Canyon.[67] They highlight briar blooms that, with their pink and yellow puffballs, look like something meant to adorn a child's shoelace rather than a High Plains succulent.[68] They reveal chollas dancing in the wind.[69] Whether the photographs portray cottonwood leaves, grassy valleys, or tufts of dry-looking grass, they emphasize quite clearly the diversity that marked a stretch of river long characterized as barren.[70]

Despite the obvious differences between the ideals of Brazos as South and Brazos as West, they share two common themes. First, artistic representations of the Lower, Middle, and Upper Brazos consistently pay attention to the lives of those individuals who lived along the length of the river. For example, singers, folklorists, and painters represented the river as a place of life and death, tying it to the humanity that alternately flourished and floundered along its banks. This emphasis on the individuals who lived within the watershed and dealt with the realities of Brazos River outbursts speaks to the humanity that persevered in the face of slavery and persecution, flood and drought, deportation and violence—the life that could flourish if given freedom from Brazos tantrums. More important, the cultural artifacts that contribute to the ideal of the Brazos as a place of life speak poignantly if indirectly to the ties that bound Brazos dwellers to the land. In the face of devastating droughts and demoralizing floods, people chose to remain in this watershed not only for economic reasons but also because they had forged connections with the land. Those connections, which differed from one end of the Brazos to the other, could be built around events that were devastating as often as they were pleasant, and they generally provided sufficient incentive for Brazos dwellers to continue wooing, pursuing, and cajoling their willful river.

For twentieth-century poet Scott Lennox, the river helped to form his very identity—it offered him life in a figurative sense. In the poem "What the River Taught Me," he admits that he had discovered deep truths about the purpose and meaning and strategy of life by studying this willful river.[71] The Brazos, flowing at different depths and varying speeds, had something to say about the pace of life itself: the river abided by its own rhythms without thought of those forces that offered resistance. Lennox wrote the poem after development projects had altered the flow of the river, yet the capricious waters that continued to frustrate and to haunt would-be developers of this river (flowing high and then low despite the presence of dams) offered him an entirely different vision. The variability of the river, in this case, provided a reason for Scott Lennox to reevaluate his lifestyle—to learn the lessons of "pushing hard, too often overflowing my own banks," to learn the value of "holding on, and letting go," and to live as a river stone, "nestled into the riverbed, settled, safe."[72]

Second, the artists who celebrated the Brazos as either South or West generally ignored any evidence of improvement within the watershed. The lack of developmental features is, in fact, astounding. It is to be expected that artists would emphasize pastoral homesteads over titanic dams, but the near total lack of attention to changes in the built environment is notable. One of the more famous artists to depart from this general rule, John Graves, uses the river as the setting for a farewell canoe trip in 1957 and the subject of a now-iconic book.[73] The narrative that he published at the end of his journey, *Goodbye to a River*, addresses the impending loss of the Brazos River to the era of dams but also discusses more generally the effects of development on the landscape: "Charlie Goodnight and the Ezra Shermans and their children and grandchildren all combined have burned out and chopped out and plowed out and grazed out and killed out a good part of that natural world they knew, or didn't know, and we occupy ourselves mainly, it sometimes seems, in finishing the job."[74] The book, in other words, speaks to the unending scuffle over America's resources, most notably her rivers.

Upon moving to Texas, Paul Christensen wrote and published a book that comments specifically on the lack of cultural attention toward development, dedicating a large portion of the text to the loss of a simpler style of life. Christensen believes that the state in its entirety had experienced such a loss, but he argues that the loss of a simpler life is reflected most aptly along the Brazos River: "There was no funeral over it. Only one book seemed to have grasped the significance of the moment: Graves's *Goodbye to a River* (1960). On its surface, Graves bids farewell to an undammed Brazos River on the eve of its being manipulated, ending a certain way of life along both banks. But it is also a farewell to an era in Texas."[75]

In the mind of this modern-day migrant, the fate of the Brazos was the fate of the state, the fate of an entire American livelihood. For Christensen, "a Huck Finn world of small, sleepy farms, . . . a life condensed enough to put into a roomy pocket of your overalls" was dying, and the loss of this lifestyle meant a severing of the connection with the frontier that defined American life.[76]

The idea of loss expressed in his literary piece is echoed in a song written by Rattlesnake Annie, titled "Goodbye to a River." What she laments in the lyrics to this song—what might be lost to the progressive march of a developmental impulse—are the raw ingredients that inspired other artists to memorialize the river in their own way: the damming of a river and the need to cry, the covering of lands by that water and the idea that such loss could be justified through the "advancement of man."[77] The song, adopted by the West German branch of Greenpeace as their anthem, expressed Rattlesnake Annie's sorrow at losing what she viewed as the more natural landscape of the Brazos River to the era of large-scale dams.[78]

Though they ultimately produced pieces that incorporated different mediums and emphasized different tropes, singers, photographers, writers, painters, and folklorists used a variety of art forms to capture the culture of the Brazos River and to express artistically their expectations for the watershed. Whether depicting this space as a part of the Western culture of cowboys and Indians or the Southern culture of slaves and cotton, artists incorporated the Brazos into their work, changing the river while immortalizing it. The end result of their efforts is rarely representative of the collective experience of Brazos life. Instead, paintings of a wide, still river and songs about a topophilic attachment to a particular place generally speak to a romanticized and mythologized view of the Brazos River (albeit one that might speak to the dark realities of slavery as well as the economic promise of navigation).

Still, the sheer number of cultural artifacts produced along this river is noteworthy, for it suggests that the story of the Brazos is, in many ways, the story of Texas. From the formal beginnings of this state at the town of Washington-on-the-Brazos to its role as a link between South and West, the history of Texas is inextricably tied into the history of the Brazos. That connection endows the river with a relevance that defies its otherwise regional nature and helps to explain the extent of cultural consumption about this river.[79] The Brazos River, for example, found its way into the genres of jazz and classical music by the late twentieth century.[80] The Crusaders recorded a jazz number known as the "Brazos River Breakdown," covered by an accomplished Swedish trombonist named Nils Landgren, and Chuck Pinnell, likewise, produced a disc of classical and acoustic guitar titled "Twelve Rivers," which placed the Brazos alongside such iconic rivers as the Shenandoah and the Rio Grande, the Mississippi and the Jordan.[81] The river's inclusion in popular music also extended into the realm of rock and pop. Billy Walker and Marty Robbins performed "Cross the Brazos from Waco" as did Old Dog Revival; Whiskeyboat sang "The Brazos River Turnaround"; and, ZZ Top immortalized the river in "Chevrolet."[82]

The cultural production that has persisted along the Brazos is significant for still another reason: the ideals reflected in these artifacts served as opiates for what proved ultimately to be an impossible dream of development for the Brazos River. The songs and paintings and civic celebrations reflect the different ways in which individuals and groups engaged the reality of daily life along the river, coming to know it and coming to know themselves through it, and also speak to a continuing inability to reconcile reality with expectation. As a result, artistic creations became one more tool with which individuals could ascertain personal, as well as national, attitudes about progress, development, and change. These artifacts, contributing quietly to a visual culture of development, bring light to the ways in which thought and activity have become intertwined in the muddy waters of the Brazos River, and they speak also to the still more muddied efforts of developers to shape those waters.

CHAPTER THREE

Immigrants, Improvements, and Agricultural Ideals along the Lower Brazos River

If Texas that promised land, should be all like this, I would advise a person to live on one of those great heaps of sand we see something [*sic*] dug out of cellars, for a month or six weeks before he comes here, that will give him an idea of this part of the country at least.

—S. M. WESTEWELT TO LEWIS, 1841

The evil influences are manifold. Water is becoming exceedingly scarce; wells are drying up, tanks ditto, and old Brazos for the first time in eighteen years, has ceased to flow gulfward; pools of the aqueous element only lingering in its wealth of bed, which can not [*sic*] last a fortnight longer at the rate they are now draughted upon by the stock of the surrounding country. Truly, a water famine is now imminent.

—U. BET, "Waco Correspondence," *Galveston Daily News*, 1874

If a comparison is made between the conditions existing at the mouth of the Brazos River and those at the mouth of the South Pass of the Mississippi River and at the Sulina branch of the Danube, the comparison will be favorable to the Brazos.

—BRAZOS RIVER CHANNEL AND DOCK COMPANY, *Facts With Reference To The Brazos River Enterprise*, 1890

IN 1833, THE BRAZOS RIVER overflowed its banks. The lower third of the river stretched to an average width of three to four miles during this overflow, leaving newly arrived immigrants little choice but to watch as muddy swaths of water buried their crops, homes, and livestock.[1] In 1842, the Brazos poured out of its banks once again, prompting another round of exclamations from people living in low-lying areas. John Washington Lockhart, an early settler in the bottoms, reminisced about this second flood in an 1893 editorial, noting that "the water was from ten to fifteen and in some low places twenty feet high in the bottoms."[2] Averaging more than one moderate to severe flood per decade, still more overflows between 1821 and 1890 prompted similar reports of devastation as witnesses noted livestock, trees, and even homes tossing about in the river.[3] The *Matagorda Gazette*, for example, reported that the 1859 flood carried away the entirety of the Richmond railroad bridge, and after the 1876 flood, the *Galveston Daily News* reported that "the main Brazos rose so as to cover the tops of the telegraph poles."[4]

Despite such graphic examples of destruction, people living along this river knew that floods represented only one form of Brazos peril. Periods of drought interrupted these overflows, bookending times of high water with years of extreme low water.[5] John Washington Lockhart described the drought of the late 1830s in that same 1893 article: "In consequence of this drouthy condition the river got to be very low. It looked for a time that it would stop running. In 1840 or 1841 Mr. Tillotston Wood . . . and myself rode from Washington to Hidalgo falls, some seven miles by land, and perhaps double that distance by the river, along the bed of the river, never once having to leave it, but crossing from the point of one sand bar to the other."[6]

Other sources reported similar problems with low water and rain-starved crops, often echoing some variation of Henry Caufield's 1859 lament—"if it don't rain soon we are done for this season."[7] The *Galveston Daily News*, which reported on the topic in 1874, repeated the refrain: "The old Brazos for the first time in eighteen years, has ceased to flow. . . . It is distressingly aggravating, and a darned dry subject to contemplate."[8]

The resources and economic potential of the watershed were undeniably impressive, but the opportunities born of the river too often went unrealized as crops dried out within sight of a diminished river or molded within the overflows of a mighty one. Contemporary Texans, as a result, both reflected on and bemoaned an inconstant river, grieving over the combined effects of irregular rains, unstable soils, shallow banks, and wide floodplains. Despite the reality of dashed hopes and tangible loss, emigrants and settlers and lawmakers began to boast of and to plan for the river's potential immediately upon their arrival to the watershed. They envisioned a new landscape based on their ideals of productive improvement, and they worked to construct projects that might realize those same expectations. This constant, if initially intellectual, struggle, between the imagined potential of the Brazos and the reality of its limitations guided the earliest decades of riparian development. More specifically, agricultural losses initiated improvement of the Brazos River as individuals along the lower third of its reaches turned to technological solutions that would moderate the river's flow, enhance navigational possibilities, and insert agricultural commodities into an economic market.

Brazos River improvement projects would ultimately take the form of transnational diversion schemes and hydroelectric dams, but they were modeled initially on the local and regional transportation systems that had remade, and were continuing to remake, the rivers of the southern and eastern states. As the Industrial Revolution transformed life in this nation during the early and mid-nineteenth century, national faith in technology grew apace, and it was within this context of emergent technocracy and navigation-centric development that settlement of the Lower Brazos River by Euro-American and American immigrants occurred. Indeed, white Americans began to populate the Mexican province of Texas in 1821, two decades after Robert Fulton successfully completed a voyage on the steamer *Clermont* and four years after construction began on New York's Erie Canal.[9]

Entrenchment of a technological faith was thus gradually realized within the watershed, but it did not immediately appear along the Brazos River, at least in part because the population itself grew uncertainly in the early years of settlement. During the first half of the nineteenth century, the population of the Brazos Basin expanded in fits and starts. American and European emigrants moved into what was then the Mexican state of Coahuila and Texas during the 1820s, enticed by impresarios such as Stephen F. Austin and their promises of free land. However, this influx slowed dramatically in the 1830s. Fearful of the expanding American population in Texas, the Mexican government tightened immigration laws at that time, most notably through an 1830 act that prohibited further settlement. This prohibition did not halt immigration by white Americans and Euro-Americans entirely, but the population would increase only gradually until the Texas Revolution and, later, the annexation of the Republic of Texas officially opened the land to wanderers from outside the Mexican nation.[10] At that point, the settlement that had centered along the Lower Brazos River would begin to spread dramatically and rapidly into the Middle Brazos River valleys and very gradually into the flat, elevated lands of the Upper Brazos River.

Although slavery was not legal in Texas, the slave population also expanded steadily (if slowly), generally paralleling the growth of the immigrant population. In direct contradiction to agreements made with the Mexican state, the introduction of slaves was not only allowed by colonizers such as Austin but also actively encouraged. For example, an 1821 advertisement for the Brazos colonies informed its readers that "Six hundred and forty acres of land will be granted to the head of each family, and in addition to that, three hundred and twenty acres to a man's wife, one hundred and sixty acres for each child, and eight acres for each slave."[11] As a result of such inducements, by the start of the Civil War the Brazos River Basin included a population of slaves that, depending on the specific geography under discussion, either matched or came close to matching the densities seen along other Deep South rivers.[12]

As had been the case in other southern states, corporate boosters did much to facilitate the increasing population in Texas, playing up the possibilities of the landscape in speeches, pamphlets, and travel guides. A promotional pamphlet published in 1881 by the South Western Immigration Company spoke, for example, of the richness and fertility of the Brazos Valley, not only comparing it favorably to other farming regions in the United States but also boasting of its superiority to the famed Nile Delta.[13] An 1894 pamphlet published by Charles Cutter used similar rhetoric to build interest in Waco, calling the city a health resort and touting the benefits of local natatoriums (swimming pools and clubs that often incorporated mineral waters), artisanal wells, and a healthy environment.[14] But the role of these boosters was necessarily limited by two factors. First, these purveyors of hope and expectation were not especially common along the Brazos River until the mid- to late nineteenth century (evidenced by the dates of publication above). Second, the promotionals produced by these professional boosters usually offered only general inducements to settlement along the Brazos.

As a result, the individuals that lived within the watershed arguably did more to attract people to the Brazos River than did corporate boosters. Where institutionalized boosterism offered grand overviews based on (at best) brief visits to the watershed, the lay boosterism of lawyers and housewives and merchants provided concrete, place-specific endorsements of the regional landscape. Brazos laypeople publicized their thoughts on the potential of the river in letters, articles, songs, and memoirs throughout the nineteenth century, and these written descriptions played a vital, if informal, role in drawing people to the region.

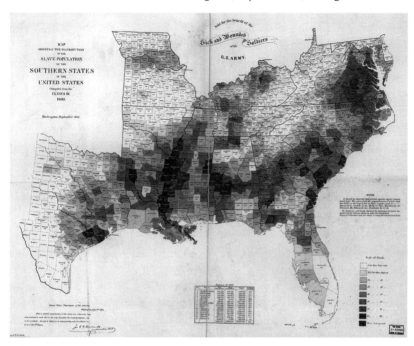

E. Hergesheimer's *Map showing the distribution of the slave population of the southern states of the United States* (1861). Courtesy the Library of Congress, Geography and Map Division.

As early as 1836 and consistently through 1890, lay boosters spoke of the Brazos River as the "Mississippi of Texas" and compared it favorably to the region of the Nile River.[15] They likened the landscape, with its arable pastureland and ample floral species, to the biblical land of Canaan and described it as "flowing with milk and honey."[16] These informal boosters also defined the landscape as a place where one's expectations were "more than realized" and envisioned a not-too-distant day when its ports would rival those of London, Liverpool, Chicago, or New York.[17]

Though the subject of these letters, articles, and memoirs varies dramatically from one source to the next, common themes emerge—most notably, the agricultural potential of the land and the perception of the land's healthiness. Nineteenth-century boosterism focused primarily on the former, on the fertility of the land and the profits to be made from that productiveness. Emphasizing the size of the crops as well as the richness of the soils, emigrants portrayed the Brazos River landscape as a region naturally suited to the cultivation of cotton, corn, peaches, potatoes, oranges, sugarcane, and even grapes.[18] Colonel Edward Stiff used his 1840 travel guide to declare, "The Brassos bottoms throughout, are perhaps inferior to no soil on the globe."[19] In a similar manner, other sources of the early and mid-nineteenth century described the riverscape as a land "very rich and fertile!" and labeled it a country "the produce of which will be sufficient to stock the world."[20] In one of the more overt examples of Brazos braggadocio, James Decatur Cocke used an 1838 pamphlet to note the pervasive presence of cotton "grown to the height, commonly, of from *eight* to *twelve* feet."[21]

Even when such sources did not explicitly mention agriculture, they still boasted of the land's bountiful production. That productivity was directly linked with economic opportunities in some sources. For example, Alexander Thomson wrote in an 1833 letter, "I think if you can wind up your business, and have enough left to bring you to this country, you would do much better than to go to the Choctaw, or Chicasaw purchase; for if you still wish to merchandise you can do far better here than in any part of the U.S., and if you wish to farm and raise stock, I have never seen or heard of any country equal to it."[22]

Still other boosters felt no need to find utilitarian value in the land, instead commenting strictly on its beauty or abundance. In 1844, Alden Jackson referred to the Little River, a tributary of the Brazos, as "the land of beauty."[23] An unnamed individual traveling from Austin to Hempstead in 1875 granted the Brazos Valley a still more evocative label, dubbing it the "garden of Texas."[24]

As late as the 1880s, people still often wrote of the river's unparalleled fertility, often contrasting that potential with what they described as the worn-out lands of the Deep South states and encouraging their brethren to take up a westward migration so as to take advantage of the Brazos splendor.[25] The boosterism of other regions even referenced the fertility of the Brazos River. An advertisement in Jacob de Cordova's 1856 travel guide, for instance, boosted the reputation of land for sale on the San Jacinto River by noting that it was "equal to that of the Brazos in its productive qualities, and being situated immediately on first-rate navigation, it is admirably adapted to the raising of Vegetables, Melons etc., for the Galveston Market."[26] In a similar manner, in 1881 the South Western Immigration Company used the "famed bottoms" of the Brazos River as the standard for Texas productivity when it advertised fertile lands for sale along the Trinity and Rio Grande Rivers.[27]

The agricultural potential of the Brazos Basin immediately engaged the minds and pens of Brazos dwellers, but as these same men and women lived and worked in the watershed, they began to formulate another line of thought about the river's potential. Though less common than agricultural praise, boosters (both lay and professional) also began to characterize the Brazos as a place of healing and vitality. Immigrants and visitors wrote frequently on the subject to family in other states between the 1830s and 1880s, telling of renewed health and praising their newly gained freedom from various fevers.[28] In a move that catered to the contemporary fascination with the human body and its sensitivity to environmental factors, out-of-state physicians and boosters even began to prescribe for the infirm a visit to the Brazos River, insisting that the climate of the region and the artisanal waters of the basin were curative.[29]

These individuals believed that the waters of the river could heal bronchitis, asthma, rheumatism, dyspepsia, syphilis, sore eyes, eczema, and a multitude of chronic blood, skin, liver, and kidney troubles.[30] William Smith wrote in 1839 that the town of Velasco promised "as great advantages as any of the sea-bathing resorts," and half a century later, the City of Waco echoed those beliefs in an advertisement for the 1894 Cotton Palace, calling itself "The Geyser City, the coming Health Resort of the World."[31] Correspondingly, Brazos cities constructed mineral wells and built natatoriums that catered to visitors hoping to cure common ailments as well as more exotic diseases.[32] The so-called curative powers of these waters thus bore enormous implications for the Brazos economy.

Despite the glowing reports, however, the riverscape also gained a reputation for sickliness among some groups. People living in or visiting the Lower Brazos River most commonly complained of dysentery, cholera, measles, and influenza (also known as the grippe) and usually attributed this sickliness to the inconsistent rain patterns.[33] Concerned women talked of fevers, irritated fathers lamented the swamps, and emigrants complained broadly of the moist air.[34] A. Somervell, for example, spoke expressively and memorably about the sickliness of the land in 1833, noting that "disease and death stalk abroad in the land defying . . . medical skill."[35] An 1833 letter from John R. Jones to James F. Perry expressed concerns over disease, death, and malaise still more clearly when it called Brazoria and its environs "the most sickly and dangerous section of country on the whole continent.[36] An occasional epidemic only added to the perception that the Brazos could be a place of death as much as of life.[37]

Whatever the reality of life, Texas immigrants generally wrote glee-fully about their good fortune in settling on the Lower Brazos River, essentially mythologizing the river even while planning for its short-comings.[38] W. B. Dewees, a visitor to Coahuila and Texas, summarized the prevailing thought in an 1823 letter. Using broad strokes of an ex-travagant style, he described the Brazos as a land beyond compare, noting that "the lands in this country are so rich and beautiful, and the climate so healthy and delightful, as to be of itself an inducement suffi-ciently strong to attract many roving adventurers to this beautiful par-adise of America."[39] Edward King echoed these same sentiments in an account of his 1874 travels: "What beautiful retreats by the Brazos!"[40] The commonalities that marked these (and other) proclamations sug-gested that, for many migrants, the passage of time had done little to dim enthusiasm for the land's potential. Immigrants were occasionally disillusioned by the gap between reality and reputation along the Lower Brazos River, but for the most part, settlers spoke exuberantly of the river's unparalleled healthiness, interminable beauty, and near-mythic fertility.[41]

The boosterism that flourished along the Lower Brazos became in-creasingly grandiose as settlement progressed during the nineteenth century. Indeed, later generations would dismiss many such sentiments as mere puffery, simple advertising, but these commendations, whatever their accuracy, served two practical purposes. First, the praise that cor-porate and lay boosters lavished on the riverscape offered hints as to why emigrants would, after encountering the reality of the river, remain along the Brazos. The people living in this watershed during the nine-teenth century found themselves in a land subject to frequent inunda-tions and devastating interludes of drought. "The disaster is so appalling that description is not possible," cried an Ohio newspaper after the 1899 flood.[42] Given the reality of life, immigrants earnestly and pur-posefully weighed their decisions to remain rooted in the watershed, and the descriptions that they provided of the river corridor in personal accounts unmask the ties that rooted them to the land and countered recurring inconveniences.

Several factors secured these individuals to the land, binding them to an unruly river and encouraging permanent settlement during an age when Americans were still quite mobile. In some cases, migrants did not have the financial resources to leave the Brazos Basin. Although the financial burden differed from one family to another and one decade to another, many families staked all their capital on a move to Texas.

Making a second move shortly thereafter was simply not an option. In other cases sheer stubbornness kept Brazos families moored to a difficult waterway as individuals determined to make a life from the land that they or their parents had carved out of the proverbial wilds. Most individuals, however, seem to have decided that the possibilities of the watershed simply outweighed any risks associated with droughts, floods, and other riparian events.[43] The economic returns that could be gained from a plot of cultivable land were enticing, and the very real fertility of the riverscape, in their opinion, justified occasional losses to overflows or low flows.

In addition to offering insight into the mentality of early settlers, these many forms of boosterism served a second, equally significant purpose. Beginning in 1821 with the much-mythologized arrival of Stephen F. Austin, Americans encountered this river in large numbers for the first time. As part of the process of emigrating and settling and beginning anew, they overlaid onto the physical landscape a series of symbolisms that spoke to how they envisioned an improved Brazos. These symbolisms emerged from daily interactions with the landscape and reflected the ways in which people prioritized land use, dealt with Brazos outbursts, and interpreted a newly encountered land. For instance, people like Mary Austin Holley and John Washington Lockhart contributed thousands of examples of boosterism to the collective reputation of the Brazos River during the nineteenth century, which in turn fostered competing ideas about what form the river should take. This process gradually linked the Brazos River with specific, contextualized ideas about development—connecting boosterism with project and thought with activity, and ultimately giving substance to the abstract ideals that people formed about the river.

That process of what might be called representation most commonly affirmed one of three ideas about the river—the Brazos should be a place of constant flow, a place of agricultural production, and/or a place of navigation. Perhaps the most common representation was the first, that of a constant Brazos. Indeed, people living along or near the Brazos River pushed almost universally for improvement as a means of mitigating the river's flashy nature. When visitors and settlers talked of the river's "flashy" nature, they were not simply speaking from a place of frustration. Instead, they referenced an ecological reality. The river almost always ran high or low, disrupting budgets, travel, shipping, and agriculture, and never quite offering a consistent streamflow. Consequently the river initially acted as an impediment to, rather than a catalyst for, the development that so many individuals in the Brazos Basin desired. Lockhart, as seen, noted both droughts and overflows in the 1830s and 1840s, even testifying to floodwaters that sent "buffaloes, wild horses and smaller game . . . floating down the river intermixed with driftwood."[44] P. R. Christiansen expounded on that same problem of flow in an 1897 newspaper article, suggesting that development projects should "keep the river running evenly all the time instead of being a roaring, destructive torrent part of the year and the balance of the time hidden in shoals."[45]

The inability of the Brazos River to offer a remotely consistent flow of water through its banks meant that steamboats grounded on sand-bars, crops rotted on barges, families lost their homes to raging waters, and settlers questioned the wisdom of migrating to the basin.[46] Such a reality could only hinder the growth of an emerging capitalist economy. The Brazos and Galveston Railroad, incorporated by Sam Houston on May 24, 1838, published a pamphlet in 1839 addressing these very frustrations and concerns:

Nature has been more bountiful to Texas in climate, in luxuriance of soil, and in the value and variety of products, than in the facilities of commerce. The lands in the Brazos valley are the finest in the world, and by remedying the defects of the disemboguement of the river, the planters will have advantages superior to those of any country.[47]

The Brazos and Galveston Railroad intended with those words merely to justify the company's creation of a railroad in sparsely populated Texas, but its pamphlet nonetheless drew attention to and expounded upon the problems impeding the river's productive use.[48]

A constant Brazos would allow, in turn, for the realization of another vision—the Brazos as a place of agricultural productivity.[49] The economy of the region relied heavily on agricultural production during the nineteenth century: as the crops went, so went the emerging market. Thus, the fickle waters of the Brazos wrought very real havoc on the stability of the region and undermined any hope that good crops would lead to good economic returns. As a general rule, both Lower and Middle Brazos River farmers engaged in multicrop subsistence farming on small pieces of land in the first decades after settlement began in the 1820s.[50] Immigrants reported cultivation of cotton as early as 1833, but corn, sweet potatoes, Irish potatoes, oats, wheat, millet, rye, and peaches were grown in equal and, at times, greater numbers on Brazos lands.[51] By the 1840s, these same farmers more commonly engaged in single-crop farming that commoditized cotton and, less frequently, sugar; by the century's end, they would see a general but marked decline in agricultural production along their stretch of river.[52] Along the Upper Brazos River, the pattern was somewhat different. Early settlers, who populated this region at the same time that cotton production began to accelerate along the coast, initially grew a variety of crops (especially the cereals) and very little cotton.[53] However, cotton became a staple of the Upper Brazos economy at the same time that it declined further downstream, testament to the impact of reclamation and irrigation on the productivity of these more arid lands.

The people living in this basin, however, did not merely cultivate crops. Although the Upper Brazos River would become most closely tied to the cattle culture during the late nineteenth century, farmers along the length of the river often engaged in animal husbandry during the nineteenth century. Cattle and hogs accounted for the vast majority of livestock, constituting by the 1890s anywhere from 88 percent to 99 percent of the economy that grew up around animal husbandry.[54] Other historic sources reinforced the information found in this census data and, more importantly, affirmed that farmers kept both crops and livestock during the early and mid-nineteenth century. Letters from the Caufield family, who lived along the Middle Brazos River, indicated that during the 1850s, individuals scattered across family farms often put much of their land into wheat and corn and little, if any, into cotton.[55] Additionally, the Caufield family engaged in both farming and stock raising in the antebellum years.[56] Other families within the Brazos Basin also participated both in animal husbandry and multicrop farming from the 1840s to the 1870s.[57]

The social, economic, and physical landscapes that early settlers built also included the industrial mechanisms responsible for processing agricultural goods. Industry was fairly absent along the Brazos River during the early and mid-nineteenth century, but it became increasingly common in the watershed as the century progressed. The town of Towash, located at a natural ford, boasted a water-powered flour mill by the end of the century.[58] Waco, San Felipe, Independence, Navasota, and most of the Lower Brazos towns could brag, likewise, of a few grain elevators, flour mills, icehouses, and cotton mills by 1900.[59] Purportedly the Baylis Gin in East Waco was the first cotton gin west of the Mississippi, and a man named Henry Gregg lived on a Brazos bottom farm that employed a steam gin.[60] Because the industry that thrived along this river dealt almost exclusively with the processing of agricultural goods and made use almost solely of waterpower, it became entangled in questions of river improvement and economic expansion.

The agricultural economy that grew up around Brazos farms generally was open only to a handful of immigrant (usually western European) or American settlers. However, the growth of that economy was predicated heavily, as it was in other southern states, upon slave labor during the antebellum years.[61] Slave owners rarely invoked the term *slave* in their letters, referring more obliquely to the institution and their role in it: "Do you wish to hire some Negroes? I have six or eight to hire if you want them come down soon as I shall dispose of them in a few days."[62] Yet, as demonstrated by frequent references in letters, articles, and deeds, Africans and African Americans working in the Lower and Middle Brazos River fields were more likely to be slaves than free men and women and, later, sharecroppers or even convicts rather than landowners.[63]

As early as 1821 and consistently throughout the antebellum years, historical sources referenced "young negroes" used as farm labor and individuals "bound in body and mind."[64] Slave laborers were usually brought into the state by their owners during this period but were also, at times, sold in Texas as part of an illicit slave trade that operated along the Brazos coastline.[65] These individuals had few if any rights, and their livelihoods were generally not considered in decisions about water or land use. Still, their contributions to the economy as a form of agricultural labor were often described as indispensable. In the postbellum years, Hispanic individuals and individuals of Chinese descent also became associated with agricultural labor and experienced a similar form of dispossession.[66]

The ability of white Americans to dictate water use and development generally had a detrimental effect on the daily lives and future prospects of other demographic and socioeconomic classes, but these subaltern groups would have benefited from any attempts to control the Brazos River. Sources frequently noted, for example, that African American families were disproportionately impacted by flood events because they often, though not always, lived in low-lying, flood-prone areas and worked as agricultural laborers.[67] An 1868 article from the Saint Joseph newspaper noted, for instance, that "a flood in the Brazos river, in Texas, washed away seventeen negroes and the grain crop."[68] The work that Brazos dwellers undertook on behalf of flood control

Undated photograph of a cotton gin near Waco; purportedly, this was the first cotton gin built west of the Mississippi River. Courtesy the Texas Collection, Baylor University, Waco, Texas.

may have been directed at white settlers, but it often offered black families security from floodwaters that in turn lessened the economic instability that many of them endured.

Similar stories in nineteenth-century newspapers indicated that, whatever their race, poor farmers struggled to put food on their tables after flood and drought events. If wealthy farmers and large landowners found it difficult to absorb the emotional and economic costs of Brazos outbursts, poor farmers (regardless of their race) were frightfully ill-equipped to rebuild their homes, replant their crops, and renew their faith in the river's potential. Though his status as a small landowner spared him many of the strains felt by less affluent farmers, Watt Caufield discussed the difficulties of forging a life along the Brazos River in an 1857 letter: "No excitement in this country only hard times on account of no rains to make bread to live on."[69] In short, class, as well as race, determined if and how individuals were able to enjoy the resources of the Brazos River and to what extent that enjoyment might be shaped by drought and overflow events.

The desire to capitalize on the river's productivity quickly became interconnected with yet another representation, that which saw the

Brazos as a place of navigation. For many Brazos dwellers, success in commercial agriculture meant little without a reliable, cost-effective means of transportation.[70] Colonel Stiff surely echoed the thoughts of many when he suggested that "the natural facilities for prosecuting a foreign commerce is, if possible, of more importance than the fertility of the soil."[71] Consequently, the search for a dependable source of transportation became something close to an obsession. Merchants, buyers, and farmers discussed the need for a transportation network while developers, boosters, and engineers discussed the practicality and design of that hoped-for network. As late as 1893, Major Charles Allen of the Army Corps of Engineers noted that "the lands bordering Brazos River are exceedingly fertile and productive but the farmers along the river, especially so above Bolivar, labor under the disadvantage of having to haul their products to railroad points separated by long distances."[72]

Hence, as agricultural output increased and the economy expanded during the nineteenth century, Texans turned increasingly not only to the production and processing of agricultural goods but also to their distribution.[73] The dreams of businessmen, boosters, housewives, and farmers for a commercially viable Brazos trade had some basis in reality. The cities of Galveston and Houston, whose hinterlands reached deep into the watershed, competed for the lucrative trade of Brazos farmers during the mid- and late nineteenth century.[74] Moreover, many roads, canals, and rails linked these established cities with the Brazos River. Jacob de Cordova noted that relationship between Brazos produce and city markets in his 1856 immigrant guide.[75] Burke's immigrant handbook, published in 1883, also noted as much in an advertisement for the Houston and Texas Central Railway: "The Houston & Texas Central Railway penetrates the interior of Texas on a line commanding the products and trade of the most fertile region in the world. From Houston to its junction with its Northwestern Branch, at Bremond, it has upon its left the rich valleys of the Brazos."[76]

To realize these expectations, the people of the Brazos envisioned a transportation network that involved roads and bridges as well as rivers and rails, but the latter two commanded the most attention. Although the railroad would eventually reign over all hoped-for networks, this dominance was not possible until the late nineteenth century. As a result, during the first decades of settlement, the Brazos River became the natural artery for much of the agricultural commerce in Texas (and the site of tremendous debate about the expansion of transportation routes).[77] Lawmakers, boosters, settlers, and tourists alike spoke of the potential for steam navigation along the river and went so far as to plant ports several hundred miles inland, speaking to the depth of this particular desire for the river.[78] Mary Austin Holley also expressed a considerable amount of optimism about a Brazos steam economy in the letters that she sent during her 1830 tour of Stephen F. Austin's colonies: "Never, was a river better calculated than the Brazos, whether we consider its depth, its placid current, or unobstructed channel, for the perfect operation of the steam engine."[79]

Such interest coincided with a broader national interest in steam-powered navigation, but the dreams for navigation along the Brazos were tempered by the geological realities of the river. The Brazos River was naturally navigable but only in very small sections. Boats could usually navigate forty miles inland from the mouth, and in good stages of water with three-foot draft boats, they could navigate as much as one hundred miles inland.[80] On very rare occasions, captains could ply their light draft boats as far north as the town of Washington, located 250 miles from the mouth and already well known for its role in the Texans' war for independence.[81] Although steamboat traffic disappeared almost entirely from the Brazos River by 1860, it became somewhat regular along the lower reaches of the river between the 1830s and 1850s. Several times a week, merchants were able to send agricultural goods along the river, residents were able to receive goods, and travelers were able to journey from one Brazos city to another.

Letters, financial reports, and memoirs discussed these navigational events both with gusto and with frequency. Newspapers lauded the arrival of the *Liberty*, *Laura*, and *Lafitte* at Brazos ports.[82] Letters referenced the anchoring of the sloop *Natchez* off the Brazos Bar, the travels of the steamer *Mustang*, the use of the cotton-clad "yelor Stone" by General Sam Houston, and the journeys of boats such as the *Hiawatha* and *Cayuga* and *Lizzie Fisher*.[83] Bills of lading spoke to economic growth and also to schooners and sloops and steamboats that visited Brazos towns with increasing regularity.[84] As early as 1828 (and consistently by the 1840s), the people living in this watershed even began to brag that Brazos cotton was shipped as far away as Liverpool, England, and Veracruz, Mexico, as well as to domestic ports such as New York and New Orleans.[85]

Some navigation, then, was already taking place along the Brazos River without the aid of improvements. However, inland farmers and coastal merchants alike decried the geological factors that limited navigation. A shallow bar located at the mouth of the river proved most problematic.[86] The bar, which "render[ed] the entrance to this river both expensive and danger[ou]s," was created and recreated as ocean swells blocked the river in its attempts to empty loads of silt and sand into the Gulf of Mexico.[87] Early visitors to the Brazos Basin commented often on the bar and the obstacles that it presented both to navigation and to commerce. In the course of his 1837 tour of Texas, for example, Andrew Forest Muir expounded on the perils of the bar, eventually coming to the unhappy conclusion that it "never can be removed."[88] Muir also noted that this Brazos bar was "so extremely dangerous" and had caused so many "repeated wrecks" that the insurance companies in the United States had begun to refuse policies "upon any vessels entered for this port at any premium."[89] George Hammeken likewise discussed the "risk of crossing the Brazos Bar" and the effects of those dangers on insurance in an 1848 letter to James Perry.[90]

Many boats met their end on this bar, caught in or dashed against its beds.[91] However, it also became somewhat common for boats to find that they could neither enter nor exit the river channel.[92] Indeed, S. M. Westewelt found himself stranded on a boat at the bar of the river for two days. He ultimately arrived in Brazoria, Texas, by exiting the boat at San Luis Island, ferrying to the mainland, and engaging a horse for the trip to Velasco and Brazoria.[93] Likewise, a man named Stephen wrote a letter complaining, "We lay at anchor off the river 9 days before we could get an opportunity of sending a boat on shore, and on the return we received the very agreeable intelligence that there was only two feet of water on this tormenting sand bank, so that all hope of getting in was effectually cut off."[94] As a result of such dangers, Holley described the moment of arrival as a moment of great anxiety as well as joy—"all hands pray for fair weather, and *whistle for favouring gales*."[95]

Though such dangers seemed enough to justify the need for improved navigation, Brazos dwellers also spoke of a desire to grow the regional economy. This expansion could mean simply an increase in the size of the Brazos economy, but laypeople also pushed for an agricultural market open to individuals otherwise excluded. The fertility of the river's surrounding landscape had allowed a small number of people to amass large quantities of wealth since settlement began in the 1820s (a wealth largely derived from the sale of agricultural products like cotton and cane). This concentration of wealth came at the expense of groups, free and unfree alike, who either did not have the resources to increase their holdings or toiled for the benefit of another. In an effort to assuage the individuals who sat on the wrong side of this economic structure, developers and lawmakers, at times, supported navigation for reasons that seemed magnanimous, socially conscious even.

The Brazos River Channel and Dock Company overtly played up that rhetoric in an 1890 pamphlet: "All the great streams flowing into the Gulf of Mexico bear upon their waters a traffic of vast consequence to the business of the South; they are natural, while the railways are artificial highways. The first can be used by everybody, the latter only by those who have the money."[96] P. R. Christiansen, likewise, noted, "it is the cost of moving produce from one point to another that keeps people poor."[97] Such discourse suggests that river traffic offered a more democratic option for farmers than railroads, a refrain that would echo throughout the Brazos Basin for decades. There is no definitive evidence to suggest that the economy became substantially more open to poorer families as navigation expanded, and such openness was clearly not intended for African American families. But the mere hope that success might one day be realized by a greater number of people was enough to promote an interest in development among individuals otherwise excluded from the economic benefits of improvement and the potential windfall of large-scale farming.

In short, the reputation of the Brazos River during the nineteenth century was generally quite favorable, something that was reflected in Brazos boosterism and also in the ways that people idealized the landscape. William Kennedy published his travel memoirs in 1841 and, in a moment of honesty that grew into verbal ecstasy, noted:

> The stranger who journeys along the low lands of the Brazos, during the drenching days of the short winter of Texas, when the natural roads over the rich alluvial soil are broken into sloughs, and the creeks swollen into unfordable torrents, will probably anathematise the country. . . . But were the same person to arrive in spring or autumn, and mounting a good horse, ascend from the coast to the interior, where the path winds along limpid brooks and gentle vales, through a wilderness of flowers, varied by clustering evergreens and fairy groves, his heart could hardly fail to dilate with emotions of grateful joyousness and to ejaculate, in the silent temple of Nature, "Methinks it is good to be here!"[98]

Reports like this prompted boosters, lawmakers, laypeople, and developers to imagine a grandiose future for the waterway. However, the people of the Brazos River nonetheless questioned the value of local resources in a world where floods and droughts kept their towns isolated from larger markets, subject to frequent economic loss, and unappealing to incoming settlers.

The development projects that were proposed for the Lower Brazos River employed technological solutions to bridge, at least in theory, that disconnect between an idealized Brazos and the natural limitations of the river. These schemes served as avenues for taming a river of "great impetuosity," and they offered an opportunity for realizing some of the dreams of Brazos dwellers.[99] The projects began, however, not with draft pencils and hammers but with the formation of improvement associations. Several local associations formed during this time, including the New Orleans and Texas Navigation Company (ca. 1830s), the Brazos Steam Association (1848), and the Brazos Internal Improvement and Navigation Company (1866).[100] Frustrated citizens also organized the Brazos River Harbor Association, the Freeport Harbor Association, and the Brazos River Channel and Dock Company during the mid- and late nineteenth century.[101] These associations generally formed in cities along the lower third of the river, and they focused almost exclusively on the need for a transportation network.

Capitalizing on the growing tide of public pressure that accompanied the formation of these groups, lawmakers began calling for legislation that would fund development of the Brazos River and, more immediately, would determine what projects should be undertaken. Despite that legislative pressure, funds rolled in, but slowly. The State Legislature of Texas and the United States Congress authorized funds for improvement, most noticeably through a series of River and Harbor Acts.[102] Private groups—such as the Waco Board of Trade—also commissioned surveys of the river at this time and allocated money toward its improvement.[103] Although funds often proved insufficient for the task at hand, interest in the development of this river quickly reached into all levels of government.

Thus armed with public support, enabling legislation, and a slew of surveys, boosters and lawmakers set to work on three noteworthy projects for the Lower Brazos River. These projects—a canal project, a port project, and dredging operations—began in the mid-1800s, continued into the mid-1900s, and became the first in a long line of proposals meant to reconcile the land to its limitations and to the expectations of boosters and settlers. The earliest of these projects centered on the construction of a canal to link the river with Galveston Bay, a more promising—and more established—shipping point than any site along the Brazos.[104] The idea of an inland waterway that connected the state's major rivers (and, in turn, linked them with the coastline) had been anticipated by the earliest settlers along the Brazos River. As early as 1841, William Kennedy predicted that "when there is sufficient capital in the country, an internal navigation will be opened along the coast from the Sabine to the Rio Grande."[105] Indeed, the proposed canal also reflected a broader impulse to rein in the nation's waterways for the purposes of navigation. Certainly, Brazos boosters did not envision a canal on the scale of that which linked the cities of Albany and Buffalo in New York, but the commercial and technological success of the Erie Canal—as well as the completion of canals like the Santee in South Carolina—sparked a very real, very lasting interest in canal-building along the Lower Brazos.[106]

Proponents of this first development project expected that the canal would elevate the Brazos River to a more important place within the state economy by concentrating regional trade along a single waterway. But this objective meant different things to different groups. The Galveston and Brazos River Navigation Company constructed the canal in hopes of "affording an uninterrupted channel, with four feet water at low tide, from the city of Galveston to the Brazos" and creating a lucrative trade between the shipping point at Galveston Bay and the productive farmlands along the river.[107] Farmers sought to reduce freight rates by creating a viable competition for the railways, and they anticipated reduced insurance costs and increased use of the river as a result of the canal.[108] Families living in isolated communities often wanted nothing more than a tangible link to population centers and a more dependable method to send and receive goods.

In 1850, Texans began work on this ambitious project. Although the government eventually involved itself in the canal, private individuals initially undertook the work.[109] Acting through the auspices of the Galveston and Brazos Navigation Company, these individuals intended to create a corridor ten miles long, fifty feet wide, and roughly three to four feet in depth.[110] Creating a canal of such size required an initial output of labor (e.g., cutting and shaping the canal) but also required consistent dredging after construction to remove the silt that built up naturally in the waterway. The channel, which came to be known as the Brazos-Galveston Canal, was completed in 1854 and opened early in 1855.[111]

Despite the fanfare that graced the canal's opening, the effectiveness of this project was questioned immediately. Complaints centered most often on the construction costs. In 1854, J. A. Paschal estimated that "the amount already expended is $70.993.33, and the estimated Cost of completion to the River is $35.000."[112] To the consternation of men such as Paschal, the cost for construction (excluding maintenance) eventually topped $340,000.[113] Another problem facing proponents of the project was the canal's availability. At times, Texans traveled along the canal with ease. For example, fishing boats, small market craft, and even stern-wheel riverboats occasionally plied the river and its canal during cotton season.[114] Tipton Walker used the canal on October 19, 1855, to travel from Galveston to the Brazos via the *Major Harris*, and the steamer *Fort Henry* traveled from the Brazos to Galveston in 1857.[115] Blockade runners also made use of the canal during the Civil War, turning to it as a means of bypassing Union ships along the coastline. However, minimal flows of water—what scientists call a low streamflow—and high rates of sedimentation often made the canal more or less impassable to all but the lightest of craft.[116]

The project, so lauded at the outset, was pushed to the side during the late 1860s as a result of these very real concerns, but the idea of creating a channel between the Lower Brazos River and Galveston Bay persisted. Proponents of Brazos navigation revived this original canal project at the turn of the century, hoping (like their predecessors) to provide inland populations with a transportation artery.[117] Farmers cheered the network that would result from the successful completion of this project, and they were joined in that refrain by merchants, boosters, engineers, and even the individuals who gathered oysters from nearby bays.[118] But developers intended that this canal would serve a much grander purpose than intrabasin navigation. The federal government purchased the original, eleven-mile long canal in 1902 at a cost of $30,000 and promptly set out to integrate that project into a larger network of coastal channels. Intending at the time to construct an inland waterway along the length of the Texas coast, the Army Corps of Engineers envisioned an ambitious, but not entirely exceptional, canal system that would incorporate the existing Brazos-Galveston Canal, create a canal from Matagorda Bay to the Brazos River, and then link these Brazos arteries with a series of canals between the Rio Grande and the Sabine River.[119]

This new version of an old Brazos project not only traversed an extant canal but also crossed the substantially sized Galveston Bay. As a result, work largely centered on dredging operations to remove silt, logs, and clay and then reinforcing the banks of the canal with that debris.[120] At the time of purchase in 1902, government documents had noted that the Brazos-Galveston Canal was not then in use, that it had a ruling depth of only eighteen inches, and that private ownership of this canal hindered development of the Texas coastline.[121] Much to the chagrin of Brazos boosters, workers with the Army Corps of Engineer would later record similar observations about this second iteration of a regional canal. Nevertheless, the government spent much of the first two decades in the twentieth century clearing the Galveston and Brazos canal from obstructions so that it could be opened once again to light draft navigation.[122]

Despite the fact that this project engaged the regional population and built off of a foundation provided in earlier endeavors, the canal disappointed proponents immediately. For one thing, developers hoped that the canal would provide an accessible inland waterway for navigational interests, but this second Brazos-Galveston canal (like its forerunner) was generally navigable only for light draft vessels. Travelers' guides often boasted that the canal would be nine feet in depth and sixty feet in width, but in reality these numbers reflected the maximum depth and width as envisioned on paper by engineers.[123] The channel actually had a ruling depth between three feet to five feet and a maximum width of closer to forty feet.[124] Furthermore, the canal needed frequent maintenance and constant dredging, costing additional tens of thousands of dollars each year.[125] For example, dredging and cutting operations along a particular stretch of canal were deemed "complete" in 1912, yet the government allocated $10,000 in 1913 and another $15,000 in 1914 for additional dredging along that same stretch of canal between West Galveston Bay and the Brazos.[126]

As had been the case with the first canal project, use of the second Galveston and Brazos Canal was suspended and renewed several times as maintenance alternately became more or less necessary. Despite these setbacks, the canal would eventually become part of a larger, more commercially viable project.[127] The inland canal that the federal government constructed to follow the Texas coast was subsumed within a venture known as the Gulf Intracoastal Waterway during the 1920s and 1930s. The Intracoastal Waterway (still in use today) would ultimately stretch from Brownsville, Texas, to St. Marks, Florida, connecting all of the Gulf Coast harbors along this reach. Even before construction of the Texas intercoastal canal, Brazos boosters foresaw the economic value of such an endeavor. The possibility for regional markets even prompted one individual to announce in 1910 that "the greatest asset which the public of Brazoria County and the State of Texas owns is the Intracoastal Canal."[128] Ambition and intent, then, had not been lacking in the currents of the Brazos channels.

In the end, the Brazos-Galveston Canal became the first in a long line of development projects that promised much and accomplished relatively little along this unruly river. The second improvement project revolved around a different goal—the construction of jetties and the deepening of the river near the mouth of the Brazos—but accomplished little more than the canal. This development project effectively sought to create a substantial, preferably public, port for the Lower Brazos River. The port-and-jetty project that developers proposed spoke to a far-reaching interest in developing urban markets for agricultural goods. Commerce and navigation in New Orleans had expanded considerably after the construction of jetties near the Heads of Pass on the Mississippi River, and it seemed reasonable to Brazos developers that jetties might accomplish the same on their waterway.

The port project, moreover, engaged a long-standing, deeply held belief that the Brazos River needed a substantial harbor and the business that harbor would provide. As early as 1837, Muir elaborated on the need for a port in his travel memoirs, complaining that "the country upon the Brazos is really fertile and yields most abundantly, yet the harbor at the mouth of the stream is little better than none at all."[129] An 1891 newspaper article reiterated the need for a port, noting that "Texas has longed for a deep water seaport" and speaking of the Brazos mouth as an ideal site.[130] The location of the intended Brazos harbor was free from barrier islands and other external obstructions; as a result, many boosters deemed it favorable in comparison to that of the more established Galveston hub, which seemed limited in its reach by a conspicuous bay.[131] In the minds of port advocates the Brazos mouth offered natural advantages that, if fully employed, would allow the riparian economy to compete with the gulf's only other major port, New Orleans.[132]

Improvement of the Brazos mouth seemed to offer benefits to navigation advocates further upstream as well. An 1897 article, perhaps, phrased it best in quoting P. R. Christiansen: "Once [they] get a good port at Velasco . . . the navigation of the Brazos river will follow as a matter of course."[133] In the opinion of port supporters, the city of Velasco (a small town near the mouth of the Brazos River) was positioned to become a shipping and receiving point not only for Texas trade but also for trade from South America and the breadth of the United States.[134] Indeed, an 1890s map likened Velasco to Liverpool, and a contemporaneous article from the *San Antonio Daily Light* called Velasco "the best harbor for ships and the easiest of entrance of any on the Gulf coast of Mexico."[135] Even if the work could not create a port that would supersede that of New Orleans or Galveston, proponents imagined a cooperative network of ports that would integrate the Brazos harbor. In the words of the *Galveston Daily News*: "When the Panama Canal is completed Texas will be full of ports. There will be room, business and glory enough for all of them, and we will need them all."[136]

Despite that public support, the construction and maintenance of these jetties proved immediately to be a complicated endeavor. Work on the jetties by the federal government began in 1881 and continued until 1887.[137] At that point, the project ended because funding had run out.[138] The Brazos River Channel and Dock Company, a private company dedicated to the river's improvement, picked up the port-and-jetty project in 1888.[139] Despite the involvement of a veteran engineer named E. L. Corthell (who worked under the direction of James Buchanan Eads to construct the jetties at the mouth of the Mississippi River), this project was nevertheless abandoned and renewed multiple times over the next decade. Ultimately, the Brazos River Channel and Dock Company constructed a pair of jetties running parallel to each other for a distance of 4,500 to 5,000 feet.[140] These jetties were transferred to the federal government in 1899, at which point the Army Corps of Engineers became involved in maintenance operations.[141]

Despite the amount of time and funding allocated to the project, the jetties were not considered a success even at the time of their completion. The frustrations that stemmed from their perceived failure were evidenced by a pamphlet that the pro-development Channel and Dock Company published in 1890: "The work that has been done by the United States Government . . . has left no special effect upon the bar, as the work is practically destroyed, and it was at no time prosecuted with sufficient funds."[142] Several factors contributed to the arguable failure of the jetties. Most obviously, financial concerns became a significant problem for developers. The cost for this project was originally estimated at $522,890, but the United States government alone spent more than three times that amount.[143]

The economic woes were quite real, but the underlying reason for the failure of these jetties was not one that revolved around financial considerations. Rather, these nineteenth-century jetties (like the projects that would supersede them) did not effectively account for the geological realities of the riverscape. The jetties, for example, required constant upkeep due to the high sediment loads within the river.[144] The river's streamflows were often not sufficient to carry the sediment beyond the Brazos bar, so no sooner had the jetties been built before dredging was required to keep the channel operable.[145] To the consternation of engineers and developers, natural disasters as well as innate geology could contribute to the problem. The storms of 1886 deposited significant loads of silt in the Brazos River, and the Galveston Hurricane of 1900 destroyed the towns of Quintana and Velasco and subsequently "filled in the 20 foot depth that had been accomplished by dredging in the harbor."[146]

As with the canal project, however, the hope for an established port and a substantial system of jetties was not long forgotten. This port-and-jetty project was revived but a decade after it had been shunted aside, and the second iteration of a long-standing hope for Brazos commerce would ultimately reflect many of the underlying motivations behind the original improvement plan. Proponents of a Brazos port still emphasized, for example, the commercial possibilities of their agriculturally rich surroundings. They also employed rhetoric similar to that used by earlier advocates for improvement, overtly emphasizing "the duty of the government to assume direct charge of this Mississippi of Texas, complete its improvements under the efficient methods approved by the corps of engineers and enable it to discharge its natural mission as a carrier."[147] Not surprisingly, then, support was great for this later port-improvement project.

Building on the port-and-jetty projects of the mid-nineteenth century, the federal government resumed work on the Brazos jetties in the early twentieth century after regaining ownership of them in 1899. Local developers and Army Corps of Engineers employees intended specifically to create a deepwater harbor through the construction of jetties extending several thousand feet into the Gulf Coast; they also hoped to develop the infrastructure that made up the physical harbor itself.[148] Little work was completed on the harbor improvements, but developers did complete a pair of jetties. These jetties lessened the effects of shoaling within the river corridor and also increased, at least temporarily, the depth of water over the Brazos Bar. Although any success was momentary, boosters nevertheless maintained that a deepwater port had been obtained.[149]

Despite these tenuous moments of victory, this port-and-jetty project disappointed proponents before the projects were even completed. Most problematic of all, improvement of the river's mouth still required continual upkeep.[150] Permanent changes to the depth or flow of the river proved elusive, and shoaling, the buildup of sediment (particularly sand) along the bed of a river, proved to be a particularly vexing problem. Additionally, construction costs mounted to alarming levels, escalating quickly as the work pushed onward. Total appropriations for the project surpassed $298,000 in 1910, and in 1913 an additional $125,000 was appropriated by the government for the project. Lawmakers were forced to allocate still another $455,000 toward the jetty project in 1917, primarily to finance maintenance operations that centered on that longtime problem of sedimentation.[151] As a result of these difficulties, the Chief of Engineers for the Corps of Engineers formally recommended in 1923 that improvement of the jetties be abandoned.[152]

Given the long history of support within the Brazos watershed for a harbor, these jetties arguably failed not because the project lacked popular support but because the project could not overcome the effects of frequent shoaling, inconstant streamflows, and the buildup of silt at the mouth. But even these issues and prior failures could not permanently derail the pursuit of a Brazos harbor. Most Brazos River projects at the midcentury point focused on dam building and the increasingly pressing issue of flood control; hence, support for developing the river's mouth still remained highly dependent on where Brazos boosters called home. In other words, the focus on dams and flood control along the Upper Brazos River overshadowed, but did not supplant entirely, a lingering push for port improvements, navigation, and economic growth in coastal communities.[153]

Developers began once again to focus their attention on a port-and-jetty project during the 1930s and 1940s, doing so with similar motives but a slightly different location. In 1929, the Army Corps of Engineers had created a new endpoint for the Brazos River, cutting a diversion channel that connected with the Gulf of Mexico three miles from the original mouth. The proponents of this mid-twentieth-century Brazos port largely ignored the question of jetties and instead emphasized a port project that would provide a channel with a depth of 22 to 25 feet and an average width of 150 feet.[154] Commercial boosters, in particular, hoped that the creation of an extensive harbor at the city of Freeport would finally permit developers to engage the resources of the Brazos River Basin in a way that was profitable as well as efficient.[155] That process required the creation of a structure large enough that it could rival the shipping power of Houston and also accommodate the agricultural production of the Brazos Valley. Developers intended, in short, to strengthen the economic situation of the watershed by creating a "modern deep sea general cargo port."[156]

The Committee on Rivers and Harbors in the House of Representatives considered the third round of hoped-for improvements to the Freeport Harbor as early as 1930, and in 1949, Mr. Russell Wait began examining the economic feasibility of developing the Brazos port.[157] The plan to improve Freeport Harbor—which included the construction of turning basins, wharfs, channels, and berths—could be considered a success in that the physical constructions survived and contributed at times to economic growth, but it certainly represented the last gasp of the dream of navigation for this river.[158] Moreover the port project, like so many other improvement efforts, unraveled somewhat amid the reality of dredging, maintenance, and commercial atrophy.

There was immediate concern, for instance, about the cost of the port improvements. As early as September 1, 1931, approximately $3,160,000 had been expended on the port improvements (which were "completed" late in 1931).[159] These costs did not account for maintenance "by dredging, by jetties at the harbor entrance and by a diversion dam in the Brazos River."[160] That these improvements and expenditures on maintenance were "essential to the development of a first class port" only reinforced an unsettling economic reality. . . . maintaining a Brazos River harbor could only be done with a continual flow of funds.[161]

Developers also questioned the permanence of the improvements. Even with periodic dredging, ships were in constant danger of grounding on the sandbars that littered the streambed.[162] More important still, developers nursed concerns about the amount of commerce that might be gained by these expenditures, arguing that current levels of commercial use on the Lower Brazos River were simply not sufficient to warrant port improvements. In fact, a congressional document from 1931 maintained that the port improvements should have as their primary goal the *expansion* of commerce: "The principal justification for increased channel dimensions does not . . . lie in providing deeper and wider channels for the existing commerce, but must rest primarily upon the possibility that greater depth and width will result in the development of additional commerce."[163] Existing commerce, in other words, could not alone justify the financial cost of developing the harbor. Despite the grand intentions and very real hopes, a report dated May 1, 1950, concluded that the improvements advocated by the Master Plan for the proposed Port of Freeport were ultimately cost prohibitive.[164]

The third of the Lower Brazos River improvement projects emerged around the turn of the twentieth century and targeted the stretch of river between Washington and Velasco.[165] Developers, focusing not on the creation of new canals or structures but on the maintenance of the existing river channel, intended that the project would work in tandem with the preceding proposals to expand navigational possibilities along the length of the Brazos River corridor.[166] Estimated initially at a cost of $225,000 and totaling nearly twice that amount in the end, this project, like the others, was authorized and completed in sections.[167] The first stage of the project, begun in June of 1896, prioritized the channel between the cities of Velasco and Richmond.[168] Developers later shifted the substance of the work to the stretch of river between Richmond and Old Washington. Because the project focused on maintaining a natural corridor, it primarily involved the removal of snags, shoals, and overhanging trees.[169] However, some amount of levee work, meant to provide an element of flood control, complemented the project.[170]

The seemingly simple nature of this improvement project did not guarantee any measure of success. The project of improvement between Washington and Velasco was completed in 1916, and maintenance operations continued until 1923. At that point, the government suspended dredging operations on the Lower Brazos River, noting a near-complete lack of traffic. The explanation was readily apparent: despite well-intentioned efforts to remove snags, smooth shoals, or trim overhanging trees, the river remained only temporarily improved. Removal of snags, for example, could never be considered complete as new snags emerged almost continually. In 1910, snag boats working a thirty-two-mile stretch of the Lower Brazos destroyed 399 snags, 92 stumps, 704 logs, and 13,553 leaning trees; trimmed 21 leaning trees; cut 5,980 shore snags; and dredged 2,455 feet of shoals.[171] In the month of August in 1915, snag boats working along this same stretch removed 44 large snags and 168 small snags and also cut 2,024 overhanging trees.[172]

Clearly, the work of maintaining the river channel could not easily be accomplished in any long-term sense, if it could be accomplished at all. In addition, a 1910 War Department Report noted that freight rates had not been influenced by maintenance operations. The report, offering a harsh and unwanted truth, commented that "no commerce of any note has developed, nor can any be expected until the Brazos River is improved from its mouth up to Waco."[173] It was not sufficient, in other words, to improve one small section of the river for small increments of time. These maintenance operations failed to maintain the river corridor, failed to expand use of the river, and failed to slow the growing power of railways—a trifecta of shortcomings that only the most confident of Brazos dwellers could ignore.

Still, proponents of navigation used even the temporary success of this project as evidence that their hopes for the river were, in fact, realistic. In 1905, Captain Edgar Jadwin of the Army Corps of Engineers, Texas congressman Robert Lee Henry, and Waco mayor James Baker steamed down the Brazos River, traveling from San Felipe to Richmond via the *Col. Riche*.[174] Reports from the trip, printed in regional newspapers, revealed that these men believed that dredging work had improved navigation prospects measurably.[175] Those positive reports prompted still more words of confident expectation in regional papers. In the words of the *Galveston Daily News*, "as soon as boats can come down the Brazos River they can also come through to Galveston" and, by implication, to the ports of more distant nations.[176]

Despite the obvious differences between canals and ports and dredge boats, a rather important commonality characterized these earliest improvement projects, endowing them with a significance that belied their seemingly minor place and brief role in the narrative of development. Specifically, a desire to duplicate the model of development in place along other rivers of the southern states prompted boosters, lawmakers, and developers to promote projects centered on economic and navigational growth. These nineteenth-century efforts to cultivate navigational routes and agricultural markets within the Lower Brazos River Basin, in turn, became a foundation upon which later developers would undertake far more ambitious projects and a lens through which Brazos dwellers at large would ultimately revisit their ideas about development. These early efforts at improvement, in other words, may not have wrought many lasting changes along the river corridor, but they did bring the national conversation about river development and the southern dialogue on navigation to the Brazos.

Moreover, the work of boosters, developers, and lawmakers pointed to the ways in which different groups experienced and reacted to what a twentieth-century reporter would call the "wild and woolly Brazos."[177] Agricultural markets and economic opportunities seemed genuinely to have been within reach for these early Brazos developers, but the reality of improvement along the Lower Brazos River still differed substantially from the various expectations of those who engaged the river on a daily basis. For some, improvement of this riverscape became a means of maintaining psychological ties with homes they had left behind and of recreating imagined communities based on similar uses of the river. For others, improvement of the Brazos promised economic opportunities based in agricultural fields and economic markets. Yet the hope for nearly all the groups living along the lower third of the river was a space of improved navigation. The hope for an improved Brazos ran so deep that not even the occasionally crushing reality of these nineteenth-century projects could halt the push for development; hope and expectation remained thoroughly intact.

CHAPTER FOUR

Locks, Dams, and a Hope for Navigation along the Middle Brazos River

After this flood will come sickness undoubtedly, and what a week ago was the fairest part of Texas is now almost a God-forsaken wilderness. The waters of the Brazos have for six days covered its lands from six to thirty feet; where a week ago there were on every land fields of cotton and corn and thousands of acres of melons, today there is slimy mud over all the vegetation.
— "HAVOC OF THE FLOOD," *Perry Advertiser*, 1899

Down along the Brazos River we have as rich and populous a country as God's sun ever shone upon. The Nile or any other river of the World does not produce as much. We come to you today and ask you to knock at the door of Congress, not because we have any fight to make on the railroads, not because we have any sentimental idea that we want transportation rates to Waco, but because we need the navigation of the Brazos River to carry the products produced from the soil of that rich valley.
— J. W. RIGGINS, Trans-Mississippi Commercial Congress, 1906

In the improvement of the Brazos River and making it navigable from its mouth to Waco, the government has undertaken a work which is destined to be of far-reaching influence on the inland commerce of Texas.
— "LOCK-AND-DAM BEING BUILT," *Galveston Daily News*, 1910

ON MAY 21, 1913, the *Waco Semi-Weekly Tribune* devoted a very small amount of space to an article on government-sponsored development of the Brazos River. This *Tribune* article, entitled "Improving the 'Mississippi of Texas,'" was not particularly long on words, but it spoke broadly and pointedly to the expectations of Progressive Era Texans.[1] More specifically, the article outlined a need for riparian control along the Brazos, invoked an almost-unshakeable faith in the idea of technological progress, and applauded government efforts toward navigation. It also affirmed what the activity of lawmakers and engineers would have likewise revealed: failed canal projects in the 1850s had not dimmed the hope for a restrained Brazos, and failed dredging operations in the 1870s had not dampened the enthusiasm for a productive river. The reform-minded, industry-inclined individuals of this period still envisioned and advocated for an improved river despite nearly eighty years of ineffective development along the ecologically variable, frustratingly capricious Brazos River.

Moving beyond and working through a perceived inability in the past to tame this river, people within the watershed still supported the ideal of improvement wholeheartedly. Moreover, they continued to believe in their ability to create a riparian highway from the inconstant waters of the Brazos River.[2] This preference for navigation still correlated nicely with ongoing efforts in southern states, with what might be called that Southern model of riparian development. Oversized lock structures were constructed frequently and in great number along southern rivers in the years that framed the turn of the century, remaking the Cape Fear in North Carolina, the Ocklawaha in Florida, the Black Warrior in Alabama, the Trinity in Texas, and the Chattahoochee in Georgia.[3] Boosters would not succeed in constructing permanent locks along the Middle Brazos River, but through their continued support of navigation projects, they nevertheless planted themselves within a concentrated, regional push for navigation.

This focus on navigation within the Brazos Basin and more traditionally southern states contrasted with ongoing projects in other regions. Expansion into the western states during the mid- and late nineteenth century had made pressing the issue of aridity for people living west of the Mississippi. Increasing calls for riparian correction, in turn, gradually prompted a dialogue about projects that might transfer water from areas of supposed feast to areas of obvious famine. Developers in those western states and territories—momentarily interrupted in their efforts by the Civil War—began once again in the last decades of the nineteenth century to propose projects that would infuse federal oversight into development and would address issues such as water scarcity and resource allocation.[4] That budding impulse toward reclamation and irrigation would gradually emerge along the Brazos River, tying the waterway into the "go-go years of dam-building" and instating within the watershed a new model of riparian development. But that commitment would not coalesce along the Brazos until the 1920s.

Instead, as the 1890s ended and the new century began, the attention of Brazos dwellers still rested firmly on a model of development that emphasized navigation over flood control and agricultural markets over irrigation. Along the Middle Brazos River, engineers, developers, and lawmakers focused on a single project in their effort to tame the unruly waters of the Brazos and, through that, to make greater use of the river as a traffic corridor. This improvement project, which centered on building structures that incorporated both locks and small-scale dams, was ultimately cast aside, but it nevertheless proved significant to the broader story of development. Specifically, development of the Middle Brazos River during the late nineteenth and early twentieth centuries incorporated industrial techniques into the construction of new navigation projects and, by doing so, gave new form to a long-standing dream for an expanded agricultural economy.

This second round of navigation projects emerged from within the context of an urbanizing, modernizing, and socially fluid world. More to the point, the proponents of these Middle Brazos River locks began their work in an age that has been given a somewhat ambiguous label—the Progressive Era. Generally described as the period between 1890 and 1917, scholars quickly came to view the Progressive Era, with its focus on productivity and efficiency, as a time of reform. This era encompassed Prohibition, women's rights, and the Niagara Movement as well as a broader push to reform labor laws, food safety, and national parks. Richard Hofstadter memorably calls this "a rather widespread and remarkably good-natured effort of the greater part of society to achieve some not very clearly specified self-reformation."[5]

The schemes that Brazos developers proposed for the middle third of the river built off of that broader movement, seeing potential for greater productivity in the still wild waters of the Brazos. Granted, these Progressive Era Texans shared with their earlier counterparts a vision for the river that emphasized "economic use," but their beliefs with regard to development exposed ongoing changes within the broader political and socioeconomic landscapes.[6] Indeed, by the beginning of the 1890s, the developers and dwellers of this watershed had been wrestling with an unimproved river for more than half a century. These past projects did nothing to dampen the technocratic spirit that ruled the watershed, but they did prompt developers, gradually but undeniably, to alter their approach.

First, residents of the watershed continued to envision a navigable river that could bring Brazos River crops into regional, national, and international markets. The individuals who settled the Middle Brazos Basin often possessed social ties with southern states, having moved from the South or from downstream towns that had, themselves, been populated by southerners. These individuals carried their ideals about navigation and agricultural economies with them. The endwaters of the Brazos River, moreover, flowed through abandoned plantations en route to the famously fertile plains of the Gulf Coast, providing an ecological (as well as a cultural) link to Southern ideals. As a result, the projects that were proposed for the middle stretch of the river emphasized the benefits of a riparian-based agricultural market and the allure of navigation in ways that both reflected and relied on the improvement projects already completed along rivers such as the Mississippi, the Ocklawaha, or the Chattahoochee.

Almanacs, advertisements, and editorials confirmed that continuing fixation with expanded river traffic. Advertisements in the *Texas Almanac and State Industrial Guide* for 1910, for instance, referred to Waco as "The Head of Brazos Navigation" and also tied the future of that city to an economic structure dependent on agriculture, noting that "Waco is the center of Cotton Production, and with the opening of the Brazos and Panama Canal to navigation Waco is destined to be the greatest interior shipping point in the Southwest."[7] A one-cent postcard from the era, likewise, foresaw in Waco the head of Brazos navigation, anticipating this reality with a colorized image of men conversing around a trifecta of almost comically undersized boats.[8] As one of the larger cities in Texas, Waco attracted a good deal of attention from boosters and developers—the city even hosted during this era a minor league baseball team named the Waco Navigators. However, navigation interests lavished promise onto other cities as well, most notably those along the Lower River. An article in the *Galveston Daily News*, for example, expanded on the future of Velasco in 1913, reminding its readers that "three great highways of commerce touch Velasco—the Brazos River, the Intercoastal Canal and the Gulf of Mexico, all three of which are giving cheap transportation and creating business for the town."[9]

People living along the Middle (and Lower) Brazos River around the turn of the century held conferences on the subject of navigation, formed committees in cities such as Waco and Navasota, and purchased boat lines in anticipation of regular steam service.[10] Newspapers even expressed hope that one day there might be a "boat for every town."[11] These advocates for progress proved remarkably tenacious, persisting in their expectation of improved navigation despite, among other

Undated postcard proclaiming Waco the "Head of Navigation, Brazos River."
Courtesy the Texas Collection, Baylor University, Waco, Texas.

disheartening developments, the increasing power of the rail industry. Boosters and lawmakers began talking about the construction of a Houston and Brazos railroad as early as 1840 (hoping to inspire "a new impulse to enterprise"), and railways traversed this riverscape by the early 1850s. By the late nineteenth century, the Gulf, Colorado and Santa Fe Railway; the Houston and Texas Central Railway; the Missouri-Kansas-Texas Railroad; the Fort Worth and Rio Grande Railway; and the St. Louis, Arkansas, and Texas Railway were just some of the railroads that worked the watershed.

Boosters, developers, lawmakers, and laypeople seem genuinely to have hoped that an improved Brazos River might displace the railroads and permit the regulation of freight rates.[12] But the irony is that the railroads would have benefited, and indeed did benefit, from early efforts at riparian improvement—even those projects that prioritized expanded navigation over flood control. The reason is simple, if unexpected: neither rail nor river traffic alone could adequately connect the isolated cities of the Brazos Basin during the nineteenth century, so projects to improve the waterway for navigation extended the reach of the rails as well.[13] The benefit was real enough that the railroad companies became involved in the push for navigation. The Texas Railroad, Navigation and Banking Company worked "to connect the waters of the Sabine and Rio

Grande rivers by means of internal navigation, with the privilege of constructing branch canals and branch railroads in every direction."[14] The Brazos Internal Improvement and Navigation Company, likewise, acted "in the interest of the Houston and Texas Central Railway for the purpose of improving the Brazos River for navigation," and in 1872, the Houston and Great Northern Railroad involved itself in improvement efforts along the Brazos.

Still, as in many rural areas, residents along the Brazos continued to believe that rail rates were excessive, and this frustration fueled the push for improved navigation in place of expanded rail access along the river.[15] Colonel Henry R. Roberts noted as much in an 1898 newspaper article: "There can be no doubt that the opening of the Brazos river to navigation by small boats and barges, and the establishment at its mouth of a port for vessels drawing eighteen or twenty feet, would reduce the rate for transportation throughout the whole valley."[16] Nine years later, Congressman John M. Moore made the point still more clearly: "The object in improving and making navigable our waterways is to give the people cheap transportation, and the opening of the Brazos River and the use of this river as a means of transportation will be of great benefit by way of reduction of freight rates."[17]

Second, Progressive Era Texans crafted this new round of projects during a time of burgeoning growth for industry, a growth that shaped the contemporaneous New South movement and also increased regional faith in technological solutions. As a result, the projects that engineers and developers envisioned for the Brazos became increasingly grand both in size and in scope. They also became more geographically dispersed as developers and engineers began to focus on improvement schemes that targeted stretches of the river geographically removed from projects that had centered on the coastline. In a world that had molded heavy metals, conquered mountains through explosive mixtures, automated the process of manufacturing, and harnessed natural processes for the sake of industry, it only made sense that something could finally be done about the volatility of the Brazos River landscape.[18]

Developers and engineers, eschewing the small-scale projects popular during most of the nineteenth century, turned to increasingly grand, technologically based solutions for such timeless problems as floods, drought, and navigability. They turned to locks and dams built to a size not practical in earlier years, and in their operations they used steamers and boats much larger than in previous decades. These same individuals admittedly struggled to find technologically based solutions for the recurrent headaches that manifested as high waters, shoaled streambeds, and mobile sand beds, but the people living in this watershed continued nonetheless to advocate the application of these solutions to riparian outbursts and to uphold a developmental narrative based not on failure but on success. As a result, the tendency toward the large and technologically impressive would only solidify over the next few decades (culminating, in many ways, in the large-scale dams of the mid-twentieth century).

Third, the fundamental motivation for improving the Brazos River shifted toward the end of this second phase of development. Although the hope for a reliable transportation network persisted into the twentieth century, the very real need for flood control began to match any lingering desire for extended navigation and so the navigation hopes embodied by locks and dams would be cast aside. In their place, developers gradually began to emphasize the need for flood control and to envision the large-scale dams that would ultimately be constructed along the Upper Brazos during the mid-twentieth century.[19] Though floods had always featured prominently in the lives of Brazos dwellers, the budding interest in flood control spoke plainly and unhesitatingly to a growing problem with overflows.

Newspapers wrote frequently of "fatal cloudbursts," local leaders bemoaned "scenes of woe and misery," and streets transformed into rivers throughout the basin.[20] An 1899 article in the *Galveston Daily News* provided a particularly graphic account of Brazos crops damaged by a recent flood: "The stench from sour corn, carcasses and decaying vegetation is terrible. Cotton is totally covered by water, is black and dead, roots and all . . . one confirmed drowning (a black man) with most people missing now found."[21] One year later, the *Galveston Daily News* reported that a flood along the Leon River, a tributary of the Middle Brazos, had washed out the Gulf, Colorado and Santa Fe Railway Bridge not once but twice within the span of several weeks.[22] There is no evidence to suggest that the number of floods had increased significantly since 1821, but the damage wrought by such overflows undoubtedly escalated over time as the regional population grew.

More horrifying still, in an account that defies belief, newspapers reported in 1913 that the Colorado and Brazos Rivers had merged along the coastline. Floodwaters had quickly gathered along upstream reaches of these rivers, creating a continuous plane of water more than forty miles in width that terrified populations downstream.[23] This fantastic

Photograph of Elm Street in East Waco, taken by C. M. Seley during the 1908 floods. Much to the chagrin of people living and working in East Waco, this side of the town flooded far more frequently than the higher-elevated West Waco, and scenes like this became relatively common. Courtesy the Texas Collection, Baylor University, Waco, Texas.

tale of a riparian union may simply have been a frenzied response to a devastating flood, but when considered next to the other reports of destruction, a clear picture of unruliness along the Brazos River emerges.[24] Flooding remained a reality of life, with one 1905 article noting three overflows in three consecutive weeks.[25] As a result, interest in power, reclamation, and flood control slowly began to supersede projects oriented around navigation, agriculture, and local control. The desire to erect flood-control structures grew apace, and by 1929, the aspiration for flood control along the Brazos River would be matched only by a determination to see those structures realized.

Still, the realities of frequent floods, limited navigation, and technological hitches initially did little to deter Progressive Era developers from their stated plans to turn the muddy waters of the Middle Brazos into a waterway on par with such historically significant rivers as the Mississippi, Nile, or Danube. The people living along the Brazos still believed in the potential of the waterway and gloried exuberantly, if somewhat mistakenly, in the "freight possibilities of the river."[26] This

Photograph of several Waco bridges during the 1913 flood. The waters of the
Brazos River have risen to within a few feet of the bridges. Courtesy the Texas
Collection, Baylor University, Waco, Texas.

confidence about the exceptional possibilities of the watershed, in turn,
prompted many people to view improvement of the river corridor as not
only a necessity but also a right. The *Galveston Daily News* committed
to such a stance in an 1898 article, noting that "the rich Brazos country
is entitled, at the hands of the government, to the facilities to expand the
power to requite its industries and swell the volume of national exploita-
tion. No forecast can measure the limit of its production."[27] Earlier in
that same article, the paper put it even more succinctly: "Every condition
emphasizes the righteous claim of the broad Brazos territory to reach the
most distant foreign and domestic markets of the sea."[28]

With these broader changes shaping their plans for improvement,
lawmakers, developers, and laypeople developed a project for the
Middle Brazos River that worked from a purpose both brutally simple
and blatantly ambitious: to "[improve] the economic condition of what
is recognized as the greatest agricultural, industrial and commercial
section of this great State, by reason of the productive power of the
lands, when unmolested by overflows."[29] Although some attention was
paid to flood control in the River and Harbor Acts that authorized the
project and in the propaganda that flourished in Texas, developers
plainly hoped to prioritize navigation. More specifically, engineers envisioned a two-pronged purpose for this project: to secure navigation
from Washington to Waco, and to join this stretch of the river with
naturally navigable portions of the river below Washington. To improve
the prospects of navigation along the Middle Brazos River, the Army
Corps of Engineers proposed eight lock-and-dam structures that would
use a small-scale dam and a single lock to raise water levels in areas
otherwise plagued by shoals, falls, and bars.[30] Collectively, these locks
and dams would create sixty-seven miles of coupled pools, leaving

roughly one hundred miles of river to be managed or transformed by other methods.[31]

Enabling legislation for this project initially provided funds for four of the eight locks and dams, what would be named Lock-and-Dam Nos. 1, 3, 6, and 8.[32] Lock No. 1, near Navasota, was completed in 1915.[33] Lock No. 8, near the city of Waco, was completed early in 1916.[34] Lock No. 3, near the city of Hearne, and Lock No. 6, near Marlin, Texas, were begun in 1916 but never completed.[35] The remaining locks were never built.[36] Just as the benefits of these improvements, if completed, would have been felt unevenly, construction was also felt differently by different racial and economic groups. Immigrants and nonwhite Americans provided much of the labor for these locks while white Americans generally acted as overseers.[37] Logs maintained at Lock No. 8 noted, for example, the following individuals: Constiano Orjel (Mexican): Laborer; V. M. Field (American): Timekeeper; A. H. Olson (Norwegian): Master. The logs also noted thirty-three "Mezicans" and a number of "Negro" roustabouts.[38]

The people living within the watershed were optimistic about the prospects for this heretofore grandest of Brazos projects and with seemingly good reason. Sources reported that the Army Corps of Engineers believed the river to be "susceptible to improvement for navigation purposes, for the reason that it has more water than the other rivers of the State."[39] Moreover, witnesses before a congressional committee reported that "the completion of the project would provide practically the same facilities for navigation as can be secured between Old Washington and the mouth without the use of locks and dams."[40] Accordingly, engineers and laypeople alike began to imagine and to believe that the completion of these structures would allow barge lines to begin operating between Waco and Navasota.[41] It was commonly hoped that these barge lines would, in turn, connect with an assortment of lines that the Seaboard and Gulf Steamship Company promised between Navasota and Velasco and with a line that already connected the cities of Velasco and Freeport in Texas with New York City.[42]

Support for this project flourished quickly and conspicuously, largely because it promised benefits not only to the people living between Washington and Waco but also to the people living along the Upper and Lower Brazos Rivers. On one hand, the lock-and-dam project brought hope to farmers who lived inland. The Lower and Middle Brazos Rivers flowed through a region that was still agriculturally productive, and developers continued to promote the river as an ideal means of shipping

Army Corps of Engineers photograph from November 8, 1912, that shows the site for Lock-and-Dam No. 1, complete with shoals below the pass. Courtesy the National Archives and Records Administration, Southwest Division, Fort Worth, Texas.

perishable produce. In the hoped-for world that might emerge from a locked and dammed Brazos, "eggs, poultry, vegetables, fruits, live stock and other freight, taken on board late one afternoon, can be delivered next morning at a destination one hundred miles or more distant."[43] On the other hand, this project interested individuals advocating more generally for riparian control.[44] In January 1901, Captain C. S. Riche of the Army Corps of Engineers estimated "that six-foot navigation, for eight months in the year, could be obtained from Old Washington to Waco, by an expenditure of $3,500,000."[45] Such numbers not only cheered advocates for navigation but also encouraged people still hoping to combat the growing power of the railways.[46]

Despite the widespread public enthusiasm, the project would be haunted by disagreements about its feasibility.[47] As early as 1918, the district engineer wrote letters encouraging the continuation of the work while the Board of Engineers for Rivers and Harbors spoke out against continuing the improvement project.[48] The Corps of Engineers, in response to such squabbles and to concerns over funding, suspended

Undated photograph from the 1910s of laborers working to build Lock-and-Dam No. 8 near Waco. Courtesy the Texas Collection, Baylor University, Waco, Texas.

work at Lock Nos. 3, 6, and 8 several times. As noted above, engineers completed two lock-and-dam structures, began construction of two more structures, and never began construction on the remaining four structures. The eight-lock-and-dam project along the Brazos River, then, was largely considered a failure. Even the overly zealous could not consider this project a success.

The reasons for the seeming failure of this project were manifold. First, financial considerations proved to be an insurmountable obstacle. The cost was estimated initially at $300,000 per lock-and-dam structure in House Document 705, but the cost of the structures exceeded the estimates without exception.[49] Construction of Lock No. 1 had cost more than $400,000 as of 1913 (two years before its completion), and that amount did not include all of the iron and steelwork.[50] Likewise, Lock No. 8 had already amassed bills totaling $514,860.62 by 1915 (one year before its completion).[51] Opponents of the lock-and-dam project noted also that it would be impossible to attract sustained river traffic with the mere *months* of navigability promised by the Army Corps of Engineers. A failure to expand river traffic would, in turn, undermine any chance at lowering rail rates.[52] As a result of these financial and geological obstacles, the corps began recommending in 1919 that expenditures for the project be limited to the maintenance of specified locks, suggesting that the remaining lock projects be abandoned.

Second, an increasing disparity between the dreams for the river and the natural limitations of the landscape undermined this project from the beginning. All classes of people had cheered the lock-and-dam project, but financial considerations, disagreement over the placement of locks, and structural failures at Lock Nos. 1 and 8 put to an end the river's grandest Progressive Era project.[53] The primary issue, however, lay in a false hope about what could genuinely be accomplished along this waterway. Although governmental employees fumed over projects that went unused, the reality is that the Brazos River could not sustain regular navigation. The geological realities of the river corridor simply would not allow it, and at the center of such geological issues was the depth of the river. For example, developers quickly found that, along its length, the Brazos River was relatively shallow.[54] Because the river often disgorged a less-than-average flow, these depths permitted the navigation only of light draft vessels. Adding to the problems of navigational interests, the average depth measurements often used as a baseline in congressional decisions did not account for the sandbars that populated the river or the natural changes in the river's streambed.[55]

Additionally, an irregular streamflow proved problematic for the workers who labored to develop the navigational possibilities of this river. The flood of 1913, for instance, caused roughly $20,000 in losses.[56] Two years later, engineers at Lock No. 8 were forced yet again to request additional funds because of damage wrought by recent floods. Engineer C. S. Riche, who noted "three rises in the river flooding the cofferdam during the past two months," commented on the problems created by these high waters in a letter to his superiors: "This request for additional funds has become necessary on account of the frequent rises in the river flooding the cofferdam, filling the foundations with deposit of silt, washing out the puddle backing and doing other damage, which has entailed a great deal of additional expense."[57]

Engineers also struggled with the river's tendency toward a low streamflow, which made it difficult to pool water behind the dams. On June 11, 1912, Charles Schuster reported a rather dramatic but maddening discovery to the army corps: namely, a mere eight to ten inches of water then flowed through the Brazos River near Waco (the site of Lock No. 8).[58]

Third, the erodible nature of the Brazos soils also worked to change the river's depth and to create new problems for advocates of improvement.[59] Employees working for the Army Corps of Engineers noted, for instance, "cut-offs and caving banks" at the sites for Lock Nos. 3, 4, 6, and 8.[60] A letter from John Watt, an engineer employed at Lock No. 8, similarly indicated that the river was slowly but undeniably filling in at the construction site.[61] More specifically, Watt's 1917 letter reported, "the channel profile of surveys of 1909 and 1917 . . . shows the river to have filled about 4 to 5 feet in front of Waco."[62] The erodible soils of the Middle Brazos River also created more dramatic problems for Brazos River developers. Though the process was exceedingly gradual, the combined effect of floods and droughts on unstable soils encouraged a migratory river channel. With time, the river shifted course, and the once-grand structures of the locks and dams were gradually cast aside by the river itself, left to endure as quiet relics far removed from the streambed. The lock-and-dam near the city of Waco, for example, would ultimately testify to the dreams of this period from its new location in a field where cattle kept company.

Finally, the slope of the Brazos River presented additional difficulties. The change in elevation from Waco to Washington averaged 1.3 feet per miles, but the incline did not change evenly. For example, the average fall per mile of water surface between Lock Nos. 1 and 2 was 0.85 feet; the average fall per mile of water surface between Lock Nos. 5 and 6 was closer to 1.95 feet.[63] The elevation, then, could change at a rate of less than 1.0 foot per mile or close to 2.0 feet per mile. These statistics demonstrated what engineers would slowly discover about the geology of the river bed, namely: "to obtain the desired navigation by open channel methods alone would require an alteration of the slopes in many places to an extent which is impracticable."[64]

In addition to the interruptions brought on by geological and financial problems, the lock-and-dam project was undone by the Brazos population itself. Popular support for improvement generally remained strong along the Middle Brazos River throughout this period, but the individuals who called loudly for development exhibited relatively little interest in actually making use of the improvements that were enacted on the river. A refusal or inability to use completed improvement projects rapidly became a source of frustration as engineers, lawmakers, and boosters introduced increasingly costly projects during the mid-twentieth century. C. W. Payne of the Army Corps of Engineers, for example, asked his colleague and superior, Captain Riche, to get involved in marshaling support for the lock-and-dam projects during the 1910s.[65] Waco judge John N. Lyle went so far as to propose in 1915 that the people of the basin either build small-scale projects that would encourage local navigation or stop complaining and start using the channels already constructed along the Lower Brazos.[66]

At times, this lack of use reflected disagreements about the projects themselves. For example, boosters, developers, corps engineers, and city officials disagreed about the number and location of locks and dams.[67] Although the lock-and-dam project never gained much traction, sources from the 1910s are littered with references to a larger project that envisioned more than twenty-six lock-and-dam structures on the Brazos River.[68] At other times, proponents of riparian development disagreed about the economic feasibility of different projects. One Frank Morgan, for instance, wrote a somewhat scathing letter to the Army Corps of Engineers that called the eight-dam, eight-lock project "a waste of money" and argued that "any improvement undertaken should provide a sufficient number of dams to give slack water for as far down the river below Waco as locks and dams are necessary."[69]

In short, for every Colonel Robert or Captain Riche who proclaimed that improvement of the river through locks and dams would be worthwhile even at the cost of millions of dollars, dozens more insisted that projects be limited in scope financially or be written to benefit a larger population. For the government groups involved in designing, sponsoring, and funding Brazos River projects, the lack of popular use that often accompanied those disagreements translated into a seeming lack of popular support. Judge Lyle and C. S. Riche exchanged correspondence in 1915 in which they agreed that "in the non-use of the portion of the Brazos already improved lies the danger of the government abandoning the [lock-and-dam] project."[70] The National Waterways Board, likewise, commented that "the use of improved channels, in many instances, has not been commensurate with the expense incurred, and there is a lack of progressiveness in providing suitable freight carrying facilities, and a failure to provide modern terminal equipment."[71]

The successes and failures of nineteenth-century projects along the Lower Brazos River—the first iterations of what would be a persistent dream of riparian control—had demonstrated to engineers, developers, and lawmakers that the mighty Brazos would not be tamed easily. As a result, advocates for change dreamed still more fantastical dreams for the Middle Brazos River during the Progressive Era, developing a lock-and-dam project that they hoped would expand navigational opportunities, undo the fickle flows of the river, and defy the power of the railways. Congressman John M. Moore, who both hailed from and represented Fort Bend County, offered a striking commentary on that sense of expectation in a 1907 article: "I want to see the river made navigable from its mouth to Waco, the jetties at its mouth repaired and extended, the bar removed and the harbor at Velasco and the mouth of the great river be, as it should be, one of the finest and safest on the Texas Gulf coast; the Brazos valley, one of the most fertile sections of this great country of ours, come into its inherent rights and prosper beyond compare and blossom as the rose."[72]

The need for improvement seemed undeniable, and the impetus, unstoppable. Indeed, many people would have agreed with the *Galveston Daily News* when it declared in 1906 that "there is no doubt that the Brazos River can be made navigable. There is no doubt about the wisdom of making it so. It is a cold-blooded Business proposition in which fact and figures will rule."[73] Still, the journey toward an improved and restrained Brazos River was not made any easier by this unity of thought.

The groups and individuals who advocated development of the watershed during this period struggled mightily to reconcile their plans for the Brazos with the geological realities of the river, to tailor their fluid (but no less sincere) hopes for change to projects that could in fact be realized. These pushers of improvement removed shoals and trimmed trees only to watch as natural forces undid what little progress industrial tools had wrought. They erected lock-and-dam structures and then watched the river shift course, isolating those monuments to industry in the fields of local farmers.[74] In the midst of that place that dashed expectations but still nourished hope, the people of this river began to alter their approach to issues of water, moving past a deeply personal dream of navigation and barges and agricultural commodities to a more immediately necessary domain of dams and reservoirs.

CHAPTER FIVE

Big Dams and Big Dreams along the Upper Brazos River

These men of the west have vision. They keep their eyes open. They do not need to be shown. They have been shown by the pioneers of this mighty movement under the skies of Texas. From its source to the place where it empties its waters into the Gulf of Mexico the Brazos should be dammed and huge reservoirs to contain impounded water should be constructed in the years to come. And this is what is going to happen in Texas.

— "FLOOD WATER CONTROL," *Port Arthur News*, 1925

Due to the flooded condition of this part of the country, caused by the over-flow of our rivers, much property and many crops are distroyed [*sic*] yearly. It is believed that this condition can be eliminated only by building the dams designed in the Brazos Project.

—NELLIE HUCKWORTH TO THE HONORABLE W. R. POAGE, 1938

Though flood waters have been rolling down Texas rivers from the Sabine to the Guadalupe this week, the Brazos has misbehaved worst of all. The Brazos is a chronic offender. It is Texas' own Ol' Man River, often leaving its natural domain to inundate a valley which winds 700 miles from the Staked Plains to the Gulf. Sooner or later, Texas will have to do something about the Brazos flood problem.

— "TEXAS FLOODS," *Galveston Daily News*, 1940*

IN 1935, 161 INDIVIDUALS from Rule, Texas, sent a petition to their newly elected congressman, George Mahon. This petition advocated the improvement of a still-unruly Brazos River, citing potential benefits for flood control, power generation, drought relief, and economic

*It is worth noting that this article was written after completion of the Possum Kingdom Dam, a structure described by many as the lynchpin to any Brazos flood project.

development: "We, the undersigned citizens of Rule, Haskell County, Texas, respectfully petition you to lend your undivided support in the approval of a bill which will be presented to Congress at any early date, calling for a $50,000,000.00 loan to the Brazos River Conservation and Reclamation District for the purpose of constructing 12 major dams."[1] *We . . . respectfully petition you to lend your undivided support*—with those words, people living in a small town in a sparsely populated region of the Texas Panhandle voiced the needs, frustrations, and desires of generations of Texans who knew the perils of Brazos living all too well.

The residents of Rule lived in close proximity to the Double Mountain Fork of the Brazos River in a region that endured dust storms, flash floods, long droughts, and the evocatively named Marfa Monsters (short-lived, torrential thunderstorms that often washed out the land and rearranged local soils). Consequently, the men and women who sent this petition would have been achingly, personally familiar with the swings from drought to flood, high water to low, that plagued the Brazos Basin.[2] These petitioners, however, were but one group in a long line of Brazos victims. Their frustrations reverberated in newspapers across the state as editors, otherwise distanced by place and philosophy, published strikingly similar tales of destruction and spoke collectively of the river as a "chronic offender."[3] Brazos dwellers from generations past had also spoken of a temperamental river, and they surely would have identified with the emotions laid bare in the opening petition.

In response to continuing outcries, lawmakers began to pursue what Congressman W. R. Poage later called the "full and complete development of the Brazos."[4] A 1938 letter from A. L. Monteith underscored the narrow mindset that guided these desperate proponents: "I see only one solution and that is a quick action in the building of these dams."[5] Previous development projects had more closely aligned the Lower and Middle Brazos with southern rivers and had emphasized navigation, agricultural production, and economic markets. This new round of projects, which largely emerged between 1929 and 1958, adopted a different model of development: one that prioritized federal funds, multiuse dam projects, and power generation. Accordingly, the construction (or, more accurately, the attempted construction) of dam structures along the Upper Brazos River spoke to a broader desire to institute a dam-centric model of development within the western states and also to the difficulty of realizing that model within the Brazos Basin.

Mounting frustrations with flood events during the late nineteenth and early twentieth centuries swept Brazos developers into a position where improvement more closely resembled the dams of the Columbia, Tennessee, or Colorado Rivers rather than the locks of the Mississippi or Cumberland, and that focus on dams between the 1930s and 1950s ushered in what would ultimately be the most successful period for improvement along the Brazos River. But development did not move forward more easily because of the narrowed focus or the multiplicity of like projects. The ratio of failed or abandoned projects to completed projects still skewed dramatically toward the former during this period, as it had during the days of levees, jetties, and locks. In addition to geological and economic obstacles, the perceived needs of people living along the Upper Brazos River continued to conflict with the needs of people living along the Lower and Middle Brazos Rivers. The result was that development interests along the length of the river continued to compete one with the other. Still, the oftentimes fruitless attempts to dam the Brazos proved significant beyond the region within which this river flowed.

Most notably, the shift in focus away from earlier riparian models reflected ongoing changes to the national landscape. Completion of Hoover Dam on the Colorado River ushered in a period in which America's rivers were dammed at an astonishing rate. President Franklin Delano Roosevelt oversaw the structure's dedication in September of 1935, and by October of the following year, the hydroelectric capabilities of Hoover Dam had generated power that lit the infrastructure of Los Angeles and the imaginations of Los Angelenos. Hoover Dam was not the first large-scale dam to be built in the United States. Nor was it the first dam to be built using either the arch or the gravity structure, designs that would characterize most oversized dams in the United States. However, this mass of concrete and steel was the tallest dam in the world upon its completion and one of the first multipurpose structures to dot the western half of the United States, so it quickly came to symbolize the promise of technological intervention in the West.

The construction of Tennessee Valley Authority, or TVA, projects during the New Deal Era provided a similar impetus for dam-building projects. In the case of the TVA project, developers and engineers incorporated multiuse dam structures within the Tennessee River watershed into a single, unified vision for riparian, social, and economic improvement. The TVA obviously worked to improve a watershed no longer part of what Americans viewed as "the West," but the work of this agency nevertheless spoke to a broad interest in multiuse projects, especially when those projects also promised a solution to the long-standing problem of aridity.

During this period of accelerated dam building, engineers raised massive structures on such rivers on the Columbia and the Snake, but even as dams began to remake the rivers of the West, navigational projects endured along many rivers in the south and southeast. Barges and boats, for example, continued to make use of locks, levees, and small-scale dams, bringing some amount of commercial growth to the towns that dotted rivers such as the Mississippi, Savannah, Tennessee, Cumberland, and Chattahoochee. The diminishing interest in river traffic along the Brazos River, in other words, did not emerge from unified, national shifts in thought but from local concerns that emphasized deliverance from floods. The expansion of railways and roadways, the growth of cities within the watershed, the parallel rise in costs that followed each flood event, the declining price for Brazos crops—all these forces served to de-emphasize riparian commerce and to elevate flood control as the current end toward which improvement schemes would work.

Dam building along the Brazos would differ somewhat from what was accomplished along other western river systems. The geology of the Brazos changed so radically from mouth to source that it proved close to impossible to implement a single vision for development within the watershed, and developers were consequently forced to apply different visions for development to the different sections of the river. Still, the river traffic that Lower and Middle Brazos River dwellers had sought to encourage in prior decades was more or less forgotten as flood control surpassed navigation as the pressing issue. In fact, many Texas lawmakers and laypeople began to view navigation as, at best, an unattainable ideal and more likely as a distraction and an irresponsible use of funds. Congressman O. H. Cross made the point clearly when he testified before the Committee on Flood Control in the House of Representatives during a 1935 hearing: "We do not expect to have this stream navigable. . . . I do not think it is feasible for navigation."[6] The *Fort Worth Star-Telegram*, in a particularly memorable quote from 1951, went so far as to claim that "'not even a rowboat' could navigate the Brazos River in Texas 250 miles from the Gulf of Mexico."[7]

Brazos developers, for the most part, happily surrendered their hopes for navigation in exchange for a more attainable dream—flood control along the upper third of the river. The perceived lack of navigability even became an asset by midcentury. The Brazos River Conservation and Reclamation District, for example, used that deficiency to argue that it did not need the permission of the Federal Power Commission to build hydroelectric dams within the watershed.[8] The Federal Power Commission, a precursor to the Federal Energy Regulatory Commission, oversaw hydroelectric development on navigable rivers during this time and regulated electric rates along those same rivers. The Regulatory Commission did not concern itself with waterways that were not navigable, and so Texas newspapers now proudly reminded their readers that "there has been no commerce on the Brazos during the memory of any living man."[9]

Amid this nascent focus on dam building, two United States congressmen—William Robert (W. R.) Poage and George Mahon—became indelibly linked with the issue of Brazos improvement, working in tandem to maintain interest in the development of a river that had withstood similar attention for more than a century. Representing the cities of Waco and Lubbock respectively, these men influenced politicians beyond their sphere of geographic influence. For example, they collectively sponsored bills in the Texas Senate, the Texas House of Representatives, and the United States House of Representatives, operating within different levels of the United States and Texas governments to jointly champion the improvement of Texas's longest in-state river. Other individuals likewise worked political angles to secure improvement within the watershed. Judge and congressman J. J. Mansfield helped the Brazos River Conservation and Reclamation District to obtain Works Progress Administration support for Possum Kingdom Dam, and several Texas governors became involved in improvement efforts as well. Still, W. R. Poage and George Mahon dictated the tempo of improvement during the twentieth century. It was largely because of their efforts, for example, that men such as Lyndon B. Johnson and Harold Ickes ultimately agreed to fund Brazos improvement.[10]

Regardless of the roles they played, the attempts of Poage, Mahon, and other lawmakers to moderate the river's flow spoke both to their persistence regarding so-called hot issues and to the real needs of Brazos dwellers. That desire to improve the watershed and to eliminate (or, at a minimum, to reduce) the effects of droughts and floods became institutionalized in 1929, when Texas lawmakers agreed to form the Brazos River Conservation and Reclamation District, renamed the Brazos River Authority in 1953. According to a pamphlet published in 1936, the Texas legislature created this agency "to control flood waters on the Brazos River."[11] An undated application for Public Works Administration funds confirmed that emphasis, stressing the district's desire to alleviate the damage caused by "recurrent, devastating floods in the valley of the Brazos River" and calling these frequent flood events a "public calamity."[12] The State of Texas created this extra-governmental agency to manage the financial, physical, and social development of a watershed that nearly surpassed the state of Pennsylvania in size, and its creation marked a turning point in the way that policy makers approached development. Never before had a public agency been given oversight over an entire major river basin.[13]

Enveloped within the purpose of this organization was a simple but notable idea that would gradually take shape in the political mind—efforts toward flood control along the Upper Brazos River would help to alleviate flooding along the Middle and Lower Brazos River as well. Accordingly, even as the Reclamation District worked to define its bureaucratic and institutional roles during the late 1920s and early 1930s, Texas lawmakers began to craft solutions for the recurring issue of Brazos River floods and to garner support for the proposals that resulted. John Norris (founding member of and chief engineer for the Reclamation District) offered one of the earliest endorsements for a dam project in a 1934 pamphlet: "Through storage alone can the menace be removed and the damaging flood flows be held within harmless bounds . . . released to provide a usable volume during the times when nature fails to provide sufficient for our purposes."[14] That same year, Dick Vaughan offered a more general endorsement of dam building in an article for the *El Paso Herald-Post*: "Plans are almost complete to take the footloose old Brazos river, which winds over one-sixth of Texas, frequently changing its course, covering millions of acres in flood or disappearing entirely in drouth, and make a consistent river of it."[15]

The politicians who dealt with the political debris that resulted from Brazos River outbursts understood that floods and droughts were a pressing problem within the basin; indeed, they could not help but know of the river's destructive capacity. But they also understood that many rivers in this nation undergo fluctuations in their streamflow, periodically poring over their banks or diminishing to little more than ephemeral streams. It was not enough for Brazos boosters to ask for federal monies to be spent on improvement; instead, the men and women involved in Brazos River development needed to demonstrate the urgency and the legitimacy of their requests for funding. To that end, the Brazos River Conservation and Reclamation District and the House of Representatives Committee on Flood Control sought testimony from local residents about the need for flood-control structures.

A Mr. Buchanan provided a particularly distressing look into the devastating nature of these frequent flood events at a 1935 hearing before the House of Representatives Committee on Flood Control. Speaking specifically of the 1921 flood, Buchanan remembered: "I myself and two or three others were staying on top of the house, and had to stay there 5 or 6 days, because the ferryboat was leaking. We would take turn about bailing the ferryboat out night and day to keep it from sinking and losing those mules. Every now and then a house would rise up and go off down the river."[16]

In an effort to further illustrate his feelings about frequent flooding, Buchanan penned and subsequently shared a poem that suggested he had found a solution to the question of Brazos perils: "Farewell to the Brazos bottoms, I bid you a long adieu. I may migrate to hell some day, But I'll never return to you."[17]

Mr. Buchanan was but one individual to provide testimony, and congressional representatives ultimately found meaning in the sheer volume of letters submitted by sheriffs, farmers, mayors, and housewives.[18] These witnesses may have exaggerated the frequency or severity of flood events, but an ecological reality underpinned (and brought legitimacy to) their complaints. More specifically, the Brazos River still ran low at times, leaving rich agricultural land thirsty in an often-humid climate; the river still topped its banks at other times, devastating the immovable and forcing the mobile into flight. It was no surprise to these Brazos dwellers that newspapers of the 1930s continued to balance their descriptions of the "monstrous flood hazard of this stream" and a "rain-gorged Brazos River" with pieces suggesting that dams would even out the inconsistent flow of the river and limit loss of life and property.[19] It even became commonplace during the 1930s for newspapers to speculate, in the days following flood events, on what damage could have been prevented by the presence of a dam structure.[20]

However, people living in the watershed had come to believe by this point that only a series of dams would address the "urgent necessity" of flood control.[21] "The butcher, the baker, the candle-stick maker—yes, everyone in Bell County is interested in the Brazos River dam project"—in the opinion of John Clarkson (and presumably many others), only a succession of dams could now prevent the overflows that periodically swelled and pitched and coursed through Brazos towns.[22] According to the *El Paso Herald-Post*, proponents of development believed that a multidam project would ultimately allow them to tame the "Old Man River of Texas, the Brazos" and to trade "a 900-mile pain in the neck for a natural resource which would rival oil in value."[23] Whatever the validity of these perspectives, they set in a motion a series of dam projects that would not pacify the river but would ultimately bring to light the centrality of a dam-centric model of development within the Brazos watershed.

The Brazos River Conservation and Reclamation District, in conjunction with the State Board of Water Engineers and the Ambursen Engineering Corporation, proposed the first large-scale dam project in 1936, a plan known simply as the Brazos River Project. The Brazos River Project, which advocated the construction of thirteen dams, constituted the Brazos River Authority's first master plan for the river and the first coordinated dam project for the Brazos Basin. The plan focused on the Upper Brazos River—though it did not exclude the Middle Brazos River entirely—and tentatively sited five large-scale dams along the main stem of the river and eight dams along the tributaries, privileging the following locations: Breckenridge Dam (Clear Fork), Seymour Dam (Salt Fork), Possum Kingdom Dam (Brazos River), Turkey Creek Dam (Brazos River), Inspiration Point Dam (Brazos River), de Cordova Bend Dam (Brazos River), Bee Mountain Dam (Brazos River), Whitney Dam (Bosque River), Lampasas Dam (Lampasas River), Leon Dam (Leon River), San Gabriel Dam 1 (San Gabriel River), San Gabriel Dam 2 (San Gabriel River), and Navasota Dam (Navasota River).[24]

The House Committee estimated that the project would cost $35 million for the construction of these major dams and an additional $15 million for the construction of what they called "minor dams."[25] Flood control alone could not justify such extensive expenditures along the Brazos, not in light of the failed projects of earlier eras and the growing demand nationally for federal funding. An application for Public Works Administration funds confirmed as much, admitting that "if it can be said that the District has a primary objective, that objective is flood control" but also conceding that "flood control dams cannot be self-liquidating and for that reason dams and reservoirs designed exclusively for flood control are not contained in this application."[26] As a result, while the project centered on flood control, the purposes of the Brazos Project were fourfold: (1) flood control, (2) water conservation for irrigation, industrial, and municipal purposes, (3) soil conservation and reclamation, and (4) hydroelectric power production.[27]

Developers chose to prioritize construction of Possum Kingdom Dam—authorized in 1935, begun in 1938, and completed in 1941—and with those efforts, the era of big dams officially commenced along the

Brazos River.[28] Federal monies could have been used on any of the thirteen dams, but the Brazos River Conservation and Reclamation District and the civic leaders from several Brazos River counties decided that a dam at this location would contribute to flood control and drought alleviation in greater and more lasting ways than at any other Brazos site.[29] The area chosen for the dam also lent itself to a large-scale structure, something that could not be said along much of the Brazos River: the preferred site for Possum Kingdom Dam included limestone cliffs that facilitated the erection of abutments for the dam structure.[30] The federal government authorized $3,001,598 for this individual project, but Morris Sheppard Dam, which impounded Possum Kingdom Lake, was ultimately constructed at a cost of roughly $9 million, nearly triple what the district had estimated.[31] As a result of that discrepancy, the Works Progress Administration did not remain involved in the construction of Possum Kingdom, ultimately excusing itself from the project.

After completing the Possum Kingdom Dam, developers began work on the Whitney Dam, an Army Corps of Engineers project intended "for control of floods and for regulation of streamflow for power development and other beneficial uses."[32] As with the Possum Kingdom Dam, the Whitney Dam was to be used primarily for flood control and only secondarily for other beneficial uses. Although engineers and developers believed that the Morris Sheppard Dam would provide the greatest amount of flood control within the Brazos River Basin, they argued that the Whitney Dam would also play a crucial role in flood-control efforts along the river.[33] In particular, developers and engineers believed that the Whitney Dam—located near the junction of the Upper and Middle Brazos Rivers—could eliminate increased streamflow and, consequently, floods for people living downstream more readily than could the Possum Kingdom Dam.

With these words of faith and hope in mind, popular support grew quickly for this second Brazos dam.[34] Representatives from the chambers of commerce for the cities of Cleburne, Meridian, Waco, Whitney, and Hillsboro even planned a celebration "to be held when the first dirt is broken on the Brazos River dam project at Whitney."[35] Mapping work commenced for the site as early as 1937, but construction did not begin until 1947 and was not completed until 1951, delayed by the ongoing war effort and by the allocation of funds to that cause.[36] Engineers put the cost of Whitney Dam at $8.5 million in 1939 and the capacity at 500,000 acre-feet, but the cost quickly increased to several times that

Families looking over the Possum Kingdom Dam at a site near Breckenridge,
Texas. Courtesy Basil Clemens Photograph Collection, Special Collections,
University of Texas at Arlington Library, Arlington, Texas.

amount.[37] The final cost for this dam increased to between $30 million
and $42 million by the late 1940s, though it is unclear if this rather
sizeable increase was due simply to incorrect estimates and unexpected
geological issues.[38] Whatever the explanation for the spiraling costs, the
final numbers certainly outpaced the initial estimates.

Proponents of the thirteen-dam project only built two large concrete
dams along the Brazos River during the 1930s, 1940s, and 1950s. They
succeeded, however, in also building a small earthen dam on the Leon
River during this period. Engineers and corps officials completed the
surveys and mapping for the Leon River in 1937, and after beginning
work in 1949, the Army Corps of Engineers completed construction on
the Lake Belton project in 1954.[39] This dam impounded the Leon River
with a rolled-earth fill structure in an area where the banks elevated
steeply.[40] Construction of Lake Belton, authorized by the 1946 Flood
Control Act and modified by the 1954 Flood Control Act, cost an estimated $17 million.[41]

Although completion of the remaining dams proved difficult,

problems with this Brazos River Project did not halt dam-building momentum along the river. When the thirteen-dam project stalled in the 1950s, lawmakers and developers drafted a new plan for the Brazos River, a six-dam project that centered on the Brazos River tributaries and revolved around a proposal drawn up by the Army Corps of Engineers rather than the Brazos River Authority.[42] Specifically, the secretary of the army recommended that six flood-control dams be built on the tributaries of the river, a recommendation that was, in turn, authorized by the Flood Control Act of 1954.[43] The Public Works Sub-Committee in the House of Representatives authorized $40 million for the project with a total estimated cost of between $92 million to $158 million. This six-dam project envisioned dams on the Bosque River near Waco (an expansion of the existing Lake Waco), on the Leon River in Comanche County, on the Lampasas River near Belton, on the San Gabriel River in Williamson County, on the Navasota River near Bryan, and on Yegua Creek near Somerville.[44] Of these proposed sites, the Lampasas and San Gabriel locations had originally been proposed as part of the thirteen-dam project.

The Army Corps of Engineers succeeded in building four of the proposed dams, but the process of funding and constructing these dams extended through three decades. For example, the corps completed mapping and fieldwork for most of these locations by 1940 but would not complete Stillhouse Hollow Lake on the Lampasas River until 1968; they completed Granger Lake Dam on the San Gabriel River in 1980.[45] The Army Corps of Engineers also constructed Lake Georgetown on the San Gabriel River in 1979, though it is not clear if they constructed the dam as part of the initial thirteen-dam plan, the six-dam plan, or through an independent push.[46] The corps completed the expansion of Lake Waco in 1964. Moreover, the Brazos River Authority succeeded in building Somerville Dam on Yegua Creek, a proposed flood-control site unique to this six-dam plan, in 1967.[47]

The proposed dam for the Navasota River proved to be the most problematic of all the projected sites.[48] Although the Brazos River Authority impounded Lake Limestone behind Sterling C. Robertson Dam in 1978, more than six sites were proposed and/or considered for the reservoir.[49] Two of the best-known locations included the Millican Dam site, at river mile 24.05, and the Ferguson Dam site, proposed for river mile 36.5 on the Navasota River.[50] The families and individuals who lived along the Navasota River argued passionately over these two dam sites, and both proponents and opponents of development continued to debate the construction of Millican Dam into the late twentieth century. Even with the difficulties surrounding the Navasota River site, this six-dam project proved to be one of the more successful of the proposed dam projects. There were many reasons for this success, but the end of the Second World War, the return of prosperity during the 1950s, and the feverish public support that accompanied a renewed emphasis on flood control unquestionably helped the Army Corps of Engineers.

The Brazos River Conservation and Reclamation District proposed yet another six-dam project during the 1950s, a project that both complemented and competed with the thirteen-dam project and six-dam project discussed above.[51] This project proposed the enlargement of Possum Kingdom and the construction of reservoirs at Hightower, Bee Mountain, Inspiration Point, de Cordova Bend, and Turkey Creek.[52] Proponents of improvement would have recognized the sites in this project: these dams, staggered along the main stem of the Upper Brazos River between Morris Sheppard and Whitney Dams, were originally included in the larger thirteen-dam project. The cost was estimated somewhere around $181 million, but the district intended to finance some portion of the costs. Indeed, newspaper articles and Brazos River Conservation and Reclamation District records alternately suggested that the Authority would finance roughly $131 million through the sale of power or that the dams "would not cost taxpayers one cent."[53]

In the course of developing the new six-dam project, the Reclamation District (known by now as the Brazos River Authority or BRA) again emphasized flood control, but in a dramatic shift, the BRA prioritized hydroelectric power production.[54] In truth, these dams were "considered to be valuable primarily for power" and to have only "incidental flood control storage benefits."[55] Part of the explanation for that shift was due to financial considerations: the Brazos River Authority hoped that power development at these dams could fund the full cost of development.[56] Developers and boosters hoped that this variation of the multidam project would trap the "wasted water" that continued to flow through the river's banks by building a "250-mile chain of lakes that will make the river, in effect, one great lake from Whitney Reservoir upstream to Possum Kingdom Reservoir."[57] The luckless inhabitants of the often-flooded towns along the Brazos surely hoped for some relief from the problems of water feast and famine.

In addition to power generation, the Brazos River Authority also promoted irrigation as an important benefit of the six-dam project.

Writing during a time when the science of ecology daily gained both intellectual ground and widespread understanding, the Brazos River Authority noted in a pamphlet that the dams of the upper reaches of the river would benefit those individuals who lived further downstream: "Two hundred thousand acres of the Brazos River bottoms between Waco and Richmond could be irrigated profitably with foreseeable water supplies, instead of the 30,000 acres now under irrigation. Forty thousand acres in the Little River Valley alone could be made to pay with irrigation. . . . Farm income makes for prosperity."[58]

Although the Brazos River Authority emphasized conservation and power generation in official propaganda, flood control continued to be a fixation for people living along and working with the Brazos. Such a reality surely motivated the *Waco Tribune-Herald* when it declared in a 1956 article that "power generation at Brazos River dams is really a secondary consideration."[59] That same article even argued, "the chief value of the dams spaced along the Brazos between [Whitney and Possum Kingdom Dams] will be in their storage of water."[60] Glossy pamphlets and thoughtfully worded releases, in other words, could not entirely sway the everyday people of this watershed into adopting wholesale this new representation.

Developers and engineers only succeeded in building one of the six dams: de Cordova Bend Dam, an earth-filled structure near Granbury, Texas. Unfortunately, the building process never proceeded smoothly at the de Cordova Bend Dam (which impounded Lake Granbury). Authorities completed the surveys and mapping work in 1937, attempted to begin construction in 1951, stalled, received a state permit in 1966 to formally begin construction, and completed the dam in 1969.[61] As would later be the case at Sterling C. Robertson Dam on the Navasota River, the Brazos River Authority used monies earned from the sale of power to fund the construction of the de Cordova Bend dam.[62] Whether the model could have been successfully incorporated into the construction of the remaining six dams is debatable, but it hardly mattered. Opposition to the dam program mounted quickly.

As with other development projects, financial concerns contributed to the failure of this basin project. Engineers reported as early as 1956, for example, that the costs of the project outweighed its benefits.[63] But economics did not undermine the six-dam project. Although a handful of individuals believed that a "holiday land" would grow up around a Brazos that was both dammed and tamed, most people living in the basin did not agree with or support the ideas propelling this project.[64] Opponents were roughly divided into three groups. First, some water users preferred the focus on power but thought that the power generated at these dams would actually cost more to produce than it would ultimately be worth on the market.[65] There seemed to be little reason to support the expenditure of tens of millions of dollars on these dams if they would not, in fact, lower costs for the individuals who purchased power through Brazos utilities.

Second, in a world where floodwaters wreaked havoc on Brazos lands with some regularity, many people argued that the six-dam project focused too much on power and too little on flood control.[66] Flood control continued to be a fixation for people living along and working with the Brazos, despite the official interest in power generation. This was especially true near the junction of the Middle and Upper Brazos Rivers, where the original dam project had been proposed. A sizeable number of Brazos dwellers prioritized flood control over power production, an issue that shaped their daily lives in less damaging and less dramatic ways, and they preferred projects that adopted the same emphasis.

Finally, some individuals feared that people living further downstream would see a decline both in the quality and the quantity of their water if the Brazos River Authority succeeded in building these dams along the upper reaches of the river.[67] The Lower Brazos River Water Users Committee, for example, published a pamphlet in which they declared that they supported the six-dam project of the Army Corps of Engineers over that of the Brazos River Authority because they believed that it offered more equitable use of the river's resources.[68] Residents from Cameron, Texas, along the Middle Brazos River, likewise, wrote to Senator Poage in 1956 to voice their opinions regarding equitable use of Brazos water. Although this letter saw a highly limited circulation, it laid bare the frustrations of many Lower Brazos River inhabitants when it noted that "it was rather irksome to us in Cameron to know that people on the Gulf by the mere giving of notice could have water released for industrial purposes when we had so much difficulty securing a release of a very small amount of water for municipal purposes."[69]

In the face of mounting opposition, the Brazos River Authority published a circular in 1957 titled *Let's Build Dams!*[70] The circular addressed a variety of issues, speaking to people whose homes would be flooded by the construction of these dams (e.g., individuals living in Graham, Texas), people who might see a decline in their water quality as a result of the construction of these dams (e.g., the residents of the Lower Brazos River), and people generally concerned with high electric costs.[71] In addition to concerns over the prevention of floods, that last question proved to be particularly important. Questions over the sale and allocation of power had plagued Brazos development as early as 1936, when some Texans became concerned that the proposed construction of Possum Kingdom as a hydroelectric dam would not do anything to lower electricity rates in Texas.[72] But concerns over power became more problematic with this six-dam scheme because it seemed to sacrifice flood control completely for electricity rates still deemed far too high.

In addition to the projects discussed above, the Brazos River Authority proposed a five-dam project that targeted the more arid regions of the Upper Brazos River watershed. Focusing almost exclusively on the formative tributaries of the river, the agency began discussing these dams during the 1940s but did not formulate a cohesive plan for the individual structures until the 1950s. The five-dam project would have expanded on several existing low-water dams and also proposed new structures at South Bend (Brazos River), Breckenridge (Clear Fork), Nugent (Clear Fork), and the twin Seymour Dams (Salt Fork and Double Mountain Fork).[73] As with other dam projects, the development scheme included a few structures that were initially considered as part of other projects. Moreover, the Brazos River Authority hoped that these dams would, like their hypothetical predecessors, prevent the "'waste' of flood waters" by controlling the flow of the Brazos River and maximizing effective use of the river's waters.[74] However, because this area experienced more famine than feast in terms of average water levels, developers intended that the project would focus as well on increasing the amount of available water through a strategy of reclamation.

Local and regional populations along the upper third of the river perhaps feared a water shortage above almost any other form of riparian problem because it was the most frequent visitor of destruction. Indeed, the ultimate hope of developers like C. M. Caldwell was that "not a drop of West Texas water will pass the 98th meridian on its way southeastward."[75] Mayor A. C. Humphrey of Stamford, Texas, concurred: "We've grappled for six years now with a serious water situation. It has been alarming at just how close we were to the edge."[76] Despite a good deal of support for the project, especially in the northern and western counties of Texas, the plan never gained much traction. Ranchers opposed several of these dams, most notably

Photograph from 1937 of families playing near a low-water dam on the Brazos River near Breckenridge, Texas. Courtesy Basil Clemens Photograph Collection, Special Collections, University of Texas at Arlington Library, Arlington, Texas.

the Breckenridge Dam.[77] The reservoir, if constructed, would have covered roughly 15,500 acres of prime ranchland in an area early settled by pioneering, ranching Texas families, and this prospect led to an outpouring of disapproval. The Matthews family, who owned a sizeable portion of the land that would have been inundated by the dam, expressed the sentiments of many when it published a statement noting, "We will not fight a new lake, if they really want to build one on the Clear Fork, . . . but we will certainly fight one at this site."[78] Such displacement was a common consequence to dam building, but it was still an undesirable one to the families who would have fallen victim to permanently heightened waters.

The cities that would have used the water in that reservoir, such as Abilene and Sweetwater and Stamford, also demonstrated resistance to this proposed dam scheme. Most commonly, the individuals representing these cities expressed concerns that the water in the Clear and Salt Forks would not meet their standards for potability. Increased chloride and sulphate levels, in their opinion, endowed the already-scarce water with an odor and flavor that many people found distasteful.[79] So high were the salt levels along the main stem of the Upper Brazos that many people living within this portion of the watershed believed that only the water of Double Mountain Fork was potable.[80] Indeed, officials representing the city of Abilene noted that they considered the water unfit for municipal use.[81] The *Abilene Reporter-News* echoed those thoughts, noting that "the two 'Seymour' dams are needed to separate the 'bad' water of the Salt Fork from the 'good' water of the Double Mountain Fork."[82]

A proposal for an independent dam on the Upper Brazos River in the 1940s complemented these series of dam projects. Although little is known about the project, contemporary newspaper articles referenced a reservoir to be sited on the Double Mountain Fork, the Bob Baskin Dam. This venture, which would have involved the Bureau of Reclamation in the process of Brazos River dam building, proposed "a dam on the Double Mountain Fork that would serve, among other purposes, the function of recharging irrigation wells in the Haskell County area."[83] Proponents of this dam, like the proponents of the Brazos River Authority's Upper Brazos River plan, emphasized very different ideals than those of the individuals living in the occasionally water-rich, flood-prone areas of the Lower and Middle Brazos River. Flood control factored into the equation only tangentially; these dams sought instead to secure a water supply for municipal and agricultural uses.[84]

The bureau never built this dam, and seemingly never even moved into the construction process. As with dams along other stretches of the river, economics and hydrology undermined the hopes of Bob Baskin developers before the project could proceed to that point. Most notably, engineers estimated that construction of the dam and reservoir site would have cost $25.5 million. Given concerns over evaporation from the reservoir and the potability of the water, escalating costs (which were difficult to avoid, as evidenced by the experience at other Brazos dams) would not be tolerated. The cost for the large reservoir simply could not be justified, particularly when the structure would almost exclusively aid irrigation interests over the interests of municipalities.

Finally, in addition to a thirteen-dam project, a six-dam project, a second six-dam project, a five-dam project, and a single-dam project, a handful of boosters began talking during the 1950s and 1960s about a twenty-three-dam project for the Brazos River.[85] Boosters proposed this especially enormous dam project as part of a comprehensive state water project that included other reclamation proposals.[86] The addition of yet another set of propositions spoke to Texans' continued faith in technology and improvement and also to their continuing frustration with the lack of control over this river. This development project also reflected a persistent belief in the exceptional potential of the Brazos itself and grew from a long-held but growing conviction on the part of locals that "we need to tame our streams, and make them do our bidding."[87] Few newspapers or letters mentioned the largest of projects; they did not even publish a list of the dams. Yet, proponents of the project very clearly insisted that they hoped to provide benefits "for all the people" and to integrate these many structures into an "over-all pattern for fullest development of the river's potential."[88]

As evidenced by the long list of would-be dams, the individuals living within the Upper Brazos River watershed struggled mightily to tame their river between 1929 and 1958. They struggled also to adjust their expectations for the potential of the river to the natural limitations of the watershed. That disconnect between expectation and reality had shaped and shadowed Brazos development for a full century along every section of the river, but its role in the imperfect improvement of the Brazos Basin is especially clear in the efforts of developers to introduce hydroelectric power generation and flood control to their watershed. Developers ultimately constructed three dams on the main stem of the river and six dams on its tributaries, but tangible and symbolic issues of power hindered improvement of the Upper Brazos. On one hand, progress on these projects slowed and, at times, ground entirely to a halt as municipalities and agencies debated the details of who should sell the power and at what cost. On the other hand, these projects were undone by disagreements that arose as the inhabitants of the Lower, Middle, and Upper Brazos Rivers sought to reconcile their own expectations for the river with those of people who lived in geologically, as well as geographically, different areas or who simply disagreed with the prioritization of flood control versus power generation.

Still, despite those setbacks, the engineers, politicians, and everyday people of the Upper Brazos River Basin sincerely believed that their thirteen-dam plan would succeed in holding back a surging flow of high waters, and that it would overcome the problems with money and geology and politics that had plagued so many improvement schemes. They also believed, to varying degrees, that the six-dam plans of the Brazos River Authority and the Army Corps of Engineers would manipulate the waters of this river to desirable ends. That faith in technology prompted countless editorials that waxed eloquently about the possibilities of the Brazos River. One editorial, for example, appeared in a 1935 edition of the *Freeport Facts* and stated confidently that Whitney Dam held the "definite promise for relief to lower Brazos River Basin residents from flood menaces."[89]

Such confidence had some basis in reality. Multiple large-scale dams were constructed during the mid-twentieth century, and some measure of flood control, power generation, and water reclamation was achieved. Yet, many Brazos dwellers remained skeptical that either permanent relief or an improved Brazos had actually been obtained. "Little has been done to protect against floods on the Brazos River"—M. C. Tyler surely echoed the frustrations of many generations of Brazos dwellers when he penned those words in a 1939 memo.[90] It was little surprise, then, to people living at the time when the era of dam building along the Upper Brazos rolled over into a still more ambitious project for riparian improvement. The impetus for development was still strong, and a new generation of developers was poised to demonstrate the extent of their commitment to the idea of a tamed Brazos.

CHAPTER SIX

Importation and Diversion along a Still-Untamed Brazos

We need to think boldly, even dream a little of future generations, but the first thing we need to do is to plan soundly and execute vigorously to catch up with the problems that have already overtaken this generation and must be met head-on if succeeding generations are to have a future in Texas.

—COLONEL STANLEY G. REIFF, "[Water Conservation along the Brazos River]," 1960

Our Nation has been blessed with a bountiful supply of water; but it is not a blessing we can regard with complacency. . . . Our available water supply must be used to give maximum benefits for all purposes—hydroelectric power, irrigation and reclamation, navigation, recreation, health, home and industry.

—PRESIDENT JOHN F. KENNEDY TO LYNDON B. JOHNSON, 1961

They make jokes about Texas and bigness, but the time may well come when the whole nation will bless the day when Texans learned to think big. This first attempt of yours to work out a big water-sharing project may or may not succeed. But bless you for making the attempt.

—LT. GEN. F. J. CLARKE, lecture, 1970

DURING THE LATTER HALF of the twentieth century, issues of water scarcity and water surplus still preoccupied the individuals who lived within the Brazos Basin. But nearly a century and a half of unpredictability along the waterway had prompted some individuals to begin calling a bit more insistently for a solution than had their forebearers. Ogallala Slim was one such personality. Tall and gaunt, this jean-clad man tended cattle in the North Plains of Texas during the 1960s. Ogallala also traveled the plains in the company of his shorter, squatter friend Frisco to teach people about conservation. These Brazos cowboys ruminated on the

A comic book titled *Ogallala Slim* (ca. 1960s) that the North Plains Water
Conservation District published to teach people about regional water issues.
Courtesy the North Plains Groundwater Conservation District, Dumas, Texas.

quality of regional water sources, stressed the importance of irrigation for local farmers, lectured on the process of water formation in the Ogallala Aquifer, and accomplished all of these things from the pages of a comic book published by the North Plains Water Conservation District.

The authors of this comic book included a substantial amount of practical information in their texts and illustrations, but they concluded Ogallala Slim's journey with panels that demonstrated visually the consequences of water use and misuse. The second to last panel featured a spaceship, a wasted and barren landscape, and a short but illustrative title—"Time: FUTURE??"—while the final panel imagined a more agreeable future where "with conservation and wise use of water, we will continue to grow and prosper."[1] These twin panels offered equally hyperbolic views of the future, but the authors took up the mantra of technocratic faith, clearly believing that the people of the North Plains could and would realize a bright future (if they only made better use of their water resources).

"You never miss the water 'till the well goes dry"—Ogallala Slim and the North Plains Water Conservation District focused largely on a water shortage. Still, their concerns with the supply and behavior of regional water resources spoke plainly to the frustrations and fears that had haunted people living in the Brazos Basin since 1821 and had driven improvement of the watershed during that same period.[2] The average booster, developer, and lawmaker likely never saw this comic and never became acquainted with Slim, but many of them would have chimed in with a similar story about water needs.

Having watched as the large-scale dams of previous decades provided some amount of flood control, proponents of development soon turned to schemes that would dwarf those structures in terms of ambition, potential, cost, and size. For example, developers proposed during the 1960s to divert water from the Columbia River, Missouri River, Arkansas River, and Mississippi River to the Brazos and to import water from Canada, California, and East Texas.[3] Politicians sought during the 1970s to pump water from West Texas playas into West Texas aquifers, and laypeople suggested the use of nuclear technology and soil conservation to solve a perceived water crisis. Though more prospective dams were cast aside during the mid-twentieth century than ever were built, the seeming success of the structures that developers did complete had merely fed the regional belief that technology could, and indeed would, exert control over the still-unruly waters of the Brazos River.

This last round of improvement projects, accordingly, existed in continuity with earlier attempts at development. As had been the case with the simple levee projects, the titanic dam projects, and everything in between, the importation and diversion projects proposed between 1958 and 1980 were born out of a desire to aid those people who engaged the river on a daily basis and were undone by an unwillingness (or inability) to overcome the geological, social, and economic costs of development. More important, these projects spoke to the ways in which regional opinions on development had shifted to engage the needs of a population that, once far more mobile, had begun to sink deep roots into a watershed that included dense clusters of people on fertile lands and scattered groupings of people on arid lands.

The projects of this period, however, also represented a notable departure from the developmental approach that had flourished since 1821. In what would be the last major period of improvement within the Brazos River Basin, developers excluded projects that prioritized the needs of any single section of the river, choosing instead to treat the Brazos as a cohesive whole and to alter its ecological shortcomings through a unified, holistic approach to improvement. Development of this watershed as a single unit during the second half of the twentieth century thus shed light both on prior impulses and on new concerns—expanding on a story of developmental woe, geological frustration, political action, and social determination that had persisted since the 1820s.

Although the projects of the mid- to late twentieth century remained entirely theoretical, both proponents and architects of these improvement schemes nonetheless crafted their plans within the social context of their time. First, these schemas downplayed flood control as an independently pressing issue and yielded to a surging preference for multiuse projects that prioritized reclamation and recreation as well as flood control and irrigation. Before the mid-twentieth century, projects often focused on a single issue. Lock-and-dam structures offered the hope of improved navigation, canals rerouted waters for the purpose of agricultural expansion, and levees fought the natural tendencies of ocean currents. True, developers had envisioned and constructed large-scale, multiuse reservoirs between the 1930s and 1950s, envisioning dams that would generate power and moderate streamflows, restrain floodwaters and provide recreation.[4] However, even these multiuse reservoirs generally prioritized either flood control or power development, labeling any other benefits as secondary. Although single-use projects persisted into the mid- and late twentieth century, any lingering preference for such projects gradually became subsumed within conversations that focused on multiuse proposals.

The projects of this fourth stage of development consequently represented a somewhat dramatic shift away from the earlier method of improving the river. Not only had navigation disappeared almost entirely as an objective of development, but developers, engineers, and lawmakers had also begun to focus on projects that addressed a multiplicity of issues. In part, this shift in emphasis stemmed from pervasive fears about global and national population growth. World leaders paid increasing attention to the issue of population during the 1960s, noting that an expanding population would result in more rapid use of natural resources. *The Population Bomb*, written by Paul Ehrlich and published in 1968, was so closely linked with the enveloping fear about overpopulation that its title became a rhetorical framework in its own right. The book, in any case, spoke clearly to the growing fears over population growth, opening with a title page that bore these words: "While you are reading these words four people, most of them children, will die of starvation—and twenty-four more babies will have been born."[5]

Proponents of Brazos development used these fears to champion their cause, emphasizing place-specific, temporally confined statistics that newspapers in the basin repeated ad nauseam. Russell Bean, for example, sent a pamphlet to George Mahon that centered on fears of overpopulation, starvation, and crisis: "Today in 1973 we have about 3.5 billion people on earth crowding the ability of 3.5 billion acres of farmland to supply food. We are told that population will double in about 35 years in spite of all efforts to the contrary. So, how are we going to feed 7 billion people with 3.5 billion acres of farmland?"[6]

Newspapers insisted, likewise, that the population in the Brazos Basin would increase by 150 percent between 1976 and 2010, with most of that growth concentrated in the Lower Brazos River Basin.[7] A 1956 article in the *Brazosport Facts* reported, in a similar vein, that the city of Lake Jackson had already outgrown a water-supply infrastructure completed only two years prior, and an article published in that same paper in 1961 contended that the population in several Lower Brazos River cities had doubled in the span of a single decade, 1950 to 1960.[8]

Concerns with a growing population in the watershed emerged at the same time that a national and at times international debate about population growth and population control moved to the front page of many newspapers and the forefront of many discussions. However, despite the sometimes consuming fears over population growth, the intellectual shift away from single-use projects also grew from an emergent under-standing of ecology and conservation.[9] During the 1940s and 1950s, large swaths of the American public began to concern themselves with issues stemming from increased globalization, the destructiveness of technology, and the finite supply of natural resources.[10] Such concerns emerged with a proto-environmental movement and anticipated a shift away from a heady focus on so-called natural areas (e.g., wildlife, wil-derness, etc.) and toward human-centered problems (e.g., pollution, public health, etc.).

The opening of the atomic era, for instance, cultivated a new con-sciousness as scientists and lawmakers began to realize the destructive forces of modern technology. In his tome on the evolution of ecological ideas, Donald Worster addressed the point extensively: "Under the threat of the atomic bomb a new moral consciousness called environ-mentalism began to take form, whose purpose was to use the insights of ecology to restrain the use of modern science-based power over nature."[11] As scientists linked recent technological advances with escalating envi-ronmental decline, they increasingly began to emphasize the biological effects of river development, the benefits and dangers of multipurpose dams, and the importance of conservation and reclamation services.[12] That development of an ecologically minded, national conscious, in turn, shaped improvement of the Brazos River as people began to revisit the seeming successes and failures of past projects and to reconsider the supposed justification for any given project.

Second, the push for improvement of the Brazos River was crafted and considered within the context of broader schemes for water devel-opment in Texas. The fate of the watershed gradually became inte-grated into plans to protect the future of the state's resources more broadly. This shift in perspective effected a striking change within the watershed as developers adopted a more holistic approach to develop-ment, incorporating multiple rivers into Brazos improvement projects (or, alternately, incorporating the Brazos River into multiriver develop-ment schemes). That regional focus manifested itself most visibly in the actions of the Texas Water Development Board, a state agency that provided "leadership, planning, financial assistance, information, and education for the conservation and responsible development of water for Texas."[13]

The general purpose of improvement projects in this state, however, remained relatively unchanged. As with many Brazos-centric projects, statewide plans for riparian development sought to mitigate the effects of both drought and flood events.[14] The key difference: developers now sought to resolve these issues across the state's waterways and without sacrificing attention to other riparian concerns. The continuing fixation with droughts and floods reflected a continuing problem with these same events. For example, although the erection of multiple large-scale dams within the watershed moderated the river's wide swings in flow, flood and drought events remained an all-too-frequent reality for people in the Brazos Basin. Indeed, newspaper articles still viewed this river as one of the worst offenders in the state when judged by the economic costs of its fluctuations in streamflow.[15] Between 1955 and 1980, the Lower and Middle Brazos Rivers inundated the cities of Dennis, Mineral Wells, Freeport, and Columbia.[16] Additionally, along the less flood-prone Upper Brazos River, floods in 1978 left the citizens of Albany, Eliasville, and Crystal Falls without electricity and stranded on elevated hilltops.[17] The flood of 1976 enacted still more damage, and in a rather stunning display of defiance, the engorged waters of the Brazos River poured over the dams that peppered the upper reaches of the river.[18]

But as had been the case during the previous century, drought events worked in conjunction with flood events to make more difficult the daily lives of Brazos dwellers.[19] The large reservoirs created by Brazos dams provided some irrigation water, but extended periods of low streamflow and little rain continued to kill crops, impair livestock, and frustrate the residents of the Brazos watershed. Evaporation from these oversized bodies of water only worsened the situation, bringing grief to Texans during especially dry years and casting some doubt on the wisdom of prior projects. Michael Bakula, an administrative assistant with the Brazos River Authority, commented on some of the problems that still plagued the watershed in a 1989 interview with the *Brazosport Facts.* He noted, for example, that drought events increased the already high saline content of the river by allowing the intrusion of salt into the main stem of the rivers.[20] Surely echoing the thoughts of many along the length of this river, Bakula ended his interview with a plea and a hope: "We're just praying for the normal spring rains to fill us up."[21]

The individuals living within the Brazos Basin between 1821 and 1980 would never have agreed on how to approach the question of development, but they would certainly have agreed that floods, droughts, and other ecological calamities wrought very real damage. Many things had changed within the Brazos Basin since 1821, but much had remained the same: the destruction brought about by the alternating tandem of flood and drought continued both to complicate and to encourage improvement within this watershed, and the devastation receded little as the decades passed. Throughout 1957, for example, regional and state newspapers reported on stories similar to one that would be printed in the *Waterloo Courier*: "Farmers in many Texas river lowlands who hadn't made a good crop in seven years of drought Tuesday saw this year's plantings succumb to floods."[22] Nearly forty years later, the *Waco Tribune-Herald* gave voice to similar frustrations in a 1997 article, even insisting at one point that "margaritas on the porch at sunset don't taste as good when the riverfront view consists of little more than a muddy stream."[23]

Third, improvement of the Brazos River also came to be considered within a national push for riparian development. The process of developing this river during the late twentieth century, accordingly, promoted new organizations as agents of change. In 1958, the United States Congress created the U.S. Study Commission, a temporary federal agency that worked toward the improvement of rivers across the nation.[24] One branch of this organization, the U.S. Study Commission–Texas, was charged specifically with the development of rivers in the state of Texas and with the integration of those rivers into a national plan for riparian control. The commission oversaw development in all the major river basins confined within the state (a total of eight) and the adjoining coastal areas and also sought to create a unified policy of development for what was a sizeable territory.[25]

Congress gave the commission authority over the entire state "for the specific purpose of making a comprehensive, integrated, and cooperative study of the land and water resources of eight river basins in Texas."[26] Establishment of the U.S. Study Commission thus marked something of the end of large-scale, single-purpose, independently conceived projects on the Brazos River. Local groups would continue, from time to time, to call for the construction of a single dam and reservoir, but there was little room for institutions, however large, that focused exclusively on any single development purpose. There was no recognized place in this world for a project in which the Army Corps of Engineers worked exclusively toward navigation and flood control while the Bureau of Reclamation, working one hundred miles further west, prioritized irrigation and hydroelectric power.[27] The Brazos River Authority could no longer prioritize the Lower Brazos River over the dams of upstream dwellers; this approach simply would not serve in a world inundated with ecological awareness and concerned with the equity of multiuse considerations.

Photograph, taken by Windy Drum Photography around 1956, of irrigation methods used in regional cotton fields. Courtesy the Texas Collection, Baylor University, Waco, Texas.

In light of these pressing social considerations, the law establishing the commission specifically directed that any development plans consider twelve different benefits: flood control, domestic and municipal water use, navigation, reclamation, hydroelectric power, soil conservation, forest conservation, wildlife and fisheries, recreation, salinity and sediment, pollution abatement and public health, and the still-vague catchall, "other beneficial and useful purposes."[28] Some of these benefits existed in contradiction to others, so different projects obviously placed differing amounts of emphasis on these points. But the intention was clear. The national government intended, by addressing a collection of problems rather than any single concern, to maximize the effectiveness of federal expenditures and to respond to a multitude of public concerns. By giving oversight of development projects to a single organization, all these benefits could, in theory, be weighted effectively and fairly throughout the state and its various river basins. U.S. Study Commission projects in that sense were the realization of a vision for full development that had been coalescing for decades.

Congress also hoped that streamlining the process of improvement by giving it to a single organization would "expedite development of the land and water resources in the eight river basins."[29] The commission existed, however, solely to make recommendations. The U.S. Study Commission–Texas did not, indeed could not, oversee the actual construction of any projects, and this lack of power would consistently prove significant, hindering construction of the infrastructure necessary for that vision of an improved system of rivers.[30]

Finally, people engaging the realities of the Brazos River between 1958 and 1980 remained optimistic about the possibility of harnessing its resources. Proponents of development, with few exceptions, did not look over the watershed and see a landscape littered with failed levees, abandoned lock-and-dam structures, and dams writ only as blueprints. They saw instead a landscape whose problems, though real and daunting, were ultimately dwarfed by the resources of the time. This optimism, this technocratic faith, persisted in the midst of developmental failure as well as success. Indeed, advocates for development projects of this scale could only have conceived of their diversion and import schemes in an age of continued, and perhaps accelerated, technological faith.

In 1967, Stewart L. Udall, then secretary of interior, made a comment in an interview that rather fittingly reflected that mindset: "In Interior, we like to think that even the impossible is possible where the good of mankind is involved."[31] His words, quoted in an article about a Brazos River–Mississippi River diversion scheme, could have easily been used to justify any of the increasingly grandiose improvement schemes imagined along Texas's longest in-state river. But this optimism—which made the schemes of the 1960s and 1970s possible—was rooted (perhaps unexpectedly) in the experiences of prior decades. Locks, canals, channels, and dams consistently failed to offer anywhere near the measure of control that proponents of improvement sought, but these same projects offered varying amounts of real, if temporary, success. As a result, they provided hope to people living in an age of expanding technology that developers of this river might finally find success where others had failed.

An assortment of projects for improvement of the Brazos River flourished between 1958 and 1980, but the most prominent and significant of the projects proposed during this time were the diversion schemes and water-import studies that sought to link basins and rivers in different states as well as different regions.[32] These water-transport schemes proposed in-state, interstate, and even transnational diversion, but they all sought to remedy the same problem—a lack of water in some areas and a so-called overabundance of water in other areas. Lieutenant General F. J. Clarke offered insight into the rationale behind these projects in a 1970 letter to George Mahon: "The clue to the water problems of the High Plains lies not in competing for water, but rather in the principle of sharing."[33]

None of these diversion and importation projects enjoyed widespread support, but a sizeable minority of politicians and laypeople in the Brazos Basin advocated some form of in-state diversion. The proposed in-state projects, seeking to undo the apparent disparities that nature herself had wrought, generally recommended the transfer of water from East Texas rivers to West Texas and South Texas landscapes, and they depended on an actual imbalance in the water resources available to different regions. Reports indicated, for example, that developers of one in-state project based their project on an assumption that "there is approximately 2½ million acres feet of excess water in Eastern Texas over and above an additional 500,000 acre feet in the Sabine that is being held back without present or future commitment."[34]

Interstate diversion plans, in contrast, sought to redirect water from the generally well-watered floodplains of the Midwest and Mississippi Valley to the far more arid plains of Texas. Although they followed the same principles as in-state diversion schemes, these interstate projects boasted a more expansive geographic reach and, accordingly, required more time, money, and flexibility for their completion. Such projects also necessitated cooperation between states, so they habitually stressed the idea that water was a problem for the droughty and the flood prone alike. The *Big Spring Daily Herald* emphasized the ubiquitous nature of the water problem in a 1968 article, paying special attention to the implications for development and reminding readers in this case of "the urgent need for additional water."[35]

The most noteworthy and longest lasting of the interstate projects proposed to divert water from the Mississippi River to West Texas and eastern New Mexico using a North Texas canal.[36] Working in the background of this Mississippi-Brazos diversion project was an organization known as Water, Inc.[37] Water, Inc., which held its organizational meeting on May 24, 1967, worked with politicians such as George Mahon to realize the diversion and importation projects that at least some portion of Brazos River residents envisioned.[38] The authors and supporters of this project targeted the Mississippi as their hoped-for source of Brazos water because they believed that it boasted a constant surplus of water, dumping on average 700 million cubic feet of "unused water" out of its mouth each second.[39] Though not formally connected with the project, Floyd Dominy (commissioner of the Bureau of Reclamation) reiterated this point in a 1968 interview. The commissioner overtly equated unused water with lost water and noted that "the Mississippi River flows more than 400 million acre feet of water a year into the Gulf of Mexico and this looks like a good potential source of surplus water."[40]

Although the Brazos-Mississippi project never was completed or even begun, engineers and boosters compiled the preliminary work rather quickly and immediately began drumming up support for what was an admittedly ambitious project. A Bureau of Reclamation report in 1968 even formed some tentative conclusions about this project. Most notably, the report insisted that "it is physically feasible to transport the projected 2020 requirements of 16.5 million acre-feet per year from the lower Mississippi River system to West Texas and Eastern New Mexico if it is determined that there are surplus waters in the Mississippi River available to meet these requirements." The report also warned that "regardless of the route, the cost per acre-foot for delivering water from the lower Mississippi River system to irrigators in the study area appears certain to exceed substantially their ability to pay for such water."[41] Despite the cautionary words about heightened costs, people living in water-stricken West Texas proved to be particularly accepting of the project. It spoke to their need for water explicitly and so boosters and businessmen as well as farmers embraced the idea that the transfer of surplus water between basins could "prevent productive land from reverting to desert."[42]

In addition to the Mississippi-Brazos project of Water, Inc., other developers proposed an interstate scheme that would have drawn water from the Arkansas River. This project, known as Operation

Southwest, engaged many of the same concerns and assumptions as other diversion schemes. The most basic assumption behind Operation Southwest was that the state of Texas needed to augment its current water supply by somewhere between 10 and 12 million acre-feet of water each year.[43] Despite the dire implications of such an imbalance, the organizational structure revealed a firm belief in the ability of man to mold the landscape to fit his needs: "The key to success is for us to get together and to move these leaders positively and constructively. The initial thrust is to create a NASA-sized organization, backed by firm national commitment."[44] Developers intended to begin this project in July of 1973 and to complete the diversion project during the summer of 1980, but little (if any) work was ever accomplished to those ends.[45] Indeed, this project (like many Brazos River projects) remained almost completely theoretical.

In addition to Mississippi-Brazos and Arkansas-Brazos import schemes, yet another group of politicians proposed a diversion scheme that would have imported water from the Missouri River to the Brazos watershed.[46] Although this scheme involved a tributary of the Mississippi River, its proponents did not intend to use the Mississippi as a corridor for moving the water. Rather, they expected to divert water upstream at specifically constructed sites and to channel water from there to Texas. Named the Beck Proposal, this entirely theoretical, arguably elaborate project would have diverted the Missouri River below Fort Randall Reservoir in Nebraska, lifted the waters through a series of dams and canals to the Texas Panhandle, and subsequently carried the water through the plains of Texas to an endpoint near Hobbs, New Mexico.[47] The work was never begun. Such a project could only have been envisioned by a people convinced of the legitimacy of technocratic solutions, but even this project did not represent the boldest plan of this developmental period.

In addition to the above projects, boosters proposed two diversion projects during this period that were transnational in nature. If the logistics of constructing in-state and interstate diversion schemes were daunting, the detailed coordination needed in planning, implementing, and maintaining a transnational diversion scheme was still more taxing. One of these two transnational schemes proposed to import water from Canada to the Brazos Basin.[48] The other proposed to link Southern California with the Texas Gulf Coast by way of the United States–Mexico border.[49] Little is known about the first project aside from its submission as a possible solution to Brazos variability, but the company that proposed the California-Texas project intended that the diversion canal "would be multipurposed, lumping irrigation, navigation and recreation in one ditch 1000 [feet] wide and 100 [feet] deep."[50]

As with the in-state and interstate projects, the proponents of these transnational projects hoped to address very real, very pressing concerns with water—problems that in their estimate afflicted every region of the nation in one way or another. Advocates of these schemes argued, for example, that the canals would open up millions of acres of land to farming, create new jobs and possibly new towns along the waterway, generate inland ports along the waterway, save money on shipping costs, decrease transit time for shipping, and offer an inland line of defense during wartime.[51] These projects were never considered seriously by politicians and engineers, but the Canada-Texas and California-Texas projects, nonetheless, sparked some amount of debate among laypeople and journalists, debates that spoke to the continuing need for riparian control.

The preceding in-state, interstate, and transnational diversion schemes targeted a single source of water, but proponents of improvement also recommended projects that would have imported water from multiple sources, combining in-state diversion and interstate importation. The Texas Water Plan, a $10 billion dollar project to be funded through federal and state agencies, was one such project.[52] The plan effectively envisioned a Trans-Texas diversion program and a multistate importation project that would have incorporated pipelines, canals, dams, and reservoirs.[53] Lee Jones of the *Big Spring Daily Herald* outlined the specifics of the project in a 1968 article: "Surplus Mississippi River water would be pumped from Louisiana to the irrigated farm land of the South Plains and then across hundreds of miles of desert to El Paso. Another system of canals and pipelines would carry surplus water from the Sabine River east of Beaumont, plus some Mississippi River water, to the fruit and vegetable farmlands of the Lower Rio Grande Valley."[54]

Collectively, this infrastructure would have created sixty-eight new dams and reservoirs in the state, allowed the importation of 12 million to 13 million acre-feet of water annually from the Mississippi River, and transported an undisclosed amount of water from East Texas along the Trans-Texas Canal.[55]

In the initial stages of the Texas Water Plan, developers alternately proposed the importation of water from the Colorado, Columbia, and Missouri Rivers.[56] Ultimately, however, developers agreed to divert water from two water-rich areas—the Mississippi River and East Texas—and to transfer that water to the more arid lands of West and South Texas.[57] Regardless of the source, where other water plans sought to address the projected needs of the twenty-first century, the Texas Water Plan grew from an assumption that "Texas does not have enough water within its boundaries to meet all its needs beyond 1985."[58] The plan, accordingly, emphasized a looming water shortage that developers characterized as "urgent" and even "critical."[59] Believers of the water crisis anticipated very real, very lasting effects on the economic, political, and social makeup of Brazos cities if the water problems were not addressed. Specifically, lawmakers predicted a reduction in irrigated farmland from 5.1 million to 2.2 million acres in West Texas alone.[60] A 1968 article in the *Corpus Christi Times* envisioned a similar future if the needs of Brazos water users went unmet: "The alternative [to this plan] is a return to dryland farming over millions of acres and an inadequate water supply for several cities."[61]

For people living in more arid regions, the Texas Water Plan seemed to resolve not only an ecological crisis but also an issue of equity and ethics. Many West Texans, for instance, gloomily anticipated that their economies would "fall into decay unless we are fortunate enough to secure surplus surface water from the Columbia, the Colorado, the Mississippi, the Missouri, or from other out-of-state source."[62] These individuals believed, fairly or not, that their way of life depended rather literally on continued irrigation and on improvement of the Brazos River, and they also charged that the economy of development had long favored downstream users of the Brazos River.[63] For people living in the supposedly water-rich areas, the problem was quite different. Businesses, families, and lawmakers living in East Texas, for example, disagreed vehemently with the idea that they had water to spare.

Despite the anticipation and fanfare, the Texas Water Plan eventually met the same fate as every other Brazos diversion project. It promised change and excited expectation but ultimately failed (under the combined weight of geological, social, and economic concerns) to become much more than a theoretical grasp at greater riparian control. In other words, the proliferation of conflicting and competing diversion schemes only reaffirmed a long-held truism along this river: though the target of projects built around good intentions and real needs, the Brazos could never live up to the expectations attached to it by ranchers, managers, and fathers tired of water concerns.

Plans to shift water from the Missouri, the Mississippi, and the Arkansas Rivers; from Canada and California; and from East Texas failed to gain much traction even in the midst of a pressing problem with water famine along the Upper Brazos River. Several factors worked against the import projects that were proposed during this period, but financial concerns offered the most significant obstacle. The Brazos River Channel and Dock Company abandoned its economically flaccid port project; the Army Corps of Engineers forsook its financially prohibitive lock-and-dam structures; and, the Brazos River Authority discarded their monetarily unattainable dams. Likewise, the success of these diversion schemes came down, at least in part, to questions of cost and profit.

In 1972, George Mahon wrote a letter to one Raymond Turnbull that highlighted the influence of financial considerations on what were perceived, by their proponents, to be life-saving projects. Mahon, after deliberating on the "magnitude" of the project, reminded Mr. Turnbull that "there have been many exciting and elaborate projects proposed which have great merit but of course cost remains the overriding consideration."[64] A contemporaneous article from the *Big Spring Daily Herald* echoed those sentiments but used the high costs as a means of justifying federal intervention: "Action by and within the state of Texas alone, even on a large scale, is not enough, because the water resources now available to Texas are not sufficient to meet the economically justified future water needs of the entire state."[65] No matter the severity of the looming water crisis or the desperation of petitioners, economics still often determined if these projects could begin.

Second, the authors of these projects struggled to overcome the geologic realities that continued to shape and oftentimes to deter development of the Brazos River corridor. The financial costs of a multibillion-dollar Texas Water Plan caused very real disquiet, but the geological concerns of these diversion schemes—sedimentation, evaporation, salination, inequities in water supply, and so forth—proved equally problematic for proponents of Brazos River improvement. Most obviously, transferring water from one basin to another necessitated that the donor basin actually support a sufficient volume of water. A 1961 letter to Austin Hancock insisted that "it is not contemplated that water will be transferred from one basin to a second basin without first satisfying existing irrigation rights and the municipal and industrial water requirements of the first basin," but this offered little solace to many individuals living in what were perceived to be areas of hydrological excess.[66] As a result, deciding what exactly constituted a source of "surplus" water often became a point of contention. People living along the Lower Brazos River, for instance, insisted (oftentimes stridently, sometimes bitterly) that they needed all the water coursing through their section of the waterway, and they pointed to a growing population as evidence.[67]

It was not sufficient, however, for developers to reconcile their projects to geological concerns. In this age of grassroots action and environmental awareness, the proponents of these projects needed to define the physical process of diversion (and to catalog the infrastructure necessary for that process) in a way that the public could embrace and understand. Most of the diversion and importation plans proposed the use of concrete-lined canals to transport water from areas of surplus to areas of shortage.[68] Moreover, the state increased in elevation toward the west so in-state diversion canals would need to lift the water that coursed through them, an admittedly complicated and unenviable task.[69] A state, nay, an entire subregion of the United States, lined and pitted with concrete ditches—this image prompted an outcry among a growing group of individuals who were concerned with the ecological effects of river development.[70] Mrs. Margaret Hill Hancock of Austin, president of the Conservation Federation of Texas, expressed such concerns in a letter that was published in a 1968 edition of the *Abilene Reporter-News*, noting that the Texas Water Plan "[would] make ditches of natural streams and mud banks of our rivers."[71]

Third, questions of equity undermined the construction and, thus, the success of these development projects. The question of diverting and importing water dredged up more than a century of old concerns that politicians and developers favored certain areas and certain types of development, a political as well as a geological issue. The Texas Water Plan provided a case in point. People living in East Texas complained that the plan withdrew too much of their so-called surplus water.[72] Crying in near unison, "no excess here," they argued that the plan disproportionately benefited people living in South Texas.[73] People living in West Texas, in contrast, argued that the plan did not provide them with enough water and that it disproportionately benefited people living along the coast.[74] Downplaying the moans of people in West Texas who thought the diversions to their region insufficient, lawmakers in Austin continued to insist that "West Texas and New Mexico will gain trillions of gallons of water annually if the Texas Water Plan becomes a reality."[75]

Public opposition emerged from out-of-state donor basins as well as from within the Brazos Basin. A group of people from the Lower Mississippi River Valley submitted a petition "opposing any diversions which might jeopardize any projects, either present, or future, which might require the retention of any or all of this presently surplus water for use in this Valley."[76] This opposition incorporated a rhetoric that was simultaneously broad and ambiguous: residents of the Lower Mississippi River would not sacrifice their projects—whatever and whenever and wherever those projects might be—for the dreams of a neighboring basin. Environmentalists also voiced their opposition to the Mississippi-Brazos and Missouri-Brazos projects. Oftentimes their opposition reflected a concern with the health of the donor waterways. "As you know, the area below New Orleans is famous for trapping, shrimping, and abundant wildlife otherwise. The first link in the chain of fish life would begin in the shallows of these swamps"— thus began a note to George Mahon warning of such environmental considerations.[77]

The opposition in West Texas to the Texas Water Plan (indeed, to several of these diversion plans) also reached extraordinary levels. Individuals living in towns such as Abilene, Sweetwater, Graham, and Rule often made statements to the effect that their needs had been "written off."[78] The *Abilene Reporter-News* offered almost-daily updates on the subject of importation during the 1960s, arguing repeatedly that the plan provided no "up-stream transfer to bring surplus East Texas water to West Texas," instead transferring water only to less arid, downstream areas.[79] A resolution written by the Abilene Chamber of Commerce even went so far as to argue that the Texas Water Plan would "seriously impede and even block future development and population growth of all of Texas west of the 99th meridian."[80]

So seemingly ill suited were the proposals of the Texas Water Plan for West Texas that politicians and civic boosters predicted "dry times ahead for West Texas."[81] R. N. Wagstaff (attorney and spokesman for the City of Abilene) spoke pointedly on the subject in a 1966 article: "We will not sit idly by out here in West Texas and see Lower Brazos water transferred to other areas for 'inferior' uses."[82] Politicians and civic leaders outside of Abilene joined in the chorus of frustration. George Mahon noted in a 1966 interview that he was "alarmed and disappointed" by the plan's lack of attention to West Texas; G. H. Nelson (a Lubbock attorney and chairman of the Plains Water for the Future

Committee) and John Ben Shepperd (president of the West Texas Chamber of Commerce) also publicized their disapproval.[83]

Lastly, competition and conflict between agencies contributed to the failure of these diversion schemes. The State of Texas, for instance, seemingly developed its fifty-year water plan without taking into account the work of the U.S. Study Commission–Texas. Furthermore, as part of the state's 1966 Master Plan, the Texas Water Development Board proposed to use the Brazos River as a canal to transport water from the northeast to the Rio Grande Valley and proposed also to build ten new reservoirs along the river, improvements that would have necessarily interfered with other plans to transport water to the river. Moreover, half of the reservoirs included in this plan were unique to the Development Board while the other half of the dams were included in the Brazos River Authority Plan—namely, Inspiration Point, Hightower, Bee Mountain, South Bend, and Turkey Creek. These import and diversion schemes also operated separately from the Brazos River Authority's Master Plan for the Brazos River, which (theoretically) should have dictated the manner by which all future development of the basin would proceed.[84] Such bureaucratic conflict could only have complicated development of a river that had proven, time and again, a seeming willingness to defy man-made expectations.

In addition to this extra-agency conflict, intraorganizational disputes interrupted improvement, most notably with the activities of the multibranched U.S. Study Commission. In a 1959 letter, William Whipple lamented that administrators working in other regional U.S. Study Commission offices could not possibly appreciate the difficulty of working in an intrastate office. He noted, for example, that "attitudes for and against this plan color everything the Commission members here are apt to do. Moreover, the Chairman George Brown, instead of being a long-standing friend of the Corps as Mr. Woodruff is, has primary interests in the Houston area."[85] Concern for water rights and private-property rights took priority for many Texans over diversion schemes that promoted shared water usage, and that reality unquestionably hindered any designs to remove water from one region for the benefit of another.

These diversion and importation projects, which dominated the thoughts and rhetoric of developers between 1958 and 1980, seemed outlandish even to some contemporaries. Indeed, they seemed almost implausibly bold, and they were complemented by lay projects, never considered seriously, that were equally bold. One individual, for example, recommended a three-dimensional concept "in which all water in the atmosphere, on the surface or in the ground is to be treated as one whole supply."[86] Still another source recommended the work of one Dr. Donald Patton, who wanted to apply atomic energy to the arena of river development. Dr. Patton argued that atomic energy could be put to diverse uses: "digging reservoirs with one gigantic blast, fracturing underground strata to form artificial acquifiers [sic] for storage; and even blowing the silt out of silted up reservoirs, making them useful for many more years."[87]

Long gone were the days when a lock-and-dam structure on the Middle Brazos or a channel along the Lower Brazos could be deemed sufficient to tame the riverscape of the state's Old Man River. The different improvement projects proposed for the Brazos River Basin during the second half of the twentieth century were, as a result, both varied and grand, encompassing stirring failures and memorable propositions with no real successes. Despite the fact that this era unquestionably resulted in fewer successes than any other period of development, the people of the Brazos River continued to dream of "that Old river being harnessed to where it cannot do so much damage in flood times."[88] The adoption of atomic energy to the Brazos River watershed—why not consider that during an age of nuclear technology and in a geography of water shortage? Likewise, transnational canals and three-dimensional schemas surely seemed no less absurd or unrealistic than had large-scale dams and intercoastal canals during their first days of consideration.

This period of development, in other words, echoed a chorus long sung within the valley—a chorus that entwined desperation and hope and connected the projects of the earliest Brazos boosters with the seemingly ostentatious proposals of a more technologically advanced time. Proponents of improvement had undoubtedly turned to much more ambitious projects since the first immigrants looked to the Brazos, saw its shortcomings, and began envisioning canals and ports, but the general commitment to improvement remained relatively unchanged despite the passage of years. People living along the Lower and Middle Brazos Rivers still privileged an ideal of development that emphasized agriculture and commerce; these ideas had simply been modernized and industrialized since the early years of simple canals and jetties. People living along the Upper Brazos River still emphasized an ideal of development centered on questions of aridity and low streamflow. Ogallala Slim, then, had it somewhat wrong—at least some Brazos peoples began preparing for shortages long before the possibility of a population-induced crisis even seemed feasible, but they did so in ways that rarely brought about their desired results or drew support from people along the length of this still-untamed river.

CHAPTER SEVEN

A Defiant Brazos and the Persistence of Its People

When flood time comes the upper Brazos goes out of its banks. Its waters are carried into the lower country and in years gone by they have cast death and devastation to the people in the lower valley who till the soil. In a quarter of a century the losses have aggregated $250,000,000, and that vast sum would have harnessed the waters of the upper and lower Brazos and provided a never failing supply of water all the year round for irrigation purposes.

—"FLOOD WATER CONTROL," *Port Arthur News*, 1925

I have had too much experience in the past in trying to develop the River only to find that spokesmen for the lower reaches objected to whatever was proposed. Frankly, I have come to doubt whether most of the people from Hempstead south want any development on the River.

—W. R. POAGE TO MARSHALL CROFT, 1959

Its waters supported that ancient plant life that fed those now-extinct creatures that roamed the area millions of years ago. Its currents washed and formed the land and the coast line. Its muddy waters flowing into the Gulf told the shipwrecked Cabeza de Vaca that land and a great river was near his flimsy raft. He called it Brazos de Dios—the Arms of God. It was used as a source of food and water by early Texas man, later his relative the Indian. It was a means of transportation for Stephen F. Austin and the Old Three Hundred. . . . In short, the Brazos River has seen everything that has happened in Brazoria County and early Texas. It is the witness.

—"THE GREAT BRAZOS: WITNESS TO HISTORY," *Brazosport Facts*, 1976

IN 1957 JOHN GRAVES canoed the Brazos River with only his dachshund as company. He launched a canoe—filled with supplies, self, and canine companion—just downstream from Possum Kingdom Lake, and he completed the journey three weeks later near Glen Rose, Texas. Graves paddled this river still largely unimproved not only to confront and to enjoy its predictably erratic flow but also to mourn its impending loss to the era of big dams. Both the Army Corps of Engineers and the Brazos River Authority had proposed multidam projects for the Brazos River during the 1950s: the first project, centering on the Brazos tributaries and the second project, centering on a section of the main stem that stretched from Possum Kingdom to Whitney Dam.

The latter of the two projects most concerned Graves. Completion of these dams would have altered in fundamental ways a river that he first came to know as a child. Though his fears were never fully realized, Graves believed this to be the last journey he would make down the Brazos, and so he planned a trip to travel down a river that still manifested in some places as an unfettered river of rapids, oaks, and sandbars. At the end of his voyage, Graves published an account of his trip under the title *Goodbye to a River*.[1] This book, as with the trip that inspired it, was intended to be a eulogy, a heartfelt adieu from a man to a river that he had loved. Instead, *Goodbye to a River* has commonly been credited with saving the Brazos from the very development that Graves feared. That praise is somewhat misplaced—financial considerations, geological realities, and even public opinion had already begun to undermine the Brazos River Authority's proposed hydroelectric dam project by the time Graves published his book in 1960. Still, there is no doubt that *Goodbye to a River* helped to cultivate appreciation for and awareness of this river, transforming it into the frontispiece for those who objected to further development.

The book could be adapted to those ends because it spoke, abstractly but still fervently, to the very character of the Brazos River. It celebrated the natural variability of the riverscape and championed that which might be lost through the building of dams. As a result, the book laced itself into a story of development that incorporated past impulses, reflected current thoughts, and anticipated future issues. The book also spoke to a story of regional identity. Graves focused very specifically on the proposed construction of large-scale dams, but he essentially described in *Goodbye to a River* a much broader story of knowing and being known. Indeed, Texans in northwest, central, and south-central Texas have come to know the Brazos River through their efforts to develop it, and the projects that have resulted from that commitment to improvement have involved far more than what might be suggested by the visual terrain of large-scale dams.

During the nineteenth century, city governments and regional improvement associations advocated dredging operations and the construction of canals and ports along the lowermost reaches of the Brazos River, and they insisted that these schemes would improve navigational possibilities, encourage economic growth, and fuel urban development. The engineers who worked near the turn of the century claimed that locks would regulate the flow of the Middle Brazos, and they believed that these structures would not only increase river traffic but would also weaken the still-swelling power of the railroads. Later advocates for riparian control, acting with new technological capabilities but a similar resolve, believed that dams along the Upper Brazos River might light entire regions, resolve the question of aridity, and check the damaging effects of frequent floods. A final group of advocates, working in conjunction with a host of regional and national agencies, treated the river as a single unit; they envisioned diversion and import projects that might regulate the flow of an entire watershed, and they dared to suggest that tools as fearsome as atomic energy might be harnessed for the development of water resources.

In short, the projects that developers proposed along the Brazos River between 1821 and 1980 became a mechanism by which people within this watershed—both those with great political authority and those with little authority outside of what they might themselves exert as a member of the public—could examine their own expectations and thus engage and reengage ideas about the shape, form, and purpose of riparian development. One generation of developers might prioritize navigation and another, flood control; one group of engineers could envision single lock-and-dam structures while another group could plan for large-scale dams that might literally stop the waters of the Brazos. Developers during the 1850s worked toward population growth, and developers in the 1970s feared that same growth. What role should new technologies, economic opportunities, ethical conundrums, or future considerations play in current plans for development? The answer was largely dependent on where Brazos residents chose to call home.

Such questions about the purpose of improvement obviously influenced decision makers on a regional scale, but changes to the ideal of development on this small stage also reflected the ways in which Americans in different eras and vastly different regions defined their ideas on development. In particular, a rather widespread faith in technological achievement—a technocratic conviction, as it were—marked the development schemes of both the Brazos Basin and the nation at large. The developers who rethought and, ultimately, revised the purpose of development within the Brazos Basin transitioned from projects oriented around navigation to projects that fixated on dams and depended on new industrial processes. In a similar manner, lawmakers and laypeople, boosters and engineers once had thought primarily of small-scale projects to encourage navigation along the Tennessee River; these same individuals later witnessed the creation of a colossal political structure during the 1930s that linked the issues of flood control, economic development, power generation, and continued navigation within the river valley. There is obviously a link between the efforts of Brazos developers and the broader efforts of Americans to tame this nation's water resources.

Still, this is ultimately a story about the Brazos River—about the people who have poured their hopes and frustrations (as well as their time and energy) into the possibility of improving a defiant river. With that in mind, this narrative of Brazos River development ends with a dialogue, not of what might have changed in the lives of Brazos dwellers (hopefully, the relative impact of the development projects is now clear) but of those aspects of life that might have remained relatively unchanged as developers instituted first one project and then another within the Brazos Basin. To put it plainly, the projects that were proposed for the Brazos River watershed between 1821 and 1980 were connected by commonalities that defied those who equated progress with dams alone and challenged those with hubris enough to think change might come easily. Behind the shifting ideals of development and hidden by the increasingly grandiose projects of a frustrated people are skeins of continuity that tie together nearly two centuries of improvement along an unruly river, and these continuities speak—in a clear, bold voice—to the concerns that motivated Brazos dwellers to propose first one model of development and then another.

Four themes prove particularly persistent in the narrative of Brazos development. First, flood and drought events shaped the lives of the earliest Texas emigrants and continued to darken the dreams of farmers, merchants, and entrepreneurs after dams and locks and canals had seemingly remade the river corridor. Flood control transformed into a singular fixation only during the mid-twentieth century, and drought remediation did not become a specific end goal until that same period. Yet the realities of high water and low nevertheless shaped life in the Brazos Basin from the earliest days of settlement. Overflows remained a fact of life along this waterway even after dams had done their part to make these events less frequent and, it might be hoped, less severe, and low flows remained a similarly vexing problem.

Photograph by C. M. Seley of the Cotton Belt Railroad Bridge in Waco during the 1908 flood. Courtesy the Texas Collection, Baylor University, Waco, Texas.

So severe and frequent were these moments of high and low water that newspapers from the 1820s to the 1980s constructed what was effectively a discourse of destruction, offering graphic accounts of widespread devastation and human suffering.[2] Overflows and high waters—a water excess—resulted in such shockingly visible damage that flood events often garnered more frequent attention than drought events. An 1899 article from the *Marshfield Times*, for example, talked poignantly about the losses that people within this watershed endured from frequent flooding and revealed the power of these events in the public mind: "Rain is descending as if the heavens were dissolving. The Brazos, though it is flowing over the roofs of buildings that were supposed to stand upon ground never reached by the greatest floods, is still rising, and its shores are lined with thousands of wet, hungry and naked negroes, who have recently been rescued from treetops, ginhouses and floating cabins."[3]

As a result of the attention paid to this particular form of disaster by developers and engineers as well as laypeople, reports of "angry waters" became common throughout the basin during both the nineteenth and twentieth centuries, as did reports of death and injury.[4] Some of these floods (such as the waters that poured through Baylor University's campus in 1989) began not in the Brazos itself but in the drainage ways

Photograph of the Brazos River near Waco during the 1913 flood; in this case, spectators have journeyed to the bridge to view the unusually high waters of this record flood. Courtesy the Texas Collection, Baylor University, Waco, Texas.

meant to corral floodwaters, but even the failure of drainage systems spoke to a persistent problem with water excess. However, floods never represented the only hazard.

Although drought events often resulted in more gradual and thus more subtle damage than flood events, they could enact more long-term harm. While in the throes of drought events, farmers regularly reported that they were in danger of losing entire crops, and ranchers lamented, in a similar manner, that they would soon be forced to sell off any livestock that had not already succumbed to thirst or hunger.[5] West Texans felt the effects of such droughts most acutely, but people living throughout the watershed knew all too well the realities of low water.[6] Lawmakers became especially concerned with the "sufferers of successive droughts" during the mid-twentieth century (noting in editorials, letters, and legislation that proposals for improvement had too often ignored the issue of water famine), but moments of low flow had been a source of exasperation from the earliest days of settlement.[7]

Second, all-too-frequent experiences with floods and droughts led people living in the watershed to assume regularly that the river was

Photograph of a flood near the Darrington Prison Unit, taken in 1965. Courtesy the Texas Department of Criminal Justice, Austin, Texas.

not quite what it could be. Consequently, people living in the watershed believed (and acted on a belief) that the river could and indeed should be remade to better reflect their expectations. Improvement seemed a logical decision. If floods and droughts led to both economic and physical damage and if technology existed that might remedy that damage, then the river should be improved so that agriculture would thrive, cities would grow, and homes would be spared the ravages of angry waters. This mantra most obviously played out in the interplay between nineteenth-century boosterism and early development projects, but the developers and dwellers of this river corridor continued to idealize the river into the twentieth century. If anything, their expectations for the river multiplied as improvement projects grew in both size and expense and as technological advances made it possible, in theory, to satisfy still greater ambitions.

Despite the fact that developers failed more often than they succeeded, dams were built and levees constructed. Improvement was realized to some extent. Yet people living in the basin during the 1820s,

Photograph of the Baylor University Bookstore after heavy rains in 1989 flooded nearby Waco Creek. Courtesy the Texas Collection, Baylor University, Waco, Texas.

1870s, 1930s, and onward continued to view this river as insufficiently improved.[8] A letter from W. R. Poage in 1959 to one of his constituents clearly spoke to the annoyance of individuals who felt like little had been done to temper the Brazos waters; the letter also revealed the annoyance of those individuals who had worked (but had often failed) to realize that same riparian restraint: "You . . . say that you have waited in vain for many years, and 'To date, little has been accomplished since the original steps that gave the water users and citizens of the watershed Possum Kingdom Dam. Much in the way of public and private money has been expended.' It seems to me that this is a very unfair and unfactual statement. It seems to me that a good deal has been done since the construction of Possum Kingdom Dam."[9]

The letter that Poage received merely echoed countless other expressions in the same line. Given how much was at stake, disagreements frequently arose as people questioned how development should look and at what pace it should progress.[10] In other words, the narrative of development that shaped the Brazos River (in literal as well as figurative ways) is one neither of outright failure or undeniable success.

Third, mounting frustrations over the twin problems of water feast and water famine as well as a persistent belief that the river was not what it could be prompted generations of Texans to commit themselves to the physical improvement of the watershed. People living throughout the Brazos Basin became invested in the process of developing the river corridor, at times acting out a near-blind devotion to improvement. Between 1821 and 1980, federal, state, and local organizations proposed (and gave at least some serious consideration to) the following large-scale development schemes for the Brazos River: multiple canal projects, multiple jetty and port projects, multiple dredging projects, a lock-and-dam project, a thirteen-dam project, two six-dam projects, a five-dam project, a twenty-three-dam project, a single-dam project, and also diversion schemes between the Brazos River and East Texas, Canada, Southern California, and the Missouri, Mississippi, and Arkansas Rivers.[11] Some of these projects, admittedly, overlapped (feeding one into the other), but the sheer number of proposals along this river is nevertheless noteworthy.

Much to the chagrin of drought- or flood-weary Brazos dwellers, the different (and often contradictory) visions of development propagated along the length of the river made improvement, already mired in fiscal dialogues and geological limitations, that much more difficult. Still the men and women, dreamers and laborers, who worked on behalf of Brazos development were nothing if not enthusiastic. The *Galveston Daily News* reflected on such zeal when it opined in a 1906 article that the "great work being accomplished in the State, is enough to make any good citizen feel like taking off his hat and yelling; 'Hurrah for Grand Old Texas!'"[12] A 1956 article from the *Waco News-Tribune* reinforced that sense of optimism, using a different rhetoric but incorporating the same sense of expectation: "We have only scratched the surface of the potential usefulness of the Brazos River, but the potential is still there if we can muster the brains and the energy to harness it."[13] When considered from the broader perspective of time, people living within the watershed were unquestionably committed to their vision of a tamed waterway, and that commitment wavered little even in the face of what some might call developmental failure, riparian defiance, or even technological woe.

Despite the long list of attempted projects and the undeniable commitment to improvement, those projects that were considered a long-term success were few in number. The canal projects were eventually subsumed within the economically successful Gulf Intracoastal Waterway, but neither iteration of the Brazos canal attracted sustained use. Most successful were the dam schemes, which ultimately resulted in the construction of thirteen dams within the Brazos River watershed. These dams shaped the ecological health of the Brazos River in ways both undeniable and daunting—streamflows evened out, alluvial depositions diminished, flood events lessened, fish numbers declined, recreational activities increased, algae populations expanded, water temperatures dropped, and lakefront properties blossomed. Still, even these large-scale structures did not provide anything near the amount of control that people had hoped to achieve over the river.[14] To put it bluntly, unadulterated zeal for improvement of the Brazos River did not necessarily lead to success.

Finally, despite the very real enthusiasm and the perceived need for control over this waterway, economic considerations and geological nuances worked in tandem to undermine development projects. From an economic perspective, developers and laypeople sought improvement of the river corridor both as a means of expanding their economies and as a way of preventing economic losses. The Brazos River Basin had been almost completely oriented around agriculture during the nineteenth century, and it continued to be heavily agricultural during the twentieth century. Accordingly, floods and droughts could shake the entire foundation of the regional economy, or they could bolster the economy of the entire watershed by propagating a bumper crop.[15] The developers and dwellers of this corridor intended that the latter would hold true more often than the former, and so they sought to mitigate the high and low flows, if not eradicate them completely. Indeed, a 1946 letter insisted that the purpose of Army Corps development projects was to "prevent rivers running wild, destroying wealth rather than creating it."[16]

Yet, advocates for improvement were also forced to give serious consideration to the escalating costs of development projects. A 1937 article in the *Denton Record-Chronicle* offered an apt, if not entirely refreshing, summary of the situation: "The trouble which has held up construction of the Possum Kingdom Dam on the Brazos River in Palo Pinto County is typical of what happens when ambitious ideas strike the obstacles of reality."[17] Elaborating still further, the *Chronicle* insisted that many "big ideas" had been undone by "cold realities" along the state's Old Man River.[18] Complaints about unchecked costs were frequent and not limited to the obviously complex projects of the mid- to late twentieth century. The Brazos-Galveston Canal (1850s) exceeded its estimated cost by 300 percent, individual lock-and-dam structures (1910s) cost two to three times more than the initial estimates, and the cost of Whitney Dam, which had been estimated at $8.5 million in 1939, increased to between $30 million and $42 million by the late 1940s.[19] Riparian control might have been an important dream in this basin and, at times, a rather literal matter of life and death, but economic costs played a determinative, undeniable role in shaping the prospects of development along the Brazos.

Still, while economic considerations did much to shape the tempo and direction of development—constraining ambition, limiting scale, halting construction, and prompting conversation, dollars and cents alone could not have undermined these riparian improvement efforts. Geological considerations proved equally and, oftentimes, more important in determining which projects could be completed and which would necessarily be abandoned. In truth, geology lay at the center of the swelling costs for many Brazos River projects. An escalating disconnect between what people imagined possible for this river and what the river itself seemed capable of ceding made development both costly and arduous.[20] An article in the *Waco Tribune-Herald* from 2004 spoke both to that disconnect and to the long history of perceived failure, using a particularly graphic metaphor to describe the consequences: "For many years it was like a recurring boil on Waco's nose. One day the city would be dressed for success with its Suspension Bridge vista gleaming. The next day, Lake Brazos would be Brazos Puddle."[21]

Collapsing banks, high sediment loads, and the continual buildup of snags worked together to lessen the efficiency of multiple iterations of a Brazos Canal. Both the Brazos port and the Brazos jetties failed to counter the combined influence of the Brazos bar and the riparian sediments. The lock-and-dam structures were undone, at least in part, by floods that washed through, over, and around the gates that developers hoped would mediate streamflows and aid navigation. The list of geological frustrations could be extended, but the import of these examples is clear: the geology of this river frequently acted in contradiction to the expectations that individuals attached to this watershed. That was true along the individual sections of this river—Lower, Middle, and Upper—and was still more true when development of the river came to be considered as a whole. It should have been no surprise, then, that developers and dwellers of the lower third of the Brazos River disagreed with boosters and businessmen along the upper thirds of the river about the proper form, direction, and pace of development.

In the end, developers never quite reconciled reality to expectation, and the river never quite yielded to the impulses of human control. But those truths do not define the total story: failure is not the word to describe the narrative of development that emerges along a river alternately called "lordly," "wild," and "mighty." The projects geared toward improvement of the Brazos River, as well as the threads of continuity that quietly linked those otherwise disparate plans, reveal a story of developmental woe. But they also make clear that the capricious waters of this river, as damaging and stubborn as they may have been, were matched by the determined spirit of generations of people. The ambitions for development had been grand—the Brazos River Channel and Dock Company intended, for example, that the town of Velasco would eclipse both Chicago and Liverpool as a port city.[22] The collapse of these projects was, in many ways, equally grand. Still, lawyers, doctors, housewives, and politicians continued to craft their plans for the Brazos River, and engineers, developers, and boosters continued to work toward those plans and to give tangible form to the hopes that people had attached to the physical landscape.

William Robert Poage—champion, lawmaker, and occasional doubter—spoke to those ambitions and to that general commitment to improvement in a 1957 letter to one H. S. Hilburn: "I enthusiastically agree that every potential resource of the river and all of its tributaries should be developed fully. I want to see a complete flood control program installed. . . . But flood control is not enough. We need *Flood Prevention*; that is, we need upstream work on all of these tributaries and on every one of the tributary creeks that make up the Brazos watershed."[23]

Discussions of the river's erratic behavior so dominated everyday life that they even became symbolic of life's troubles more broadly considered. An advertisement for the Brookshire State Bank, for example, transformed the Brazos into a much more general symbol for hardship after a 1913 overflow, noting: "The Brazos Flood is the most perplexing question that confronts the people of Brookshire today, and a way of securing a safe guard in business transactions in every day life is another."[24]

Despite the grand ambitions and the real needs dictating development, the "best-laid plans of engineers and politicians" simply could not vanquish the realities of the landscape.[25] Projects crumbled beneath the weight of expectation and failed to stand as bulwarks of progress, and in that disconnect is the story of this river. That imperfect improvement, that curtailed development, has frustrated people hoping to fully tame an unruly river, but it is actually within that interstitial space (that place between success and failure) that continuity has quietly persisted. More to the point, the constant struggle between expectation and reality underpins the narrative of the Brazos River. This history must be told both through abandoned locks and stalwart dams; it is a story of continuity that persists in the midst of a push for change and the tale of a river that defies what people define as progress. Upon a bedrock of technocratic faith, people constructed locks, dug canals, built dams, and envisioned ports, and when all was said and done, many were left to wonder whether they had in fact resolved that Brazos River problem.

Appendix A

OVERVIEW OF IMPROVEMENT PROJECTS

1850–1854	Canal project
1888–1891	Jetty project
1896–1905	Dredging project
1899–1923	Jetty project
1905–1915	Lock-and-Dam project
1910–1914	Canal project
1930–1950	Port project
1930s	13-Dam project (ACOE)
1940s	1-Dam project
1950s	6-Dam project (BRA)
1950s	6-Dam project (ACOE)
1960s	23-Dam project
1960s	Diversion scheme (East Texas)
1970s	Diversion scheme (Canada)
1970s	Diversion scheme (Missouri River)
1970s	Diversion scheme (Mississippi River)
1970s	Diversion scheme (Arkansas River)
1970s	Diversion scheme (Southern California)

Appendix B

GEOLOGICAL TIMELINE

ERA	PERIOD	CHRONOLOGY (M.Y.A.)*
Cenozoic	Quaternary	0.01–1.60
	Tertiary	1.60–65
Mesozoic	Cretaceous	65–145
	Jurassic	145–200
	Triassic	200–250
Paleozoic	Permian	250–290
	Pennsylvanian	290–330
	Mississippian	323–360
	Devonian	360–408
	Silurian	408–439
	Ordovician	439–510
	Cambrian	510–570

* This chart has been compiled using data from a number of governmental and public sources and reflects the author's interpretation of the current debate on the delineation of geological eras.

**m.y.a. = millions of years ago

Notes

Introduction

1. Dick Vaughan, "Federal Government Funds May Help Tame Erratic Brazos River, Provide Irrigation, Electric Power, and Protection from Floods," *El Paso Herald-Post*, December 4, 1934, www.newspaperarchive.com.
2. W. R. Poage to John D. McCall, February 22, 1957, box 639, file 5, Poage Papers. Poage Legislative Library (Waco, TX).
3. Marc Reisner, *Cadillac Desert: The American West and Its Disappearing Water* (New York: Penguin, 1993), 145.

Chapter One

1. Roger Norman Conger, *The Waco Suspension Bridge* (n.p.: n.p., 1963?), 182.
2. A. R. Roessler, *Map No. 59: Texas* (Washington, D.C.: Engineer's Office, Department of the Gulf, 1865), Map Annex, Special Collections, University of Texas at Arlington (hereinafter SC-UTA).
3. John McPhee popularized the phrase "deep time" in his foundational work, *Basin and Range* (New York: Farrar, Straus, and Giroux, 1981). The concept of deep time simply accounts for the very long history of the earth, its geologic history as well as the period of written history.
4. For a table of the geological timeline, see appendix B.
5. Frederick W. Rathjen, *The Texas Panhandle Frontier* (Lubbock: Texas Tech University Press, 1998); John P. Brand, "Cretaceous of Llano Estacado," *Report of Investigations—No. 20* (Austin: Bureau of Economic Geology, University of Texas, November 1953); West Texas Geological Society, *Cenozoic geology of the Llano Estacado and Rio Grande Valley, GuideBook Field Trip No. 2* (Texas: West Texas Geological Society, November 1949); Richard Phelan and Jim Bones, *Texas Wild: The Land, Plants, and Animals of the Lone Star State* (New York: Dutton, 1976), 90; Peter Bird, "Formation of the Rocky Mountains. Western United States: A Continuum Computer Model," *Science* 239, no. 4847 (March 1988).
6. Robert T. Hill, "Classification and Origin of the Chief Geographic Features of the Texas Region," *American Geologist* 5 (January 1890); Robert T.

Hill, "Geography and Geology of the Black and Grand Prairies, Texas," in *Twenty-First Annual Report of the United States Geological Survey to the Secretary of the Interior, 1899–1900*, ed. Charles D. Walcott (Washington, D.C.: Government Printing Office, 1901), 65–69, 71–73; J. C. Frye et al., "Caliche and Clay Mineral Zonation of Ogallala Formation, Central-Eastern New Mexico," *New Mexico Bureau of Geology & Mineral Resource Circular* 144 (1974); Donald E. Trimble, "The Geologic Story of the Great Plains: A nontechnical description of the origin and evolution of the landscape of the Great Plains," in *Geological Survey Bulletin 1493* (Washington D.C.: Government Printing Office, 1980), http://library.ndsu.edu/exhibits/text/greatplains/text.html; Robert J. Finley and Thomas C. Gustavson, "Lineament Analysis Based on Landsat Imagery, Texas Panhandle," *Bureau of Economic Geology Circular* 81, no. 5 (1981); Sharon Judd, "Prehistoric Cultural Resources in the Central Llano Estacado and Western Rolling Plains of Texas" (master's thesis, Texas Tech University, 1977), 13–23; Brand, "Cretaceous of Llano Estacado."

    7. John A. Wilson, "Tertiary Shorelines, Texas Coastal Plain," *Palaeogeography, Palaeoclimatology, Paleoecology* 5, no. 1 (July 1968), 135–40; Ali Chowdhury and Mike J. Turco, *Geology of the Gulf Coast Aquifer, Texas* (Austin, TX: Water Resources Planning, Texas Water Development Board, 2011), http://www.twdb.state.tx.us/wrpi/rwp/3rdRound/2011_RWP/RegionK/Files/Engr_Notes_and_Calcs/WaterMgmtStrat/Enhanced_Recharge_Lwr_Basin/Misc_Info/Gulf_Coast_Aquifer_Geology.pdf, 23–27.

    8. Army Corps of Engineers (hereinafter ACOE), "Memorandum Report on the Economic Justification from a Flood-Control Standpoint of the 13-Dam Brazos River Valley Project" (January 25, 1937), box 6, folder 9, FW17—"Subject Files Relating to the Construction of Possum Kingdom Dam, 1936–1937" (hereinafter FW17), Record Group 77—Records of the Army Corps of Engineers, Southwest Division (hereinafter RG 77), National Archives and Records Administration—Southwest Division (Fort Worth, TX) (hereinafter NARA); "Flood Damage Study for Main Stem and Major Tributaries, Work Assignment 11.2," (April 1961), box 12, folder 6, SW6—"U.S. Commission Study—Texas, 1958–1960" (hereinafter SW6), RG 77, NARA; District Engineer to Chief of Engineers, February 6, 1919, box 10, folder 2, G6—"Examination and Survey Files, 1908–1948" (hereinafter G6), RG 77, NARA.

    9. H. A. Montgomery, to Division Engineer, Gulf of Mexico Division, January 25, 1937, box 6, folder 9, FW17, RG 77, NARA; M. C. Tyler, memorandum, June 23, 1939, box 1426, file 44, W. R. Poage Papers, Poage Legislative Library (Waco, TX) (hereinafter POAGE); M. C. Tyler to Secretary of War, memorandum, June 23, 1939, box 12, folder 3, G6, RG 77, NARA; Alston V. Thoms and John L. Montgomery, *The Archeological Resources of the Brazos River Basin: A Summary Statement* (Lubbock: Department of Anthropology, Texas Tech University, 1977), 31; "Flood Damage Study for Main Stem and Major Tributaries, Work Assignment 11.2," (April 1961); District Engineer to Chief of Engineers, February 6, 1919; ACOE, "Memorandum Report on the Economic Justification."

    10. M. C. Tyler to Secretary of War, memorandum, June 23, 1939, NARA; memorandum by M. C. Tyler, June 23, 1939, POAGE; H. A. Montgomery to

Division Engineer, January 25, 1937; ACOE, "Memorandum Report on the Economic Justification."

11. Terry Jordan, "Evaluation of Vegetation in Frontier Texas," *Southwestern Historical Quarterly* (hereinafter *SHQ*) 76, no. 3 (January 1973); Amiel Weeks Whipple, *Diary of a journey from the Mississippi to the coasts of the Pacific with a United States government expedition*, vol. 1 (London, England: Longman, Brown, Green, Longmans & Roberts, 1858); Josiah Gregg, *Commerce of the prairies, or, the journal of a Santa Fé trader: during eight expeditions across the great western prairies, and a residence of nearly nine years in northern Mexico* (Philadelphia, PA: Moore, 1849); William B. Parker, ed., *Notes taken during the expedition commanded by Capt. R. B. Marcy, U.S.A. through unexplored Texas, in the summer and fall of 1854* (New York: Hayes and Zell, 1856), 79; [*Aerial View of the Brazos River*], ca. 1930s, box 257, folder "Waco Aerial Views—1930s," Photograph File—"Waco, Texas," Photograph Collection (hereinafter PHOTO), Texas Collection, Baylor University (Waco, TX) (hereinafter TXBU); *A Memorial and biographical history of McLennan, Falls, Bell and Coryell Counties, Texas* (Chicago, IL: Lewis, 1893), 69; Walter Keene Ferguson, *Geology and Politics in Frontier Texas, 1845–1909* (Austin: University of Texas Press, 1969); William Kennedy, *The Rise, Progress, and Prospects of the Republic of Texas*, vol. 1 (London: Hastings, 1841); Bureau of Economic Geology, University of Texas at Austin, *Vegetation/Cover Types of Texas* (Austin: University of Texas, 2000), Map Collection, Perry-Castañeda Library, University of Texas at Austin (hereinafter PCL), http://www.beg.utexas.edu/UTopia/images/pagesizemaps/vegetation.pdf; Nagle, "Irrigation in Texas," *USDA Bulletin* 222 (Washington, D.C.: Government Printing Office, 1910); Verne Huser, *Rivers of Texas* (College Station: Texas A&M University Press, 2004); Phelan and Bones, *Texas Wild*; ACOE, "Memorandum Report on the Economic Justification"; Thoms and Montgomery, *Archaeological Resources*.

12. Proof, "Report on Prelim. Exam. of Brazos River Texas, House Doc. No. 298, 66 Congress" (Washington, D.C.: Government Printing Office, 1919), box 4, folder BR3-1, E.FW18—"Records of the Dallas Engineer Office" (hereinafter E.FW18), RG 77, NARA; Edgar Jadwin to Brigadier General A. Mackenzie and Lieut. Col. Clinton B. Sears, July 11, 1905, box 10, folder 3, G6, RG 77, NARA; Louis Giraud, *Velasco, the first & only deep water port on the coast of Texas: the commercial hope of the Trans-Mississippi by Louis Giraud* (St. Louis, MO: n.p., ca. 1892), Map Annex (hereinafter MAP), SC-UTA; Society for the Diffusion of Useful Knowledge, *Central America, including Texas, California, and the Northern States of Mexico* (London, England: Charles Knight & Co., 1842), 126/12 #00327, MAP, SC-UTA; Jesse Olney, *Map of Texas to illustrate Olney's School Geography*, in *Map of the United States, Canada, Texas & Parts of Mexico to Illustrate Olney's School Geography*, ed. David Robinson and Jesse Olney (New York: Pratt, Woodford, 1844); Weniger, *Explorers' Texas*, 162–63; District Engineer to Chief of Engineers, February 6, 1919; Kennedy, *Republic of Texas*, vol. 1, 35.

13. Weniger, *Explorers' Texas*, 162–63; Pichardo, *Treatise on the Limits of Louisiana and Texas*.

14. Giraud, *Velasco*, 3.

15. Colonel Edward Stiff, *The Texas emigrant: being a narration of the adventures of the author in Texas, and a description of the soil, climate, productions, minerals, towns, bays, harbors, rivers, institutions, and manners and customs* (Cincinnati, OH: George Conclin, 1840; repr.: Waco, TX: Texian Press, 1968), 10; Homer S. Thrall, *A pictorial history of Texas, from the earliest visits of European adventurers, to A.D. 1879: embracing the periods of missions, colonization, the revolution, the republic and the state, also a topographical description of the country* (New York: N. D. Thompson, 1885), 26; memorandum by M. C. Tyler, June 23, 1939, POAGE; M. C. Tyler to Secretary of War, memorandum, June 23, 1939, NARA; Thoms and Montgomery, *Archaeological Resources*, 3, 31; H. A. Montgomery to Division Engineer, January 25, 1937.

16. Thoms and Montgomery, *Archaeological Resources*, 31.

17. War Department, Office of the Division Engineer, "Brief of Report on Flood in Brazos River, Texas," April 14, 1937, box 6, folder 9, FW17, RG 77, NARA; District Engineer to Chief of Engineers, February 6, 1919; ACOE, "Memorandum Report on the Economic Justification."

18. L. L. Foster, *Forgotten Texas Census: First Annual Report of the Agricultural Bureau of the Department of Agriculture, Insurance, Statistics, and History, 1887–1888* (Austin: Texas State Historical Association, 2001), 68; Phelan and Bones, *Texas Wild*, 142.

19. ACOE, "Memorandum Report on the Economic Justification."

20. Soil Conservation Service, United States Department of Agriculture (hereinafter SCS-USDA), "Soil Survey of Austin and Waller Counties, Texas," (1984), http://soils.usda.gov/survey/online_surveys/texas; SCS-USDA, "Soil Survey of Brazoria County, Texas," (1981), http://soils.usda.gov/survey/online_surveys/texas; SCS-USDA, "Soil Survey of Brazos County, Texas," (2002), http://soils.usda.gov/survey/online_surveys/texas; SCS-USDA, "Soil Survey of Washington County, Texas," (1981), http://soils.usda.gov/survey/online_surveys/texas; SCS-USDA, "Soil Survey of Burleson County, Texas," (2005), http://soils.usda.gov/survey/online_surveys/texas. Bottomland soils most frequently take the form of (reddish-brown, gray, or dark-brown) clay, (reddish-brown) silty clay loam, (reddish-brown) silt loam, (gray or gray-brown) clay loam, or (brown) loam. Less frequently, the surface layer will consist of (reddish-brown or brown) silt loam or (brown) fine sandy loam. Alluvial soils commonly consist of (pale-brown) sandy loam, (pale-brown, light gray, or yellow-brown) fine sandy loam, (dark-brown) loamy fine sand, (dark brown or dark-gray) clay, or (dark-brown) loam.

21. SCS-USDA, "Soil Survey of Austin and Waller Counties, Texas"; SCS-USDA, "Soil Survey of Brazoria County, Texas"; SCS-USDA, "Soil Survey of Brazos County, Texas"; SCS-USDA, "Soil Survey of Burleson County, Texas"; SCS-USDA, "Soil Survey of Washington County, Texas."

22. SCS-USDA, "Soil Survey of Austin and Waller Counties, Texas"; SCS-USDA, "Soil Survey of Brazoria County, Texas"; SCS-USDA, "Soil Survey of Brazos County, Texas"; SCS-USDA, "Soil Survey of Burleson County, Texas"; SCS-USDA, "Soil Survey of Washington County, Texas." The soils in these

series include the Benchley, Boonville, Kurten, Singleton, Spiller, Tremona, Kenny, Padina, Silstid, Bieberville, Renish, and Catilla series. Of these series, the Silstid, Spiller, Singleton, Kurten, Boonville, and Benchley series are most common outside of the Coastal Plains. Surface layers commonly take the form of (dark-brown or gray-brown) fine sandy loam, (yellow-brown or dark-brown) loamy fine sand, (pale-brown) fine sand, (dark-gray) clay, (gray or gray-brown) clay loam, (brown) loamy sand, or (brown) sandy loam.

23. SCS-USDA, "Soil Survey of Austin and Waller Counties, Texas"; SCS-USDA, "Soil Survey of Brazoria County, Texas"; SCS-USDA, "Soil Survey of Brazos County, Texas"; SCS-USDA, "Soil Survey of Burleson County, Texas"; SCS-USDA, "Soil Survey of Washington County, Texas."

24. SCS-USDA, "Soil Survey of Austin and Waller Counties, Texas"; SCS-USDA, "Soil Survey of Brazoria County, Texas"; SCS-USDA, "Soil Survey of Brazos County, Texas"; SCS-USDA, "Soil Survey of Burleson County, Texas"; SCS-USDA, "Soil Survey of Washington County, Texas." Soils most commonly take the form of (brown) fine sand, (brown, dark-gray, or gray-brown) fine sandy loam, (brown or gray-brown) loamy fine sand, (dark-brown or gray-brown) sandy loam, (reddish-brown) sandy clay loam, (gray-brown) loam, (dark-gray or gray-brown) clay loam, or (gray-brown, dark-brown, reddish-brown, or gray) clay. Less common are soils of (dark-brown) loam. Some of these prairie soils are explicitly associated with deep, nonsaline locations. Surface layers take the form of (dark-gray) clay loam, (reddish-brown or dark-gray) clay, (dark-gray or pale-brown) loam, (reddish-gray) silty clay loam, (dark gray-brown) silt loam, or (brown) fine sandy loam.

25. George C. Furber, *The Twelve Months Volunteer* (Cincinnati, OH: U. P. James, 1857), http://scholarship.rice.edu/jsp/xml/1911/27093/1/aa00376. tei.html; Burke, *Burke's Texas almanac and immigrant's handbook for 1883, with which is incorporated Hanford's Texas state register* (Houston, TX: J. Burke, 1883); De Witt Clinton Baker, ed., *A Texas scrap-book: Made Up of the history, biography, and miscellany of Texas and its people* (New York: A. S. Barnes and Company, 1875); Amos Andrew Parker, *Trip to the West and Texas: Comprising a journey of eight thousand miles, through New-York, Michigan, Illinois, Missouri, Louisiana and Texas, in the autumn and winter of 1834–5. Interspersed with anecdotes, incidents and observations* (Concord, NH: White and Fisher, 1835), 131–33; Andrew Jackson Sowell, *Early Settlers and Indian Fighters of Southwest Texas* (Chicago, IL: A. C. Jones, 1900), 293–95; A. W. Moore, "A Reconnaissance in Texas in 1846," *SHQ* 30, no. 4 (April 1927); William Fairfax Gray, *From Virginia to Texas, 1835* (Houston, TX: Gray, Dillaye, 1835–1837), 42; W. N. Bryant, *All About Texas Boiled Down for 25 Cents, As It Was, As It Is! And As It Will Be!* (Dallas, TX: W. N. Bryant, 1879); Gregg, *Commerce of the Prairies*; Fisk, *A Visit to Texas: being the journal of a traveller through those parts most interesting to American settlers. With descriptions of scenery, habits, &c. &c.* (New York: Goodrich & Wiley, 1834), 12.

26. Geyata Ajilvsgi, *Wildflowers of Texas* (Fredericksburg, TX: Shearer Publishing, 2003); Lady Bird Johnson Wildflower Center, "Native Plant Database," Lady Bird Johnson Wildflower Center, University of Texas, http://

www.wildflower.org/plants; National Resources Conservation Service, PLANTS Database, Natural Resources Conservation Service, United States Department of Agriculture, http://plants.usda.gov; Furber, *Twelve Months Volunteer*; Baker, *Texas Scrap-Book*; Parker, *Trip to the West and Texas*; Sowell, *Early Settlers*; Moore, "Reconnaissance in Texas"; Gray, *From Virginia to Texas*, 1835.

27. William L. Bray, "Distribution and adaptation of the Vegetation of Texas," *Bulletin of the University of Texas* 82 (1906), 70–71; Richard Francaviglia, *Cast Iron Forest* (Austin: University of Texas Press, 1998), 8; Mary Austin Holley, *Texas. Observations, historical, geographical and descriptive: in a series of letters, written during a visit to Austin's colony, with a view of a permanent settlement in that country, in the autumn of 1831* (Baltimore, MD: Armstrong & Plaskitt, 1833); Ferdinand Roemer, *Texas: with particular reference to German immigrant and the physical appearance of the country* (Austin, TX: German-Texas Heritage Society, 1935), 3–5; Benjamin Tharp, *The Vegetation of Texas* (Houston, TX: Anson Jones Press, 1939), 31–33; Carmine A. Stahl and Ria McElvaney, *Trees of Texas: An Easy Guide to Leaf Identification* (College Station: Texas A&M University Press, 2003); Robert A. Vines, *Trees of East Texas* (Austin: University of Texas Press, 1977); Robert A. Vines, *Trees of North Texas* (Austin: University of Texas Press, 1982); Thrall, *Pictorial History of Texas*, 25; Foster, *Forgotten Texas Census*, 74; Giraud, *Velasco*, 10–12; Gregg, *Commerce of the Prairies*, 19.

28. David J. Schmidly, *Texas Mammals East of the Balcones Fault Zone* (College Station: Texas A&M University Press, 1983), 13; Letter to George Barnard, March 22, 1835, box 2B106, folder 4—"Deeds 1843–1859," George Barnard Papers (hereinafter BARNARD), TXBU; "Buffalo in Texas— Civilization Advancing Backward," *Milwaukie Sentinel*, June 15, 1844, www.newspaperarchive.com; "Severe Winter in Texas," *Watertown Chronicle*, April 4, 1849, www.newspaperarchive.com; George Wilkins Kendall, *Narrative of the Texan Santa Fe Expedition, comprising a description of a tour through Texas, and across the great Southwestern prairies . . .* (London: Wily & Putnam, 1844), 87–88; William B. Davis and David J. Schmidly, *The Mammals of Texas* (Austin: University of Texas Press, 2004); Walter W. Dalquest and Norman V. Horner, *Mammals of North-Central Texas* (Wichita Falls, TX: Midwestern State University Press, 1984); Kennedy, *Republic of Texas*, vol. 1, 159; SCS-USDA, "Soil Survey of Austin and Waller Counties, Texas;" SCS-USDA, "Soil Survey of Brazoria County, Texas;" SCS-USDA, "Soil Survey of Brazos County, Texas;" SCS-USDA, "Soil Survey of Burleson County, Texas;" SCS-USDA, "Soil Survey of Washington County, Texas."

29. Kennedy, *Republic of Texas*, vol. 1, 159; SCS-USDA, "Soil Survey of Austin and Waller Counties, Texas;" SCS-USDA, "Soil Survey of Brazoria County, Texas;" SCS-USDA, "Soil Survey of Brazos County, Texas;" SCS-USDA, "Soil Survey of Burleson County, Texas;" SCS-USDA, "Soil Survey of Washington County, Texas."

30. National Museum of History, Smithsonian Institution, "North American Mammals," Smithsonian Institution, http://www.mnh.si.edu/mna/ search_ name.cfm; Letter to George Barnard, March 22, 1835; "Buffalo in

Texas—Civilization Advancing Backward;" "Severe Winter in Texas;" Kendall, *Texan Santa Fe Expedition*; Kennedy, *Republic of Texas*, vol. 1, 159; SCS-USDA, "Soil Survey of Austin and Waller Counties, Texas;" SCS-USDA, "Soil Survey of Brazoria County, Texas;" SCS-USDA, "Soil Survey of Brazos County, Texas;" SCS-USDA, "Soil Survey of Burleson County, Texas;" SCS-USDA, "Soil Survey of Washington County, Texas"; Davis and Schmidly, *Mammals of Texas*; Schmidly, *Texas Mammals*; Dalquest and Horner, *Mammals of North-Central Texas*.

31. C. M. Hubby to John Adriance, April 20, 1845, box 127, folder "Correspondence 1843–1845," John Adriance Papers, 1832–1903, Dolph Brisco Center for American History, University of Texas at Austin (hereinafter CAH-UT); Manuel Jared E. Groce to Mr. Powel, April 11, 1833, #23–1123, Samuel May Williams Papers (hereinafter WILLIAMS), Galveston and Texas History Center, Rosenberg Library (Galveston, TX) (hereinafter GTHC); Mary Austin Holley, Letter III from Bolivar, Texas, December 1831, in Mary Austin Holley, *Letters of an Early American Traveler, Mary Austin Holley, Her Life and Her Works, 1784–1846* (Dallas, TX: Southwest Press, 1933), 110; Holley, Letter IV from Bolivar, Texas, December 1831; Andrew Forest Muir, *Texas in 1837: An Anonymous, Contemporary Narrative* (Austin: University of Texas Press, 1958), 64.

32. "Journal of Stephen F. Austin on his First Trip to Texas," *SHQ* 7, no. 4 (1904); James Breeden, ed., *A Long Ride in Texas: The Explorations of John Leonard Riddell* (College Station: Texas A&M University Press, 1994).

33. M. Whilldin, *A Description of Western Texas* (Galveston, TX: Galveston, Harrisburg & San Antonio Railway Company, 1876), 23; "Great Bargains in Good Lands!," *Civilian and Gazette*, April 28, 1857, www.newspaperarchive.com; Letter from Wheelock, April 17, 1858, in *Civilian and Galveston Gazette*, April 27, 1858, www.newspaperarchive.com; "Up the Country," *Galveston Daily News*, August 7, 1866, www.newspaperarchive.com; "Editorial Correspondence," *Galveston News*, November 22, 1853, www.newspaperarchive.com; "Special Correspondence," *Galveston Weekly News*, October 13, 1857, www.newspaperarchive.com; "Robertson County," *Galveston Weekly News*, February 3, 1857, www.newspaperarchive.com; "Valuable Tract of Land on the Brazos," *Civilian and Galveston Gazette*, September 23, 1851, www.newspaperarchive.com; "Valuable sugar land for sale," *Civilian and Galveston Gazette*, November 23, 1852, www.newspaperarchive.com; "Land for Sale," *Civilian and Galveston Gazette*, November 23, 1852, www.newspaperarchive.com; "Brazos River Land for Sale," *Civilian and Galveston Gazette*, November 23, 1852, www.newspaperarchive.com; "Land for Sale," *Civilian and Galveston Gazette*, December 21, 1844, www.newspaperarchive.com; "General Land Agent," *Civilian and Galveston Gazette*, April 21, 1847, www.newspaperarchive.com; Kennedy, *Republic of Texas*, vol. 1, 14.

34. Kennedy, *Republic of Texas*, vol. 1, 22; Muir, *Texas in 1837*.

35. Thrall, *Pictorial History of Texas*, 26; Thoms and Montgomery, *Archeological Resources*, 3, 7.

36. Thoms and Montgomery, *Archeological Resources*, 7.

37. U.S. engineers Office, "Report on Hydrology of the Site, Design Requirements, and Probable Benefits from Construction—Possum Kingdom Dam, Brazos River, Texas" (November 7, 1936), box 4, folder 7, FW17, RG 77, NARA, 2.

38. "Flood Damage Study for Main Stem and Major Tributaries, Work Assignment 11.2" (1961).

39. William P. Zuber to Mrs. T. E. Murrelle, October 7, 1907, box 1, folder 5, GA19, William Physick Zuber Papers (hereinafter ZUBER), SC-UTA; Phelan and Bones, *Texas Wild*, 142.

40. *History of McLennan, Falls, Bell and Coryell Counties, Texas*, 72; ACOE, "Memorandum Report on the Economic Justification."

41. Bob Poage, *McLennan County before 1980* (Waco: Texian Press, 1981), 2; Patricia Ward Wallace, *Waco: Texas Crossroads* (Woodland Hills, CA: Windsor Publications, 1983), 10; Karl Kibler and Tim Gibbs, "Archeological Survey of 61 Acres along the Bosque River, Waco, McLennan County, Texas," *Technical Reports* 69 (Austin, TX: Prewitt and Associates, Cultural Resources Services, 2004), 1.

42. Surface layers most commonly take the form of (reddish-brown or brown) silt loam, (dark-brown) fine sandy loam, (reddish-gray, reddish-brown, dark-brown, gray-brown, or dark-gray) clay, (dark-gray or brown) silty clay, (reddish-brown or dark-brown) silty clay loam, or (gray-brown or dark-brown) clay loam. Less frequently, these surface soils take the form of (gray-brown) silty clay, (gray-brown or dark-gray) calcareous silty clay, or (gray-brown or brown) loam; SCS-USDA, "Soil Survey of McLennan County, Texas" (2001), http://soils.usda.gov/survey/online_surveys/texas; SCS-USDA, "Soil Survey of Robertson County, Texas" (2007), http://soils.usda.gov/survey/online_surveys/texas; SCS-USDA, "Soil Survey of Milam County, Texas" (2004), http://soils.usda.gov/survey/online_surveys/texas; SCS-USDA, "Soil Survey of Falls County, Texas" (1978), http://soils.usda.gov/survey/online_surveys/texas; SCS-USDA, "Soil Survey of Brazos County, Texas"; SCS-USDA, "Soil Survey of Burleson County, Texas."

43. SCS-USDA, "Soil Survey of McLennan County, Texas"; SCS-USDA, "Soil Survey of Robertson County, Texas"; SCS-USDA, "Soil Survey of Milam County, Texas"; SCS-USDA, "Soil Survey of Falls County, Texas"; SCS-USDA, "Soil Survey of Brazos County, Texas"; SCS-USDA, "Soil Survey of Burleson County, Texas."

44. These soils include the Aledo, Bolar, Crawford, Denton, Eckrant, Purves, Ferris, Heiden, Houston Black, Austin, Fairlie, Stephen, Benchley, Crockett, Luling, Satin, and Rosanky series. Less common are soils in the Lott, McLennan series. Surface layers most commonly take the form of (gray-brown) gravelly clay loam, (dark-reddish-gray, dark-gray, gray-brown, or brown) clay, or (dark-brown or gray-brown) silty clay, (brown, dark-gray, or gray-brown) clay loam, (dark-brown or gray-brown) fine sandy loam, (reddish-brown) sandy clay loam, (pale-brown, gray, or gray-brown) loam, (dark-gray) silty clay loam, (brown) loamy fine sand, or (gray-brown) calcareous clay.

45. SCS-USDA, "Soil Survey of McLennan County, Texas"; SCS-USDA, "Soil Survey of Robertson County, Texas"; SCS-USDA, "Soil Survey of Milam

County, Texas"; SCS-USDA, "Soil Survey of Falls County, Texas"; SCS-USDA, "Soil Survey of Brazos County, Texas"; SCS-USDA, "Soil Survey of Burleson County, Texas."

46. SCS-USDA, "Soil Survey of McLennan County, Texas"; SCS-USDA, "Soil Survey of Robertson County, Texas"; SCS-USDA, "Soil Survey of Milam County, Texas"; SCS-USDA, "Soil Survey of Falls County, Texas"; SCS-USDA, "Soil Survey of Brazos County, Texas"; SCS-USDA, "Soil Survey of Burleson County, Texas." These soils fall in the Houston Black, Eddy, Burlewash, Kurten, Altoga, Zack, Zulch, and Silstid series. Less common are soils in the Slidell and Sanger series. Surface soils most commonly take the form of (brown or yellow-brown) clay loam, (dark-brown) silty clay, (pale-brown, reddish-brown, or gray-brown) fine sandy loam, (brown or yellow-brown) loamy fine sand, (reddish-brown) sandy clay loam, (pale-brown or gray-brown) loam, (dark-gray) silty clay loam, (gray-brown or pale-brown), (pale-brown) fine sand, or (dark-gray) clay.

47. Thomas B. Robinson, *Thomas B. Robinson Diary (1865–1866)*, GA47, Thomas Robinson Diary, SC-UTA, 1653; Rachel Plummer, *Narrative of the capture and subsequent sufferings of Mrs. Rachel Plummer during a captivity of twenty-one months among the Comanche Indians* (Waco: Texan Press, 1968), 5; O. T. Hayward et al., *A Field Guide to the Grand Prairie of Texas: Land, History, Culture* (Waco, TX: Baylor University, 1992), 7; Bray, "Vegetation of Texas," 71; Jordan, "Vegetation in Frontier Texas," 235; Roemer, *Texas*, 3–5; Thrall, *Pictorial History of Texas*, 25; Thoms and Montgomery, *Archeological Resources*, 7; Burke, *Texas Almanac*; Sowell, *Early Settlers*, 293–95; Fisk, *Visit to Texas*, 12; Gregg, *Commerce of the Prairies*.

48. Tharp, *Vegetation of Texas*, 31.

49. "Statement of Marshall H. D. W. Smith Jr., Assistant Engineer of the Texas and Pacific Railway," in United States Senate, Committee on Irrigation and Reclamation of Arid Lands, *Report on the Special Committee of the United States Senate on the Irrigation and Reclamation of Arid Lands* (Washington, D.C.: Government Printing Office, 1890), 142; United States Census, *Report on cotton production in the United States: also embracing agricultural and physico-geographical description of the several cotton states and of California* (Washington, D.C.: Government Printing Office, 1880); E. H. Templin, *Soil Survey: McLennan County, Texas* (Washington, D.C.: U.S. Government Printing Office, 1958), 6; Edward Dale Leach, "Maximum Probable Flood on the Brazos River in the City of Waco" (master's thesis, Baylor University, 1978), 40; Kibler and Gibbs, "Archeological Survey," 1; Tharp, *Vegetation of Texas*, 31; Plummer, *Narrative of the capture*, 5; Jordan, "Vegetation in Frontier Texas," 235; Hayward et al., *Field Guide*, 7, 16.

50. SCS-USDA, "Soil Survey of McLennan County, Texas"; SCS-USDA, "Soil Survey of Robertson County, Texas"; SCS-USDA, "Soil Survey of Milam County, Texas"; SCS-USDA, "Soil Survey of Falls County, Texas"; SCS-USDA, "Soil Survey of Brazos County, Texas"; SCS-USDA, "Soil Survey of Burleson County, Texas"; Stahl and McElvaney, *Trees of Texas*; Vines, *Trees of East Texas*; Vines, *Trees of North Texas*; Thrall, *Pictorial History of Texas*; Foster,

Forgotten Texas Census; Giraud, *Velasco*, 10–12; Gregg, *Commerce of the Prairies*.

51. Bray, "Vegetation of Texas," 70–71; Gregg, *Commerce of the Prairies*, 19; Tharp, *Vegetation of Texas*, 31–33; Francaviglia, *Cast Iron Forest*, 8; Roemer, *Texas*, 3–5; Stahl and McElvaney, *Trees of Texas*; Vines, *Trees of East Texas*; Vines, *Trees of North Texas*; Thrall, *Pictorial History of Texas*; Foster, *Forgotten Texas Census*; Giraud, *Velasco*, 10–12.

52. Ajilvsgi, *Wildflowers of Texas*; Lady Bird Johnson Wildflower Center, "Native Plant Database"; National Resources Conservation Service.

53. Davis and Schmidly, *Mammals of Texas*; Dalquest and Horner, *Mammals of North-Central Texas*; Schmidly, *Texas Mammals*.

54. Davis and Schmidly, *Mammals of Texas*; Schmidly, *Texas Mammals*; Dalquest and Horner, *Mammals of North-Central Texas*; National Museum of History, Smithsonian Institution, "North American Mammals."

55. Kendall, *Texan Santa Fe Expedition*, 94.

56. W. B. Dewees, letter, July 16, 1822, in W. B. Dewees, *Letters from an Early Settler of Texas* (Louisville, KY: Morton & Griswold, 1852), 28.

57. *Autobiography of John Wirt [or Wurts] Cloud*, box 31, folder 31.18, MS 17, Andrew Forest Muir Papers (hereinafter MUIR), Woodson Research Center (hereinafter WRC), Fondren Library, Rice University (Houston, TX) (hereinafter RICE), 4–5; Thrall, *Pictorial History of Texas*, 28 (quotation); Kennedy, *Republic of Texas*, vol. 1, 16.

58. H. A. Montgomery to Division Engineer, January 25, 1937; M. C. Tyler, memo, June 23, 1939, POAGE; M. C. Tyler to Secretary of War, memorandum, June 23, 1939, NARA.

59. Thrall, *Pictorial History of Texas*, 41; Phelan and Bones, *Texas Wild*, 92; Thoms and Montgomery, *Archeological Resources*, 3, 7; H. A. Montgomery to Division Engineer, January 25, 1937.

60. ACOE, "Memorandum Report on the Economic Justification."

61. SCS-USDA, "Soil Survey of Stephens County, Texas," (1994), http://soils.usda.gov/survey/online_surveys/texas; SCS-USDA, "Soil Survey of Palo Pinto County, Texas," (1981), http://soils.usda.gov/survey/online_surveys/texas; SCS-USDA, "Soil Survey of Bosque County, Texas," (1980), http://soils.usda.gov/survey/online_surveys/texas; SCS-USDA, "Soil Survey of Young County, Texas"; SCS-USDA, "Soil Survey of McLennan County, Texas"; Natural Resources Conservation Service. These soils are predominantly in the Lincoln, Westola, Padgett, Clearfork, Clairemont, Wheatwood, Bosque, Frio, Ovan, Tinn, Yahola, Santo, and Krum series. Surface layers are most commonly (reddish-yellow) sandy loam, (brown) fine sandy loam, (reddish-brown or light-brown) loam, (reddish-brown, brown, or gray) clay, (gray or brown) silty clay, or (brown or gray-brown) clay loam. Less frequently, these soils take the form of (reddish-brown) silty clay loam or (reddish-brown) silt loam.

62. These soils include the Grandfield, Sagerton, Gowen, Bastrop, Apalo, Krum, Gageby, Thurber, Minwells, Bastsil, Gholson, and Frio Series. These soils are most commonly (light-brown or dark-brown) loamy fine sand, (gray-brown or brown) fine sandy loam, (gray-brown) loam, (gray-brown) calcareous

clay, (gray-brown or brown) calcareous clay loam, or (dark-brown or reddish-brown) fine sandy loam. Less frequently, they take the form of (dark-gray-brown) calcareous silty clay loam or (brown) silty clay.

63. SCS-USDA, "Soil Survey of Stephens County, Texas"; SCS-USDA, "Soil Survey of Palo Pinto County, Texas"; SCS-USDA, "Soil Survey of McLennan County, Texas"; SCS-USDA, "Soil Survey of Bosque County, Texas"; SCS-USDA, "Soil Survey of Young County, Texas"; Natural Resources Conservation Service, PLANTS Database; Natural Resources Conservation Service, SOIL. Within the uplands, the Minwells, Branyon, Bremond, Burleson, Mabank, Payne, Wilson, and Thurber series are associated with non-alluvial land that is nonetheless in relative proximity to streambeds. Surface layers are most often (dark-brown) fine sandy loam, (gray-brown) clay loam, (yellow-brown) loam, (gray-brown) fine sandy loam, or (dark-gray) clay. Less frequently, these soils will take the form of (gray-brown) calcareous clay or (gray-brown) calcareous silty clay.

64. SCS-USDA, "Soil Survey of Stephens County, Texas"; SCS-USDA, "Soil Survey of Palo Pinto County, Texas"; SCS-USDA, "Soil Survey of McLennan County, Texas"; SCS-USDA, "Soil Survey of Bosque County, Texas"; SCS-USDA, "Soil Survey of Young County, Texas"; Natural Resources Conservation Service, PLANTS Database.

65. SCS-USDA, "Soil Survey of Stephens County, Texas"; SCS-USDA, "Soil Survey of Palo Pinto County, Texas"; SCS-USDA, "Soil Survey of McLennan County, Texas"; SCS-USDA, "Soil Survey of Bosque County, Texas"; SCS-USDA, "Soil Survey of Young County, Texas"; Natural Resources Conservation Service, PLANTS Database. The upland soils associated with the Central Texas prairies are in the Windthorst, Cranfill, Eckrant, Denton, Purves, Tarrant, Ferris, Heiden, Houston Black, Slidell, Sanger, Aledo, Bolar, Crawford, Denton, Eckrant, Purves, Thurber, Austin, Eddy, Fairlie, Lott, McLennan, and Stephen series. Moreover, the surface soils most commonly take the form of (brown) calcareous gravelly clay loam, (gray-brown) gravelly clay loam, (dark-brown or gray-brown) silty clay, (dark-brown, gray-brown, or yellow-brown) fine sandy loam, (brown) stony fine sandy loam, (reddish-brown) loam, (gray-brown or dark-brown) clay loam, (brown) sandy loam, or (reddish-brown, reddish-gray, gray-brown, dark-gray, or brown) clay.

66. "Hidalgo Falls Dam," *Galveston Daily News*, January 31, 1909, www.newspaperarchive.com; Zebulon M. Pike, *Exploratory travels through the western territories of North America, comprising a voyage from St. Louis, on the Mississippi to the source of that river* (London: Longman, 1811); Burke, *Texas Almanac*, 124; Kennedy, *Republic of Texas*, vol. 1, 34–35; Holley, letter IV from Bolivar, Texas, December 1831, 113; Phelan and Bones, *Texas Wild*, 126.

67. SCS-USDA, "Soil Survey of Garza County, Texas," (1975), http://soils.usda.gov/survey/online_surveys/texas; SCS-USDA, "Soil Survey of Throckmorton County, Texas," (2004), http://soils.usda.gov/survey/online_surveys/texas; SCS-USDA, "Soil Survey of Young County, Texas," (2009), http://soils.usda.gov/survey/online_surveys/texas; SCS-USDA, "Soil Survey of Baylor County, Texas"; Frye et al., "Caliche and Clay Mineral Zonation"; Finley and

Gustavson, "Lineament Analysis"; Judd, "Prehistoric Cultural Resources."

68. Stahl and McElvaney, *Trees of Texas*; Vines, *Trees of East Texas*; Vines, *Trees of North Texas*; Thrall, *Pictorial History of Texas*; Foster, *Forgotten Texas Census*; Giraud, *Velasco*, 10–12; Gregg, *Commerce of the Prairies*.

69. "The Wagon Road," *Galveston Weekly News*, November 24, 1857, www.newspaperarchive.com; Stahl and McElvaney, *Trees of Texas*; Vines, *Trees of East Texas*; Vines, *Trees of North Texas*; Thrall, *Pictorial History of Texas*; Foster, *Forgotten Texas Census*; Giraud, *Velasco*, 10–12; Gregg, *Commerce of the Prairies*.

70. Ajilvsgi, *Wildflowers of Texas*; Lady Bird Johnson Wildflower Center, "Native Plant Database"; National Resources Conservation Service.

71. Kendall, *Texan Santa Fe Expedition*, 94; Dalquest and Horner, *Mammals of North-Central Texas*; Davis and Schmidly, *Mammals of Texas*; Schmidly, *Texas Mammals*.

72. Davis and Schmidly, *Mammals of Texas*; Schmidly, *Texas Mammals*; Dalquest and Horner, *Mammals of North-Central Texas*; National Museum of History, Smithsonian Institution, "North American Mammals."

73. Sam H. Lyonto to R. L. Ballon, December 17, 1893, box 2B106, folder "Correspondence: Business/Legal 1893," BARNARD, TXBU; B. Hanna to George W. Barnard, April 3, 1893, box 2B106, folder "Correspondence: Business/Legal 1893," BARNARD, TXBU.

74. Randolph Barnes Marcy, *Thirty Years of Army Life on the Border* (New York: Harper and Brothers, 1866), 180; Burke, *Texas Almanac*; Baker, *Texas Scrap-Book*.

75. Kendall, *Texan Santa Fe Expedition*, 107–8.

76. Ibid., 102.

77. *Map of Texas Showing Major Vegetative Regions*, in Davis and Schmidly, *Mammals of Texas*; Dan Flores, *Caprock Canyonlands: Journeys into the Heart of the Southern Plains* (Austin: University of Texas Press, 1990), 5; Schmidly, *Texas Mammals*; M. C. Tyler, memorandum, June 23, 1939, POAGE; memorandum, M. C. Tyler to Secretary of War, June 23, 1939, NARA.

78. John Miller Morris, *El Llano Estacado: Exploration and Imagination on the High Plains of Texas and New Mexico, 1536–1860* (Austin: Texas State Historical Association, 1997), 2; Frye et al.; Finley and Gustavson, "Lineament Analysis"; Judd, "Prehistoric Cultural Resources."

79. Parker, *Expedition Commanded by Capt. R. B. Marcy*, 10, 161; Marcy, *Thirty Years of Army Life*, 180; Baker, *Texas Scrap-Book*, 464; Olney, *Map of Texas*; Thrall, *Pictorial History of Texas*, 41; Rathjen, *Texas Panhandle Frontier*; Phelan and Bones, *Texas Wild*, 89; Morris, *El Llano Estacado*.

80. *Texas Almanac and State Industrial Guide Volume 1904* (Galveston, TX: Belo, 1904), 73; William L. Bray, "The Ecological Relations of the Vegetation of Western Texas," *Botanical Gazette* 32, no. 3 (September 1901); Thrall, *Pictorial History of Texas*, 41 (quotation); Hill, "Classification and origin of the chief geographic features of the Texas region"; Hill, "Geography and Geology of the Black and Grand Prairies, Texas," 1; Phelan and Bones,

Texas Wild, 128.

81. James F. Meline, *Two thousand miles on horseback, Santa Fe and Back: A summer tour through Kansas, Nebraska, Colorado, and New Mexico, in the year 1866* (New York: Hurd and Houghton, 1867), 309; Phelan and Bones, *Texas Wild*, 89.

82. Phelan and Bones, *Texas Wild*, 90.

83. Flores, *Caprock Canyonlands*, 5.

84. Natural Resources Conservation Service; SCS-USDA, "Soil Survey of Garza County, Texas"; SCS-USDA, "Soil Survey of Throckmorton County, Texas"; SCS-USDA, "Soil Survey of Young County, Texas"; SCS-USDA, "Soil Survey of Baylor County, Texas." The soil survey for Garza County, through which the Double Mountain Fork flows, lists the Dalby series, but the USDA Soil Series places the soils of this series only in far west Texas. I have chosen to include the series in this list, but the discrepancy should be noted. The predominant soils of the alluvial plains are in the Dalby, Grandfield, Gowen, Sagerton, Leeray, Rowena, and Enterprise series. Most commonly, these soils take the form of (reddish-brown or gray-brown) clay, (light-brown) loamy fine sand, (gray-brown or dark-brown) loam, (gray-brown) silty clay, or (reddish-brown or gray-brown) clay loam. The terraces themselves tend to consist of (dark-brown or reddish-brown) fine sandy loam that is particularly deep, while upland soils in proximity to the Brazos River tend to consist of (dark-brown) fine sandy loam or (reddish-brown) calcareous fine sandy loam.

85. The uplands are commonly populated by soils in the Vernon, Tillman, Owens, Lueders, Throck, Miles, Bluegrove, Thurber, Sagerton, Winters, Jolly, and Rowena series; soils in the Bluegrove, Newcastle, Mereta, Rotan, and Tobosa series can be found in lesser amounts. They most commonly take the form of (reddish-brown, red, dark-gray-brown, or yellow-brown) calcareous clay, (reddish-brown, gray-brown, or dark-brown) clay loam, (dark-brown) calcareous clay loam, (reddish-brown) loam, or (gray-brown) silty clay loam. Less frequently, these soils take the form of (yellow-brown) stony clay or (brown) fine sandy loam.

86. Natural Resources Conservation Service; SCS-USDA, "Soil Survey of Garza County, Texas"; SCS-USDA, "Soil Survey of Throckmorton County, Texas"; SCS-USDA, "Soil Survey of Young County, Texas"; SCS-USDA, "Soil Survey of Baylor County, Texas."

87. The soils of the broken lands are often of the Vernon, Mobeetie, and Berda series. The soils of the broken lands are moderately deep, well-drained soils that take the form of (reddish-brown) clay loam, (dark-brown) calcareous fine sandy loam, or (brown) loam.

88. Thrall, *Pictorial History of Texas*, 41; Thoms and Montgomery, *Archeological Resources*, 3, 7; H. A. Montgomery to Division Engineer, January 25, 1937; Morris, *El Llano Estacado*, 2 (quotation); Frye et al., "Caliche and Clay Mineral Zonation"; Finley and Gustavson, "Lineament Analysis"; Judd, "Prehistoric Cultural Resources."

89. Ajilvsgi, *Wildflowers of Texas*; Lady Bird Johnson Wildflower Center, "Native Plant Database"; National Resources Conservation Service; Frye et al., "Caliche and Clay Mineral Zonation"; Finley and Gustavson, "Lineament

Analysis"; Judd, "Prehistoric Cultural Resources"; SCS-USDA, "Soil Survey of Garza County, Texas"; SCS-USDA, "Soil Survey of Throckmorton County, Texas"; SCS-USDA, "Soil Survey of Young County, Texas"; SCS-USDA, "Soil Survey of Baylor County, Texas."

90. SCS-USDA, "Soil Survey of Garza County, Texas"; SCS-USDA, "Soil Survey of Throckmorton County, Texas"; SCS-USDA, "Soil Survey of Young County, Texas"; SCS-USDA, "Soil Survey of Baylor County, Texas."

91. Dalquest and Horner, *Mammals of North-Central Texas*; Davis and Schmidly, *Mammals of Texas*; Natural Resources Conservation Service; SCS-USDA, "Soil Survey of Garza County, Texas"; SCS-USDA, "Soil Survey of Throckmorton County, Texas"; SCS-USDA, "Soil Survey of Young County, Texas"; SCS-USDA, "Soil Survey of Baylor County, Texas"; Schmidly, *Texas Mammals*.

92. Davis and Schmidly, *Mammals of Texas*; Schmidly, *Texas Mammals*; Dalquest and Horner, *Mammals of North-Central Texas*.

93. "Flood Damage Study for Main Stem and Major Tributaries, Work Assignment 11.2" (1961).

94. [*Waco Flood of 1902*], 1902, folder "Waco—Events—Floods—1902," PHOTO, TXBU; *High Water, East Waco*, 1908, folder "Waco—Events—Floods—1908" (hereinafter FOLDER 1908), PHOTO, TXBU; C. M. Seley, *Cotton Belt R. R. Bridge*, 1908, FOLDER 1908, PHOTO, TXBU; C. M. Seley, *Elm Street, East Waco, Texas*, 1908, FOLDER 1908, PHOTO, TXBU; *The Brazos on a Rampage*, 1909, FOLDER 1908, PHOTO, TXBU; *Elm Street, East Waco, 1909*, 1909, folder "Waco—Events—Floods—1909," PHOTO, TXBU; [*Waco Flood*], 1913, folder "Waco—Events—Floods—1913" (hereinafter FOLDER 1913), PHOTO, TXBU; C. M. Seley, *Elm Street, East Waco, 1913*, 1913, FOLDER 1913, PHOTO, TXBU; C. M. Seley, *Brazos River, 1913*, FOLDER 1913, PHOTO, TXBU; [*Brazos in Flood*], 1913, FOLDER 1913, PHOTO, TXBU; Fred Gildersleeve, [*Brazos in Flood*], 1918, folder "Waco—Events—Floods—1918," PHOTO, TXBU; Fred Gildersleeve, [*Waco in Flood*], 1918, folder "Waco—Events—Floods—1918," PHOTO, TXBU; [*Waco in Flood*], 1936, folder "Waco—Events—Floods—1936," PHOTO, TXBU; [*Roiling Floodwaters*], 1936, folder "Waco—Events—Floods—1936," PHOTO, TXBU; [*Waco in Flood*], 1989, folder "Waco—Events—Floods—1989" (hereinafter FOLDER 1939), PHOTO, TXBU; [*Baylor in Flood*], 1989, FOLDER 1989, PHOTO, TXBU; [*Baylor Bookstore in Flood*], 1989, FOLDER 1989, PHOTO, TXBU; [*Baylor Campus in Flood*], 1989, FOLDER 1989, PHOTO, TXBU; [*Brazos at High Water*], n.d., box 261, folder "Waco—Brazos River," Photograph File—"Waco, Texas," PHOTO, TXBU; "[*Brazos Flood*]," n.d., box 261, folder "Waco—Brazos River," Photograph File—"Waco, Texas," PHOTO, TXBU; United States House of Representatives, *H.R. 6198: A Bill to Control Flood Waters of the Brazos River and Its Tributaries in the State of Texas* (Washington, D.C.: Government Printing Office, February 28, 1935), 20; John Washington Lockhart, "Boating on the Brazos: First Trip of the 'Mustang' to Washington—A Regular Packet Line Afterward—The Terrible Overflow of 1842—Interesting Reminiscences," *Galveston Daily News*, February 12, 1893, in John Washington Lockhart,

Sixty Years on the Brazos: The Life and Letters of Dr. John Washington Lockhart, 1824–1900 (Ann Arbor, MI: Argonaut Press, 1930); Gail Hathaway to District Engineer, May 23, 1936, box 7, folder 2, FW17, RG 77, NARA; John Henry Brown, *History of Texas from 1685 to 1892* (St. Louis, MO: Daniell, 1893), 531; H. A. Montgomery to Division Engineer, January 25, 1937; ACOE, "Memorandum Report on the Economic Justification." The years for these severe floods: 1822, 1833, 1836, 1842, 1843, 1852, 1859, 1866, 1869, 1875, 1876, 1884, 1885, 1889, 1899, 1900, 1902, 1908, 1909, 1913, 1918, 1921, and 1922.

95. "The Lamentable Flood in Texas," *New York Herald*, July 23, 1869, www.newspaperarchive.com.

96. "Texas Much Poorer in Money, but Not in Life—Revised Reports Indicate that Most of Lower Brazos Flood Sufferers Are Safe," *World*, July 7, 1899, www.newspaperarchive.com; "Miles of Floods in Texas," *Herald*, July 8, 1899, www.newspaperarchive.com.

97. "During the Brazos Flood," *Postville Review*, September 15, 1899, www.newspaperarchive.com.

98. Lockhart, "Boating on the Brazos."

99. Daniel J. Prikryl and Jack Johnson, *Waco Lake, McLennan County, Texas: An Inventory and Assessment of Cultural Resources* (Austin, TX: Prewitt and Associates, 1985), 32.

100. Breeden, ed., *Long Ride in Texas*, 42.

101. ACOE, "Memorandum Report on the Economic Justification;" H. A. Montgomery to Division Engineer, January 25, 1937; Proof, "Prelim. Exam. of Brazos River Texas" (1919); District Engineer to Chief of Engineers, February 6, 1919.

102. War Department, "Flood in Brazos River, Texas."

103. "Brazos River, Texas," series 1, folder AR406 1-10-1, *Fort Worth Star-Telegram* Photographs, SC-UTA.

104. Alston V. Thoms, et al., "Native American Land Use in the Yegua Creek Basin and Vicinity: Ethnohistoric and Archeological Records," in *Yegua Creek Archaeological Project: Survey Results from Lake Somerville State Parks and Trailway, East-Central Texas*, ed. A. V. Thoms (College Station: Texas A&M University Press, 2004), 35–48; William C. Foster, *Historic Native Peoples of Texas* (Austin: University of Texas Press, 2008); William C. Foster, ed., *The La Salle Expedition to Texas: The Journal of Henri Joutel, 1684–1687*, trans. Johanna S. Warren (Austin: Texas State Historical Commission, 1998).

105. J. Phil Dering and J. Bryan Mason, eds., *Prehistoric and Historic Occupation in Central Brazos County, Texas, Archaeological Investigations of Two City Parks: Veterans Park and Athletic Complex and Lick Creek Park, College Station, Texas* (College Station: Texas A&M University Press, 2001), 14.

106. Manuel de Mier y Teran, "Notice of the Indian tribes who are known to inhabit the department of Texas, with the tribe of families that compose each tribe, the area in which they live, and the fields in which they camp" (June 9, 1828), Eberstadt Collection, box 3N180, folder 2, CAH-UT; Manuel

de Mier y Teran to President Guadalupe Victoria, March 28, 1828, in Manuel de Mier y Teran, *Texas by Teran: The Diary Kept by General Manuel de Mier y Teran on His 1828 Inspection of Texas*, ed. Jack Jackson (Austin: University of Texas Press, 2000), 29; Prikryl and Johnson, *Waco Lake*, 28.

107. Father Marion A. Habig, *Spanish Texas Pilgrimage: The Old Franciscan Missions and Other Spanish Settlements of Texas, 1632–1821* (Chicago, IL: Franciscan Herald Press, 1990); Herbert Bolton, *Athanase de Mézières and the Louisiana-Texas frontier, 1768–1780: documents pub. for the first time, from the original Spanish and French manuscripts, chiefly in the archives of Mexico and Spain; tr. into English* (Cleveland, OH: Clark, 1914), 32; Thoms and Montgomery, *Archeological Resources*, 26.

108. Marion to Governor Pedro del Barrio Junco y Espriella, memorandum, July 26, 1749, in *Documentary Series 7, Letters and Memorials of Fray Mariano de Los Dolores y Viana, 1737–1762* (San Antonio, TX: Old Spanish Missions Historical Research Library, 1985), 62; Marion to Governor Pedro del Barrio Junco y Espriella, July 16, 1749, in *Letters and Memorials of Fray Mariano de Los Dolores y Viana*, 57; "Instancia, y razones representadas al exmo. Sor Virrey para la fundacion de X.[n] Xavier" (n.d.), 2Q237, folder 766, Transcripts from Santa Cruz de Queretero, 1750–1767, Spanish Missions in Texas and California, 1691–1825 (hereinafter TRANSCRIPTS), CAH, 171–72; Fray Mariano Dolores to Señor Governor and Captain General [Leg. 19. No. 65], 2Q237, folder 768, TRANSCRIPTS, CAH, 71–80; "Informe del R. P. Fr. Benito de Sta Ana al Exmo. sobre la fundacion de Sn Xavier [K.N. 32, Leg. 6]" (1752), 2Q237, folder 768, TRANSCRIPTS, CAH, 154–63; Marion to Fr. Guardian Francisco Xavier Ortiz, March 6, 1762, in *Letters and Memorials of Fray Mariano de Los Dolores y Viana*, 344.

109. "Instancia, y razones representadas al exmo. Sor Virrey para la fundacion de X.[n] Xavier" (n.d.), 2Q237, folder 766, TRANSCRIPTS, CAH, 171–72; Fray Mariano Dolores to Señor Governor and Captain General [Leg. 19. No. 65], 2Q237, folder 768, TRANSCRIPTS, CAH, 71–80; "Informe del R. P. Fr. Benito de Sta Ana al Exmo. sobre la fundacion de Sn Xavier [K.N. 32, Leg. 6]" (1752), 2Q237, folder 768, TRANSCRIPTS, CAH, 154–63; Marion to Governor Pedro del Barrio Junco y Espriella, July 16, 1749, in *Letters and Memorials of Fray Mariano de Los Dolores y Viana*, 57.

110. Debbie Cunningham, ed., "Notes and Documents: The Domingo Ramon Diary of the 1716 Expedition into the Province of the Tejas Indians: An Annotated Translation," *SHQ* 110, no. 1 (July 2006); Eleanor Claire Buckley, "The Aguayo Expedition into Texas and Louisiana, 1719–1722," *SHQ* 15, no. 1 (July 1911); Fray Mariano de los Dolores to Don Diego Ramon, 2Q237, folder 766, TRANSCRIPTS, CAH, 201; *Letters and Memorials of Fray Mariano de Los Dolores y Viana*, 57–58; "Informe del R. P. Fr. Benito de S.[ta] Ana al Exmo. sobre la fundacion de S.[n] Xavier [K.N. 32, Leg. 6]," 154–63.

111. Marion to Rev. Fr. Preacher, Fray Miguel Pinilla, December 9, 1752, in *Letters and Memorials of Fray Mariano de Los Dolores y Viana*, 183 (first quote); "Informe del R. P. Fr. Benito de Sta Ana al Exmo. sobre la fundacion de Sn Xavier [K.N. 32, Leg. 6]," 154–63 (second quote).

112. Fray Mariano Delores to Señor Then.ᵗᵉ D.ⁿ Ju. Galban, April 12, 1750, "Ynforme del th.ᵉ Galvan sobre S.ⁿ Xav.ʳ y carta escrita al dho. el año de 1750 [K. Legajo 19. No. 90]," 2Q237, folder 768, TRANSCRIPTS, CAH, 5.

113. Herbert E. Bolton, *Texas in the Middle Eighteenth Century: Studies in Spanish Colonial History and Administration* (Berkeley: University of California Press, 1915), 138; "Reminiscences of J. H. Fulcher, A Grandson of Abigail (McLennan) Fokes," October 27, 1835, in Malcolm McLean, *Papers concerning Robertson's Colony in Texas, October 15, 1835, through January 14, 1836*, vol. 12 (Arlington: University of Texas at Arlington Press 1985), 167.

114. "Reminiscences of J. H. Fulcher"; Bolton, *Texas in the Middle Eighteenth Century*, 138.

115. Antonio Gramsci, *Prison Notebooks*, vol. 1 (New York: Columbia University Press, 2010).

116. Dr. Doyle Eastland to C. S. Riche, sick roll, October 31, 1913, box 7, folder 419a, FW18, RG 77, NARA; Dr. Doyle Eastland to C.S. Riche, sick roll, January 31, 1913, box 7, folder 419a, FW18, RG 77, NARA; Dr. Doyle Eastland to C. S. Riche, sick roll, February 28, 1913, box 7, folder 419a, FW18, RG 77, NARA; Dr. Doyle Eastland to C. S. Riche, sick roll, March 31, 1913, box 7, folder 419a, FW18, RG 77, NARA; Dr. Doyle Eastland to C. S. Riche, sick roll, April 30, 1913, box 7, folder 419a, FW18, RG 77, NARA; Dr. Doyle Eastland to C. S. Riche, sick roll, June 30, 1913, box 7, folder 419a, FW18, RG 77, NARA; Dr. Doyle Eastland to C. S. Riche, sick roll, July 31, 1913, box 7, folder 419a, FW18, RG 77, NARA; Dr. Doyle Eastland to C. S. Riche, sick roll, August 31, 1913, box 7, folder 419a, FW18, RG 77, NARA; Dr. Doyle Eastland to C. S. Riche, sick roll, September 30, 1913, box 7, folder 419a, FW18, RG 77, NARA; Dr. Doyle Eastland to C. S. Riche, sick roll, November 30, 1913, box 7, folder 419a, FW18, RG 77, NARA; Dr. Doyle Eastland to C. S. Riche, sick roll, December 31, 1913, box 7, folder 419a, FW18, RG 77, NARA.

117. Benedict Anderson, *Imagined Communities: Reflections on the Origin and Spread of Nationalism* (New York: Norton, 2006).

Chapter Two

1.   Mary Austin Holley, *Texas. Observations, historical, geographical and descriptive: in a series of letters, written during a visit to Austin's colony, with a view of a permanent settlement in that country, in the autumn of 1831* (Baltimore, MD: Armstrong & Plaskitt, 1833).

2.   Mary Austin Holley, "Brazos Boat Glee," 1838, Sheet Music, A Guide to the Texas Composers Collection, 1836–1968 Dolph Briscoe Center for American History, University of Texas at Austin (hereinafter CAH-UT); Mary Austin Holley, "Brazos Boat Glee," (New York: Firth and Hall, 1838), reel 27 no. 1314, microfilm collection, Special Collections, University of Texas at Arlington (hereinafter SC-UTA).

3.   In terms of cultural theory, this is the idea of différance versus difference. For more information on these ideas see Jacques Derrida, particularly his

essay "Cogito and the History of Madness," in Alan Bass, trans., *Writing and Difference* (New York: Routledge, 1978).

4.   Earl Wesley Fornell, *The Galveston Era: The Texas Crescent on the Eve of Secession* (Austin: University of Texas Press, 2009); M. Edwards to J. E. Sumner, May 19, 1836, GA 21, folder 7, William Ransom Hogan Papers 1934–1946 (hereinafter HOGAN), SC-UTA; M. Edwards to George Knight, May 19, 1836, GA 21, folder 7, HOGAN, SC-UTA; "James W. Fannin, slave trader & importer," in Brazoria County Probate Records, case no. 162 (estate of James W. Fannin), GA 21, folder 8, HOGAN, SC-UTA; Sean Kelley, "Blackbirders and *Bozales*: African-Born Slaves on the Lower Brazos River of Texas in the Nineteenth Century," *Civil War History* 54, no. 4 (December 2008).

5.   Lynn Willoughby, *Flowing Through Time: A History of the Lower Chattahoochee River* (Tuscaloosa: University of Alabama Press, 1999); John O. Anfinson, *The River We Have Wrought: A History of the Upper Mississippi* (Minneapolis, MN: University of Minnesota Press, 2005); John M. Barry, *Rising Tide: The Great Mississippi Flood of 1927 and How It Changed America* (New York: Simon and Schuster, 1990); Jim Kimmel, *Exploring the Brazos River: From Beginning to End* (College Station: Texas A&M Press, 2011); Pamela Puryear and Nath Winfield, *Sandbars and Sternwheelers: Steam Navigation on the Brazos* (College Station: Texas A&M Press, 1976).

6.   Ronald E. Shaw, *Erie Water West: A History of the Erie Canal, 1792–1854* (Lexington: University Press of Kentucky, 1990); Peter L. Bernstein, *Wedding of the Waters: The Erie Canal and the Making of a Great Nation* (New York: Norton, 2006); Carol Sheriff, *The Artificial River: The Erie Canal and the Paradox of Progress, 1817–1862* (New York: Macmillan, 1997); Patrick Vincent McGreevy, *Stairway to Empire: Lockport, The Erie Canal, and the Shaping of America* (New York: SUNY Press, 2009); Terry K. Woods, *Ohio's Grand Canal: A Brief History of the Ohio and Erie Canal* (Kent, OH: Kent State University Press, 2008); Ronald E. Shaw, *Canals for a Nation: The Canal Era in the United States, 1790–1860* (Lexington: University Press of Kentucky, 1993).

7.   J. Frank Dobie, *Southwestern Lore* (Hatsboro, PA: Folklore Associates, 1931); Polly Redford, *Raccoons and Eagles: Two Views of American Wildlife* (New York: Dutton Publishing, 1965), 40–43; A. W. Eddings, "How Sandy Got His Meat," in Stith Thompson, *Round the Levee* (Austin: Texas Folkloric Society, 1916), 47–49; John A. Lomax, *Folk Song U.S.A.: The 111 Best American Ballads* (New York: Duell, Sloan & Pearce, 1947), 6.

8.   William Wilis Greenleaf, "Uncle Israel Changes His Mind," in John Mason Brewer, *Dog Ghosts* (Austin: University of Texas Press, 1958), 17–18.

9.   Ibid., 17–18.

10.   Anderson Shaw, "Sit Down, Self!," in Brewer, *Dog Ghosts*, 37–38; "Cussing for the Church," in John Mason Brewer, *The Word on the Brazos* (Austin: University of Texas Press, 1953), 11–12; "Elder Lott's Sunday Night Sermon," in Brewer, *Word on the Brazos* ,12–13; "Reverend Carter's Twelfth Anniversary Sermon," in Brewer, *Word on the Brazos*, 17–19; "The Tale of the Three Preachers," in Brewer, *Word on the Brazos*, 21–22; "Brother Gregg

Identifies Himself," in Brewer, *Word on the Brazos*, 32–34; "The Old Preacher's Will and the Young Wife," in Brewer, *Word on the Brazos*, 34–35; "Uncle Ebun and the Sign of the Shooting Star," in Brewer, *Word on the Brazos*, 39–40; "Sister Patsy's Error," in Brewer, *Word on the Brazos*, 22; "The Wrong Man in the Coffin," in Brewer, *Word on the Brazos*, 22–23; "What Major Buford Knows," in Brewer, *Word on the Brazos*, 23–25; "How Elder Samuels Was Saved," in Brewer, *Word on the Brazos*, 26–28; "Sister Liza and the New Pastor," in Brewer, *Word on the Brazos*, 28–29; "Halley's Comet and Judgment Day," in Brewer, *Word on the Brazos*, 30–32; "The Hare-Lipped Man and the Speaking Meeting," in Brewer, *Word on the Brazos*, 43–44; "The Complaining Church Sister," in Brewer, *Word on the Brazos*, 52–54; "Sister Sadie Washington's Littlest Boy," in Brewer, *Word on the Brazos*, 54–56; "Uncle Charlie Gets Directions," in Brewer, *Word on the Brazos*, 56–57; "The Haunted Church and the Sermon on Tithing," in Brewer, *Word on the Brazos*, 64, 66–67; "The Lord Answers Sister Milly's Prayer," in Brewer, *Word on the Brazos*, 67–68; "The Baptist Negroes in Heaven," in Brewer, *Word on the Brazos*, 82–83; Jerry Mullinox, "Elder Brown's False Teeth," in Brewer, *Dog Ghosts*, 73–76; "The Moderator and the Alligator," in Brewer, *Word on the Brazos*, 45–46; "The Preacher Who Walked on Water," in Brewer, *Word on the Brazos*, 46–47; "The Sinner Man's Son and the Preacher," in Brewer, *Word on the Brazos*, 104–6.

11. Jerry Mullinox, "Deacon Wright's Confession," in Brewer, *Word on the Brazos*, 84–85; Mullinox, "Elder Brown's False Teeth," in Brewer, *Dog Ghosts*, 73–76; "Halley's Comet and Judgment Day," in Brewer, *Word on the Brazos*, 30–32.

12. "The Sunday School Scholar and the Pastor," in Brewer, *Word on the Brazos*, 71–72; "Scott Mission Methodist Church Gets a Full-Time Pastor," in Brewer, *Word on the Brazos*, 75; "John's Trip to Hell," in Brewer, *Word on the Brazos*, 90.

13. Henry Isaacs, *Road Down to the Brazos River*, in Henry Isaacs, "Paintings from the American Southwest" [hereinafter ISAACS], http://www. henryisaacs.com/?q=node/5; Henry Isaacs, *Wildflowers near the Brazos*, in ISAACS, http://www.henryisaacs.com/?q=node/5; Henry Isaacs, *Flowers Along the Brazos River*, in ISAACS, http://www.henryisaacs.com/?q=node/5; Henry Isaacs, *Wildflowers Along the Brazos River Study #1*, in ISAACS, http://www.henryisaacs.com/?q=node/5; M. E. Brannon, *Brazos River*, 2005, in "Gallery—Acrylic Paintings," Hay Bale Studio, http://haybalestudio.com/gallery/main.php?g2_itemId=48&g2_jsWarning=true.

14. Russell Cushman, Murals, in Star of the Republic Museum, Washington on the Brazos, Texas; Fisk, *A Visit to Texas: being the journal of a traveller through those parts most interesting to American settlers. With descriptions of scenery, habits, &c. &c.* (New York: Goodrich & Wiley, 1834).

15. Don Hutson, painting of Jackson Plantation (n.d.), Brazoria County Historical Museum (Angleton, TX) (hereinafter BCHM); Don Hutson, painting of Ellersley Plantation (n.d.), BCHM; Don Hutson, *painting of Patton Plantation (n.d.), BCHM.

16. Scott Lennox, *Brazos Bend*, LENNOX, http://www.scottlennoxart.

com/portfolio.cfm?nK=12868&nS=0&i=134564; Scott Lennox, *Brazos Sunrise*, LENNOX, http://www.scottlennoxart.com/portfolio. cfm?nK=12868&nS=0&i=134564; Scott Lennox, *Brazos Fall*, LENNOX, http://www.scottlennoxart.com/portfolio.cfm?nK=12868&nS=0&i=134564.

17. Sylvia Morgan, *Brazos Palmettos*, in Fine Art America, "Fine Art America" (hereinafter FAA), http://fineartamerica.com/featured/ brazos-palmettos-sylvia-morgan.html; Sheri Jones, *Brazos River*, 2010, in Sheri Jones, "Sheri Jones Painting Journal" (hereinafter SJP), http://sheriart.blogspot. com/2010/05/brazos-river-by-sheri-jones.html; Sheri Jones, *The Brazos River*, 2010, SJP, http://sheriart.blogspot.com/2010/03/brazos-river-by-sheri-jones. html; Sheri Jones, *The River at Pecan*, 2010, SJP, http://sheriart.blogspot. com/2010/03/river-at-pecan-by-sheri-jones.html; Sheri Jones, *Brazos River Beach*, 2011, in Artists of Texas, "Artists of Texas Blog," http://artistsoftexas. blogspot.com/2011/07/brazos-river-beach-by-sheri-jones.html.

18. Lee Jamison, *Austin's Last Journey*, n.d., Lee Jamison, "Lee Jamison: . murals . . fine art . . exhibits . . ." Lee Jamison (hereinafter JAMISON), http:// www.leejamison.com/history.html; Lee Jamison, *The Runaway Scrape: Loading the Yellow Stone at Groce's Plantation*, n.d., JAMISON, http://www. leejamison.com/history.html.

19. Don Hutson, painting of the steamboat *Hiawatha* (n.d.), BCHM.

20. Karl Bodmer, [*Yellow Stone*], 1832, in Ronald Howard Livingston, "The Steamboat Yellow Stone: The Lil' Steamer that Could," Reflections on the Past (hereinafter LIVINGSTON), http://brazoriaresearch.com; George Catlin, [*Yellowstone*], ca. 1832, LIVINGSTON, http://brazoriaresearch.com.

21. Russell Cushman, *Planters in the Field* (n.d.), in Blues Alley (hereinafter BLUES), Navasota, TX; Russell Cushman [*Pickers in the Cotton Field*] (n.d.), BLUES, Navasota, TX.

22. Leon Collins [*Sharecroppers with Cotton Sacks*], n.d.; Leon Collins, [*Sharecroppers with Building in Background*], n.d.; Leon Collins [*Sharecropper with Cotton Sack*], n.d.; Leon Collins, [*Sharecroppers in the field*], n.d.; Leon Collins [*Sharecroppers—Women*], n.d.; Leon Collins [*Sharecroppers—Men*], n.d.; Leon Collins [*Sharecroppers with Abraham Lincoln, Right Side*], n.d.; Leon Collins [*Sharecroppers with Abraham Lincoln, Left Side*], n.d.

23. David Woods [*Sharecroppers in a Brazos River Cotton Field*], ca. 1993, in BLUES, Navasota, TX; David Woods [*Sharecroppers in a Brazos River Cotton Field 2*], ca. 2003, in BLUES, Navasota, TX; David Woods [*Musician with Crops in Background*], n.d., BLUES, Navasota, TX.

24. Dewey Sizemore, *Cotton Farm*, n.d., BLUES, Navasota, TX; Ruth Mofford [*Sharecroppers in a Brazos River Cotton Field*], n.d., BLUES, Navasota, TX; Cushman, Murals.

25. Windy Drum Photography, [*Waco, Texas, from an Aerial View*], ca. 1950s, box 257, folder "Waco Aerial Views—1950s," Photograph File—"Waco, Texas," PHOTO, TXBU; [*First Bale*], n.d., folder "Waco—Cotton—Agriculture," PHOTO, TXBU; Windy Drum Photography [*Cotton*], ca. 1956, folder "Waco—Cotton—Agriculture," PHOTO, TXBU; Fred Gildersleeve [*Cotton in the Town Square*], 1911, folder "Waco—Cotton—Agriculture," PHOTO, TXBU; Windy Drum Photography [*Irrigation and Cotton*]," ca. 1956,

folder "Waco—Cotton—Agriculture," PHOTO, TXBU; *View of Waco and Brazos River from the Air*, ca. 1940s, box 257, folder "Waco Aerial Views— 1940s," Photograph File—"Waco, Texas," PHOTO, TXBU; *Municipal Stadium and Cotton Palace—Waco, Tex.*, ca. 1940s, box 257, folder "Waco Aerial Views—1940s," Photograph File—"Waco, Texas," PHOTO, TXBU; *Downtown Waco, 'Gem City of the Brazos,'* ca. 1940s, box 257, folder "Waco Aerial Views—1940s," Photograph File—"Waco, Texas," PHOTO, TXBU; *Downtown Waco, Showing Amicable Bldg*, ca. 1940s, box 257, folder "Waco Aerial Views—1940s," Photograph File—"Waco, Texas," PHOTO, TXBU.

26. R. Hedspeth to Adaline Earle, November 1, 1884, box 2B332, folder 5: "Personal Papers: Correspondence, 1874–1885," Graves-Earle Family Papers, 1848–1963 (hereinafter GRAVES), TXBU; Isaac Parks to Caroline Crittenden, December 23, 1862, box 2B13, folder 2: "Correspondence, 1858–1877," Isaac Parks Papers (hereinafter PARKS), TXBU; Sally Graves to Mary Earl, September 10, 1892, box 2B332, folder 7: "Personal Papers: Correspondence, 1892–1893," GRAVES, TXBU; Josephine Parks to Isaac Parks, September 24, 1876, box 2B13, folder 2: "Correspondence, 1858–1877," PARKS, TXBU; Mary to Adaline Graves, December 14, 1873, 1848–1963, box 2B332, folder 4: "Personal Papers: Correspondence, 1871–1873," GRAVES, TXBU; George Barnard to Shap[ley] Barnard, June 16, 1882, box 2B106, folder "Correspondence Personal 1882–1889," Barnard Papers (hereinafter BARNARD), TXBU; George Barnard to Shap[ley] Barnard, June 20, 1882, box 2B106, folder "Correspondence Personal 1882–1889," BARNARD, TXBU.

27. *Texas Cotton Palace*, n.d., box 2J227, folder "Photographs," PHOTO, TXBU.

28. Rebecca Sharpless, *Fertile Ground, Narrow Choices: Women on Texas Cotton Farms, 1900–1940* (Chapel Hill: University of North Carolina Press, 1999); Agnes Warren Barnes, *Waco, Texas: A Postcard Journey* (Mount Pleasant, SC: Arcadia Publishing, 1999).

29. *Unique, Original, Attractive: The Texas Cotton Palace, Waco, Texas, The First Annual Exhibition Will Open November 8 and Close December 6, 1894* (Waco, TX: Brooks & Wallace Printing House, 1894), box 2J227, folder "Promotional Materials," Texas Cotton Palace Papers (hereinafter COTTON PALACE), TXBU.

30. Ibid.

31. Neil Foley, *The White Scourge: Mexicans, Blacks, and Poor Whites in Texas Cotton Culture* (Berkley: University of California Press, 1997); "Waco Cotton Palace," *Galveston Daily News*, November 18, 1910, www.newspaperarchive.com; Texas Cotton Palace Ass'n, mailer to R. J. Parsons, December 12, 1910, box 2J227, folder "Promotional Materials," COTTON PALACE, TXBU; Sharpless, *Fertile Ground*.

32. Robert Perkinson, *Texas Tough: The Rise of America's Prison Empire* (New York: Macmillan, 2010); Bruce Jackson, *Wake Up Dead Man: Afro-American Worksongs from Texas Prisons* (Cambridge, MA: Harvard University Press, 1972); Matthew Mancini, *One Dies, Get Another: Convict Leasing in the American South, 1866–1928* (Columbia: University of South Carolina Press,

1996); Donald R. Walker, *Penology for Profit: A History of the Texas Prison System, 1867–1912* (College Station: Texas A&M University Press, 1988); Anne M. Butler, *Gendered Justice in the American West: Women Prisoners in Men's Penitentiaries* (Champaign: University of Illinois Press, 1999).

33. "Convicts on Repair Work," *Galveston Daily News*, July 25, 1899, www.newspaperarchive.com; "Burleson Convict Farms Investigated," *Galveston Daily News*, March 1, 1910, www.newspaperarchive.com; "Convicts Shoot Way to Freedom; Flee in Swamp," *Steubenville Herald-Star*, July 28, 1928, www.newspaperarchive.com; "Body is Found in River Here," *Freeport Facts*, December 24, 1931, www.newspaperarchive.com.

34. Jackson, *Wake Up Dead Man*, vii.

35. Ibid., 311.

36. Ted Gioia, *Work Songs* (Durham, NC: Duke University Press, 2006), 35; Ernest Williams, "Ain't No More Cane on the Brazos," *Field Recordings Vol. 6: Texas (1933–1958)*, 1997, Document Records; Lonnie Donegan, "Ain't No More Cane on the Brazos," *Lonnie*, 2008, Hallmark Records; The Tex-i-an Boys, "Ain't No More Cane on the Brazos," *Songs of Texas*, 1961, Folkway Records; Bob Dylan, "Ain't No More Cane," *The Basement Tapes*, 2009, Columbia/Legacy; Harvey Reid, "Ain't No More Cane," *Steel Drivin' Man*, 2008, Woodpecker Records; Ollabelle, "Ain't No More Cane," *Before This Time*, 2008, Yep Roc Records; Dennis Monroe, "Ain't No More Cane on the Brazos," *Released*, 2005, Dennis Monroe; The Band of Heathens, "Ain't No More Cane," *Live at Antone's*, 2008, BOH Records; Lyle Lovett, "Ain't No More Cane," *It's Not Big It's Large*, 2007, Curb/Lost Highway; Paul Austin Kelly, "Ain't No More Cane on the Brazos," *Unleashed on America*, 2006, Walking Oliver Productions; Chris Bryant, "Ain't No More Cane," *Please Be Patient With Me*, 2009, Chris Bryant; Great American Taxi, "Ain't No More Cane on the Brazos," *FestivaLink Presents Great American Taxi at Old Settler's Music Festival, TX, 4/16/09*, 2009, festivalink.net; Professor Louie and the Crowmatrix, "Ain't No More Cane," *Whispering Pines*, 2009, Woodstock Records; Powder Mill, "Ain't No More Cane," *Live in Carter County*, 2011, Powder Mill.

37. Ernest Williams, "Ain't No More Cane on the Brazos," *Deep River of Song: Big Brazos: Texas Prison Recordings, 1933 and 1934*, 2000, Rounder Select.

38. Sugarcane Collins, "One Wing Frank," *Way Down the River*, 2006, A. Collins. Other songs, which alternately reference the Brazos River or Fort Bend County as a burning hell, are mentioned in Alan Lomax, *The Land Where the Blues Began* (New York: Pantheon Books, 1993), 283; Alan Mullen, *The Man Who Adores the Negro: Race and American Folklore* (Champaign: University of Illinois Press, 2003), 80; Charles K. Wolfe, *The Life and Legend of Leadbelly* (Cambridge, MA: Da Capo Press, 1999), 79.

39. Alan Lomax, *American Ballads and Folk Songs* (New York: Macmillan, 1934), 193.

40. Jackson, *Wake Up Dead Man*, 148–49.

41. It's been speculated that famous bluesman Lightnin' Hopkins might be responsible for this song; there's no evidence to back up that claim, but Hopkins

did record several songs about Tom Moore, one of four Moore brothers who farmed this area on the Brazos River.

42. William A. Owens, *Tell Me a Story, Sing Me a Song: A Texas Chronicle* (Austin: University of Texas Press, 1983).

43. Ernest Williams, "Ain't No More Cane on the Brazos."

44. *Cane Fields Line*, n.d., folder "Agriculture," Texas Prison Museum (Huntsville) (hereinafter PRISON); *Bailing & Loading Hay*, n.d., folder "Agriculture," PRISON; *Black Hoe Squad*, n.d., folder "Wardens, Kelley," PRISON; *Boss Horse Cotton Picking*, n.d., folder "Agriculture," PRISON; *Capt McGill*, n.d., folder "Wardens, McGill," PRISON; *Cotton Picker 1964b*, 1964, folder "Units Old, Scott Retrieve," BK 189, PRISON; *Cotton Pickers*, n.d., folder "Agriculture, Field Work," PRISON; *Cotton picking*, n.d., folder "Agriculture, Crops," PRISON; *Cotton Sacks*, n.d., folder "Agriculture, Field Work," PRISON; *Cotton Scale*, n.d., folder "Units Old, Lease Farms, Terrell Farms, Rogers Plantation, Terrell 2," PRISON; *Irrigation*, n.d., folder Units Old, Darrington, Darrington 101," PRISON; *Picking Cotton 65*, 1965, folder "Agriculture," PRISON; *Picking Cotton*, n.d., folder "Agriculture," PRISON; *Plowing Corn*, n.d., folder "Units Old, Central, Imperial, New," PRISON; *Sugarcane Workers*, n.d., folder "Units Old, Imperial, New," PRISON; *Untitled 2*, n.d., folder "Wardens, McGill," PRISON.

45. *Cotton Pickers*, n.d., folder "Agriculture, Field Work," PRISON; *Cotton picking*, n.d., folder "Agriculture, Crops," PRISON; *Cotton Sacks*, n.d., folder "Agriculture, Field Work," PRISON; *Picking Cotton 65*, 1965, folder "Agriculture," PRISON; *Untitled 2*, n.d., folder "Wardens, McGill," PRISON; *Plow*, n.d., folder "Agriculture, Crops," PRISON.

46. *Officer on a Horse, Garden 1*, n.d., folder "Units Old, Clemens," BK 96 Clemens 1971–1973, PRISON; *Cabbage Convicts*, n.d., folder "Agriculture," PRISON.

47. John Adams, *Damming the Colorado: The Rise of the Lower Colorado River Authority, 1933–1939* (College Station: Texas A&M University Press, 1990); Richard White, *The Organic Machine: The Remaking of the Columbia River* (New York: Macmillan, 1996); Katrine Barber, *Death of Celilo Falls* (Seattle: University of Washington Press, 2005); Roberta Ulrich, *Empty Nets: Indians, Dams, and the Columbia River* (Corvallis: Oregon State University Press, 1999); Mark Fiege, *Irrigated Eden: The Making of an Agricultural Landscape in the American West* (Seattle: University of Washington Press, 1999); Robert Kelly Schneiders, *Big Sky Rivers: The Yellowstone and Upper Missouri* (Lawrence: University of Kansas Press, 2003); Robert Kelly Schneiders, *Unruly River: Two Centuries of Change Along the Missouri* (Lawrence: University of Kansas Press, 1999); William Lang and Robert Carriker, eds., *Great River of the West: Essays on the Columbia River* (Seattle: University of Washington Press, 1999); James Aton and Robert McPherson, *River Flowing from the Sunrise: An Environmental History of the Lower San Juan* (Logan: Utah State University Press, 2000); Philip Fradkin, *A River No More: the Colorado River and the West* (New York: Knopf, 1981); Douglas Littlefield, *Conflict on the Rio Grande: Water and the Law, 1879–1939* (Norman: University of Oklahoma Press, 2009); Fred Phillips, *Reining in the Rio Grande:*

People, Land, and Water (Albuquerque: University of New Mexico Press, 2011); Marc Reisner, *Cadillac Desert: The American West and Its Disappearing Water* (New York: Penguin, 1993); Paul Horgan, *Great River: The Rio Grande in North American History* (Middleton, CT: Wesleyan University Press, 1991); Evan Ward, *Border Oasis: Water and the Political Ecology of the Colorado River Delta, 1940–1975* (Tucson: University of Arizona Press, 2003); William deBuys, *Salt Dreams: Land and Water in Low-Down California* (Albuquerque: University of New Mexico Press, 1999); Peter Carrells, *Uphill against Water: The Great Dakota Water War* (Omaha: University of Nebraska Press, 1999); Jeffrey Stine, *Mixing the Waters: Environment, Politics, and the Building of the Tennessee-Tombigbee Waterway* (Akron, OH: University of Akron Press, 1993); G. Emlen Hall, *High and Dry: The Texas–New Mexico Struggle for the Pecos River* (Albuquerque: University of New Mexico Press, 2002); David Billington and D. C. Jackson, *Big Dams of the New Deal Era: A Confluence of Engineering and Politics* (Norman: University of Oklahoma Press, 2006); David Billington, D. C. Jackson, and Martin Melosi, *The History of Large Federal Dams: Planning, Design, and Construction in the Era of Big Dams* (Washington D.C.: Government Printing Office, 2005); Donald Worster, *Rivers of Empire: Water, Aridity, and the Growth of the American West* (New York: Oxford University Press, 1992).

48. Elliott West, *The Contested Plains: Indians, Goldseekers, and the Rush to Colorado* (Lawrence: University Press of Kansas, 1998); Sucheng Chan, *This Bittersweet Soil: The Chinese in California Agriculture, 1860–1910* (Berkeley: University of California Press, 1989); William Goetzmann, *Exploration and Empire: The Explorer and Scientist in the Winning of the American West* (New York: Knopf, 1966); Ramon Gutierrez, *When Jesus Came, the Corn Mothers Went Away: Marriage, Sexuality, and Power in New Mexico, 1500–1846* (Stanford, CA: Stanford University Press, 1991); Patricia Limerick, *The Legacy of Conquest: The Unbroken Past of the American West* (New York: Norton, 1987); Rodman Paul, *Mining Frontiers of the Far West, 1848–1880* (New York: Holt, Rinehart, and Winston, 1963); Elmer Sandmeyer, *The Anti-Chinese Movement in California* (Champaign: University of Illinois Press, 1991); Patricia Limerick, *Trails: Toward a New Western History* (Lawrence: University Press of Kansas, 1991); William Cronon, *Nature's Metropolis* (New York: Norton, 1992); Reisner, *Cadillac Desert*.

49. C. C. Augur to Colonel R. S. Mackenzie, September 30, 1873, in Ranald S. Mackenzie, *Ranald S. Mackenzie's Official Correspondence Relating to Texas, 1873–1879* (Lubbock: West Texas Museum Association, 1968); C. C. Augur to Assistant Adjutant General, September 30, 1873, in Mackenzie, *Official Correspondence*; Scott Zesch, *The Captured: A True Story of Abduction by Indians on the Texas Frontier* (New York: Macmillan, 2005).

50. Tom Mauchahty-Ware, "Brazos River Song," *Sunrise*, 1989, Tandem Music Group.

51. Henry Van Dyke, "Texas: A Democratic Ode, Part 1: Wild Bees," *Poetry Journal* 1, no. 4 (1913), 153.

52. Edgar Rice Burroughs, "The Roughneck," *Boston Globe*, August 11, 1922, www.newspaperarchive.com; Zane Grey, "Twin Sombreros," *San Antonio*

Express, April 23, 1940; Zane Grey, "Twin Sombreros," *San Antonio Express*, February 15, 1940, www.newspaperarchive.com; Zane Grey, "Twin Sombreros," *San Antonio Express*, February 5, 1940, www.newspaperarchive.com.

53. Captain Mayne Reid, *The Death Shot: A Romance of Forest and Prairie* (London: Chapman and Hall, 1873); Captain Mayne Reid, *The Man-Eaters and Other Odd People: A Popular Description of Singular Races of Man* (New York: Routledge, 1860); Captain Mayne Reid, *The Boy Hunters; or, Adventures in Search of a White Buffalo* (Boston, MA: Ticknor and Fields, 1853); Albert Pike, *Gen. Albert Pike's Poems with Introductory Sketch* (Little Rock, AR: A. W. Allsopp, 1900), 531.

54. Larry McMurtry, *Lonesome Dove: A Novel* (New York: Simon and Schuster, 1985); Larry McMurtry, *Comanche Moon: A Novel* (New York: Simon and Schuster, 1993); Larry McMurtry, *Dead Man's Walk: A Novel* (New York: Simon and Schuster, 1995); Larry McMurty, *Buffalo Girls: A Novel* (New York: Simon and Schuster, 1990); Larry McMurty, *Horseman, Pass By* (New York: Penguin, 1961); Larry McMurtry, *Folly and Glory*, The Berrybender Narratives no. 4 (New York: Simon and Schuster, 2001); E. Roy Hector, *Escape from Hell's Corner* (Bloomington, ID: iUniverse, 2003); E. Roy Hector, *Brazos River Marauders* (Bloomington, Indiana: iUniverse, 2007); Cormac McCarthy, *Blood Meridian, or, The Evening Redness in the West* (New York: Random House, 1985); Lucia St. Clair Robson, *Ride the Wind* (New York: Ballantine, 1985); Steve Wilson, *The Spider Rock Treasure: A Texas Mystery of Lost Spanish Gold* (Austin, TX: Eakin Press, 2004); Lester Galbreath, *Campfire Tales: True Stories from the Western Frontier* (Houston, TX: Bright Sky Press, 2005); Robert Ervin Howard and Rusty Burke, *The End of the Trail: Western Stories* (Lincoln: University of Nebraska Press, 2005); Caroline Clemmons, *Brazos Bride* (CreateSpace Independent Publishing Platform, 2012); Tom Meinecke, *Arms of God: From Prussia to Texas to Death in the Brazos River* (Bloomington, ID: Author House, 2010); Tom Sheehan, "Fair Exchange," in Rope and Wire, "Rope and Wire: A Western Lifestyle Online Community," Rope and Wire (hereinafter ROPE), http://www.ropeandwire.com/index.html; Tom Sheehan, "High Stakes Teacher," in ROPE, http://www.ropeandwire.com/index.html; Jack Sheriff, *Brazos Guns* (Yorkshire, UK: Dales Large Print Books, 1998).

55. Charles Reaugh, *Crossing the Brazos*, Fine Arts of Texas (hereinafter FINE ARTS), http://texaspaintings.com/frank_reaugh.htm; Charles Reaugh, *Cattle in the Brazos*, FINE ARTS, http://www.frankreaugh.com/html/frank_reaugh_gallery_12.html; Frank Reaugh, *Scene on the Brazos*, Dallas Public Library, "Texas/Dallas History & Archives Division," http://dallaslibrary2.org/texas/exhibits.htm#online.

56. Fisher County Art Society, [*Mural, Rotan, Texas*], 2007, in Jim Watson, "Brazos River Canyonlands" (hereinafter BRC), http://brazosrivercanyonlands.com/photography/scottBourland/071107037.html; Jim Clements, *Break at the Brazos*, Fine Art America (hereinafter FAA), http://fineartamerica.com/featured/break-at-the-brazos-jim-clements.html.

57. L. O. Griffith, *Whitetop Field, West Texas*, 1900, BRC, http://brazosrivercanyonlands.com/art/louisGriffith/11017.html; L. O. Griffith,

Seymour, Texas, BRC, http://brazosrivercanyonlands.com/
art/louisGriffith/14042.html; L. O. Griffith, *Valley View*, 1909, BRC, http://
brazosrivercanyonlands.com/art/louisGriffith/14044.html; Josephine Oliver,
[*Untitled*], 1932, BRC, http://brazosrivercanyonlands.com/art/
josephineOliver/13792.html; L.O. Griffith, [*Untitled*], 1900, BRC, http://
brazosrivercanyonlands.com/art/louisGriffith/11232.html; Amy Winton,
Sunflower Sea, 2007, BRC, http://brazosrivercanyonlands.com/art/
amyWinton/sunflowerSea.html; Laura Lewis, [*Untitled—Double Mountain
Fork 1*], 2008, in Laura Lewis, "Laura Lewis Professional Artist (This is my
Blog)" (hereinafter LEWIS), http://lauralynnlewis.blogspot.com; Laura Lewis,
[*Untitled—Double Mountain Fork 2*], 2008, in LEWIS, http://lauralynnlewis.
blogspot.com; Amy Winton, *Blanco Canyonscape*, in Dan Flores and Amy
Winton, *Canyon Visions: Photographs and Pastels of the Texas Plains*
(Lubbock: Texas Tech University Press, 1989), 27.

    58. Jim Watson, *Dramatic Hues Color an Iconic Sunset Viewed from
Impossible Canyon*, 2007, BRC, http://brazosrivercanyonlands.com/
photography/jimWatson/071207046.html; Scott Bourland, *Canyon Walls and
Gently Rolling Hills Hiding below the Uniform Horizon of Tablelands*,
2007, BRC, http://brazosrivercanyonlands.com/photography/
scottBourland/071106021.html; Scott Bourland, *Panorama of Western
Horizon Viewed from Impossible Canyon*, 2007, BRC, http://
brazosrivercanyonlands.com/photography/scottBourland/071106100–104.
html; Scott Bourland, *Panoramic View of Longhorn Valley*, 2007, BRC, http://
brazosrivercanyonlands.com/photography/scottBourland/071107311–313.
html; Forrest Armke, *Aerial View of the Double Mountain from Gyp Springs
Ranch*, 2008, BRC, http://brazosrivercanyonlands.com/photography/
forrestArmke/080117018.html; Forrest Armke, *Aerial View of a Large Playa
on Gyp Springs Ranch*, 2008, BRC, http://brazosrivercanyonlands.com/
photography/forrestArmke/080117040.html; Forrest Armke, *Shallow Creek
Glistens in Late Afternoon Sun along a Gully in Impossible Canyon*,
2008, BRC, http://brazosrivercanyonlands.com/photography/
forrestArmke/080117240.html.

    59. Scott Bourland, *View of the Double Mountain Fork of the Brazos
River [1]*, 2007, BRC, http://brazosrivercanyonlands.com/photography/
scottBourland/071107072.html; Scott Bourland, *View of the Double Mountain
Fork of the Brazos River [2]*, 2007, BRC, http://brazosrivercanyonlands.com/
photography/scottBourland/071107075.html; Scott Bourland, *View of the
Double Mountain Fork of the Brazos River [3]*, 2007, BRC, http://
brazosrivercanyonlands.com/photography/scottBourland/071107092.html;
Scott Bourland, *View of the Double Mountain Fork of the Brazos River [4]*,
2007, BRC, http://brazosrivercanyonlands.com/photography/
scottBourland/071107093.html; Scott Bourland, *Cattails along the River Bed
of the Double Mountain Fork of the Brazos River*, 2007, BRC, http://
brazosrivercanyonlands.com/photography/scottBourland/071107099.html;
Scott Bourland, *Wildlife Tracks on the River Bed of the Double Mountain
Fork of the Brazos River*," 2007, BRC, http://brazosrivercanyonlands.com/
photography/scottBourland/071107103.html; Scott Bourland, *View from the*

River Bed of the Double Mountain Fork of the Brazos River," 2007, BRC, http://brazosrivercanyonlands.com/photography/scottBourland/071107109. html; Scott Bourland, *Color Variations in the Soil along the River Bed of the Double Mountain Fork of the Brazos River*, 2007, BRC, http:// brazosrivercanyonlands.com/photography/scottBourland/071107114.html; Scott Bourland, *Clear, Shallow Waters along the Double Mountain Fork of the Brazos River*, 2007, in BRC, http://brazosrivercanyonlands.com/photography/ scottBourland/071107114.html; Forrest Armke, *A Winding Gulch on Gyp Springs Ranch*, 2008, BRC, http://brazosrivercanyonlands.com/photography/ forrestArmke/080117063.html.

60. Dan Flores, *Blanco Canyon Autumn*, in Flores and Winton, *Canyon Visions*, 68; Dan Flores, *Fluvanna Overlook*, in Flores and Winton, *Canyon Visions*, 90; Amy Winton, *Double Mountain Fork Afternoon*, in Flores and Winton, *Canyon Visions*, 91.

61. Dan Flores, *Storm over Turkey Mesa*, in Flores and Winton, *Canyon Visions*, 6; Dan Flores, *Falling Mesas Sunset*, in Flores and Winton, *Canyon Visions*, 76; Dan Flores, *Venus Rising*, in Flores and Winton, *Canyon Visions*, 104; Dan Flores, *The Morning the Sky Was on Fire*, in Flores and Winton, *Canyon Visions*, 105.

62. Dan Flores, *Blanco Mounds*, in Flores and Winton, *Canyon Visions*, 38.

63. Dan Flores, *Mount Blanco*, in Flores and Winton, *Canyon Visions*, 26.

64. Ibid.

65. Stephanie Chambers, *Purple Stem of a Prickly Pear Hides in a Bed of Dormant Grass Blades*, 2008, BRC, http://brazosrivercanyonlands.com/ photography/stephanieChambers/080117473.html; Scott Bourland, *Lofty Red Cliffs Shadow Big Rough Creek*, 2007, BRC, http://brazosrivercanyonlands. com/photography/scottBourland/071106003.html; Scott Bourland, *A Towering Hoodoo along Big Rough Creek*, 2007, BRC, http://brazosrivercanyonlands.com/ photography/scottBourland/071106012.html; Scott Bourland, *Mesquites, Cedars and Tall Grasses Covering the Canyon Floor along Big Rough Creek*, 2007, BRC, http://brazosrivercanyonlands.com/photography/ scottBourland/071106015.html; Scott Bourland, *Escarpments in Impossible Canyon*, 2007, BRC, http://brazosrivercanyonlands.com/photography/ scottBourland/071106037.html; Scott Bourland, *Blooming Cholla from Impossible Canyon*, 2007, BRC, http://brazosrivercanyonlands. com/photography/scottBourland/071106070.html; Scott Bourland, *Rugged Escarpment Plunges into Impossible Canyon*, 2007, BRC, http:// brazosrivercanyonlands.com/photography/scottBourland/071106084.html; Scott Bourland, *Typical Canyonlands Landscape Form Abraded by Wind and Water Erosion in Impossible Canyon*, 2007, in BRC, http:// brazosrivercanyonlands.com/photography/scottBourland/071106117.html; Scott Bourland, *Grasses along a Canyon Ridge Trail with Mesquite Trees in the Background*, 2007, BRC, http://brazosrivercanyonlands.com/photography/ scottBourland/071106091.html; Scott Bourland, *Detail of a Small Shallow Gulley in Impossible Canyon*, 2007, BRC, http://brazosrivercanyonlands.com/ photography/scottBourland/071106112.html; Scott Bourland, *Rugged Topography in Impossible Canyon Evoke Images of a Rough and Rutted*

Badland, 2007, BRC, http://brazosrivercanyonlands.com/photography/ scottBourland/071106115.html; Scott Bourland, *View of a Water and Wind Sculpted Draw at the Headwater of Impossible Canyon*, 2007, BRC, http:// brazosrivercanyonlands.com/photography/scottBourland/071106120.html; Scott Bourland, *Gnarled Trunk of Weathered Lifeless Mesquite Tree*, 2007, BRC, http://brazosrivercanyonlands.com/photography/ scottBourland/071107179.html; Forrest Armke, *Weather-Beaten Mesa on Gyp Springs Ranch Strikes a Dramatic Pose Against a Backdrop of Vast Tablelands and Rugged Cliffs*, 2008, BRC, http://brazosrivercanyonlands.com/ photography/forrestArmke/080117055.html; Forrest Armke, *Colorful and Rugged Terrain of a Tableland Mesa Provides an Archetypal Image of a Western Badland*, 2008, BRC, http://brazosrivercanyonlands.com/ photography/forrestArmke/080117058.html.

66. Scott Bourland, *Golden Crownbeard (Verbesina encelioides) Basks in the Morning Sun on the Banks of the Double Mountain Fork of the Brazos River*, 2007, BRC, http://brazosrivercanyonlands.com/photography/ scottBourland/071107121.html; Scott Bourland, *Blue Stem Illuminated by Morning Light*, 2007, BRC, http://brazosrivercanyonlands.com/photography/ scottBourland/071106058.html; Scott Bourland, *Opuntia spinosbacca (Spiny-Fruited Prickly Pear)*, 2007, BRC, http://brazosrivercanyonlands.com/ photography/scottBourland/071106077.html; Scott Bourland, *Shoots from a Yucca Plant form a Starburst Pattern in Impossible Canyon*, 2007, BRC, http://brazosrivercanyonlands.com/photography/scottBourland/071106109. html; Scott Bourland, *Late Autumn Foliage along the Banks of a Canyon-Fed Creek that Flows into the Double Mountain Fork of the Brazos River in Longhorn Valley*, 2007, BRC, http://brazosrivercanyonlands.com/ photography/scottBourland/071107249.html; Forrest Armke, *Thickets of Dormant Mesquites Look like Islands in a Sea of Grasslands*, 2008, BRC, http://brazosrivercanyonlands.com/photography/forrestArmke/080117187. html; Forrest Armke, *Evergreen Cedars and Tow-Colored Grasses Swirling in the Wind*, 2008, BRC, http://brazosrivercanyonlands.com/photography/ forrestArmke/080117273.html; Bourland, *Mesquites, Cedars and Tall Grasses Covering the Canyon Floor along Big Rough Creek*; Bourland, *Grasses along a Canyon Ridge Trail with Mesquite Trees in the Background*; Bourland, *Blooming Cholla from Impossible Canyon*; Chambers, *Purple Stem of a Prickly Pear Hides in a Bed of Dormant Grass Blades*.

67. Dan Flores, *Juniper and Moon and Sky*, in Flores and Winton, *Canyon Visions*, 42.

68. Dan Flores, *Sensitive Briar Blooms*, in Flores and Winton, *Canyon Visions*, 50.

69. Dan Flores, *Dance of the Chollas*, in Flores and Winton, *Canyon Visions*, 54.

70. Dan Flores, *Late October Cottonwoods*, in Flores and Winton, *Canyon Visions*, 82; Dan Flores, *Double Mountain Badlands*, in Flores and Winton, *Canyon Visions*, 58; Dan Flores, *Yellow House Moonrise*, in Flores and Winton, *Canyon Visions*, 98.

71. Scott Lennox, "What the River Taught Me," in Scott Lenox, LENNOX, http://www.scottlennoxart.com/Text_page.cfm?pID=3686.

72. Ibid.

73. John Graves, *Goodbye to a River: A Narrative* (New York: Knopf, 1960).

74. Ibid., 159.

75. Paul Christensen, *West of the American Dream: An Encounter with Texas* (College Station: Texas A&M Press, 2001), 39.

76. Ibid.

77. Rattlesnake Annie, "Goodbye to a River," *Rattlesnakes and Rusty Water,* 1980, Rattlesnake Records.

78. Kathleen Hudson, *Women in Texas Music: Stories and Songs* (Austin: University of Texas Press, 2007).

79. Gov't Mule, "Broke Down on the Brazos," *By a Thread,* 2009, Evilive; Hank Thompson and the Brazos Valley Boys, *Song of the Brazos Valley,* 1996, EMI Special Products; Dub Miller, "Livin' on Lonestar Time," 2001; Lyle Lovett, "Walk Through the Bottomland," *Pontiac,* 1988, Curb; Lyle Lovett and Robert Earl Keen, "Front Porch Song," *The Party Never Ends,* 2003, SUGAR HILL; Roger McGuinn, "The Brazos River," *Treasures from the Folk Den,* 2001, Appleseed; Lovett, "Texas River Song"; Hiatt, *The River Knows Your Name*; David G. Dodd, *The Complete Annotated Grateful Dead Lyrics: The Collected Lyrics of Robert Hunter and John Barlow* (New York: Simon and Schuster, 2005), 22. The updated lyrics say, "Don't ease, don't ease . . . Don't ease me in. . . . I've been all night long coming home. . . . Don't ease me in"; the original lyrics say, "Don't ease, don't ease . . . Don't ease me in. . . . It's a long night, Cunningham. . . . Don't ease me in." Cunningham was reportedly a well-known businessman who lived along the Brazos River during the early twentieth century and leased convicts to work on his sugar plantations.

80. John Nugent, "Brazos River Boogie," *John Nugent,* 1992, Jazz Inspiration; Brian Marshall, "Brazos River Special," *Polish Standard Time,* 1999, Marszalek Recordings; "The Brazos River Trail," *Red River,* 2005, Naxos; Stephen Daniel Wood, *Sunset on Brazos Bend,* 2008, Stephen Daniel Wood.

81. The Crusaders, "Brazos River Breakdown," *Live in Japan,* 2004, GRP Records; Nils Landgren, "Brazos River Breakdown," *Licence to Funk,* 2007, ACT Music; Chuck Pinnell, "Brazos," *Twelve Rivers,* 2000, Mad Moon Records.

82. Hank Snow, "Cross the Brazos at Waco," *YouTube* video, 2:08, March 28, 2011, http://www.youtube.com/watch?v=vSoBbhf-zsI; Gene Stuart, "Cross the Brazos at Waco," n.d.; Old Dog Revival, "Cross the Brazos at Waco," n.d.; ZZ Top, "Chevrolet," *Rio Grande Mud,* 2007, Rhino/Warner Bros.; Billy Walker, "Cross the Brazos at Waco," *YouTube* video, 2:52, June 12, 2010, http://www.youtube.com/watch?v=fo95mPRcfds; Whiskeyboat, "The Brazos River Turnaround," *The Congress Hotel,* 2009, Whiskeyboat.

Chapter Three

1. "Following Disastrous Floods: Alarming Reports of Losses of Life in the Brasos Valley, Texas," *Naugatuck Daily News,* July 5, 1899, www.

newspaperarchive.com; "Following Disastrous Floods: Alarming Reports of Losses of Life in the Brasos Valley, Texas," *Lebanon Daily News*, July 6, 1899, www.newspaperarchive.com; John Henry Brown, *History of Texas from 1685 to 1892* (St. Louis, MO: L. E. Daniell, 1893), 530.

2. John Washington Lockhart, "Boating on the Brazos: First Trip of the 'Mustang' to Washington—A Regular Packet Line Afterward—The Terrible Overflow of 1842—Interesting Reminiscences," *Galveston Daily News*, February 12, 1893, in John Washington Lockhart, *Sixty Years on the Brazos: The Life and Letters of Dr. John Washington Lockhart, 1824–1900* (Ann Arbor, MI: Argonaut Press, 1930), 82.

3. Andrew Forest Muir, *Texas in 1837: An Anonymous, Contemporary Narrative* (Austin: University of Texas Press, 1958), 65; Robert Hancock, *Narrative of Robert Hancock Hunter, 1813–1902: From His Arrival in Texas, 1822, through the Battle of San Jacinto, 1836* (Austin, TX: Cook, 1936), 11–12; De Witt Clinton Baker, ed., *A Texas Scrap-Book: Made Up of the History, Biography, and Miscellany of Texas and its People* (New York: A. S. Barnes, 1875), 53, 193; Fisk, *A Visit to Texas: being the journal of a traveller through those parts most interesting to American settlers. With descriptions of scenery, habits, &c. &c.* (New York: Goodrich & Wiley, 1834), 30; Zebulon M. Pike, *Exploratory Travels through the Western Territories of North America* (London: Longman, 1811), 320; "Diary of Isaac Parks," September 1, 1861–June 9, 1877, box 2B13, folder 1: "Diary, 1861–1877," Isaac Parks Papers (hereinafter PARKS), TXBU; J. Minter to F. M. Willington, November 14, 1848, box 2B220, folder "Waco Village: Correspondence: 1848," Waco Village Papers, TXBU; "Late and Interesting from Texas," *Experiment*, March 29, 1843, www.newspaperarchive.com; "Latest Details from the Flood," *Galveston Daily News*, July 3, 1899, www.newspaperarchive.com; "Reports from the Rivers," *Galveston Daily News*, September 29, 1900, www.newspaperarchive.com; "Texas Much Poorer in Money, but Not in Life—Revised Reports Indicate that Most of Lower Brazos Flood Sufferers Are Safe," *World*, July 7, 1899, www.newspaperarchive.com; "The Distress is Great," *Titusville Herald*, July 7, 1899, www.newspaperarchive.com; "Relief for Flood Sufferers," *Times Democrat*, July 10, 1899, www.newspaperarchive.com; "Cotton Crops Destroyed," *Times Democrat*, July 10, 1899, www.newspaperarchive.com; "Many Lives are Lost," *Algona Republican*, July 12, 1899, www. newspaperarchive.com; "Brazos is five miles wide," *Le Mars Semi-Weekly Sentinel*, July 6, 1899, www.newspaperarchive.com; "Horrors of the Texas Floods," *Statesville Landmark*, July 11, 1899, www.newspaperarchive.com; "By Rising Water," *Sandusky Star*, July 5, 1899, www.newspaperarchive.com; "The Brazos Floods," *San Antonio Daily Light*, July 26, 1899, www. newspaperarchive.com; "1,000 Destitute," *San Antonio Daily Light*, July 7, 1899, www.newspaperarchive.com; "Heart Rending is the Situation in the Flood Stricken country," *San Antonio Daily Light*, July 7, 1899, www. newspaperarchive.com; "Brazos Flood Now Receding," *San Antonio Daily Express*, July 8, 1899, www.newspaperarchive.com; "News from Austin," *San Antonio Daily Express*, August 4, 1899, www.newspaperarchive.com; "Need Food," *Salt Lake Tribune*, July 10, 1899, www.newspaperarchive.com;

"Many Lives are Lost," *Salt Lake Tribune*, July 6, 1889, www. newspaperarchive.com; "Two Hundred are Reported Dead," *Perry Advertiser*, July 7, 1899, www.newspaperarchive.com; "Terrible Flood in Texas," *New York Herald*, July 22, 1869, www.newspaperarchive.com; "The Lamentable Flood in Texas," *New York Herald*, July 23, 1869, www.newspaperarchive.com; "The News—Condensed," *Mauston Star*, September 12, 1860, www. newspaperarchive.com; "Latest News," *Milwaukee Daily Sentinel*, September 4, 1860, www.newspaperarchive.com; "The Worst is Over," *Iola Daily Register*, July 7, 1899, www.newspaperarchive.com; "Glorious News," *Huron Reflector*, May 24, 1836, www.newspaperarchive.com; Letter to J. R. Dunn, in *Star and Republican Banner*, May 23, 1836, www.newspaperarchive.com; "Miles of Floods in Texas," *Herald*, July 8, 1899, www.newspaperarchive.com; "Rainy Season in the West," *Hagerstown Mail*, July 16, 1869, www.newspaperarchive. com; "Bad Tidings Continue," *Galveston Daily News*, September 22, 1875, www.newspaperarchive.com; "Commercial," *Galveston Daily News*, May 20, 1866, www.newspaperarchive.com; "Letter from Houston," *Galveston Daily News*, May 15, 1866, www.newspaperarchive.com; "Governor Sayers' Work," *Galveston Daily News*, July 10, 1899, www.newspaperarchive.com; "Return of Life Savers," *Galveston Daily News*, July 11, 1899, www.newspaperarchive. com; "Detroit, Tex., Sent Supplies," *Galveston Daily News*, July 19, 1899, www. newspaperarchive.com; "Too Much for Local Charity," *Galveston Daily News*, July 10, 1899, www.newspaperarchive.com; "Alto Sent Food and Seed," *Galveston Daily News*, July 10, 1899, www.newspaperarchive.com; "Damaged Crop Estimates," *Galveston Daily News*, July 11, 1899, www. newspaperarchive.com; "He Was Surprised at the Lack of Diversification," *Galveston Daily News*, July 25, 1899, www.newspaperarchive.com; "The Water at Allen Farm," *Galveston Daily News*, July 11, 1899, www. newspaperarchive.com; "The Overflow," *Galveston Daily News*, July 20, 1869, www.newspaperarchive.com; "Flood Over at Bryan," *Galveston Daily News*, July 10, 1899, www.newspaperarchive.com; "Meeting at Calvert," *Galveston Daily News*, July 10, 1899, www.newspaperarchive.com; "Water Subsiding," *Galveston Daily News*, July 9, 1899, www.newspaperarchive.com; "400 Persons May Be Drowned in Texas," *World*, July 5, 1899, www.newspaperarchive.com; "Texas Flood Fakes," *Logansport Pharos*, July 7, 1899, www.newspaperarchive. com; "During the Brazos Flood," *Marshfield Times*, September 15, 1899, www. newspaperarchive.com; "During the Brazos Flood," *Postville Review*, September 15, 1899, www.newspaperarchive.com; "Flood in Brazoria County," *Galveston Daily News*, July 9, 1899, www.newspaperarchive.com; "Many are Drowned," *Racine Daily Journal*, July 5, 1899, www.newspaperarchive.com; "Many are Starving," *Renwick Times*, July 14, 1899, www.newspaperarchive. com; "Help is Needed Now," *Galveston Daily News*, July 8, 1899, www. newspaperarchive.com; "Resume of Losses from the Brazos Valley Flood," *Galveston Daily News*, July 30, 1899, www.newspaperarchive.com; "Floods in Texas," *Galveston Daily News*, July 5, 1876, www.newspaperarchive.com; "The Floods Receding," *Galveston Daily News*, April 30, 1891, www. newspaperarchive.com; "Telegraphic Summary," *Weekly Wisconsin*, July 21, 1869, www.newspaperarchive.com; "Loss is Ten Millions," *Daily Iowa Capital*,

July 8, 1899, www.newspaperarchive.com; "At Danger Point Remain the Swirling Waters in Stricken Texas," *Daily Herald,* July 6, 1899, www. newspaperarchive.com; "Damage on the Increase Instead of Growing Less," *Kane Daily Republican,* July 7, 1899, www.newspaperarchive.com; "Aftermath," *Lima Daily News,* July 7, 1899, www.newspaperarchive.com; "Loss of Life Exaggerated," *New Era,* July 12, 1899, www.newspaperarchive.com; "General Telegraphic News," *New York Times,* September 4, 1860, www. newspaperarchive.com; "Disastrous Floods: Alarming Reports of Losses of Life in the Brasos Valley, Texas," *Naugatuck Daily News,* July 5, 1899, www. newspaperarchive.com; "Texas Towns in Peril," *News,* July 5, 1899, www. newspaperarchive.com; "Plans for Relief," *San Antonio Daily Express,* July 11, 1899, www.newspaperarchive.com; "The Floods in Texas: Alarming Reports Come from the Brasos River Bottoms," *News,* July 6, 1899, www. newspaperarchive.com; "Dispatches by Telegraph," *Daily Sanduskian,* May 14, 1851, www.newspaperarchive.com; Brown, *History of Texas,* 8–9, 531; "Following Disastrous Floods: Alarming Reports of Losses of Life in the Brasos Valley, Texas," *Naugatuck Daily News;* "Following Disastrous Floods: Alarming Reports of Losses of Life in the Brasos Valley, Texas," *Lebanon Daily News.*

4.   Excerpt from *Matagorda Gazette,* May 28, 1859, 2, c. 1, MS 17, Andrew Forest Muir Papers (hereinafter MUIR), Woodson Research Center (hereinafter WRC), Fondren Library, Rice University (Houston, TX) (hereinafter RICE); "Floods in Texas" (quotation).

5.   William Warren Rogers, ed., "'I am Tired Writing'": A Georgia Farmer Reports on Texas in 1871," *Southwestern Historical Quarterly* (hereinafter *SHQ*) 87, no. 2 (October 1983), 187; William Pool, "Westward I Go Free: The Memoirs of William E. Cureton, Texas Frontiersman," *SHQ* 81, no. 2 (October 1977), 172; Henry J. Caufield to Watson Caufield, September 25, 1860, box 2B384, folder 2 "Correspondence, 1858–1861, 1871–1872, 1888" (hereinafter FOLDER 1858), Caufield Family Papers (hereinafter CAUFIELD), TXBU; "Later from Texas," *New York Daily Times,* April 14, 1853, www. newspaperarchive.com; "News," *Sheboygan Journal,* August 6, 1857, www. newspaperarchive.com; Henry J. Caufield to Watson Caufield, July 8, 1855, box 2B384, folder 1 "Correspondence, 1847–1857" (hereinafter FOLDER 1847), CAUFIELD, TXBU; Henry J. Caufield to Lizzie Caufield, December 8, 1855, box 2B384, FOLDER 1847, CAUFIELD, TXBU; Mary Jane Caufield to Watson Caufield, July 29, 1859, box 2B384, FOLDER 1858, CAUFIELD, TXBU; M. J. Caufield to Watson Caufield, July 17, 1855, box 2B384, FOLDER 1847, CAUFIELD, TXBU; Wat Caufield to his father, June 29, 1857, box 2B384, FOLDER 1847, CAUFIELD, TXBU; Henry J. Caufieldto Wat Caufield, April 25, 1859, box 2B384, FOLDER 1858, CAUFIELD, TXBU; Henry J. Caufield to Watson Caufield, July 15, 1859, box 2B384, FOLDER 1858, CAUFIELD, TXBU; Letter to "cousin," March 4, 1888, box 2B332, folder 6: "Personal Papers: Correspondence, 1886–1891" (hereinafter FOLDER 1886), GRAVES, TXBU; Isaac Parks to John Crittenden, January 6, 1858, box 2B13, folder 2 "Correspondence, 1858–1877" (hereinafter FOLDER 1877), PARKS, TXBU; L. S. Rossletter to Victor Rose, September 23, 1880, box 2B383, folder 3 "Correspondence, 1870–March 1881," Ross Family Papers, TXBU;

R. Hedspeth to Adaline Earle, November 1, 1884, box 2B332, folder 5 "Personal Papers: Correspondence, 1874–1885," Graves-Earle Family Papers, 1848–1963 (hereinafter GRAVES), TXBU; "Diary of Isaac Parks"; Isaac Parks to Caroline Crittenden, December 23, 1862, box 2B13, FOLDER 1877, PARKS, TXBU; Josephine Parks to Isaac Parks, September 24, 1876, box 2B13, FOLDER 1877, PARKS, TXBU; U. Bet., "Waco Correspondence," *Galveston Daily News*, August 18, 1874, www.newspaperarchive.com; Lockhart, "Boating on the Brazos," 82.

6.   Lockhart, "Boating on the Brazos," 82.

7.   Ibid.; Henry J. Caufield to Watson Caufield, July 8, 1855; Henry J. Caufield to Lizzie Caufield, December 8, 1855; Mary Jane Caufield to Watson Caufield, July 29, 1859; M. J. Caufield to Watson Caufield, July 17, 1855; Wat Caufield to his father, June 29, 1857; Henry J. Caufield to Wat Caufield, April 25, 1859; Henry J. Caufield, Watson Caufield, July 15, 1859; R. Hedspeth to Adaline Earle, November 1, 1884; "Diary of Isaac Parks"; Letter to "cousin," March 4, 1888; Isaac Parks to John Crittenden, January 6, 1858; Isaac Parks to Caroline Crittenden, December 23, 1862; Josephine Parks to Isaac Parks, September 24, 1876; L. S. Ross to Victor Rose, September 23, 1880.

8.   U. Bet, "Waco Correspondence."

9.   Ronald E. Shaw, *Erie Water West: A History of the Erie Canal, 1792–1854* (Lexington: University Press of Kentucky, 1990); Peter L. Bernstein, *Wedding of the Waters: The Erie Canal and the Making of a Great Nation* (New York: Norton , 2006); Carol Sheriff, *The Artificial River: The Erie Canal and the Paradox of Progress, 1817–1862* (New York: Macmillan, 1997); Patrick Vincent McGreevy, *Stairway to Empire: Lockport, The Erie Canal, and the Shaping of America* (New York: SUNY Press, 2009); Terry K. Woods, *Ohio's Grand Canal: A Brief History of the Ohio & Erie Canal* (Kent, Ohio: Kent State University Press, 2008); Ronald E. Shaw, *Canals for a Nation: The Canal Era in the United States, 1790–1860* (Lexington: University Press of Kentucky, 1993); Kirkpatrick Sale, *The Fire of His Genius: Robert Fulton and the American Dream* (New York: Simon and Schuster, 2002); John Laurence Busch, *Steam Coffin: Captain Moses Rogers and The Steamship* Savannah *Break the Barrier* (New Canaan, CT: Hodos Historia, 2010); Jack L. Shagena, *Who Really Invented the Steamboat?: Fulton's Clermont Coup; A History of the Steamboat Contributions of William Henry, James Rumsey, John Fitch, Oliver Evans, Nathan Read, Samuel Morey, Robert Fulton, John Stevens, and Others* (Amherst, NY: Humanity Books, 2004).

10.   Thomas G. Bradford, *Texas* (New York: Weeks, Jordan, 1838); Samuel Augustus Mitchell and James H. Young, *A New Map of Texas, with the Contiguous American and Mexican States* (Philadelphia, PA: S. A. Mitchell, 1836); W. Hooker, *Map of the State of Coahuila and Texas* (n.p., ca. 1833), in Mary Austin Holley, *Texas. Observations, historical, geographical and descriptive: in a series of letters, written during a visit to Austin's colony, with a view of a permanent settlement in that country, in the autumn of 1831* (Baltimore, MD: Armstrong & Plaskitt, 1833); John Arrowsmith, *Map of Texas, compiled from surveys recorded in the Land Office of Texas, and other official surveys* (London: John Arrowsmith, 1841).

11. Stephen F. Austin, *Civil Commandant of the colony forming on the Colorado and Brazos Rivers in the province of Texas: Permission is hereby granted to _____ to emigrate and settle in the colony forming by me* (New Orleans, LA: n.p., 1821), in *Texas as Province and Republic, 1795–1845*, reel 19, no. 1082, MICROFILM, ACM.

12. E. Hergesheimer, *Map showing the distribution of the slave population of the southern states of the United States. Compiled from the census of 1860* (Washington, D.C.: Henry S. Graham, 1861), Geography and Map Division, Library of Congress.

13. South Western Immigration Company, *Texas: Her resources and capabilities: Being a description of the state of Texas and the inducements she offers to those seeking homes in a new country* (New York: E. D. Slater, 1881), 14.

14. Charles Cutter, *Cutter's Guide to the City of Waco, Texas* (Waco, TX: n.p., 1894).

15. E. D. Nash to John Adriance, August 25, 1849, box 127, folder "Correspondence 1847–1849," John Adriance Papers, 1832–1903 (hereinafter ADRIANCE), Dolph Briscoe Center for American History, University of Texas at Austin (hereinafter CAH-UT); Col. Henry M. Robert to Chief of Engineers, September 6, 1900, in Brazos River and Valley Improvement Ass'n, *Permanent organization formed at Bryan, Texas, October 12–13, 1915, for the prevention of overflows and promotion of navigation* (Waco, TX: L. S. Henry, 1915), 23; S. M. Williams to Stephen F. Austin, April 22, 1835, in Eugene Barker, ed., *The Austin Papers* (Washington, D.C.: Government Printing Office, 1924–1928), 65; Homer S. Thrall, *A pictorial history of Texas, from the earliest visits of European adventurers, to A.D. 1879: embracing the periods of missions, colonization, the revolution, the republic and the state, also a topographical description of the country* (New York: N. D. Thompson Publishing, 1885), 28; Robert I. Chester to his wife, January 3, 1836, in Malcolm McLean, *Papers concerning Robertson's Colony in Texas, October 15, 1835, through January 14, 1836*, vol. 12 (Arlington: University of Texas at Arlington Press, 1985), 539–40; "The State Press," *Galveston Daily News*, March 1, 1887, www.newspaperarchive.com.

16. A. W. Moore, "A Reconnaissance in Texas in 1846," *SHQ* 30, no. 4 (April 1927); William Fairfax Gray, *From Virginia to Texas, 1835* (Houston, TX: Gray, Dillaye, 1835–1837), [42]; W. B. Dewees, letter, July 16, 1822, in W. B. Dewees, *Letters from an Early Settler of Texas* (Louisville, KY: Morton & Griswold, 1852), 25; Fisk, *Visit to Texas*, 22–23.

17. Robert I. Chester to his wife, January 3, 1836, 539–40.

18. Manuel de Mier y Teran to President Guadalupe Victoria, March 28, 1828, in Manuel de Mier y Teran, *Texas by Teran: The Diary Kept by General Manuel de Mier y Teran on His 1828 Inspection of Texas*, ed. Jack Jackson (Austin: University of Texas Press, 2000), 34; Amos Andrew Parker, *Trip to the West and Texas: Comprising a journey of eight thousand miles, through New-York, Michigan, Illinois, Missouri, Louisiana and Texas, in the autumn and winter of 1834–5. Interspersed with anecdotes, incidents and observations* (Concord, NH: White and Fisher, 1835), 141; J. Burke, *Burke's Texas almanac and immigrant's handbook for 1883, with which is incorporated Hanford's Texas state register* (Houston, TX: J. Burke, 1883), 97; "Wanted," *Galveston*

Daily News, August 7, 1866, www.newspaperarchive.com; "Journey to Austin," *Galveston Daily News*, July 4, 1872, www.newspaperarchive.com; "Blow of Sea," *Boston Daily Globe*, September 10, 1900, www.newspaperarchive.com; William Kennedy, *The Rise, Progress, and Prospects of the Republic of Texas*, vol. 1 (London: R. Hastings, 1841); 72–73; Col. Edward Stiff, *The Texas emigrant: being a narration of the adventures of the author in Texas, and a description of the soil, climate, productions, minerals, towns, bays, harbors, rivers, institutions, and manners and customs* (Cincinnati, OH: George Conclin, 1840; repr.: Waco: Texian Press, 1968), 10; Amy E. Dase, *Hell-Hole on the Brazos: A Historic Resources Study of Central State Farm, Fort Bend County, Texas*, Technical Report Number 70 (Austin, TX: Prewitt and Associates (September 2004), 4; W. B. Dewees, letter, September 6, 1838, in W. B. Dewees, *Letters from an Early Settler of Texas*, 218–19; "Sugar Production in Texas," *Galveston Daily News*, January 1, 1900, www.newspaperarchive.com; Baker, *Texas Scrap-Book*, 53, 456; South Western Immigration Company, *Texas*; Fisk, *Visit to Texas*, 22–23, 26, 71; Henry J. Caufield to Watson Caufield, July 8, 1855; Henry J. Caufield to Lizzie Caufield, December 8, 1855; W. B. Dewees, letter, July 16, 1822, 24–25.

19. Stiff, *Texas Emigrant*, 66.

20. W. N. Bryant, *All About Texas Boiled Down for 25 Cents, As It Was, As It Is! And As It Will Be!* (Dallas, TX: W. N. Bryant, 1879), 6; Sterling C. Robertson to Eldridge B. Robertson, October 23, 1835, in McLean, *Robertson's Colony*, 129–30; W. B. Dewees, letter, July 16, 1822, 24; W. B. Dewees, letter, September 6, 1838, 218–19; Robert I. Chester to his wife, January 3, 1836, in McLean, *Robertson's Colony*, 539; "Brazoria County," *Galveston Daily News*, December 21, 1882, www.newspaperarchive.com.

21. James Decatur Cocke, *Glance at the Currency and Resources Generally of the Republic of Texas* (Houston, TX: Niles & Co. Printers, 1838), 11–12, in *Texas as Province and Republic, 1795–1845*, reel 3, no. 232, Microfilm Collection (hereinafter MICROFILM), Amon Carter Museum (Fort Worth, TX) (hereinafter ACM).

22. Alexander Thomson to William Thomson, September 22, 1833, folder 288, Thomson Family of Texas Papers, 1832–1898, MS 288, WRC, RICE.

23. Alden A. M. Jackson, letter, November 17, 1844, in *Civilian and Galveston Gazette*, December 14, 1844, www.newspaperarchive.com; Mary Austin Holley, letter III from Bolivar, Texas, December 1831, in Mary Austin Holley, *Letters of an Early American Traveler, Mary Austin Holley, Her Life and Her Works, 1784–1846* (Dallas, TX: Southwest Press, 1933), 110.

24. "From Hempstead: Ovation to Hon. Jefferson Davis," *Galveston Daily News*, May 19, 1875, www.newspaperarchive.com.

25. "The Sunny South," *Perry Pilot*, October 29, 1884, www.newspaperarchive.com; United States Census, *Report on cotton production in the United States: also embracing agricultural and physico-geographical description of the several cotton states and of California* (Washington, D.C.: Government Printing Office, 1880); "Statement of Marshall H. D. W. Smith Jr., Assistant Engineer of the Texas and Pacific Railway," in United States Senate,

Committee on Irrigation and Reclamation of Arid Lands, *Report on the Special Committee of the United States Senate on the Irrigation and Reclamation of Arid Lands* (Washington, D.C.: Government Printing Office, 1890), 142; "Journey to Austin."

26. Jacob de Cordova, *The Texas Immigrant and Traveller's Guide Book* (Austin, TX: De Cordova and Frazier, 1856), 16.

27. South Western Immigration Company, *Texas*, 21, 45.

28. M. J. Caufield to Watson Caufield, September 23, 1855, box 2B384, FOLDER 1847, CAUFIELD, TXBU; Eddie L. Carpenter to John Campbell, July 12, 1884, box 1, folder 1.6, MS 329, John Campbell Personal Papers, 1820–1906, WRC; Alexander Thomson to William Thomson, September 22, 1833; Gray, *From Virginia to Texas*, [42]; Burke, *Texas Almanac*, 102; Isaac Parks to Caroline Crittenden, December 23, 1862; R. Hedspeth to Adaline Earle, November 1, 1884.

29. Wm. R. Smith to Dr. Genl., March 11, 1839, GA 21, folder 9, William Ransom Hogan Papers 1934–1946 (hereinafter HOGAN), Special Collections, University of Texas at Arlington (hereinafter SC-UTA) (quotation); *A Memorial and biographical history of McLennan, Falls, Bell and Coryell Counties, Texas* (Chicago, IL: Lewis 1893), 71, 126; Francis White Johnson et al., *A History of Texas and Texans* (Chicago, IL: American Historical Society, 1914); Janet Valenza, *Taking the Waters in Texas: Springs, Spas, and Fountains of Youth* (Austin: University of Texas Press, 2000), 207; *Unique, original, attractive: The Texas Cotton Palace, Waco, Texas, the first annual exhibition will open November 8 and close December 6, 1894* (Waco, TX: Brooks & Wallace, 1894), box 2J227, folder "Promotional Materials," Texas Cotton Palace Papers (hereinafter COTTON PALACE), TXBU; S. H. Pope, *Geyser City Record: A Texas Journal Devoted to Agriculture, Mechanical and Realty Development, Waco, Texas, May 25, 1890* (Waco, TX: Press of the News Printing 1890), 3, 29; South Western Immigration Company, *Texas*, 193.

30. COTTON PALACE, TXBU; Pope, *Geyser City Record*; L. L. Foster, *Forgotten Texas Census: First Annual Report of the Agricultural Bureau of the Department of Agriculture, Insurance, Statistics, and History, 1887–1888* (Austin: Texas State Historical Association, 2001), 175.

31. Wm. R. Smith to Dr. General, March 11, 1839 (quotation); *Memorial and biographical History*, 126; COTTON PALACE, TXBU.

32. *Memorial and biographical history*, 71, 126; COTTON PALACE, TXBU; Pope, *Geyser City Record*, 3, 29.

33. Eliza Perry to Stephen Perry, April 16, 1844, box 2J33, folder 1 "General Correspondence, 1844," James F. Perry Papers (hereinafter PERRY), CAH-UT; Stephen S. Perry to J. H. Brown, February 1, 1858, 2J36, PERRY, CAH-UT; James F. Perry to Stephen S. Perry, June 26, 1843, 2J32, PERRY, CAH-UT; Letter from San Felipe, Texas, August 9, 1833, 2J30, PERRY, CAH-UT; Moses Bryan to James F. Perry, September 5, 1833, 2J30, PERRY, CAH-UT; James F. Perry to Stephen S. Perry, February 29, 1844, 2J33, PERRY, CAH-UT; Anson Jones, "Private memoirs," in *Memoranda and official correspondence relating to the Republic of Texas, its history and annexation* (New York: D. Appleton, 1859), 15; Adaline Graves to "my dear children," June 28, 1843, box 2B332,

folder 4 "Personal Papers: Correspondence, 1871–1873" (hereinafter FOLDER 1873), GRAVES, TXBU; "News," *Weekly Wisconsin,* September 12, 1849, www.newspaperarchive.com; "The Cholera is Coming," *Weekly Wisconsin,* April 11, 1849, www.newspaperarchive.com; N. D. Labadie, "San Jacinto Campaign," in *Texas Almanac and State Industrial Guide* (Dallas, TX: Belo, 1857), 45; George Wilkins Kendall, *Narrative of the Texan Santa Fe Expedition, comprising a description of a tour through Texas, and across the great Southwestern prairies . . .* (London: Wily & Putnam, 1844), 94–95; Baker, *Texas Scrap-Book,* 52–53; Brown, *History of Texas,* 349; Fisk, *Visit to Texas,* 24; Kennedy, *Republic of Texas,* vol. 1, 74; Stiff, *Texas Emigrant,* 10, 67.

34. Manford Eugene Jones, *A History of Cotton Culture along the Middle Brazos River* (master's thesis, University of New Mexico, 1939), 10; Vicente Filísola, *Memorias para la historia de la guerra de Tejas,* vol. 2 (Mexico City, Mexico: Imprenta de Ignacio Cumplido, 1848–1849); Noah Smithwick, *The Evolution of a State, or Recollections of Old Texas Days* (Austin, TX: Gammel, 2000), 93; Moses Austin Bryan to James F. Perry, August 3, 1840, 2J32, PERRY, CAH-UT; Moses Austin Bryan to James F. PERRY, September 10, 1840, 2J32, PERRY, CAH-UT; Kennedy, *Republic of Texas,* vol. 1, 384; Sally Graves to Addie Earl, September 10, 1892, box 2B332, folder 7 "Personal Papers: Correspondence, 1892–1893," GRAVES, TXBU; Ada to "ma," February 18, box 2B332, FOLDER 1874, GRAVES, TXBU; Mary to Adaline Graves, December 14, 1873, 1848–1963, box 2B332, folder 4 "Personal Papers: Correspondence, 1871–1873," GRAVES, TXBU; "Epidemic Probable: Serious Problem in Sanitation Confronts Texas," *Portsmouth Herald,* July 13, 1899, www.newspaperarchive.com; Mary Jane Caufield to Wat, December 6, 1857, box 2B384, FOLDER 1847, CAUFIELD, TXBU; Labadie, "San Jacinto Campaign," 45; Gray, *From Virginia to Texas,* [71], [87]; Fisk, *Visit to Texas,* 24; Baker, *Texas Scrap-Book,* 52–53; R. Hedspeth to Adaline Earle, November 1, 1884; Adaline Graves to "my dear children," June 28, 1843; M. J. Caufield to Watson Caufield, September 23, 1855; Wat Caufield to his father, June 29, 1857.

35. A. Somervell to James F. Perry, August 14, 1833, 2J30, PERRY, CAH-UT.

36. John R. Jones to James F. Perry, August 14, 1833, 2J30, PERRY, CAH-UT.

37. Letter from Richmond, Texas, February 11, 1859, 2J36, PERRY, CAH-UT; Adaline Graves to "my dear children," June 28, 1843; "The Cholera is Coming"; Baker, *Texas Scrap-Book,* 52–53; Brown, *History of Texas,* 349.

38. Thomas G. Western, "Translation of Samuel Bangs' legal petitions regarding his Texas land grant, 1830–1834, 1840," GA33, folder 1, "Translation of Samuel Bangs' legal petitions regarding his Texas land grant," 1830–1834, 1840, SC-UTA; "News by Telegraph," *Semi-Weekly Wisconsin,* February 21, 1866, www.newspaperarchive.com; Stiff, *Texas Emigrant,* 12.

39. W. B. Dewees, letter, August 29, 1823, in Dewees, *Letters from an Early Settler of Texas,* 42.

40. Edward King, *Texas: 1874: An Eyewitness Account of Conditions in Post-Reconstruction Texas* (Houston, TX: Cordovan Press, 1974), 69.

41. Parker, *Trip to the West and Texas,* 185.

42. "Havoc of the Flood," *Perry Advertiser*, July 7, 1899, www. newspaperarchive.com.

43. Alexander Thomson to William Thomson, September 22, 1833; Sterling C. Robertson to Eldridge B. Robertson, October 23, 1835, 129–30; W. B. Dewees, letter, July 16, 1822, in Dewees, *Letters from an Early Settler of Texas*, 218–19; Robert I. Chester to his wife, January 3, 1836, in McLean, *Robertson's Colony*, 539; Stiff, *Texas Emigrant*; Holley, letter III from Bolivar, Texas, December 1831.

44. James F. Perry to Stephen S. Perry, February 29, 1844; Lockhart, "Boating on the Brazos," 83 (quotation).

45. "Brazos Navigation," *Galveston Daily News*, January 16, 1897, www. newspaperarchive.com.

46. Thomas McKinney to Sam, February 4, 1839, no. 23–1648, Samuel May Williams Papers (hereinafter WILLIAMS), Galveston and Texas History Center, Rosenberg Library (Galveston, TX) (hereinafter GTHC).

47. "Brazos and Galveston Railroad Company, N[ew] Orl[eans]" (New York: L. Dillard [1839]), 3, in *Texas as Province and Republic, 1795–1845*, reel 28, no. 1344, MICROFILM, ACM; "Charter of Brazos & Galveston Rail Road," May 24, 1838, in *Texas as Province and Republic, 1795–1845*, reel 3, no. 229, MICROFILM, ACM (quotation).

48. "Brazos and Galveston Railroad Company, N[ew] Orl[eans]," 3.

49. "Cotton worm—festival—personal," *Galveston Daily News*, August 6, 1874, www.newspaperarchive.com; John C. Roberts to Gen. W. H. Hamman, August 16, 1875, box 6, folder 9, MS 006, Hamman Papers (hereinafter HAMMAN), WRC; Mary Lena Seale Stewart, "Life at Cedar Creek, Brazos County, Texas, in the 1870s," in Johnnie E. Stribling, *Twixt the Brazos and the Navasot: A Study of the Early History of Selected Communities in Northeast Brazos County, Texas, 1830–1900's* (n.p.: n.p., 1978); "To the Planters of Texas," *Civilian And Galveston City Gazette*, November 11, 1843, www. newspaperarchive.com; Mrs. Georgina Kendall Fellowes to Mr. S. G. Reed, June 6, 1937, box 8, folder 8.6, AR376, Kendall Family Papers, SC-UTA; W. P. Zuber to Mrs. J. T. Anderson, ca. 1900, box 1, folder 5, GA19, William Physick Zuber Papers (hereinafter ZUBER), SC-UTA; Stephen to Eliza Ann, November 13, 1841, GA 21, folder 13, HOGAN, UTA; Stiff, *Texas Emigrant*, 64; Lockhart, "Boating on the Brazos," 82–83; Henry J. Caufield to Watson Caufield, July 8, 1855; Henry J. Caufield to Lizzie Caufield, December 8, 1855; Foster, *Forgotten Texas Census*.

50. Daniel J. Prikryl and Jack Johnson, *Waco Lake, McLennan County, Texas: An Inventory and Assessment of Cultural Resources* (Austin, TX: Prewitt and Associates, 1985), 34–35.

51. C. M. Hubby to John Adriance, February 23, 1843, box 127, folder "Correspondence 1843–1845," ADRIANCE, CAH-UT; E. D. Nash to John Adriance, August 14, 1849; Anson Jones to Samuel Williams, October 10, 1848, no. 23–2069, WILLIAMS, GTHC; Thomas McKinney to Sam, February 22, 1839, no 23–1652, WILLIAMS, GTHC; Thomas F. McKinney to Sam, July 16, 1838, no. 23–1568, WILLIAMS, GTHC; Thomas F. McKinney to Sam, November 3, 1838, no. 23–1616, WILLIAMS, GTHC; M. A. Bryan to James

Perry, February 18, 1845, box 2J33, folder 2 "General Correspondence, January–June 1845," PERRY, CAH-UT; James Perry to John A. Merle, January 5, 1836, 2J42, PERRY, CAH-UT; James Reed, letter, February 27, 1839, 2J42, PERRY, CAH-UT; G. Gaines Lipscomb to M. A. Bryan, January 5, 1849, 2J42, PERRY, CAH-UT; Moses Austin Bryan to James F. Perry, August 31, 1840, 2J32, PERRY, CAH-UT; Moses Austin Bryan to James F. Perry, September 30, 1840, 2J32, PERRY, CAH-UT; W. W. Hunter to James, February 18, 1833, 2J30, PERRY, CAH-UT; Thomas McKinney to Sam, February 4, 1839; Moses Austin Bryan to James F. Perry, September 10, 1840; James F. Perry to Stephen S. Perry, June 26, 1843; Jones, *History of Cotton Culture*, 6; W. P. Zuber to Mrs. J. T. Anderson, ca. 1900; "Brazos and Galveston Railroad Company, N[ew] Orl[eans]," 5; Alexander Thomson to William Thomson, September 22, 1833; Stephen to Eliza Ann, November 13, 1841; Mrs. Georgina Kendall Fellowes to Mr. S. G. Reed, June 6, 1937; Stiff, *Texas Emigrant*, 64; John C. Roberts to Gen. W. H. Hamman, August 16, 1875; Stewart "Life at Cedar Creek"; Lockhart, "Boating on the Brazos," 82–83; Foster, *Forgotten Texas Census*, 9–10.

52. Stephen S. Perry to J. H. Brown, February 1, 1858.

53. M. Whilldin, *A Description of Western Texas* (Galveston, TX: Galveston, Harrisburg & San Antonio Railway Company, 1876), 35; Jones, *History of Cotton Culture*, 6; John C. Roberts to Gen. W. H. Hamman, August 16, 1875; Stewart, "Life at Cedar Creek"; Lockhart, "Boating on the Brazos," 82–83; Foster, *Forgotten Texas Census*.

54. *Texas Almanac and State Industrial Guide* (Galveston, TX: Belo, 1910); *Texas Almanac and State Industrial Guide Volume 1904* (Galveston, TX: Belo, 1904); United States Census, *Cotton Production*; Foster, *Forgotten Texas Census*; de Cordova, *Texas Immigrant*; Burke, *Texas Almanac*.

55. Henry J. Caufield to Wat, January 30, 1858, box 2B384, FOLDER 1847, CAUFIELD, TXBU; Mary Jane Caufield to Watson Caufield, July 29, 1859; Henry J. Caufield to Watson Caufield, July 8, 1855; Henry J. Caufield to Lizzie Caufield, December 8, 1855; M. J. Caufield to Watson Caufield, July 17, 1855; Wat Caufield to his father, June 29, 1857.

56. Mary Jane Caufield to Wat Caufield, October 5, 1860, box 2B384, FOLDER 1858, CAUFIELD, TXBU; Mary Jane Caufield to Watson Caufield, July 29, 1859; Henry J. Caufield to Watson Caufield, July 8, 1855; Henry J. Caufield to Lizzie Caufield, December 8, 1855; M. J. Caufield to Watson Caufield, July 17, 1855; Wat Caufield to his father, June 29, 1857.

57. Thomas Johnston to John Adriance, August 14, 1845, box 127, folder "Correspondence 1843–1845," ADRIANCE, CAH-UT; William E. Young to Watson Caufield, May 16, 1858, box 2B384, FOLDER 1847, CAUFIELD, TXBU; Henry J. Caufield to his brother, October 1, 1858, box 2B384, FOLDER 1847, CAUFIELD, TXBU; W. E. Young to Watson Caufield, May 15, 1859, box 2B384, FOLDER 1858, CAUFIELD, TXBU; E. D. Nash to John Adriance, August 14, 1849; Hancock, *Narrative*, 11; James F. Perry to Stephen S. Perry, June 26, 1843; South Western Immigration Company, *Texas*; Pool, "Westward I Go Free," 168; Baker, *Texas Scrap-Book*; Fisk, *Visit to Texas*; Burke, *Texas Almanac*; Mary Jane Caufield to Watson Caufield, July 29, 1859; Henry J. Caufield to Watson Caufield, July 15, 1859.

58. Pool, "Westward I Go Free," 168.

59. Letter from San Felipe de Austin to James F. Perry, March 21, 1831, 2J30, PERRY, CAH-UT; "Brazos Land for Sale," *Galveston Daily News*, November 14, 1857, www.newspaperarchive.com; Letter from Austin, Texas, to James Hearne, December 18, 1853, box 2B107, folder "Correspondence: Business/Legal 1836–1854 (hereinafter BARNARD), TXBU; Hancock, *Narrative*, 9; Smithwick, *Evolution of a State*, 9; G. Gaines Lipscomb to M. A. Bryan, January 5, 1849; Moses Austin Bryan to James F. Perry, August 31, 1840; Fisk, *Visit to Texas*; Isaac Parks to John Crittenden, January 6, 1858; W. P. Zuber to Mrs. J. T. Anderson, ca. 1900.

60. [*Cotton Gin near Waco, Texas*], n.d., PHOTO, TXBU; "For Sale," *Civilian And Galveston Gazette*, December 17, 1845, www.newspaperarchive. com; Judge Rufus Y. King, "Indian Attack upon the Gregg Family in 1841," in McLean, *Robertson's Colony*, 563.

61. John Brown, bill of sale for female slave named Rhoda, June 19, 1835, box 2H483, Vandale (Earl) Collection (hereinafter EARL), CAH-UT; Letter from Galveston, Texas, to Stephen Perry, April 23, 1859, 2J36, PERRY, CAH-UT; William Hansbrough and Stephen S. Perry, bill of sale for group of slaves, November 17, 1849, 2J42, PERRY, CAH-UT; M. Austin Henry to James F. Perry, December 27, 1840, 2J32, PERRY, CAH-UT; Charles D. Sayre and Stephen S. Perry, bill of sale for group of slaves, February 23, 1857, 2J36, PERRY, CAH-UT; John Brown, receipt for $400 for the sale a Negro girl named Mary, May 12, 1834, 2J31, PERRY, CAH-UT; Joshua Fletcher, contract to sell a mulatto girl named Chaney, March 1834, 2J31, PERRY, CAH-UT; Isaac Mayfield to James Perry, March 19, 1833, 2J30, PERRY, CAH-UT; Sean Kelley, "Blackbirders and *Bozales*: African-Born Slaves on the Lower Brazos River of Texas in the Nineteenth Century," *Civil War History* 54, no. 4 (December 2008); Robert H. Porter, receipt, April 2, 1845, box 2B108, folder "Legal Records: 1844–1860," BARNARD, TXBU; Red Morrow, Runafter, Ooks-ta-le, Ashes, Keyd, Segene, Standing Rock, and Cletoke, receipt for return of runaway slave, April 4, 1845, box 2B109, folder "Financial Records: 1841–1846," BARNARD, TXBU; Advertisement: "Negro woman for sale," *Civilian And Galveston City Gazette*, December 16, 1843, www. newspaperarchive.com; Stephen S. Perry to J. H. Brown, February 1, 1858; Moses Austin Bryan to James F. Perry, September 10, 1840.

62. R. R. Brown to S. S. Perry, April 15, 1855, 2J35, PERRY, CAH-UT.

63. Thomas F. McKinney to S. M. Williams, June 2, 1834, no. 23–1329, WILLIAMS, GTHC; J. G. M. Reed to J. F. Perry, January 4, 1862, 2J37, PERRY, CAH-UT; Martha Norkunas, "Narratives of Resistance and the Consequences of Resistance," *Journal of Folklore Research* 41, no. 2/3 (2004); J. H. Bird to Mary R. Barnard, March 10, 1896, box 2B107, folder "Correspondence: Business/Legal 1896," BARNARD, TXBU; "Editorial Correspondence," *Galveston Daily News*, July 4, 1865, www. newspaperarchive.com; Isaac Parks to John Crittenden, January 6, 1858; John W. Cloud, deed in Brazoria County, Texas, September 25, 1843, Deed Records of Brazoria County, in *Autobiography of John Wirt [or Wurts] Cloud*, box 31, folder 31.18, MS 17, MUIR, WRC, RICE; M. Edwards to J. E. Sumner,

May 19, 1836, GA 21, folder 7, HOGAN, SC-UTA; M. Edwards to George Knight, May 19, 1836, GA 21, folder 7, HOGAN, SC-UTA; Thomas G. Gordon to General T. J. Green, December 31, 1838, GA 21, folder 9, HOGAN, SC-UTA; S. M. Westewelt to Lewis, October 24, 1841; Stephen to Eliza Ann, November 13, 1841; Wm. R. Smith to Dr. Genl., March 11, 1839; Wat Caufield to his father, June 29, 1857.

64. Charles D. Sayre and Stephen S. Perry, bill of sale for group of slaves, February 23, 1857 (quotation); Austin, *Civil Commandant of the colony*; "Recollections of Mrs. Jane Hallowell Hill, Austin, Texas" (March 2, 1898), MS 288, folder 288, Thomson Family of Texas Papers 1832–1898 (hereinafter THOMSON), WRC; F. J. Calvert to L. W. Groce, ca. mid-1800s, box 1, folder 1, MS 240, Groce Family Correspondence, WRC; Henry J. Caufield to Watson Caufield, July 15, 1859; Henry J. Caufield to Wat Caufield, April 25, 1859; Fisk, *Visit to Texas*, 205; Lockhart, "Boating on the Brazos," 83; John W. Cloud, deed in Brazoria County, Texas, September 25, 1843; Robert I. Chester to his wife, January 3, 1836, 540.

65. Earl Wesley Fornell, *The Galveston Era: The Texas Crescent on the Eve of Secession* (Austin: University of Texas Press, 2009); M. Edwards to J. E. Sumner, May 19, 1836; M. Edwards to George Knight, May 19, 1836; Thomas G. Gordon to General T. J. Green, December 31, 1838; "James W. Fannin, slave trader & importer," in Brazoria County Probate Records, Case No. 162 (Estate of James W. Fannin), GA 21, folder 8, HOGAN, SC-UTA; Kelley.

66. In addition to the sources already cited, see Anson Jones to John Campbell, July 8, 1850, John Campbell Personal Papers, 1820–1906 (hereinafter CAMPBELL), box 1, folder 1.1, MS 329, WRC; Anson Jones to John Campbell, September 12, 1849, CAMPBELL, box 1, folder 1.1., WRC; Old Red, telegraph to Cushing, March 21, 1863, box 38, folder 38.1, MS 17, MUIR, WRC; Edward J. M. Rhoads, "The Chinese in Texas," *SHQ* 81, no. 1 (July 1977); Eliza Perry to Stephen Perry, April 16, 1844.

67. "Reminiscences of J. H. Fulcher, A Grandson of Abigail (McLennan) Fokes" (October 27, 1835), in McLean, *Robertson's Colony*, 158–59; "Found at Last," *Adams Sentinel*, March 9, 1840, www.newspaperarchive.com; "The Texas Death List is Growing," *Milford Mail*, July 13, 1899, www. newspaperarchive.com; "Drowning Near Hempstead," *Galveston Daily News*, July 9, 1899, www.newspaperarchive.com; "During the Brazos Flood," *Marshfield Times*; "During the Brazos Flood," *Postville Review*; "Resume of Losses from the Brazos Valley Flood"; "Results of the Flood"; "Texas Towns in Peril"; "The Floods in Texas: Alarming Reports come from the Brasos River Bottoms"; "Many Lives are Lost," *Salt Lake Tribune*; "Many Lives are Lost," *Algona Republican*; "At Danger Point Remain the Swirling Waters in Stricken Texas"; "The Worst is Over"; "Latest Details from the Flood"; "Miles of Floods in Texas"; "Cotton Crops Destroyed."

68. "Incidents and Accidents," *St. Joseph Herald*, June 13, 1868, www. newspaperarchive.com.

69. Wat Caufield to his father, June 29, 1857 (quotation); Henry J. Caufield to Watson Caufield, September 25, 1860.

70. George Barnard to Shap[ley Ross], October 5, 1881, box 2B109,

folder "Correspondence: Personal, 1850–1881" (hereinafter FOLDER 1850), BARNARD, TXBU; Brig. Gen. Thos. Lincoln Casey to Hon. S. B. Elkins, December 15, 1892, in *United States Congressional Serial Set*, issue 3105 (Washington, D.C.: Government Printing Office, 1893); W. A. Taylor to George Barnard, January 9, 1880, box 2B109, FOLDER 1850, BARNARD, TXBU; [*Construction of the Interurban Bridge*], ca. 1910, box 261, folder "Waco—Bridges—Interurban Bridge," Photograph File—"Waco, Texas" (hereinafter INTERURBAN), PHOTO, TXBU; [*Bridges during Flood Time*], ca. 1913, box 261, INTERURBAN, PHOTO, TXBU; [*Washington Bridge*], ca. 1913, box 261, folder "Waco—Bridges—Washington Bridge," Photograph File—"Waco, Texas" (hereinafter WASHINGTON), PHOTO, TXBU; [*Washington Bridge in Flood*], n.d., box 261, WASHINGTON, PHOTO, TXBU; [*Washington Bridge in Flood 2*], ca. 1908, box 261, WASHINGTON, PHOTO, TXBU; [*Washington Bridge with Men*], ca. 1902, box 261, WASHINGTON, PHOTO, TXBU; *H. R. M. Smith, Lee Davis, W. H. B. Higgins, Ray Lucas*, box 261, folder "Waco—Bridges—Bosque Bridge," Photograph File—"Waco, Texas" (hereinafter BOSQUE), PHOTO, TXBU; [*Bosque River Bridge*], n.d., box 261, BOSQUE, PHOTO, TXBU; Roger Norman Conger, *The Waco Suspension Bridge* (n.p.: n.p., 1963?), 195, 214, 222–23; Thomas F. McKinney to Sam, January 29, 1839, no. 23–1147, WILLIAMS, GTHC; L. Jones to Sam, January 31, 1839, no. 23–1147, WILLIAMS, GTHC; E. P. Calking, "Cotton Factors and Commission Merchants, Strand, Galveston, Texas" (July 10, 1846), in Cotton Factors in Galveston, Texas, Notice to James F. Perry, 2J33, PERRY, CAH-UT; Andrew Forest Muir, "Railroad Enterprise in Texas, 1836–1841," *SHQ* 47, no. 4 (April 1944); "Canal," *Galveston Daily News*, May 10, 1876, www.newspaperarchive.com; United States Army Corps of Engineers (hereinafter ACOE), *Report of the Chief of Engineers* (Washington, D.C.: Government Printing Office, 1875); E. B. Nichols and Co., advertisement seeking Brazos cotton, in League of Nations, *Rapport du Comité consultatif: Report of the Advisory committee* (London: Harrison & Sons, 1856); S. M. A. Butler to James F. Perry, April 24, 1848, 2J33, PERRY, CAH-UT; "Canal to Follow Gulf Coast," *Evening Gazette*, September 13, 1912, www.newspaperarchive.com; J. C. Colton to W. H. Hamman, July 28, 1874, box 6, folder 19, MS 006, HAMMAN, WRC; Major Chas. J. Allen to Gen. Thomas L. Casey, December 7, 1892, in *Letter from The Secretary of War, transmitting with letter of the chief of engineers*, United States congressional serial set, issue 3105 (Washington, D.C.: Government Printing Office, 1893), 218; E. D. Nash to John Adriance, August 18, 1849; Anson Jones to Samuel Williams, October 10, 1848; Letter from Galveston, Texas, to Stephen Perry, April 23, 1859; Muir, *Texas in 1837*, 65; Kennedy, *Republic of Texas*, vol. 2; "Need Food."

71. Stiff, *Texas Emigrant*, 144.

72. Major Chas. J. Allen to Gen. Thomas L. Casey, December 7, 1892.

73. S. M. A. Butler to James F. Perry, April 24, 1848; J. C. Colton to W. H. Hamman, July 28, 1874; "Need Food."

74. Anson Jones to Samuel Williams, October 10, 1848; Thomas F. McKinney to Sam, January 29, 1839; L. Jones to Sam, January 31, 1839;

E. P. Calking and Co., "Cotton Factors and Commission Merchants, Strand, Galveston, Texas" (July 10, 1846); Muir, "Railroad Enterprise in Texas"; "Canal," *Galveston Daily News*; ACOE, *Report of the Chief of Engineers* (1875); E. B. Nichols and Co., advertisement seeking Brazos cotton; Letter from Galveston, Texas, to Stephen Perry, April 23, 1859; Muir, *Texas in 1837*, 65; Kennedy, *Republic of Texas*, vol. 2.

75. de Cordova, *Texas Immigrant*, 12.

76. Burke, *Texas Almanac*, 97.

77. Brazos River and Valley Improvement Association, "Flood Prevention and Navigation Brazos River," September 18, 1915, box 6, 410c, E.FW18— "Records of the Dallas Engineer Office" (hereinafter E.FW18), Record Group 77—Records of the Army Corps of Engineers, Southwest Division (hereinafter RG 77), National Archives and Records Administration— Southwest Division (Fort Worth, TX) (hereinafter NARA); C. W. Payne, *The Brazos River of Texas: freight tonnage survey of Waco and territory tributary also commercial statistics and economic results of the improvement to commercial navigation* (Waco, TX: City Commission, 1916), 55.

78. Marjorie Rogers, "Port Sullivan, Once an Important Point Between Houston and Belton, the Former Seat of a Widely Known College and a Point to Which Steamboats Plied Long Ago, Loses Its Luster and Almost Becomes a 'Ghost City,'" *Houston Chronicle*, December 21, 1930, in Port Sullivan Vertical File (hereinafter PORT SULLIVAN), TXBU; John Banta, "Port Sullivan had to sink or swim on the Brazos," *Waco Tribune-Herald*, December 2, 1984, PORT SULLIVAN, TXBU.

79. Holley, letter IV from Bolivar, Texas, December 1831, 115.

80. Samuel Ellis, *The Emigrant's Guide to Texas, containing: a condensation of the laws under which the titles to land in Texas are held; a description of the most important bays, rivers & towns, with a table of distances; the tariff and revenue laws; proceedings in probate; statistics* (New Orleans, LA: T. Rea, 1839), 159, in *Texas as Province and Republic, 1795–1845*, reel 28, no. 1346, MICROFILM, ACM; Donald Jackson, *Voyages of the Steamboat Yellow Stone* (New York: Tickner and Fields, 1985), 119–20; S. M. Wilcox to William E. Anderson, June 12, 1914, box 4, folder 400, E.FW18, RG 77, NARA; District Engineer in Galveston, Texas, to Chief of Engineers, February 6, 1919, box 10, folder 2, G6, RG 77, NARA; J. C. Sanford to Division Engineer, May 26, 1919, box 10, folder 2, G6, RG 77, NARA; Proof, "Report on prelim. exam. of Brazos River, Texas, House Doc. No. 298, 66 Congress" (Washington, D.C.: Government Printing Office, 1919), box 4, folder BR3-1, E.FW18, RG 77, NARA; Parker, *Trip to the West*, 144–45; Kennedy, *Republic of Texas*, vol. 1, 159; Sterling C. Robertson to Eldridge B. Robertson, October 23, 1835 129–30; Muir, *Texas in 1837*, 65.

81. Brazos River and Valley Improvement Ass'n, *Permanent organization*, 22; Waco Business Men's Club, Committee of Brazos River Improvement, *The Improvement of the Brazos River, Texas, from Waco to Its Mouth to the Secretary of War* (Waco, TX: n.p., 1905), [4]; John Kerr Rose, *Development of the Brazos River, Texas: Aspects of Legislation and Activities by Local Interests and the Federal Government* (Washington, D.C.: Library of Congress

Legislative Reference Service, June 18, 1963), box 639, file 6, Poage Papers, Poage Legislative Library (Waco, TX) (hereinafter POAGE), 1; Stiff, *Texas Emigrant*, 63; Fisk, *Visit to Texas*, 30; Parker, *Trip to the West*, 144–45; Jackson, *Steamboat Yellow Stone*, 119–20.

82. "Trinity Project Finally Dropped," *Galveston Daily News*, June 25, 1922, www.newspaperarchive.com; Holley, *Texas*; William S. Brown to the Secretary of the Navy, June 28, 1835, box 1, folder GA 1.3, GA 1–2, Irion Family Papers 1825–1929, bulk 1826–1874, SC-UTA; Financial Records (1839), box 2N177, GA 11–12, Samuel Maas Papers 1824–1900, bulk 1834–1837, SC-UTA; "Reminiscences of J. H. Fulcher, A Grandson of Abigail (McLennan) Fokes," 158–59; "Brazos Navigation"; Kennedy, *Republic of Texas*, vol. 1.

83. George B. McKinstry to Samuel M. Williams, May 27, 1830, no. 23–0363, WILLIAMS, GTHC; Sam Houston, title bond to Lewis C. Ferguson for a league of land in exchange for ferry passage across the river, April 3, 1836, box 2H483, EARL, CAH-UT; James F. Perry to Emily Perry, April 15, 1836, 2J31, PERRY, CAH-UT; James F. Perry to Emily Perry, April 26, 1836, 2J31, PERRY, CAH-UT; Stephen S. Perry to W. Hensley, July 27, 1854, 2J35, PERRY, CAH-UT; Robert Baldwin to S. F. Perry, November 29, 1853, 2J35, PERRY, CAH-UT; Letter to James F. Perry, January 31, 1831, 2J30, PERRY, CAH-UT; Abigail Curlee, "History of a Texas Slave Plantation 1831–1863," *SHQ* 26, no. 2 (October 1922); Earl F. Woodward, "Internal Improvements in Texas in the Early 1850's," *SHQ* 76, no. 2 (October 1972); Louis E. Brister and Eduard Harkort, "The Journal of Col. Eduard Harkort, Captain of Engineers, Texas Army, February 8–July 17, 1836," *SHQ* 102, no. 3 (January 1999); "Galveston and Columbia Packet," Civilian And Galveston City Gazette, October 26, 1842, www.newspaperarchive.com; ACOE, *Report of the Chief of Engineers U.S. Army* (Washington, D.C.: Government Printing Office, 1901); Advertisement, *Civilian and Galveston Gazette*, December 2, 1843, www. newspaperarchive.com; Advertisement, *Civilian and Galveston Gazette*, November 29, 1843, www.newspaperarchive.com; "Texas in Early Days," *Galveston Daily News*, December 29, 1879, www.newspaperarchive.com; "News," *Civilian and Gazette*, November 24, 1857, www.newspaperarchive. com; "Sale of Wreck'd Cotton," *Civilian and Galveston Gazette*, May 18, 1844, www.newspaperarchive.com; "For Washington on the Brazos," *Civilian and Galveston Gazette*, May 18, 1844, www.newspaperarchive.com; "Brazos River Trade," *Galveston Weekly News*, March 1, 1859, www. newspaperarchive.com; "Steamers, Rivers," *Semi-Weekly Journal*, June 24, 1852, www.newspaperarchive.com; "Brazoria County," *Civilian and Galveston Gazette*, November 6, 1847, www.newspaperarchive.com; Advertisement, *Civilian and Galveston City Gazette*, August 24, 1842, www. newspaperarchive.com; "Passengers," *Civilian and Galveston Gazette*, April 15, 1848, www.newspaperarchive.com; "Galveston, Brazoria & Columbia Packet," *Civilian and Galveston Gazette*, April 15, 1848, www. newspaperarchive.com; Advertisement, *Civilian and Galveston City Gazette*, July 27, 1842, www.newspaperarchive.com; Advertisement, *Civilian and Galveston City Gazette*, October 26, 1842, www.newspaperarchive.com; Advertisement, *Civilian and Galveston City Gazette*, September 7, 1842,

www.newspaperarchive.com; Advertisement, *Civilian and Galveston City Gazette,* September 14, 1842, www.newspaperarchive.com; "Editorial Correspondence," *Galveston News,* November 22, 1853, www. newspaperarchive.com; "The Patriarch has Left Us," *Telegraph and Texas Register,* December 25, 1836, in *Texas As province and Republic, 1795–1845,* reel 2, no 129a, MICROFILM, ACM; "Diary of Capt'n. C. R. Perry, of Johnson City, Texas, A Texas Veteran," GA 47, folder 1, C. R. Perry Diary, SC-UTA, 1; Unnamed Document about the Brazos River, in "Facts-study on Brazos River and Freeport harbor," 2, box 31, folder 31.9, MS 346, J. Russell Wait Port of Houston Papers (hereinafter WAIT), WRC; transcript, "Recollections of James Monroe Hill" (October 19, 1897), MS 288, THOMSON, WRC; José Valdes, *Santa Anna y La Guerra de Texas* (Mexico: Imprenta mundial, 1936), box 1, folder 11, S 471.1, John A. Hulen Papers (hereinafter HULEN), Southwest Collection, Texas Tech University (Lubbock) (hereinafter TTU-SWC), 257; Sam Houston to Smith, December 8, 1855, box 1, folder 11, S 471.1, HULEN, TTU-SWC; James Morgan to Sam Houston, November 17, 1842, box 2, folder 1.11 "Correspondence 1840–1849," MS 49, Sam Houston Papers, WRC; W. P. Zuber to Mrs. T. E. Murrelle, October 3, 1907, box 1, folder 5, GA19, ZUBER, SC-UTA; Smithwick, *Evolution of a State;* Moses Austin Bryan to James F. Perry, September 10, 1840; M. Austin Henry to James F. Perry, December 27, 1840; Hancock, *Narrative;* Gray, *From Virginia to Texas,* [64], [212]; Jones, *History of Cotton Culture,* 10; Major Chas. J. Allen to Gen. Thomas L. Casey, December 7, 1892; Fisk, *Visit to Texas,* 9; Baker, *Texas Scrap-Book,* 193; W. P. Zuber to Mrs. J. T. Anderson, ca. 1900; Lockhart, "Boating on the Brazos," 84; Brown, *History of Texas,* 8; Rose, *Development of the Brazos River,* 1; Jackson, *Steamboat Yellow Stone,* 118–19.

84. G. Hammeken to Emily Perry, September 22, 1848, box 2J33, folder 7 "General Correspondence" (hereinafter FOLDER 7), 1848, PERRY, CAH-UT; G. Hammeken to James F. Perry, July 22, 1848, box 2J33, FOLDER 7, 1848, PERRY, CAH-UT; Thomas Borden to James F. Perry, January 18, 1849, box 2J33, folder 6 "General Correspondence" (hereinafter FOLDER 6), 1847, PERRY, CAH-UT; A. Austin Jr. to Stephen Perry, December 16, 1847, box 2J33, FOLDER 6, 1847, PERRY, CAH-UT; A. Parnell, bill of lading for Sloop Elizabeth at Sabine River, bound for Brazos River, April 8, 1857, 2J36, PERRY, CAH-UT; S.S. Perry, bill of lading for Schooner Alamo at Gulf Prairie, bound for Galveston, May 1856, 2J36, PERRY, CAH-UT; Paul McKnight, bill of lading for Sloop "Eliza Saul" at Galveston bound for Brazoria, October 28, 1842, 2J32, PERRY, CAH-UT; James Reed, bill of lading for the Schooner William Bryan, in New Orleans bound for the Brazos River, November 18, 1840, 2J32, PERRY, CAH-UT; James Perry, bill of lading for Schooner at New Orleans bound for Brazoria, May 30, 1833, 2J30, PERRY, CAH-UT; James F. Perry, bill of lading for Schooner "Comanche" at Quintana bound for Galveston, March 18, 1836, 2J31, PERRY, CAH-UT; James F. Perry, bill of lading for Schooner "Julius Caesar" at Brazoria bound for New Orleans, February 6, 1837, 2J31, PERRY, CAH-UT; S. F. Perry, bill of lading for Schooner "William and Maria" at Brazoria, September 12, 1853, 2J35, PERRY, CAH-UT; S. F. Perry, bill of lading for Steamboat "J.H. Bell" at Quintana

bound for Columbia, July 13, 1854, 2J35, PERRY, CAH-UT; S. F. Perry, bill of lading for Schooner "General Hamer" at Galveston bound for Brazoria, May 26, 1853, 2J35, PERRY, CAH-UT; S. F. Perry, bill of lading for Schooner "Columbia" at Gulf Prairie Landing bound for Mobile, Alabama, May 16, 1854, 2J35, PERRY, CAH-UT; S. F. Perry, bill of lading for Schooner "Skimmer" at Gulf Prairie Landing, February 14, 1855, 2J35, PERRY, CAH-UT; S. F. Perry, bill of lading for Schooner "Perpendicular" at Gulf Prairie Landing, March 16, 1855, 2J35, PERRY, CAH-UT; S. F. Perry, bill of lading for Schooner "Perpendicular" at Gulf Prairie Landing, May 11, 1855, 2J35, PERRY, CAH-UT; J. J. Davis, bill of lading for Steamer S. M. Williams at Galveston bound for Brassos River, #23–2096, WILLIAMS, GTHC; S. F. Perry, bill of lading for Schooner "Alamo" at Gulf Prairie Landing bound for Galveston, July 29, 1854, 2J35, PERRY, CAH-UT; S. F. Perry, bill of lading for Schooner "Alamo" at Gulf Prairie Landing, April 12, 1856, 2J35, PERRY, CAH-UT; S. F. Perry, bill of lading for Schooner "Alamo" at Gulf Prairie Landing, May 5, 1855, 2J35, PERRY, CAH-UT; S. F. Perry, bill of lading for Schooner "Alamo" at Gulf Prairie Landing, May 7, 1855, 2J35, PERRY, CAH-UT; S. F. Perry, Bill of lading for Schooner "Alamo" at Gulf Prairie Landing, May 26, 1855, 2J35, PERRY, CAH-UT; S. F. Perry, bill of lading for Schooner "Alamo" at Gulf Prairie Landing, December 20, 1853, 2J35, PERRY, CAH-UT; S. F. Perry, Bill of lading for Schooner "Nymph" at Gulf Prairie Landing, April 10, 1856, 2J35, PERRY, CAH-UT; S. F. Perry, bill of lading for Schooner "Nymph" at Gulf Prairie Landing, July 2, 1857, 2J35, PERRY, CAH-UT; S. F. Perry, Bill of lading for Schooner "Alex Mose" at Gulf Prairie Landing, March 19, 1856, 2J35, PERRY, CAH-UT; Moses Austin Bryan to James F. Perry, September 10, 1840.

85. J. K. Mabray to Sam, March 21, 1848, no. 23–1867, WILLIAMS, GTHC; Thomas McKinney to Sam, February 4, 1839; L. Jones to Sam, January 31, 1839; Thomas F. McKinney to Samuel M. Williams, April 21, 1834, no. 23–1316, WILLIAMS, GTHC; E. W. Gregory to Samuel M. Williams, December 16, 1833, no. 23–1237, WILLIAMS, GTHC; Elliott W. Gregory to Samuel M. Williams, February 19, 1834, no. 23–1268, WILLIAMS, GTHC; Jorge Fisher, affidavit, November 6, 1830, no. 23–0465, WILLIAMS, GTHC; F. Ganalel to Moses, Bryan, Austin & Co., December 17, 1840, 2J32, PERRY, CAH-UT; R. and D. G. Mills, to James F. Perry, February 16, 1845, 2J33, PERRY, CAH-UT; William Watson, *Adventures of a Blockade Runner, Or, Trade in Time of War* (London: T. F. Unwin, 1892), 31; "From the Army," *Star and Republican Banner*, August 7, 1846, www. newspaperarchive.com; "The Battle at Monterey," *Republican Compiler*, October 26, 1846, www.newspaperarchive.com; Stephen S. Perry to J. H. Brown, February 1, 1858; Moses Austin Bryan to James F. Perry, September 10, 1840; Moses Austin Bryan to James F. Perry, September 30, 1840; Stephen S. Perry to W. Hensley, July 27, 1854; Moses Austin Bryan to James F. Perry, September 30, 1840; James F. Perry to Stephen S. Perry, February 29, 1844; Fisk, *Visit to Texas*, 21; Kennedy, *Republic of Texas*, vol. 2; Kennedy, *Republic of Texas*, vol. 1, 91–92; Manuel de Mier y Teran to President Guadalupe Victoria, March 28, 1828, 34.

86. Seth Eastman, *Wreck on the Brazos, Texas,* 1849, no. 96.06, WILLIAMS, GTHC; George L. Hammeken to James F. Perry, October 22, 1848, box 2J33, FOLDER 7, PERRY, CAH-UT; Letter to James F. Perry, December 21, 1830, 2J30, PERRY, CAH-UT; Mirabeau B. Lamar, *Travel Journal, 1835,* MS 311, Mirabeau B. Lamar Travel Journal, WRC, http://scholarship.rice.edu/handle/1911/21658; L. Jones to Sam, January 31, 1839; Letter to James F. Perry, January 31, 1831; Muir, *Texas in 1837,* 65; Watson, *Adventures of a Blockade Runner,* 46; Parker, *Trip to the West,* 182; Stiff, *Texas Emigrant,* 63; Kennedy, *Texas Emigrant,* vol. 1, 35.

87. Stephen to Eliza Ann, November 13, 1841; "Brazos and Galveston Railroad Company, N[ew] Orl[eans]," 3 (quotation); Lamar, *Travel Journal,* 164.

88. Muir, *Texas in 1837,* 64–65.

89. Ibid.

90. George L. Hammeken to James F. Perry, October 22, 1848.

91. C. Richard King, ed., *Victorian Lady on the Texas Frontier: The Journal of Anne Raney Coleman* (New York: W. Foulsham, 1972); Holley, letter III from Bolivar, Texas, December 1831, 110; Letter, James F. Perry, December 21, 1830; Woodward, "Internal Improvements," 162; Gray, *From Virginia to Texas,* [209]; Fisk, *Visit to Texas,* 12; Parker, *Trip to the West,* 182.

92. Holley, letter II from Bolivar, Texas, December 1831, 108; S. M. Westewelt to David, March 14, 1842, GA 21, folder 13, HOGAN, SC-UTA; L. Jones to Sam, January 31, 1839; Stiff, *Texas Emigrant,* 63; Lamar, *Travel Journal.*

93. S. M. Westewelt to Lewis, October 24, 1841.

94. Stephen to Eliza Ann, November 13, 1841.

95. Holley, letter III from Bolivar, Texas, December 1831, 110.

96. Brazos River Channel and Dock Company (hereinafter BRCDC), *Facts with Reference to the Brazos River Enterprise and the "New South"* (New York: John A. Lowell & Col. Printers, 1890), 9.

97. "Brazos Navigation."

98. Kennedy, *Republic of Texas,* vol. 1, 72–73.

99. Ibid., 34–35.

100. New Orleans and Texas Navigation Company and Mexican Gulf Railway Company, *An act to incorporate the New Orleans and Texas Navigation Company, and to incorporate the Mexican Gulf Railway Company* (New Orleans, LA: Jerome Bayon, 1837), 1; Anson Jones to Samuel Williams, October 10, 1848; Brazos River and Valley Improvement Ass'n, *Permanent organization,* 22.

101. J. Russell Wait, "Report to Brazos River Harbor Navigation District," in Robert J. Cummins to Freeport Sulphur Company, July 1, 1950, box 31, folder 31.1, MS 346, WAIT PAPERS, WRC, 4.

102. Brazos River and Valley Improvement Ass'n, *Permanent organization,* 22; Wait, "Report to Brazos River Harbor Navigation District," 2; Unnamed Document about the Brazos River, 3.

103. Brazos River and Valley Improvement Ass'n, *Permanent organization,* 22–23.

104. Southern Commercial Convention, *Proceedings of the Southern Commercial Convention* (n.p.: n.p., 1871), 92; "Up the Country," *Galveston Daily News*, August 7, 1866, www.newspaperarchive.com; John Richardson, "Deep Water at Galveston," *Galveston Daily News*, December 2, 1885, www.newspaperarchive.com; "The State Press," *Galveston Daily News*, June 14, 1887, www.newspaperarchive.com; "Texas Notes," *Galveston Daily News*, May 7, 1869, www.newspaperarchive.com; J. A. Paschal to Mr. President, January 5, 1854, box 76, folder 76.11, MS 17, MUIR, WRC; "Richmond," *Galveston Weekly News*, October 13, 1857, www.newspaperarchive.com; "Arrival of the Ohio," *Newport Daily News*, April 26, 1851, www.newspaperarchive.com; "Texas Public Improvements," *Manitowoc County Herald*, March 1, 1851, www.newspaperarchive.com; Brazos River to be Important Waterway," *Galveston Daily News*, September 9, 1909, www.newspaperarchive.com; Major Chas. J. Allen to Gen. Thomas L. Casey, December 7, 1892; "Canal to Follow Gulf Coast"; Rose, *Development of the Brazos River*, 2; Thrall, *Pictorial History of Texas*, 56.

105. Kennedy, *Republic of Texas*, vol. 2, 395.

106. Albert Gallatin, *Report of the secretary of the Treasury, on the subject of public roads and canals: made in pursuance of a resolution of Senate, of March 2d, 1807* (n.p.: W. A. Davis, 1807).

107. Petition from Galveston and Brazos Navigation Company to the Legislature of Texas, December 14, 1855, box 76, folder 76.11, MS 1, MUIR 7, WRC.

108. J. A. Paschal to Mr. President, January 5, 1854; Stiff, *Texas Emigrant*, 64, 148; "Brazos Navigation."

109. Letter to Brazos Harbor Navigation District Commissioners, May 1, 1950, box 31, folder 31.2, MS 346, WAIT PAPERS, WRC, 9; Transportation Planning and Programming Division, Texas Department of Transportation, "Gulf Intracoastal Waterway—Legislative Report for 2003–2004," ftp.txdot. gov/pub/txdot-info/tpp/giww/giww04.pdf; "Galveston Beyond Brazos River Canal," *Galveston Daily News*, July 21, 1869, www.newspaperarchive.com; transcript, sworn by James B. Shaw, December 19, 1855, box 76, folder 76.11, MS 17, MUIR, WRC.

110. United States Department of War (hereinafter WAR), *Annual Reports* (Washington, D.C.: Government Printing Office, 1910); ACOE, *Report of the Chief of Engineers* (1875); Woodward, "Internal Improvements."

111. Lou Ellen Ruesink, "Taming the Brazos," *Texas Water Resources Institute* 3, no. 6 (August 1977); Allan D. Meyers, "Brazos Canal: Early Intracoastal Navigation in Texas," *SHQ* 103, no. 2 (Oct., 1999); ACOE, *A Historical summary giving the scope of previous projects for the improvement of certain rivers and harbors* (Washington, D.C.: Government Printing Office, 1915), 1858–1859; "Canal in Texas," *Weekly Wisconsin*, February 12, 1851, www.newspaperarchive.com; James B. Shaw to Tipton Walker, September 19, 1855, box 76, folder 76.11, MS 17, MUIR, WRC; petition from Galveston and Brazos Navigation Company; ACOE, *Report of the Chief of Engineers* (1875); Woodward, "Internal Improvements"; BRCDC, 21–22; Rose, *Development of the Brazos River*, 2; Unnamed Document about the Brazos River, 2.

112. J. A. Paschal to Mr. President, January 5, 1854.

113. Woodward, "Internal Improvements."

114. WAR, *Letter from the Secretary of War, transmitting, with a letter from the Chief of Engineers, report of examination of channel between Brazos River and Galveston Bay, Texas. House of Representatives, 54th Congress, 2nd session, Document 89* (Washington, D.C.: Government Printing Office, December 14, 1896), 2.

115. Tipton Walker to James B. Shaw, October 31, 1855, box 76, folder 76.11, MS 17, MUIR, WRC; "News," *Galveston Weekly News*, February 3, 1857, www.newspaperarchive.com.

116. "Arrival of the Ohio"; "Galveston Beyond Brazos River Canal"; Tipton Walker to James B. Shaw, October 31, 1855.

117. "Government Ready to Extend Inland Canal," *Galveston Daily News*, January 7, 1911, www.newspaperarchive.com; "Drainage Matters Straightened Out," *Galveston Daily News*, July 6, 1910, www.newspaperarchive.com. It should be noted that the canal of the 1850s itself echoed the dreams of local citizens who had pushed for a smaller, earlier version of a Brazos River canal. The Brazos Canal Company began construction on the Brazos Canal around 1841 but never finished the project.

118. "Drainage Matters Straightened Out."

119. ACOE, *Report of the Chief of Engineers U.S. Army* (Washington, D.C.: Government Printing Office, 1897); "Progress Made on InterCoastal Canal," *Galveston Daily News*, October 15, 1911, www.newspaperarchive. com; "Open by February 1," *Galveston Daily News*, October 26, 1906, www. newspaperarchive.com; "Millions for Rivers-Harbors," *Brookshire Times*, December 12, 1913, www.newspaperarchive.com; "Waterways Bill before the House," *Galveston Daily News*, February 12, 1910, www.newspaperarchive. com; "Major Howell Will Recommend a Preliminary Survey," *Galveston Daily News*, August 18, 1910, www.newspaperarchive.com; "Events Boiled Down," *Grand Prairie Texan*, February 11, 1910, www.newspaperarchive. com; *Texas Almanac and State Industrial Guide* (1910), 125; "Drainage Matters Straightened Out"; "Government Ready to Extend Inland Canal"; WAR, *Letter from the Secretary of War* (1896); BRCDC.

120. "Work on Texas Waterways," *Galveston Daily News* July 29, 1909, www.newspaperarchive.com; ACOE, *Report of the Chief of Engineers* (1875); *Texas Almanac and State Industrial Guide* (1910), 125; "Drainage Matters Straightened Out"; "Government Ready to Extend Inland Canal"; "Progress Made on InterCoastal Canal"; "Millions for Rivers-Harbors"; "Waterways Bill before the House"; "Major Howell Will Recommend a Preliminary Survey"; "Events Boiled Down."

121. Ruling depth is generally defined as the shallowest depth of the river at mean, low water.

122. "Coast Canal Plan," *Galveston Daily News*, January 2, 1904, www. newspaperarchive.com; "Present Transportation Facilities at Freeport," *Freeport Facts*, November 10, 1912, www.newspaperarchive.com; "To Navigate Brazos," *Galveston Daily News*, August 29, 1905, www. newspaperarchive.com; "Work on Texas Waterways."

123. Thomas Edie Hill, *Hill's reference guide for land seekers, travelers, schools, tourists, emigrants and general readers: including description and outline maps, with new method of quick-finding location, in each state of any city or village of 200 population and more* (Chicago, IL: Hill Standard Book Company, 1912), 198; Kingman to Col. Riche, October 7, 1914, box 6, folder 410, E.FW18, RG 77, NARA; S. M. Wilcox to Al W. Davis, March 15, 1913, box 5, folder 400, E.FW18, RG 77, NARA; *Texas Almanac and State Industrial Guide* (1910), 124–25; ACOE, *Report of the Chief of Engineers U.S. Army*, Part 1 (Washington, D.C.: Government Printing Office, 1910), 1648.

124. *Congressional serial set, Issue 6205* (Washington, D.C.: Government Printing Office, 1912); *Texas Almanac and State Industrial Guide* (1910), 124–25; Hill, *Reference Guide*, 198.

125. J. H. Anderson to Superintending Civil Engineer of Bureau of Yards and Docks of Navy Department, July 5, 1944, box 1, folder 8, G5— "NAVIGABLE WATERWAY FILES, 1931–1962," RG 77, NARA; WAR, *Annual Reports of the Secretary of War*, vol. 2 (Washington, D.C.: Government Printing Office, 1910), 547–49, 550; "Waterway Expenditures in Galveston District Much Bigger than in Past Year," *Galveston Daily News*, October 1, 1924, www.newspaperarchive.com.

126. "Texas to Florida Inland Waterway," *Galveston Daily News*, October 5, 1910, www.newspaperarchive.com; Kingman to Col. Riche, October 7, 1914; S. M. Wilcox to Al W. Davis, March 15, 1913; *Texas Almanac and State Industrial Guide* (1910), 124–25; ACOE, *Report of the Chief of Engineers U.S. Army*, Part 1, 1648; "Present Transportation Facilities at Freeport."

127. "BRAZORIA SHIP CHANNEL, INTRACOASTAL CANAL," in *Data for Survey Report* (1948), box 31, folder 31.2, MS 17, MUIR, WRC, [1]; "Intercoastal Canal," *Galveston Daily News*, October 9, 1910, www.newspaperarchive.com; "Texas to Florida Inland Waterway."

128. "BRAZORIA SHIP CHANNEL, INTRACOASTAL CANAL," [1] (quotation); "Canal to Follow Gulf Coast."

129. Muir, *Texas in 1837*, 120.

130. "Editorial Correspondence: The Port of Velasco," *San Antonio Daily Light*, August 29, 1891, www.newspaperarchive.com.

131. "The State Press," *Galveston Daily News*, June 14, 1887, www.newspaperarchive.com.

132. Mary C. R. Phillips, proclamation signed and witnessed by City Secretary J. R. Smith, August 15, 1888, box 2B144, folder 1 "Correspondence: 1885–1923," Edward McCrea Ainsworth Papers, TXBU; "Washington," *Galveston Daily News*, April 1, 1876, www.newspaperarchive.com.

133. "Brazos Navigation."

134. Louis Giraud, *Velasco, the first & only deep water port on the coast of Texas: the commercial hope of the Trans-Mississippi by Louis Giraud* (St. Louis, Missouri: n.p., ca. 1892), Map Annex (hereinafter MAP), SC-UTA, 11; "Editorial Correspondence: The Port of Velasco."

135. Giraud, *Velasco*, 25; BRCDC, 9; "Editorial Correspondence: The Port of Velasco."

136. "Brazos River to be Important Waterway."

137. First Lieutenant Wm. C. Langfitt to Major Chas. J. Allen, November, in ACOE, *A Historical summary giving the scope of previous projects for the improvement of certain rivers and harbors* (Washington, D.C.: Government Printing Office, 1915), 1860, 1892; ACOE, *Report of the Chief of Engineers* (1875); Unnamed document about the Brazos River, 3.

138. Unnamed document about the Brazos River, 3.

139. WAR, *Annual reports of the Secretary of War*, vol. 2, 553–54; ACOE, *Report of the Chief of Engineers U.S. Army*, Part 1, 553; "Editorial Correspondence: The Port of Velasco"; ACOE, *Report of the Chief of Engineers* (1875); ACOE, *A Historical summary giving the scope of previous projects for the improvement of certain rivers and harbors*, 1860; "Wilke v. The Teredo: Exciting Contest Between the Two at the Brazos Mouth," *Galveston Daily News*, June 16, 1889, www.newspaperarchive.com; Wait, "Report to Brazos River Harbor Navigation District," 2–3; Unnamed Document about the Brazos River, 5.

140. Brig. Gen. Thos. Lincoln Casey to Hon. S. B. Elkins, December 15, 1892; Major Chas. J. Allen to Gen. Thomas L. Casey, December 7, 1892; WAR, *Annual Reports of the Secretary of War*, vol. 2, 553–54.

141. Senate Committee on Commerce, *Report on the river and harbor [appropriation] bill [1916] (H.R. 20189)* (Washington, D.C.: Government Printing Office, 1915), 196; ACOE, *A Historical summary giving the scope of previous projects for the improvement of certain rivers and harbors*, 1860; WAR, *Annual reports of the Secretary of War*, vol. 2.

142. BRCDC, 21–22.

143. Ibid., 3, 11.

144. "Brazos Navigation."

145. "Three Jetty Bids," *Galveston Daily News*, June 29, 1905, www. newspaperarchive.com; Unnamed Document about the Brazos River, 8.

146. Wait, "Report to Brazos River Harbor Navigation District," 3; Unnamed Document about the Brazos River, 8 (quotation).

147. "Brazos River and Harbor," *Galveston Daily News*, June 20, 1898, www.newspaperarchive.com (quotation).

148. BRCDC.

149. Ibid.

150. "Work on Texas Waterways."

151. "A New Port City to Be Born," *Galveston Daily News*, October 18, 1912, www.newspaperarchive.com; League of Women Voters, Freeport Texas, *Study of Brazos River Harbor Navigation District* (n.p.: n.p., 196?), 1; Al W. Davis to S. M. Wilcox, March 11, 1913, box 5, folder 400, E.FW18, RG 77, NARA; "Millions for Rivers-Harbors"; "Waterways Bill before the House"; S. M. Wilcox to Al W. Davis, March 15, 1913; ACOE, *Report of the Chief of Engineers U.S. Army*, Part 1, 1654.

152. WAR, *Annual reports of the Secretary of War*, vol. 2, 553–54; Sam I. Graham to Secretary of War, March 22, 1916, box 8, folder 426, E.FW18, RG 77, NARA; Lt. Col. of Army Corps of Engineers to John Ehrhardt, November 1, 1916, box 8, folder 426, E.FW18, RG 77, NARA; William Barden

to R. C. Smead, October 16, 1916, box 8, folder 426, E.FW18, RG 77, NARA; Record Cards, Engineer Department, U.S. Army—Doc. File Brazos, Case No 410, Sheet No 10, October 13–31, box 6, folder 410, E.FW18, RG 77, NARA; League of Women Voters, Freeport Texas, *Study of Brazos River Harbor Navigation District*, 1.

153. By midcentury, the City of Freeport did not connect directly with the Brazos River. The Army Corps of Engineers diverted the mouth of the river in 1929.

154. United States Army Corps of Engineers, *Review of Reports on Freeport Harbor, Texas* (Galveston, TX: ACOE, Galveston District, ca. 1970).

155. Ibid.

156. *A Brief for Crandall Dry Dock Engineers, Inc.*, in Dow Wynn, Brazos River Harbor Navigation District (BRHND) to Paul Crandall, August 24, 1954, box 32, folder 32.1, MS 346, WAIT PAPERS, WRC.

157. League of Women Voters, Freeport Texas, *Study of Brazos River Harbor Navigation District*, 2.

158. "Big Celebration at Freeport on July 4th," *Freeport Facts*, June 27, 1930, www.newspaperarchive.com; "Channel Here Finished, Catt Left Thursday," *Freeport Facts*, August 1, 1930, www.newspaperarchive.com; "Public Wharf is Recommended by Wait," *Freeport Facts*, February 23, 1950, www. newspaperarchive.com; "Port Tour is Immense Success," *Freeport Facts*, February 23, 1950, www.newspaperarchive.com; "Largest Cargo in History Moves Out of Freeport's 32-Foot Harbor Today," *Freeport Facts*, February 2, 1939, www.newspaperarchive.com; "Maercky Enthusiastic over Outlook Here," *Freeport Facts*, April 25, 1930, www.newspaperarchive.com; "$100,000 Will Be Spent on Local Harbor During Next Fiscal Year," *Freeport Facts*, January 12, 1939, www.newspaperarchive.com; "Two Hydraulic Dredges Work Brazos Harbor," *Freeport Facts*, June 8, 1950, www.newspaperarchive.com.

159. ACOE, *Review of Reports on Freeport Harbor, Texas.*

160. Ibid.

161. Wait, "Report to Brazos River Harbor Navigation District."

162. ACOE, *Review of Reports on Freeport Harbor, Texas.*

163. Ibid.

164. Ibid.

165. "Year's Work on Texas Harbors," *Galveston Daily News*, September 1, 1914, www.newspaperarchive.com; "Work on Texas Waterways," *Galveston Daily News* July 29, 1909, www.newspaperarchive.com; "Capt. Riche," *Galveston Daily News*, April 11, 1904, www.newspaperarchive.com; "Navigated Canal," *Galveston Daily News*, September 23, 1904, www. newspaperarchive.com; "Velasco Notes," *Galveston Daily News*, December 28, 1894, www.newspaperarchive.com.

166. "Uncle Sam is Working to Make the Brazos Navigable," *Galveston News*, January 9, 1916, www.newspaperarchive.com.

167. U.S. Engineers Office (hereinafter ENGINEERS), *Report on Survey of Brazos River and Tributaries, Texas: Oyster Creek, Texas, Jones Creek, Texas*, vol. 1 (Galveston, TX: U.S. engineers Office, 1947), 31.

168. WAR, *Annual reports of the Secretary of War*, vol. 2 (Washington, D.C.:

Government Printing Office, 1910), 568.

169. "Brazos River: Snagboat Waco," 1911, Dallas Historical Society Collection (hereinafter DHS), www.texashistory.unt.edu; ACOE, "Brazos River: Snagboat Navasota," 1911, DHS, www.texashistory.unt.edu; "Channel Complete," *Galveston Daily News* July 8, 1906, www. newspaperarchive.com; "Matagorda-Brazos Canal," *Advocate*, June 3, 1911, www.newspaperarchive.com; "Snagboat at Columbia," *Galveston Daily News*, December 21, 1910, www.newspaperarchive.com; "Inland Waterway," *Galveston Daily News*, July 21, 1910, www.newspaperarchive.com; W. H. Lillard to Captain A. E. Waldron, December 5, 1910, box 66, folder 412, E.FW18, RG 77, NARA; C. S. Riche to Mrs. J. Alleine Brown, January 7, 1915, box 4, folder 400, E.FW18, RG 77, NAR; Al W. Davis to S. M. Wilcox, March 11, 1913, box 5, folder 400, E.FW18, RG 77, NARA; S. M. Wilcox to Al W. Davis, March 15, 1913, box 5, folder 400, E.FW18, RG 77, NARA; Record Card, Engineer Department, U.S. Army, August 2, 1916, box 6, folder 410, E.FW18, RG 77, NARA; Proof, "Report on Prelim. Exam. of Brazos River, Texas" (1919); "Work on Texas Waterways."

170. "Levee Nearing Completion," *Galveston Daily News*, July 22, 1910, www.newspaperarchive.com; "Ditching for Levee," *Galveston Daily News*, May 7, 1910, www.newspaperarchive.com.

171. ACOE, *Report of the Chief of Engineers U.S. Army*, Part 1 (Washington, D.C.: Government Printing Office, 1910), 1677.

172. Brazos River and Valley Improvement Ass'n, *Permanent organization*, 24.

173. WAR, *Annual reports of the Secretary of War*, vol. 2, 569; Endorsement to a letter sent from Board of Engineers for Rivers and Harbors, June 10, 1919.

174. "Inspection of Brazos: Capt. Jadwin, Congressman Henry and Mayor Baker of Waco Traveled from San Felipe to Richmond," *Galveston Daily News*, November 13, 1905, www.newspaperarchive.com.

175. Ibid.

176. Ibid.

177. Dick Vaughan, "Federal Government Funds May Help Tame Erratic Brazos River, Provide Irrigation, Electric Power and Protection from Floods," *El Paso Herald-Post*, December 4, 1934, www.newspaperarchive.com.

Chapter Four

1. "Improving the 'Mississippi of Texas,'" *Waco Semi-Weekly Tribune*, May 21, 1913, box 6, folder 419, E.FW18—"Records of the Dallas Engineer Office" (hereinafter E.FW18), Record Group 77—Records of the Army Corps of Engineers, Southwest Division (hereinafter RG 77), National Archives and Records Administration (Fort Worth, TX) (hereinafter NARA); J. C. Nagle, "Irrigation in Texas," *USDA Bulletin* 222 (Washington, D.C.: Government Printing Office, 1910).

2. "To Navigate Brazos," *Galveston Daily News*, August 29, 1905, www. newspaperarchive.com; "Corn on B.T. Gilbert's Land at Danbury, in Coast

Country," *Galveston Daily News*, August 24, 1913, www.newspaperarchive. com; Dick Vaughan, "Federal Government Funds May Help Tame Erratic Brazos River, Provide Irrigation, Electric Power and Protection from Floods," *El Paso Herald-Post*, December 4, 1934, www.newspaperarchive.com; "Utilize the Brazos," *Galveston Daily News*, October 13, 1906, www. newspaperarchive.com; "Congressman Moore on the Texas Waterways," *Galveston Daily News*, May 5, 1907, www.newspaperarchive.com.

    3.   *United States Congressional Serial Set, Issue 3200* (Washington, D.C.: Government Printing Office, 1895); United States Department of War (hereinafter WAR), *Annual Reports of the War Department* (Washington, D.C.: Government Printing Office, 1907).

    4.   Richard White, *It's Your Misfortune and None of My Own: A New History of the American West* (Norman: University of Oklahoma Press, 1993); Ian Tyrell, *True Gardens of the Gods: Californian-Australian Environmental Reform, 1860–1930* (Berkeley: University of California Press, 1999); Jessica Teisch, *Engineering Nature: Water, Development, and the Global Spread of American Environmental Expertise* (Chapel Hill, University of North Carolina Press, 2011); Donald J. Pisani, *From the Family Farm to Agribusinss: The Irrigation Crusade in California and the West, 1850–1931* (Berkeley: University of California Press, 1984); Mark Fiege, *Irrigated Eden: The Making of an Agricultural Landscape in the American West* (Seattle: University of Washington Press, 1999).

    5.   Richard Hofstadter, *The Age of Reform: From Bryan to FDR* (New York: Vintage Books, 1955), 5.

    6.   Col. Henry M. Robert to Chief of Engineers, September 6, 1900, in Brazos River and Valley Improvement Ass'n, *Permanent organization formed at Bryan, Texas, October 12–13, 1915, for the prevention of overflows and promotion of navigation* (Waco, TX: L. S. Henry, 1915), 23; Brazos River and Valley Improvement Association, "Flood Prevention and Navigation Brazos River," September 18, 1915, box 6, 410c, E.FW18, RG 77, NARA; H. A. Montgomery to Division Engineer, Gulf of Mexico Division, January 25, 1937, box 6, folder 9, FW17—"Subject Files Relating to the Construction of Possum Kingdom Dam, 1936–1937" (hereinafter FW17), RG 77, NARA; Endorsement to a letter sent from Board of Engineers for Rivers and Harbors, June 10, 1919, box 10, folder 2, G6—"Examination and Survey Files, 1908–1948" (hereinafter G6) RG 77, NARA.

    7.   *Texas Almanac and State Industrial Guide* (Galveston, TX: Belo, 1910), 325, 331.

    8.   "Head of Navigation, Brazos River, Waco, Texas," Postcard Collection (hereinafter POSTCARD), Baylor University, Texas Collection (Waco, TX) (hereinafter TXBU).

    9.   "Velasco: Where Rail and Sail Meet," *Galveston Daily News*, September 1, 1913, www.newspaperarchive.com.

    10.   "Navasota Conference," *Galveston Daily News*, October 7, 1906, www.newspaperarchive.com; "Waco Tenders Its Support," *Galveston Daily News*, September 1, 1906, www.newspaperarchive.com; "Navasota Meeting," *Galveston Daily News*, September 27, 1906, www.newspaperarchive.com.

11. "The New Texas Port," *Freeport Facts*, November 17, 1912, www. newspaperarchive.com; "Katy System Secures Outlet to the Gulf," *San Antonio Daily Light*, March 23, 1913, www.newspaperarchive.com; "A Port of Destiny: Freeport at the Mouth of the Brazos River," *Galveston Daily News*, September 1, 1913, www.newspaperarchive.com; "River Port Association Is to Meet in Angleton," *Galveston Daily News*, February 14, 1924, www. newspaperarchive.com; "Brazos River and Harbor," *Galveston Daily News*, June 20, 1898, www.newspaperarchive.com; "Velasco: Where Rail and Sail Meet"; "Utilize the Brazos."

12. Waco Business Men's Club, Committee of Brazos River Improvement, *The Improvement of the Brazos River, Texas, from Waco to Its Mouth to the Secretary of War* (Waco, TX: n.p., 1905), [4].

13. "To the Public," *Civilian And Galveston Gazette*, November 4, 1840, www.newspaperarchive.com; "Texas Public Improvements," *Manitowoc County Herald*, March 1, 1851, www.newspaperarchive.com; "The State Press," *Galveston Daily News*, June 6, 1888, www.newspaperarchive.com; Advertisement, *Civilian and Galveston City Gazette*, August 24, 1842, www. newspaperarchive.com; Advertisement, *Civilian and Galveston City Gazette*, July 27, 1842, www.newspaperarchive.com; Advertisement, *Civilian and Galveston City Gazette*, October 26, 1842, www.newspaperarchive.com; Advertisement, *Civilian and Galveston City Gazette*, September 7, 1842, www. newspaperarchive.com; Advertisement, *Civilian and Galveston City Gazette*, September 10, 1842, www.newspaperarchive.com; Advertisement, *Civilian and Galveston City Gazette*, September 14, 1842, www.newspaperarchive.com; Advertisement, *Civilian and Galveston City Gazette*, September 24, 1842, www.newspaperarchive.com; Advertisement, *Daily Advertiser*, February 26, 1842, www.newspaperarchive.com; "Notice! To Travelers in Texas!!," *Civilian and Gazette*, April 28, 1857, www.newspaperarchive.com; "100 Land Certificates of Six Hundred and Forty Acres Each, 64,000 Acres," *Galveston Daily News*, May 22, 1866, www.newspaperarchive.com; Letter from Wheelock, April 17, 1858, in *Civilian and Galveston Gazette*, April 27, 1858, www. newspaperarchive.com (quotation); Tipton Walker to Governor E. M. Pease, March 24, 1856, box 63, folder 63.3, MS 17, Andrew Forest Muir Papers (hereinafter MUIR), Woodson Research Center (hereinafter WRC), Fondren Library, Rice University (Houston, TX) (hereinafter RICE); Clement R. Johns to E. F. Gray, December 16, 1858, box 38, folder 38.1, MS 17, MUIR, WRC; Walter C. Hunter v. BBB&C, box 63, folder 63.1, MS 17, MUIR, WRC; Jno. C. Blassingame v. Buffalo Bayou, Brazos and Colorado Railway Co., box 63, folder 63.2, MS 17, MUIR, WRC; John A. Williams to Clement R. Johns, July 1, 1859, box 63, folder 63.2, MS 17, MUIR, WRC; Gideon Lincencum to Daniel Boone Moore and Emily Moore, April 2, 1860, in Gideon Lincencum, *Gideon Lincecum's Sword: Civil War Letters from the Texas Home Front* (Denton, TX: University of North Texas Press, 2001); George Barnard to Shap[ley] Barnard, May 1, 1882, box 2B106, folder "Correspondence Personal 1882–1889," George Barnard Papers (hereinafter BARNARD), TXBU; Topographic Map of Cleburne (1894), Topographic Map Collection (hereinafter TOPO), TXBU; Topographic Map of Granbury (1889), TOPO, TXBU;

Topographic Map of Temple (1894), TOPO, TXBU; Topographic Map of Temple (1892), TOPO, TXBU; Topographic Map of Waco (1892), TOPO, TXBU; W. A. Taylor to George Barnard, January 9, 1880, box 2B109, folder 1850, BARNARD, TXBU; "To the Public."

14. Homer S. Thrall, *A pictorial history of Texas, from the earliest visits of European adventurers, to A.D. 1879: embracing the periods of missions, colonization, the revolution, the republic and the state, also a topographical description of the country* (New York: N. D. Thompson, 1885), 296.

15. "Hidalgo Falls Dam," *Galveston Daily News*, January 31, 1909, www.newspaperarchive.com; Endorsement to a letter sent from Division Engineer of Gulf Division in New Orleans, Louisiana, May 21, 1918, box 10, folder 2, G6, RG 77, NARA; C. W. Payne, *The Brazos River of Texas: Freight Tonnage Survey of Waco and Territory Tributary also Commercial Statistics and Economic Results of the Improvement to Commercial Navigation* (Waco, TX: City Commission, 1916), 55; "Brazos River and Harbor."

16. "Brazos River and Harbor."

17. "Congressman Moore on the Texas Waterways."

18. Mother to daughter, December 12, 1901, box 2B332, folder 8 "Personal Papers: Correspondence, 1894, 1898, 1900–1904," Graves-Earle Family Papers, 1848–1963 (hereinafter GRAVES), TXBU; C. W. Payne to Colonel C. S. Riche, September 13, 1915, box 6, 410c, E.FW18, RG 77, NARA; Mary to Edward M. Ainsworth, November 25, 1924, box 2B144, folder 2 "Correspondence: 1924–1936," Edward McCrea Ainsworth Papers (hereinafter AINSWORTH), TXBU.

19. [*Waco Flood of 1902*], 1902, folder "Waco—Events—Floods—1902" (hereinafter FOLDER 1908), Photograph Collection (hereinafter PHOTO), TXBU; *High Water, East Waco*, 1908, FOLDER 1908, PHOTO, TXBU; C. M. Seley, *Cotton Belt R. R. Bridge*, 1908, FOLDER 1908, PHOTO, TXBU; C. M. Seley, *Elm Street, East Waco, Texas*, 1908, FOLDER 1908, PHOTO, TXBU; *The Brazos on a Rampage*, 1909, FOLDER 1908, PHOTO, TXBU; *Elm Street, East Waco, 1909*, 1909, FOLDER 1908, PHOTO, TXBU; [*Waco Flood*], 1913, folder "Waco—Events—Floods—1913" (hereinafter FOLDER 1913], PHOTO, TXBU; C.M. Seley, *Elm Street, East Waco, 1913*, 1913, FOLDER 1913, PHOTO, TXBU; C.M. Seley, *Brazos River*, 1913, FOLDER 1913, PHOTO, TXBU; [*Brazos in Flood*], 1913, FOLDER 1913, PHOTO, TXBU; Fred Gildersleeve, [*Brazos in Flood*], 1918, folder "Waco—Events—Floods—1918" (hereinafter FOLDER 1918), PHOTO, TXBU; Fred Gildersleeve, [*Waco in Flood*], 1918, FOLDER 1918, PHOTO, TXBU; [*Waco in Flood*], 1936, folder "Waco—Events—Floods—1936" (hereinafter FOLDER 1936), PHOTO, TXBU; [*Roiling Floodwaters*], 1936, FOLDER 1936, PHOTO, TXBU; *Annual Report of the United States Life-Saving Service for the Fiscal Year Ending June 30, 1900* (Washington, D.C.: Government Printing Office, 1901); Western Union Telegrams, box 5, folder 400, E.FW18, RG 77, NARA; "96 Lives are Lost in Flood," *Evening Gazette*, December 8, 1913, www.newspaperarchive.com; "Fatal Cloudbursts," *Lebanon Daily News*, April 28, 1900, www.newspaperarchive.com; "The Floods in Texas: Damage on the Increase Instead of Growing Less," *Kane Daily Republican*, July 7, 1899, www.newspaperarchive.com;

"Report Twenty People Drowned," *Laredo Times*, December 14, 1913, www. newspaperarchive.com; "Running Out in Low Places," *Galveston Daily News*, June 28, 1905, www.newspaperarchive.com; "Valleys are Swept," *Galveston Daily News*, May 1, 1905, www.newspaperarchive.com; "Brazos Overflow Expected," *Galveston Daily News*, May 14, 1905, www.newspaperarchive.com; "Losses by Brazos Overflows," *Galveston Daily News*, May 18, 1905, www. newspaperarchive.com; "Brazos at Waco," *Galveston Daily News*, April 9, 1900, www.newspaperarchive.com; "Brazos Rising," *Galveston Daily News*, April 9, 1900, www.newspaperarchive.com; "Brazos Valley Loss," *Galveston Daily News*, April 9, 1900, www.newspaperarchive.com; "Nineteen Drown at Brazos," *Winnipeg Free Press*, August 20, 1915, www.newspaperarchive.com; M. C. Tyler, memorandum, June 23, 1939, box 1426, file 44, W. R. Poage Papers, Poage Legislative Library (Waco, TX) (hereinafter POAGE); C. W. Payne to Colonel C. S. Riche, September 13, 1915; "Barge Line to Be Put on Brazos to Ply From Waco to Freeport, River Mouth," *Waco Daily Times-Herald*, September 10, 1915, in C. W. Payne to Colonel C. S. Riche, September 10, 1915, box 6, 410c, E.FW18, RG 77, NARA; "Brazos Crest Passing Slowly," *Corsicana Daily Sun*, December 11, 1913, www.newspaperarchive.com; "Plans for Relief," *San Antonio Daily Express*, July 11, 1899, www.newspaperarchive.com; "50 Years Ago . . . Brazos Goes on Rampage," *Galveston Daily News*, July 6, 1949, www. newspaperarchive.com; "Brazos River Falling," *Galveston Daily News*, July 3, 1905, www.newspaperarchive.com; "Waco Residents Frightened," *New York Times*, September 24, 1900, www.newspaperarchive.com; "Relief Sighted When Sky Begins Clearing in South," *Wichita Daily Times*, April 27, 1922, www. newspaperarchive.com; "Over Hundred Bodies Recovered in Texas," *Winnipeg Free Press*, September 13, 1921, www.newspaperarchive.com; "Report 100 Bodies Found Along River," *Boston Daily Globe*, September 13, 1921, www. newspaperarchive.com; "Death Toll in Flood Now Numbers 150," *Webster City Tribune*, December 12, 1913, www.newspaperarchive.com; "Trinity Project Finally Dropped," *Galveston Daily News*, June 25, 1922, www. newspaperarchive.com; "Waco Cotton Palace," *Galveston Daily News*, November 18, 1910, www.newspaperarchive.com; "Make Brazos Navigable," *Galveston Daily News*, October 27, 1899, www.newspaperarchive.com; "Extols Jadwin Paper," *Galveston Daily News*, October 25, 1905, www. newspaperarchive.com; Mary to Edward M. Ainsworth, June 19, 1917, box 2B144, folder 1 "Correspondence: 1885–1923," AINSWORTH, TXBU; Mary to Edward M. Ainsworth, November 25, 1924.

20. Inspector Crotty to John C. Kramer, May 29, 1909, box 4, folder 400, E.FW18, RG 77, NARA; "Thrown in Brazos Flood as Bridge Gives Away—Checking up Toll of Texas Tragedy," *Beatrice Daily Sun*, May 17, 1922, www.newspaperarchive.com; "Crest of Brazos Flood in Waller; 20 more Drown," *Denton Record-Chronicle*, December 8, 1913, www. newspaperarchive.com; "Plans for Relief," *San Antonio Daily Express*, July 11, 1899, www.newspaperarchive.com (second quotation); "Fatal Cloudbursts" (first quotation).

21. "Water Subsiding," *Galveston Daily News*, July 9, 1899, www. newspaperarchive.com.

22. "Washouts on Santa Fe," *Galveston Daily News*, April 9, 1900, www. newspaperarchive.com.

23. "Critical Situation Produced by Floods," *Correctionville News*, December 18, 1913, www.newspaperarchive.com.

24. "Loss is Ten Millions," *Daily Iowa Capital*, July 8, 1899, www. newspaperarchive.com; "400 Persons May Be Drowned in Texas," *The World*, July 5, 1899, www.newspaperarchive.com; "Cloudburst at Marlin," *Galveston Daily News*, August 1, 1903, www.newspaperarchive.com; "During the Brazos Flood," *Marshfield Times*, September 15, 1899, www.newspaperarchive.com; John Phillips to Sayers, telegram, July 6, 1899, Records of Joseph Draper Sayers, Texas Office of the Governor, Archives and Information Services Division, Texas State Library and Archives Commission, www.tsl.state.tx.us; "Losses by Brazos Overflows."

25. John Phillips to Sayers, telegram, July 6, 1899.

26. Proof, "Report on prelim. exam. of Brazos River Texas, House Doc. No. 298, 66 Congress" (Washington, D.C.: Government Printing Office, 1919), box 4, folder BR3–1, E.FW18, RG 77, NARA; Lieut. Colonel C. S. Riche to C. W. Payne, September 15, 1915, box 6, folder 410c, E.FW18, RG 77, NARA; Endorsement to a letter sent from Board of Engineers for Rivers and Harbors, June 10, 1919.

27. "Brazos River and Harbor."

28. Ibid.

29. Brazos River and Valley Improvement Association, "Flood Prevention."

30. "Brazos Dam Site," *Galveston Daily News*, November 10, 1905, www. newspaperarchive.com; "Site has been Selected for Lock-and-Dam No. 8," *Galveston Daily News*, November 17, 1911, www.newspaperarchive.com; "Limited Amounts for Rivers and Harbors," *Galveston Daily News*, January 25, 1910, www.newspaperarchive.com; Brazos River and Valley Improvement Ass'n, *Permanent organization*, 24; Endorsement to a letter sent from Board of Engineers for Rivers and Harbors, June 10, 1919; "Uncle Sam is Working to Make the Brazos Navigable"; "Work on Texas Waterways."

31. C. S. Riche to District Engineer and Chief of Engineers, October 20, 1914, box 6, folder 410, E.FW18, RG 77, NARA; "Inspection of Brazos: Capt. Jadwin, Congressman Henry and Mayor Baker of Waco Traveled from San Felipe to Richmond"; Brazos River and Valley Improvement Ass'n, *Permanent organization*; Endorsement to a letter sent from Board of Engineers for Rivers and Harbors, June 10, 1919.

32. "Millions for Rivers-Harbors," *Brookshire Times*, December 12, 1913, www.newspaperarchive.com; "Waterways Bill before the House," *Galveston Daily News*, February 12, 1910, www.newspaperarchive.com; Endorsement to a letter sent from Division Engineer of Gulf Division, May 21, 1918.

33. [*Lock-and-Dam No. 1, with Shoals*], November 8, 1912, box 5, folder 403a, E.FW18, RG 77, NARA; [*Lock-and-Dam No. 1*], box 5, folder 403a, E.FW18, RG 77, NARA; [*Lock-and-Dam 1, View of Dam up with Pool Full. Taken from below Lock on Left Bank*], October 20, 1914, box 10, folder 3, G6, RG 77, NARA; Elmer Self to Frank Collins, September 9, 1919, box 4, folder B. R. Leases, E.FW18, RG 77, NARA; O. R. Scott to Lieut. Col. C. S. Riche,

July 16, 1913, box 5, folder 403a, E.FW18, RG 77, NARA; Colonel C. S. Riche to E. R. Hatten, August 14, 1913, box 5, folder 400, E.FW18, RG 77, NARA; Major, letter, September 24, 1915, box 6, folder 410a, E.FW18, RG 77, NARA; Lieut. Colonel C. S. Riche to C. W. Payne, February 14, 1916, box 6, folder 410c, E.FW18, RG 77, NARA; "Second Lock Site: Located on the Brazos River Opposite Bryan—will be Surveyed This Week"; W. H. Lillard to Captain A. E. Waldron, December 5, 1910; C. S. Riche to Mrs. J. Alleine Brown, January 7, 1915; C. S. Riche to District Engineer and Chief of Engineers, October 20, 1914.

34. Fred Gildersleeve, [*Lock-and-Dam No. 8*], n.d., box 261, folder "Waco—Brazos River Lock-and-Dam" (hereinafter LOCK-AND-DAM), Photograph File—"Waco, Texas," PHOTO, TXBU; [*Panorama of Lock-and-Dam No. 8*], n.d., box 261, LOCK-AND-DAM, PHOTO, TXBU; [*Laborers at Lock-and-Dam No. 8*], n.d., box 261, LOCK-AND-DAM, PHOTO, TXBU; [*Damage at Lock-and-Dam No. 8*], August 1912, box 7, folder 419a, E.FW18, RG 77, NARA; *Lock-and-Dam No 8 Brazos River. Placing Concrete in Lock Floor. Lower End Lock*, March 5, 1913, box 7, folder 419a, E.FW18, RG 77, NARA; Fred Gildersleeve, [*Lock-and-Dam No. 8, Photo 2*], December 11, 1915, box 7, folder 419a, E.FW18, RG 77, NARA; Fred Gildersleeve, [*Lock-and-Dam No. 8, Photo 3*], December 11, 1915, box 7, folder 419a, E.FW18, RG 77, NARA; Letter to District Engineer and Chief of Engineers, July 6, 1916, box 6, folder 410, E.FW18, RG 77, NARA; H. F. Harris to John W. Henderson, July 1, 1915, box 4, folder "Lock & Dam #8," E.FW18, RG 77, NARA; Lieut. Colonel C. S. Riche to C.W. Payne, February 14, 1916; C. S. Riche to Mrs. J. Alleine Brown, January 7, 1915.

35. A. E. Waldron to Chief of Engineers, June 5, 1909, box 66, folder 412, E.FW18, RG 77, NARA; John W. Henderson to Hon. Jas. B. Baer, March 29, 1916, box 8, folder 426, E.FW18, RG 77, NARA; C. S. Riche to Mrs. J. Alleine Brown, January 7, 1915; C. W. Payne to Lieut. Colonel C. S. Riche, February 16, 1916, box 6, 410c, E.FW18, RG 77, NARA; G. W. Glass to C. S. Riche, February 25, 1916, box 8, folder 426, E.FW18, RG 77, NARA; C. S. Riche to Hon. Jas. B. Baker, July 3, 1916, box 8, folder 426, E.FW18, RG 77, NARA; C. S. Riche to Chief of Engineers, U.S. Army and Division Engineer, May 29, 1915, box 4, folder "Lock-and-Dam No. 6," E.FW18, RG 77, NARA; Frank R. Morgan to Captain A. E. Waldron, May 17, 1909, box 66, folder 412, E.FW18, RG 77, NARA; Elmer Self to Frank Collins, September 9, 1919; W. H. Lillard to Captain A. E. Waldron, December 5, 1910; Lieut. Colonel C. S. Riche to C. W. Payne, February 14, 1916; C. S. Riche to Mrs. J. Alleine Brown, January 7, 1915.

36. Lock No. 2 was proposed for river mile 302 (near Bryan/College Station); Lock No. 4 was proposed for river mile 347; Lock No. 5 was proposed for river mile 352; and Lock No. 7 was proposed for river mile 384. See A. E. Waldron to Chief of Engineers, June 5, 1909; Frank R. Morgan to Captain A. E. Waldron, May 17, 1909; Lieut. Colonel C. S. Riche to C. W. Payne, February 14, 1916; W. H. Lillard to Captain A. E. Waldron, December 5, 1910.

37. Walter Hogan to Mr. Gillette, April 10, 1919, box 6, folder B419, E.FW18, RG 77, NARA; Doyle L. Eastland to Lieut. Col. C. S. Riche and S. M. Wilcox, December 31, 1912, box 7, folder 419a, E.FW18, RG 77, NARA.

38. O. R. Scott to Major Earl I. Brown, February 9, 1912, box 7,

folder 419a, E.FW18, RG 77, NARA; Doyle L. Eastland to Lieut. Col. C. S. Riche and S. M. Wilcox, December 31, 1912.

39. "Second Lock Site: Located on the Brazos River Opposite Bryan—will be Surveyed This Week"; "Lock-and-Dam Being Built in the River Near Navasota," *Galveston Daily News*, December 11, 1910, newspaperarchive.com.

40. Proof, "Report on prelim. exam. of Brazos River Texas" (1919).

41. Edgar Jadwin to Brig. Gen. A. Mackenzie and Lieut. Col. Clinton B. Sears, July 11, 1905.

42. "Present Transportation Facilities at Freeport," *Freeport Facts*, November 10, 1912, www.newspaperarchive.com; "Navigation Board Will Meet Tuesday," *Waco Morning News*, September 10, 1915, in C. W. Payne to Colonel C. S. Riche, September 10, 1915, box 6, 410c, E.FW18, RG 77, NARA; "Opening of Freeport, New City of Texas, Wednesday, Nov. 20th, Causes Great Interest," *Wichita Daily Times*, November 17, 1912, www.newspaperarchive.com; "Katy System Secures Outlet to the Gulf"; "Velasco: Where Rail and Sail Meet"; "Barge Line to Be Put on Brazos to Ply From Waco to Freeport, River Mouth."

43. Yearbook of the Department of Agriculture (Washington, D.C.: Government Printing Office, 1907), in Payne, *Brazos River of Texas*, 291.

44. Edgar Jadwin to Brig. Gen. A. Mackenzie and Lieut. Col. Clinton B. Sears, July 11, 1905, box 10, folder 3, G6, RG 77, NARA.

45. "Second Lock Site: Located on the Brazos River Opposite Bryan—Will Be Surveyed This Week," *Galveston Daily News*, December 16, 1906, www.newspaperarchive.com; "Inspection of Brazos: Capt. Jadwin, Congressman Henry and Mayor Baker of Waco Traveled from San Felipe to Richmond"; Brazos River and Valley Improvement Ass'n, *Permanent organization*, 23–24.

46. Endorsement to a letter sent from Division Engineer of Gulf Division, May 21, 1918; Endorsement to a letter sent from Board of Engineers for Rivers and Harbors, June 10, 1919.

47. Record Cards, Engineer Department, U.S. Army—Doc. File Brazos, Case No 410, Sheet No 10, October 13–31, box 6, folder 410, E.FW18, RG 77, NARA; WAR, Board of Engineers for Rivers and Harbors, *Public Notice Relative to Proposed Improvement of Brazos River, Texas, from Old Washington to Waco* (Washington, D.C.: Government Printing Office, ca. 1910), box 10, folder 2, G6, RG 77, NARA; Morris Sheppard to Major W. J. Barden, telegram, October 28, 1916, box 6, folder 410, E.FW18, RG 77, NARA; District Engineer to Chief of Engineers, February 6, 1919, box 10, folder 2, G6—"Examination and Survey Files, 1908–1948" (hereinafter G6), RG 77, NARA; Endorsement to a letter sent from Board of Engineers for Rivers and Harbors, June 10, 1919; Proof, "Report on Prelim. Exam. of Brazos River Texas" (1919); Endorsement to a letter sent from Division Engineer of Gulf Division, May 21, 1918.

48. WAR, Board of Engineers for Rivers and Harbors, *Public Notice Relative to Proposed Improvement of Brazos River, Texas, from Old Washington to Waco*; Board of Engineers for Rivers and Harbors to Chief of Engineers, U.S. Army, June 25, 1918, box 10, folder 2, G6, RG 77, NARA; "Trinity Project Finally Dropped"; Endorsement to a letter sent from Board of Engineers for Rivers and Harbors, June 10, 1919.

49. Colonel C. S. Riche to E. R. Hatten, August 14, 1913; C. S. Riche to Mrs. J. Alleine Brown, January 7, 1915.
50. Colonel C. S. Riche to E. R. Hatten, August 14, 1913.
51. Brazos River and Valley Improvement Ass'n, *Permanent organization*, 25.
52. WAR, Board of Engineers for Rivers and Harbors, *Public Notice Relative to Proposed Improvement of Brazos River, Texas, from Old Washington to Waco*; District Engineer to Chief of Engineers, February 6, 1919; Edgar Jadwin to Brig. Gen. A. Mackenzie and Lieut. Col. Clinton B. Sears, July 11, 1905; "Hidalgo Falls Dam."
53. J. C. Sanford to Division Engineer, May 26, 1919, box 10, folder 2, G6, RG 77, NARA; Endorsement to a letter sent from Division Engineer of Gulf Division, May 21, 1918; District Engineer to Chief of Engineers, February 6, 1919; Brazos River and Valley Improvement Ass'n, *Permanent organization*, 24; Proof, "Report on Prelim. Exam. of Brazos River Texas" (1919); Endorsement to a letter sent from Board of Engineers for Rivers and Harbors, June 10, 1919.
54. S. M. Wilcox to R. C. Smead, January 11, 1919, box 10, folder 2, G6, RG 77, NARA.
55. "Emery Grounds Again after Being Floated," *Galveston Daily News*, February 18, 1920, www.newspaperarchive.com; "Rotarian Returns with Sisal and Derrick Barge Tender Tow," *Galveston Daily News*, January 28, 1920, www.newspaperarchive.com.
56. "Water Damage at Locks Is Estimated at $20,000," *Galveston Daily News*, December 23, 1913, www.newspaperarchive.com.
57. C. S. Riche to District Engineer and Chief of Engineers, May 5, 1915, box 6, folder 410, E.FW18, RG 77, NARA.
58. Char. Schuster to Major Early Brown, June 11, 1912, box 7, folder 419a, E.FW18, RG 77, NARA.
59. John C. Kramer to Captain John C. Oakes, June 3, 1909, box 4, folder 400, E.FW18, RG 77, NARA; John M. G. Watt to Chief of Engineers, November 3, 1917, box 6, folder B419, E.FW18, RG 77, NARA; "Work on Texas Waterways"; Inspector Crotty to John C. Kramer, May 29, 1909; F. P. Blums to S. M. Wilcox, December 13, 1913, box 4, folder 400, E.FW18, RG 77, NARA; District Engineer to Chief of Engineers, February 6, 1919.
60. W. H. Lillard to Captain A. E. Waldron, December 5, 1910; A. E. Waldron to Chief of Engineers, June 5, 1909; Frank R. Morgan to Captain A. E. Waldron, May 17, 1909.
61. John M. G. Watt to Chief of Engineers, November 3, 1917.
62. Ibid.
63. W. H. Lillard to Captain A. E. Waldron, December 5, 1910.
64. Edgar Jadwin to Brig. Gen. A. Mackenzie and Lieut. Col. Clinton B. Sears, July 11, 1905.
65. Lieut. Colonel C. S. Riche to C. W. Payne, February 14, 1916.
66. John N. Lyle to Colonel C. S. Riche, September 15, 1915, box 6, 410c, E.FW18, RG 77, NARA.
67. A. E. Waldron to Hon. Jas. B. Baker, September 23, 1909, box 66,

folder 412, E.FW18, RG 77, NARA; Frank R. Morgan to Captain A. E. Waldron, May 17, 1909.

68. A. E. Waldron to Chief of Engineers, June 5, 1909; Frank R. Morgan to Captain A. E. Waldron, May 17, 1909.

69. Frank R. Morgan to Captain A. E. Waldron, May 17, 1909.

70. "Navasota has the Idea on Navigation," *Waco Tribune-Herald*, 1915, in John N. Lyle to Colonel C. S. Riche, September 15, 1915, box 6, 410c, E.FW18, RG 77, NARA; Lieut. Colonel C. S. Riche to Judge John N. Lyle, September 18, 1915, box 6, 410c, E.FW18, RG 77, NARA.

71. "Navasota has the Idea on Navigation"; Lieut. Colonel C. S. Riche to Judge John N. Lyle, September 18, 1915.

72. "Congressman Moore on the Texas Waterways."

73. "Utilize the Brazos."

74. Evidence of what once were locks and dams can be found near the cities of Port Sullivan, Navasota, and Waco.

Chapter Five

1. Citizens of Rule, Texas, to Honorable George Mahon, petition, January 35, 1935, box 459, folder 13, S 653.1, "George H. Mahon: An Inventory of His Papers, 1887–1986 and undated" (hereinafter MAHON PAPERS), Southwest Collection, Texas Tech University (Lubbock) (hereinafter TTU-SWC).

2. E. D. Weaver to Honorable George Mahon, January 20, 1935, box 459, folder 13, S 653.1, MAHON PAPERS, TTU-SWC.

3. "Brazos Flood Control Plan Taking Shape," *Daily Court Review*, November 7, 1929, www.newspaperarchive.com; "Brazos Flood Menaces Waco," *Evening Independent*, September 28, 1936, www.newspaperarchive. com; "Prospects for Brazos Flood Control Good," *Freeport Facts*, December 24, 1931, www.newspaperarchive.com; "Drought-Plagued Farmers See Plantings Wash Away: Some Texas Cities Bracing for Floods," *Paris News*, April 30, 1957, www.newspaperarchive.com; "Brazos Flood Waters Are Reported Receding," *Galveston Daily News*, February 20, 1932, www.newspaperarchive.com; H. Bascom Simpson, "Wait Stresses Flood Control Survey Need," *Brazosport Facts*, December 11, 1959, www.newspaperarchive.com; "Seven Missing in Texas Flood," *Evening Independent*, November 26, 1940, www. newspaperarchive.com; "Texas Farm Goes Under During Brazos Flood," *European Stars and Stripes*, May 9, 1957, www.newspaperarchive.com; "Amarillo Without Water but Electric Lines Are Restored: Rescue Workers Comb Inundated Area for Marooned Residents," *Daily Capital News*, November 26, 1940, www.newspaperarchive.com; "Brazos Flood Perils Texas Farm Section," *Cumberland Evening Times*, May 8, 1957, www. newspaperarchive.com; "History Reveals Texas Always Prime Target for Nature's Violent Wrath," *Corsicana Daily Sun*, May 23, 1957, www. newspaperarchive.com; "Rivers and Harbors Improvement Drawn for Consideration," *Corsicana Daily Sun*, December 22, 1934, www.

newspaperarchive.com; "Waco Brazos Dam Urged," *Big Spring Daily Herald*, November 3, 1953, www.newspaperarchive.com; "Tracks Missing," *Abilene Reporter-News*, September 29, 1955, www.newspaperarchive.com; "Preliminaries on Brazos Dam Are Started," *Big Spring Daily Herald*, June 12, 1938, www.newspaperarchive.com; "Water over Oil," *Abilene Reporter-News*, September 29, 1955, www.newspaperarchive.com; "Millions Urged for Brazos Dam," *Abilene Reporter-News*, July 6, 1939, www.newspaperarchive.com; "Senate Group Gets Request for $3,000,000 Brazos Dam," *Abilene Reporter-News*, March 7, 1946, www.newspaperarchive.com; Earle Walker, "Haskell-Knox, Stonewall, Throckmorton, Dams Planned on Brazos River in Decades," *Abilene Reporter-News*, January 30, 1946, www.newspaperarchive.com; "Farmlands Washed by Hard Floods," *Big Spring Daily Herald*, April 30, 1957, www.newspaperarchive.com; "Amarillo, Texas Cut Off From World after Terrific Ice Storm—20 Inches Rain Falls in East Part of State," *Times*, November 25, 1940, www.newspaperarchive.com; "Clearing Skies May Slack Swelling Rivers in Texas," *Paris News*, September 27, 1955, www.newspaperarchive.com; "Fateful Fifty Years—the Noteworthy Events of Our Time, 1900–1949," *Tyrone Daily Herald*, January 5, 1950, www.newspaperarchive.com; "Brazos Flood Losses Set at Million," *Waco News-Tribune*, September 29, 1955, www.newspaperarchive.com; "Report on Brazos Flood Plan Sent to Senators," *Waco News-Tribune*, May 3, 1957, www.newspaperarchive.com; "Recent Brazos Flood Toll Estimate Set at $7,882,650," *Abilene Morning News*, October 15, 1936, www.newspaperarchive.com; "We Need River Control," *Abilene Morning News*, October 1, 1936, www.newspaperarchive.com.

4. W. R. Poage to Honorable Byron Skelton, June 18, 1957, box 639, file 3, folder "Project: Brazos River Authority, 1957," Poage Papers, Poage Legislative Library (Waco, TX) (hereinafter POAGE).

5. A. L. Monteith to Honorable W. R. Poage, June 7, 1938, box 1425, file 40 "Brazos, Bell, & Milam Counties—Letters for Action (1938)" (hereinafter File 40), POAGE.

6. United States House of Representatives (hereinafter HOUSE), "*H.R. 6198: A Bill to Control Flood Waters of the Brazos River and Its Tributaries in the State of Texas*" (Washington, D.C.: Government Printing Office, February 28, 1935), 5.

7. "Brazos Not Navigable, Connally Informs FPC: 'Not Even for Rowboats,'" *Fort Worth Star-Telegram*, January 19, 1951, AR 406, 7–18, Fort Worth Star-Telegram Collection (hereinafter FWSTC), Special Collections, University of Texas at Arlington (hereinafter SC-UTA).

8. Ibid.

9. Ibid.

10. W. R. Poage to Honorable George Mahon, October 10, 1938, box 459, folder 13, S 653.1, MAHON PAPERS, TTU-SWC.

11. Brazos River Channel and Dock Company (hereinafter BRCDC), *Facts with Reference to the Brazos River Enterprise and the "New South"* (New York: John A. Lowell & Col. Printers, 1890).

12. Public Works Administration (hereinafter PWA), "Form No. 158: Legal Information Supplied by Applicant," n.d., box 1426, file 44, POAGE.

13. W. R. Poage to Honorable A. L. Bronsted, February 9, 1946, box 1424, folder 27 "Whitney Dam 1945–46" (hereinafter FOLDER 27), POAGE; Citizens of Grimes and Waller Counties, in Navasota, Texas, resolution, March 5, 1935, box 459, folder 13, S 653.1, MAHON PAPERS, TTU-SWC; Abilene Chamber of Commerce, in Abilene, Texas, resolution, March 19, 1935, box 459, folder 13, S 653.1, MAHON PAPERS, TTU-SWC; W. R. Poage to Board of Directors for Marlin Chamber of Commerce, February 6, 1946, box 1424, FOLDER 27, POAGE.

14. John Norris, "Concerning the Production of Hydroelectric Power on Texas Streams" (n.d.), box 1423, folder 22, POAGE.

15. Dick Vaughan, "Federal Government Funds May Help Tame Erratic Brazos River, Provide Irrigation, Electric Power and Protection from Floods," *El Paso Herald-Post*, December 4, 1934, www.newspaperarchive.com.

16. HOUSE, *H.R. 6198*, 35; M.C. Tyler, memorandum, June 23, 1939, box 1426, file 44, POAGE, 2.

17. Ibid., 4.

18. H. P. Drought to William McCraw, October 23, 1935, box 2, folder 4, FW17—"Subject Files Relating to the Construction of Possum Kingdom Dam, 1936–1937" (hereinafter FW17), Record Group 77—Records of the Army Corps of Engineers, Southwest Division (hereinafter RG 77), National Archives and Records Administration (Fort Worth, TX) (hereinafter NARA); C. B. McQueen to Bob Poage, June 8, 1938, box 1425, file 40, POAGE; Sheriff John R. Bigham to W. R. Poage, June 9, 1938, box 1425, file 40, POAGE; Jim Neinast to Honorable Bob Poage, June 13, 1938, box 1425, file 40, POAGE; E. C. Cole to Honorable Bob Poage, June 14, 1938, box 1425, file 40, POAGE; E. M. Brown to W. R. Poage, June 8, 1938, box 1425, file 40, POAGE; Roy Case to Honorable Bob Poage, June 1938, box 1425, file 40, POAGE.

19. "Brazos Floods Soon Will Be Harnessed," *FWST*, December 2, 1936, AR 406-7-18-1, FWSTC, SC-UTA; "Seymour Project Recommended by Water Engineers," *Wichita Daily Times*, April 17, 1923, www. newspaperarchive.com; "Waco Threatened with Brazos Flood," *Paris News*, April 28, 1942, www.newspaperarchive.com; D. W. Bell to Senator, October 11, 1935, box 1425, file 40, POAGE; "Exhibit C," in Franklin D. Roosevelt to Secretary of the Treasury, September 26, 1935, box 1425, file 40, POAGE.

20. "'Wholesale Destruction' From Brazos Flood is Feared," *Morning Avalanche*, September 29, 1936, www.newspaperarchive.com; "Brazos River in Spotlight Again on Two Counts," *Waco News-Tribune*, May 22, 1956, www.newspaperarchive.com; H. A. Montgomery to F. B. Wilby, October 3, 1936, box 3, folder 2, FW17, RG 77, NARA; W. R. Poage to Honorable Winbourn Pearce, July 19, 1937, box 1426, folder 46 "Brazos River (1937–1941)," POAGE; "Report on Brazos Flood Plan Sent to Senators."

21. E. M. Brown to W.R. Poage, June 8, 1938 (first quotation); C. B. McQueen to Bob Poage, June 8, 1938 (second quotation).

22. John Clarkson to Honorable Bob Poage, June 8, 1938, box 1425, file 40, POAGE (quotation).

23. Vaughn, "Federal Government Funds May Help Tame Erratic Brazos River, Provide Irrigation, Electric Power and Protection from Floods."

24. "Editorial: The Brazos Authority," *Abilene Reporter-News*, April 1, 1953, www.newspaperarchive.com; "Federal Funds Sought for Dams Along Brazos," *Abilene Reporter-News*, July 17, 1945, www.newspaperarchive.com; "Towns Near the Proposed Reservoirs, Brazos River Conservation and Reclamation District" (n.d.), box 1423, FOLDER 22, POAGE; A. B. Thornton and Dallas Coffin Co. to Honorable George Mahon, January 25, 1935, box 459, folder 13, S 653.1, MAHON PAPERS, TTU-SWC; "Texas Senate Passes Bill to Speed Dam Construction," *FWST*, May 8, 1953, AR 406–7–18, FWSTC, SC-UTA; Joe Bomer to W. R. Poage, June 10, 1938, box 1425, file 40, POAGE; Walker, "Haskell-Knox, Stonewall, Throckmorton"; "Flood Water Control Can Redeem Millions of Acres of Texas Land," *Port Arthur News*, October 2, 1925, newspaperarchive.com; H. A. Montgomery to Division Engineer, Gulf of Mexico Division, January 25, 1937, box 6, folder 9, FW17, RG 77, NARA.

25. Bess Stephenson, "Brazos Dam Idea is Old," *FWST*, June 24, 1940, AR 406–7–18, FWSTC, SC-UTA; Herbert S. Hilburn to Honorable George Mahon, December 4, 1951, box 459, folder 1, S 653.1, MAHON PAPERS, TTU-SWC; Army Corps of Engineers (hereinafter ACOE), "Memorandum Report on the Economic Justification from a Flood-Control Standpoint of the 13-Dam Brazos River Valley Project" (January 25, 1937), box 6, folder 9, FW17, RG 77, NARA.

26. PWA, "Form No. 157, Financial Information Supplied by Texas: State File 2143-P, 9/30/38," 1938, box 1426, file 44, POAGE.

27. J. Russell Wait, "Report to Brazos River Harbor Navigation District," in J. Russell Wait to Brazos River Harbor Navigation District of Brazoria County, May 1, 1950, box 31, folder 31.3, MS 346, J. Russell Wait Port of Houston Papers (hereinafter WAIT PAPERS), Woodson Research Center, Rice University (Houston, TX).

28. Aubrey Williams to George Dern, February 3, 1936, box 2, folder 9, FW17, RG 77, NARA; T. P. Carroll to Honorable George Mahon, June 12, 1935, box 459, folder 13, S 653.1, MAHON PAPERS, TTU-SWC; George D. Babcock to Honorable George Mahon, June 15, 1935, box 459, folder 13, S 653.1, MAHON PAPERS, TTU-SWC; "Project No. 1165: Application for Allotment of Funds under Emergency Relief Appropriation Act of 1935," January 29, 1936, box 2, folder 4, FW17, RG 77, NARA; Harry Hopkins to George Dern, January 27, 1936, box 3, folder 1, FW17, RG 77, NARA; ACOE, *Annual Report of Chief of Engineers on Improvement of Rivers and Harbors in the Mineral Wells, Texas, District* (Washington, D.C.: Government Printing Office, 1938); Franklin D. Roosevelt to Mr. Secretary, September 26, 1935, in John D. McCall to Special Committee appointed for Washington Trip, July 9, 1937, box 1426, file 47, POAGE; "Work is Begun on Brazos Dam," *Abilene Reporter-News*, June 12, 1938, www.newspaperarchive.com; H. E. Fisher to R. J. Tipton, August 15, 1936, box 3, folder 2, FW17, RG 77, NARA; "Report on Losses from the Brazos River Flood in 1936," 1936, box 1423, file 24, POAGE; W. R. Poage to Roy Potts, June 9, 1938, box 1425, file 40, POAGE; B. C. Clarke to Captain P. A. Feringa, June 2, 1939, box 12, folder 3, G6— "Examination and Survey Files, 1908–1948" (hereinafter G6), RG 77, NARA; F. C. Harrington to John A. Norris, December 11, 1936, box 1, folder 4, FW17,

RG 77, NARA; "Exhibit C"; D. W. Bell to Senator, October 11, 1935; "Brazos Floods Soon will be Harnessed"; Harry Hopkins to George Dern, January 27, 1936; Brazos River Conservation and Reclamation District (hereinafter BRCRD), *The Brazos Project: What Is It?* (Temple, TX: BRCRD, 1936), box 1423, file 22 "Brazos River 1927–1934," POAGE; John D. McCall to Special Committee appointed for Washington Trip, July 9, 1937, box 1426, file 47, POAGE.

29. H. A. Montgomery to Division Engineer, September 30, 1936, box 2, folder 9, FW17, RG 77, NARA; Marion Dillingham to District Engineer, U.S. Engineers Office, August 18, 1937, box 6, folder 9, FW17, RG 77, NARA; "Texas WPA Chief Favors Brazos Work," *FWST*, August 29, 1935, AR406-7–18-8, FWSTC, SC-UTA; "First of Brazos Dams Assured," *FWST*, October 24, 1935, AR406-7–18-8, FWSTC, SC-UTA; *Possum Kingdom Dam near Breckenridge, TX*, 1941, AR317-10-17, Basil Clemons Photograph Collection (hereinafter BASIL), SC-UTA; "Possum Kingdom Now is Sheppard Lake, Dam," *FWST*, July 22, 1941, AR406-7-18-3, FWSTC, SC-UTA; "Last of Concrete is Poured at Possum Kingdom Dam," *FWST*, March 21, 1941, AR406-7-18-3, FWSTC, SC-UTA; "Possum Dam Power Sale OK," *FWST*, March 16, 1941, AR406-7-18-3, FWSTC, SC-UTA; "Dam to Serve Broad Section," *FWST*, March 15, 1941, AR406-7-18-3, FWSTC, SC-UTA; "Magnificent Scenic Playground Planned as by-Product of Possum Kingdom Dam," *FWST*, June 26, 1940, AR406-7-18-3, FWSTC, SC-UTA; "Possum Kingdom Dam is Dedicated Amid Cheers," *FWST*, July 3, 1941, AR406-7-18-3, FWSTC, SC-UTA; "Fishing in Nearby Possum Kingdom Lake Is Attractive for Mineral Wells," *FWST*, June 17, 1942, AR406-7-18-3, FWSTC, SC-UTA; "Texans Request WPA Approval of Brazos Dam," *Galveston Daily News*, July 21, 1937, www.newspaperarchive.com; Eric Haquinius to John Norris, interoffice memorandum, May 28, 1937, box 3, folder 2, FW17, RG 77, NARA; George Mahon to Howard Humphrey, March 4, 1947, box 459, folder 4, S 653.1, MAHON PAPERS, TTU-SWC; "Budget Bureau Director Says Project 'Fine,'" *FWST*, October 12, 1935, AR 406-7–18, FWSTC, SC-UTA; E. M. Markham to Harry Hopkins, June 15, 1936, box 1, folder 4, FW17, RG 77, NARA; "Brazos PWA Project Approval Demanded," *FWST*, August 4, 1938, AR 406-7–18-1, FWSTC, SC-UTA; H. A. Montgomery, District Circular No. 1, June 25, 1936, box 1, folder 5, FW17, RG 77, NARA; E. H. Marks to Division Engineer, Gulf of Mexico Division, February 17, 1936, box 2, folder 4, FW17, RG 77, NARA; B. C. Clarke to Captain P. A. Feringa, June 2, 1939; George D. Babcock to Honorable George Mahon, June 15, 1935; T. P. Carroll to Honorable George Mahon, June 12, 1935; Harry Hopkins to George Dern, January 27, 1936; ACOE, *Annual Report of Chief of Engineers on Improvement of Rivers and Harbors in the Mineral Wells, Texas, District*; "Brazos Floods Soon will be Harnessed"; W. R. Poage to Board of Directors for Marlin Chamber of Commerce, February 6, 1946; W. R. Poage to Honorable A. L. Bronsted, February 9, 1946.

30. "Model Studies of the Spillway and Stilling Basin for the Possum Kingdom Dam," *Technical Memorandum No. 111–1* (n.p.: October 3, 1936); [*Possum Kingdom Damsite*], box 6, folder 7, FW17, RG 77, NARA; *Viewing*

East Brazos River and Cliff at Possum Kingdom Dam Site, 1936, 1936, AR 317–10–16, BASIL, SC-UTA; *Possum Kingdom Dam near Breckenridge, TX.*

31. "Work on Brazos Dam Awaits Settlement of Cost Estimates," *Belton Journal,* February 11, 1937, www.newspaperarchive.com; "To Discuss Brazos Dam," *Big Spring Daily Herald,* July 19, 1937, www.newspaperarchive.com; "Ambitious but Expensive," *Denton Record-Chronicle,* August 2, 1937, www.newspaperarchive.com; Memorandum from H. A. Montgomery on September 11, 1936, box 1, folder 4, FW17, RG 77, NARA; Aubrey Williams to E. M. Markham, July 10, 1936, box 1, folder 3, FW17, RG 77, NARA; E. M. Markham to Aubrey Williams, on July 17, 1936, box 1, folder 3, FW17, RG 77, NARA; "To Start Work Soon on First of Brazos Dams," *Big Spring Daily Herald,* December 30, 1935, www.newspaperarchive.com.

32. R. A. Wheeler to Honorable W. R. Poage, March 12, 1946, box 1424, folder 27, POAGE; "House Turns Down Whitney Dam Fund," *FWST,* January 8, 1946, AR 406–7–18, FWSTC, SC-UTA; "Committee Gets Brazos Dam Plea," *FWST,* March 7, 1946, AR 406–7–18, FWSTC, SC-UTA; "Flood Damage Study for Main Stem and Major Tributaries, Work Assignment 11.2," (April 1961), box 12, folder 6, SW6—"U.S. Commission Study—Texas, 1958–1960" (hereinafter SW6), RG 77, NARA, 1; "Towns near the Proposed Reservoirs, Brazos River Conservation and Reclamation District"; HOUSE, *H.R. 6198,* 35; M. C. Tyler, memorandam, June 23, 1939, box 1426, file 44, POAGE; United States Senate (hereinafter SENATE), *S. 2092: A bill to control flood waters of the Brazos River and its tributaries in the State of Texas, to aid and improve agriculture and industrial development within said river basin, and for other purposes. 74th Congress, 1st session* (Washington, D.C., Government Printing Office, March 12, 1935), 7; H. A. Montgomery to Division Engineer, January 25, 1937; George Mahon to Howard Humphrey, March 4, 1947; Joe Bomer to W. R. Poage, June 10, 1938.

33. "Towns near the Proposed Reservoirs, Brazos River Conservation and Reclamation District"; W. T. Garrett to W. R. Poage, February 18, 1941, box 1421, folder 6, POAGE; Herbert S. Hilburn to Honorable George Mahon, December 4, 1951; HOUSE, *H.R. 6198,* 35; SENATE, *S. 2092,* 7; H. A. Montgomery to Division Engineer, January 25, 1937; Joe Bomer to W. R. Poage, June 10, 1938.

34. "Texans Plan House Fight for Dam Funds," *FWST,* March 20, 1946, AR 406–7–18–5, FWSTC, SC-UTA; "Rep. Poage Optimistic over Whitney Dam," *FWST,* October 10, 1946, AR 406–7–18–5, FWSTC, SC-UTA; "Whitney Dam Grant Okay is Announced," *FWST,* evening edition, April 16, 1946, AR 406–7–18–5, FWSTC, SC-UTA; "Brazos Dam is Taken up by Congress," *FWST,* July 6, 1939, AR 406–7–18–5, FWSTC, SC-UTA; "Texans Make Urgent Appeal for Whitney Dam Funds," *FWST,* March 7, 1946, AR 406–7–18–5, FWSTC, SC-UTA.

35. "Celebration Planned," *San Antonio Express,* May 11, 1947, www.newspaperarchive.

36. "Congressmen Fail In Attempt to Get Whitney Dam Appropriation," *Belton Journal,* February 14, 1946, www.newspaperarchive.com; "US Engineer Reports on Dam Ceremony," *Galveston Daily News,* July 8, 1947,

www.newspaperarchive.com; Eric Haquinius, inter-office Memorandum to John Norris, interoffice Memorandum, May 28, 1937; Herbert S. Hilburn to Honorable George Mahon, December 4, 1951.

37. "Millions Urged for Brazos Dam"; Larry Deister, "Harnessing Wild Texas Rivers Big Task Supervised by District Engineers Here," *Galveston Daily News*, November 13, 1949, www.newspaperarchive.com; B. C. Clarke to Captain P. A. Feringa, June 2, 1939; M. C. Tyler, memorandum, June 23, 1939, POAGE.

38. "Eastland Rock to Be Used for Big Brazos Dam," *Abilene Reporter-News*, July 9, 1948, www.newspaperarchive.com; Deister, "Harnessing Wild Texas Rivers"; Walker, "Haskell-Knox, Stonewall, Throckmorton."

39. Colonel Stanley G. Reiff, "[Water Conservation along the Brazos River]" (lecture, Sixteenth Annual Convention of Texas Water Conservation Association, Austin, TX, October 31, 1960), box 1, folder 1, SW6, RG 77, NARA; M. C. Tyler to Honorable W. R. Poage, April 11, 1939, box 12, folder 2, G6, RG 77, NARA; *Projects in Congressional District No. 11, Hon. W. R. Poage, Recommended to the President by the National Resources Committee in its Report Transmitted December 1936* (Washington, D.C.: Government Printing Office, 1936), box 1426, File 46, POAGE; F.S. Besson to Honorable W. R. Poage, March 7, 1940, box 12, folder 2, G6, RG 77, NARA; "Flood Damage Study for Main Stem and Major Tributaries, Work Assignment 11.2," (April 1961), 1; Eric Haquinius to John Norris, interoffice memorandum, May 28, 1937; "Texas Senate Passes Bill to Speed Dam Construction."

40. ACOE, *Flood Control Project, Brazos River Basin, Belton Reservoir, Leon River, Texas* (Fort Worth, TX: Army Corps of Engineers, 1954), Map Collection, TXBU; ACOE, *Flood Control Project, Brazos River Basin, Belton Dam, Leon River, Texas* (Fort Worth, TX: Army Corps of Engineers, 1954), Map Collection, TXBU; "Flood Damage Study for Main Stem and Major Tributaries, Work Assignment 11.2," (April 1961), 1; *Projects in Congressional District No. 11, Hon. W. R. Poage*; Ambursen Engineering Corporation (hereinafter AMBURSEN), Leon Dam, Site Map (n.p.: 1946), Map Collection, TXBU.

41. "Flood Damage Study for Main Stem and Major Tributaries, Work Assignment 11.2," (April 1961), 1; *Projects in Congressional District No. 11, Hon. W. R. Poage.*

42. W. R. Poage to H. S. Hilburn, July 9, 1957, box 639, file 3, POAGE; W. R. Poage to Pearl A. Neas, August 9, 1954, box 639, file 1, POAGE; W. R. Poage to Stuart Long, August 26, 1957, box 639, file 3, POAGE.

43. "Army Boss Recommends Brazos Tributary Dams," *FWST*, March 15, 1950, AR 406–7–18–1, FWSTC, SC-UTA; Loren Olmstead to Honorable W. R. Poage, July 24, 1959, box 639, file 4, POAGE; W. R. Poage to H. S. Hilburn, July 9, 1957; Reiff, "[Water Conservation along the Brazos River]."

44. "New Lake for Waco in Brazos Program," *San Antonio Express*, November 8, 1964, www.newspaperarchive.com; "Engineers Consider Six New Dams for Brazos Watershed," *Paris News*, October 21, 1947, www. newspaperarchive.com; "Six More Dams for Brazos River Project Favored," *Corsicana Daily Sun*, November 5, 1948, www.newspaperarchive.com; "Army

Boss Recommends Brazos Tributary Dams"; W. R. Poage to Pearl A. Neas, August 9, 1954; Reiff, "[Water Conservation along the Brazos River]."

45. W. R. Poage to John A. Norris, January 6, 1940, box 1424, file 29, POAGE; Eric Haquinius to John Norris, interoffice memorandum, May 28, 1937; M. C. Tyler to Honorable W. R. Poage, April 11, 1939.

46. W. R. Poage to John A. Norris, January 6, 1940; Eric Haquinius to John Norris, interoffice memorandum, May 28, 1937; F. S. Besson to Honorable W. R. Poage, March 7, 1940; Texas Senate Passes Bill to Speed Dam Construction"; M. C. Tyler to Honorable W. R. Poage, April 11, 1939; *Projects in Congressional District No. 11, Hon. W. R. Poage.*

47. *Capacity-Cost Curve for Somerville Reservoir Site, Yegua Creek* (Austin, TX: Army Corps of Engineers, 1960), box 8, SW6, RG 77, NARA; Franklin Fisher to W. A. Mahla, December 7, 1939, box 1, folder 8, G5— "NAVIGABLE WATERWAY FILES, 1931–1962" (hereinafter G5), RG 77, NARA; F. S. Besson to Honorable W. R. Poage, March 7, 1940; Eric Haquinius, inter-office Memorandum to John Norris, May 28, 1937; "Texas Senate Passes Bill to Speed Dam Construction"; M. C. Tyler to Honorable W. R. Poage, April 11, 1939.

48. Louis Williams to M. J. Asensio, December 5, 1939, box 1, folder 8, G5, RG 77, NARA; J. L. Schley to Honorable Luther Johnson, January 23, 1941, box 12, folder 2, G6, RG 77, NARA; M. C. Tyler to Honorable W. R. Poage, April 11, 1939.

49. Bob Wright, "Lake Hearing Held Monday at Groesbeck," *Mexia Daily News*, March 5, 1974, www.newspaperarchive.com; "Millican and Navasota No. 2 Reservoirs, Brazos River Basin, Texas" (May 22, 1968), box 684, folder 7, Water, Inc. Collection [unlisted collection hereinafter WATER INC], TTU-SWC.

50. "Millican and Navasota No. 2 Reservoirs, Brazos River Basin, Texas."

51. "Harnessing River is Brazos District's Job," *Abilene Reporter-News*, September 14, 1952, www.newspaperarchive.com; "Size, Location Given for Key Dams in BRA's Control Plan," *Waco Tribune-Herald*, August 2, 1956, www.newspaperarchive.com; "Brazos Dam Hopes Rise," *Waco News-Tribune*, February 25, 1956, www.newspaperarchive.com; Jules Loh, "BRA Has Special Plans for Dealing with Salt, Gypsum Polluting River," *Waco News-Tribune*, August 3, 1956, www.newspaperarchive.com; "Report on Brazos Flood Plan Sent to Senators"; John Colton, "BRA Proposes 6 Dams to Hold River Water," *Baytown Sun*, August 8, 1957, www.newspaperarchive.com; "Review of Commission Plan on Basis of Commission Action on June 5, 1961" (June 26, 1961), box 2, folder 6, SW6, RG 77, NARA; R. D. Collins to George Mahon, August 8, 1955, box 291, folder 19, S 653.1, MAHON PAPERS, TTU-SWC.

52. AMBURSEN, *Turkey Creek Dam, Site Map* (New York: AMBURSEN, 1950), Map Collection, TXBU; John A. Morris to G. F. Harley, telegram, March 4, 1939, box 1426, folder 45, POAGE; Herbert Hilburn to Honorable George Mahon, December 12, 1951, box 459, folder 1, S 653.1, MAHON PAPERS, TTU-SWC; Herbert Hilburn to Honorable George Mahon, December 5, 1951, box 459, folder 1, S 653.1, MAHON PAPERS, TTU-SWC;

H.F. 2873: A bill to authorize purchase of a portion of the bonds issued by the Brazos River Authority, an agency of the State of Texas, to finance the early development by it of the water resources of the Brazos River Basin, Texas. 84th Congress, 1st Session (Washington, D.C.: Government Printing Office, January 24, 1955), box 446, file 5, POAGE, 1–2; ACOE, "Notice of Interim Report on Review of Brazos River Authority Proposed Plan of Development, Brazos River, Texas," (September 20, 1956), in L. E. Seeman to Honorable William R. Poage, September 12, 1956, box 639, file 2, POAGE; Eric Haquinius to John Norris, interoffice memorandum, May 28, 1937; Herbert S. Hilburn to Honorable George Mahon, December 4, 1951; Brazos River Authority (hereinafter BRA), *The River* (n.p.: ca. 1950), WATER INC.

53. "Size, Location Given for Key Dams in BRA's Control Plan"; "Brazos Dam Hopes Rise" (quotation); Colton, "BRA Proposes 6 Dams to Hold River Water."

54. W. R. Poage to Marshall Croft, June 22, 1959, box 639, file 4, POAGE; *H.F. 2873*, 4; ACOE, "Notice of Interim Report on Review of Brazos River Authority Proposed Plan of Development, Brazos River, Texas"; BRA, *River.*

55. "Texas Senate Passes Bill to Speed Dam Construction"; M. C. Tyler to Honorable W. R. Poage, April 11, 1939 (quotation); W. R. Poage, *Oral Memoirs of William Robert "Bob" Poage* (Waco, TX: Baylor University Institute for Oral History), 492; BRA, *River.*

56. *H.F. 2873*, 5.

57. BRA, *River.*

58. Ibid.

59. "Five Dams on Brazos are Vital to Texas Progress," *Waco News-Tribune*, July 17, 1956, www.newspaperarchive.com.

60. Ibid.

61. "New Brazos Dam Planned," *Brazosport Facts*, December 30, 1963, www.newspaperarchive.com; W. R. Poage to Honorable G. W. Lineweaver, December 20, 1954, box 639, file 2, POAGE.

62. "Brazos Dam Power Pact Approved," *Abilene Reporter-News*, January 14, 1964, www.newspaperarchive.com; "New Brazos Dam Planned"; Eric Haquinius to John Norris, interoffice memorandum, May 28, 1937.

63. "Engineers Report Brazos Dam Costs Outweigh Benefits," *Galveston Daily News*, September 21, 1956, www.newspaperarchive.com; "Opposition Briefs to the Six-Dam Program field at Public Hearing of the Brazos River Authority" (Austin, TX: n.p., July 16, 1957).

64. "A Vast New Holiday Land," *Aspermont Star*, September 6, 1956, in University of North Texas, "The Portal to Texas History," University of North Texas Libraries, http://www.texashistory.unt.edu.

65. Colton, "BRA Proposes 6 Dams to Hold River Water."

66. "Nugent Dam Project," *Abilene Reporter-News*, August 12, 1953, www.newspaperarchive.com; "Dividing the Water," *FWST*, July 31, 1954, AR 406-7-18-4, FWSTC, SC-UTA; "Texans Seek Law Change on Brazos Dam," *FWST*, July 16, 1953, AR 406-7-18-4, FWSTC, SC-UTA; "Brazos River Dam System Is Outlined," *FWST*, July 1, 1954, AR 406-7-18-4, FWSTC, SC-UTA; Colton, "BRA Proposes 6 Dams to Hold River Water"; "Brazos River Dam

Project Criticized by Water Users," *Galveston Daily News*, November 18, 1956, www.newspaperarchive.com; Blair Justice, "Brazos River Board Member Asserts Dams Benefit Few," *FWST*, August 11, 1953, AR 406–7–18, FWSTC, SC-UTA.

67. "Brazos River Dam Project Criticized by Water Users"; Justice, "Brazos River Board Member."

68. "Comparison of Brazos River Authority's Six Dam Project with U.S. Army Engineers Authorized Reservoir Plan" (n.d.), box 639, file 3, POAGE.

69. Emory E. Camp to Honorable W. R. Poage, October 18, 1957, box 639, file 3, POAGE.

70. BRA, *Let's Build Dams!* (n.p.: n.p., August 1957), box 639, file 3, POAGE.

71. Ibid.

72. "Head of WPA Is Asked to Settle Brazos Dispute," *Corpus Christi Times*, December 9, 1936, www.newspaperarchive.com; "Hearing Slated on Brazos Dam," *Brownsville Herald*, August 15, 1948, www.newspaperarchive. com; Dick Vaughan, "Money of Taxpayers to Harness Brazos, But There'll Be No Cut in Electric Bills," *El Paso Herald-Post*, November 30, 1936, www. newspaperarchive.com; "Power Company Asks Monopoly," *El Paso Herald-Post*, January 25, 1937, www.newspaperarchive.com; "Brazos Dam Power Hearings Slated," *Denton Record-Chronicle*, May 19, 1949, www. newspaperarchive.com; "The Colonel's Comments," *Hearne Democrat*, December 4, 1936, www.newspaperarchive.com; "Selling Brazos Power to a Utility," *Hearne Democrat*, December 4, 1936, www.newspaperarchive.com; "Power Trust Reaching for Brazos Dams," *Hearne Democrat*, December 4, 1936, www.newspaperarchive.com.

73. "Harnessing River is Brazos District's Job"; "Nugent Dam Project."

74. Ibid.

75. Walker, "Haskell-Knox, Stonewall, Throckmorton."

76. Hamilton Wright, "Brazos Fork Might be Dammed, If Cities Need Water Supply," *Abilene Reporter-News*, August 1, 1948, www. newspaperarchive.com.

77. Edward H. Harte, "Minor Changes in Hubbard Water Bill Seen by Latimer," *Abilene Reporter-News*, February 18, 1955, www. newspaperarchive.com; Katharyn Duff, "From the Water Plant War at Reynolds Bend," *Abilene Reporter-News*, August 6, 1966, www. newspaperarchive.com.

78. Ibid.

79. Katharyn Duff, "If Abilene Interested, Plan for Nugent Dam Not 'Dead,'" *Abilene Reporter-News*, May 4, 1954, www.newspaperarchive.com; "Hubbard or Nugent?," *Abilene Reporter-News*, January 12, 1955, www. newspaperarchive.com; Harte; "Nugent Dam Urged, Hubbard Creek Reservoir Criticized at BRA Parley"; "Nugent Dam Project."

80. "Nugent Dam Urged, Hubbard Creek Reservoir Criticized at BRA Parley"; Hamilton Wright, "$1,500,000 'Ear-Marked' For Baskin Dam Across Brazos River," *Abilene Reporter-News*, June 28, 1944, www. newspaperarchive.com.

81. "Nugent Dam Urged, Hubbard Creek Reservoir Criticized at BRA Parley"; Hamilton Wright, "$1,500,000 'Ear-Marked' For Baskin Dam Across Brazos River," *Abilene Reporter-News*, June 28, 1944, www. newspaperarchive.com.

82. "Harnessing River is Brazos District's Job."

83. Don Tabor, "No Hope Given on Brazos Dam," *Abilene Reporter-News*, February 15, 1964, www.newspaperarchive.com; "Booster Group For Rule Dam Organizes," *Abilene Reporter-News*, January 11, 1964, www. newspaperarchive.com; "Preliminary Engineering Done for Brazos Dam in Knox County," *Abilene Reporter-News*, January 30, 1944, www. newspaperarchive.com; M. H. Brannen to George H. Mahon, October 16, 1945, box 459, folder 4, S 653.1, MAHON PAPERS, TTU-SWC (quotation); George Mahon to W. R. Johnson, December 1, 1956, box 459, folder 7, S 653.1, MAHON PAPERS, TTU-SWC.

84. Wright, "Brazos Fork."

85. *The Mighty Brazos Valley: A Look at Tomorrow* (Waco, TX: Brazos River Authority, n.d.), WATER INC, TTU-SWC; Herbert S. Hilburn to Honorable George Mahon, December 4, 1951.

86. "Hearings are Set on Six Basins," *Big Spring Daily Herald*, July 6, 1966, www.newspaperarchive.com.

87. *Mighty Brazos Valley*.

88. Ibid.

89. "Brazos Dam is in 1940 Rivers and Harbors Bill: Gives Promise of Flood Relief in Lower River Basin," *Freeport Facts*, July 13, 1939, www. newspaperarchive.com.

90. M. C. Tyler, memorandum, June 23, 1939, POAGE.

Chapter Six

1. North Plains Water Conservation District, *Ogallala Slim*, Comic Book, ca. 1960s, Water, Inc. Collection [unlisted collection hereinafter WATER INC], TTU-SWC.

2. Ibid.

3. Tom Johnson, "Water Plan Opposition Comes from East, West," *Abilene Reporter-News*, July 17, 1968, www.newspaperarchive.com; Joe Kilgore to Walter J. Wells, August 21, 1964, box 639, folder "Poage Project: Brazos River, 1959–1964," file 4, Poage Papers, Poage Legislative Library (Waco, TX) (hereinafter POAGE).

4. "Flood Damage Study for Main Stem and Major Tributaries, Work Assignment 11.2," (April 1961), box 12, folder 6, SW6—"U.S. Commission Study—Texas, 1958–1960" (hereinafter SW6), Record Group 77—Records of the Army Corps of Engineers, Southwest Division (hereinafter RG 77), National Archives and Records Administration (Fort Worth, TX) (hereinafter NARA), 1; Public Works Administration (hereinafter PWA), "Form No. 157, State File No. 2143: 'Exhibit "A" To Amend Application of September 30, 1938,'" box 1426, file 44, POAGE; E. M. Brown to W. R. Poage, June 8, 1938, box 1425,

file 40, POAGE; C. B. McQueen, letter two to Bob Poage, June 8, 1938, box 1425, file 40, POAGE; *Concerning Brazos River Conservation and Reclamation District* (n.p.: n.d.), box 1423, folder 22 "Brazos River 1927–1934" (hereinafter FOLDER 22), POAGE; PWA, "Form No. 158: Legal Information Supplied by Applicant," n.d., box 1426, file 44, POAGE; John Norris, "Concerning the Production of Hydroelectric Power on Texas Streams" (n.d.), box 1423, FOLDER 22, POAGE; PWA, "Form No. 157, Financial information supplied by Texas: state file 2143-P, 9/30/38," 1938, box 1426, file 44, POAGE; "Water Supply," *Data for Survey Report* (1948), box 31, folder 31.2, MS 346, J. Russell Wait Port of Houston Papers (hereinafter WAIT PAPERS), Woodson Research Center, Rice University (Houston, TX) (hereinafter WRC), [3]; J. Russell Wait, "Report to Brazos River Harbor Navigation District," in Robert J. Cummins to Freeport Sulphur Company, July 1, 1950, box 31, folder 31.1, MS 346, WAIT PAPERS, WRC; "Date Fixed to Open Bids on Brazos Dam," *Abilene Reporter-News*, August 22, 1937, www.newspaperarchive.com; Brazos River Conservation and Reclamation District (hereinafter BRCRD), *The Brazos Project: What is It?* (Temple, TX: BRCRD, 1936), box 1423, FOLDER 22, POAGE; "[The Brazos River is the only . . .]" (n.p.: n.d.), box 1423, FOLDER 22, POAGE; Army Corps of Engineers (hereinafter ACOE), "Memorandum Report on the Economic Justification from a Flood-Control Standpoint of the 13-Dam Brazos River Valley Project" (January 25, 1937), box 6, folder 9, FW17—"Subject Files Relating to the Construction of Possum Kingdom Dam, 1936–1937" (hereinafter FW17), RG 77, NARA; R. A. Wheeler to Honorable W. R. Poage, March 12, 1946, box 1424, folder 27, POAGE; "House Turns Down Whitney Dam Fund," *Fort Worth Star-Telegram* (hereinafter *FWST*), January 8, 1946, AR 406-7-18, Fort Worth Star-Telegram Collection (hereinafter FWSTC), Special Collections, University of Texas at Arlington (hereinafter SC-UTA); "Committee Gets Brazos Dam Plea," *FWST*, March 7, 1946, AR 406-7-18, FWSTC, SC-UTA; "Towns Near the Proposed Reservoirs, Brazos River Conservation and Reclamation District" (n.d.), box 1423, FOLDER 22, POAGE; United States House of Representatives, *H.R. 6198: A bill to control flood waters of the Brazos River and its tributaries in the State of Texas*" (Washington, D.C.: Government Printing Office, February 28, 1935), 35; M. C. Tyler, memorandum, June 23, 1939, box 1426, file 44, POAGE; M. C. Tyler to Secretary of War, memorandum, June 23, 1939, box 12, folder 3, G6, RG 77, NARA; United States Senate, *S. 2092: A bill to control flood waters of the Brazos River and its tributaries in the state of Texas, to aid and improve agriculture and industrial development within said river basin, and for other purposes. 74th Congress, 1st session* (Washington, D.C., Government Printing Office, March 12, 1935), 7; George Mahon to Howard Humphrey, March 4, 1947, box 459, folder 4, S 653.1, George H. Mahon: An Inventory of His Papers, 1887–1986 and undated (hereinafter MAHON PAPERS), Southwest Collection, Texas Tech University (Lubbock) (hereinafter TTU-SWC); Joe Bomer to W. R. Poage, June 10, 1938, box 1425, file 40, POAGE; *Concerning Brazos River Conservation and Reclamation District* (n.p.: n.d.), box 1423, FOLDER 22, POAGE.

5.   Paul Ehrlich, *The Population Bomb* (New York: Ballantine, 1968).

6.   Russell Bean, "Famine in Your Future" (1973), box 465, folder 29,

S 653.1, MAHON PAPERS, TTU-SWC.

7.   G. R. Phippen, "Planning Report 30.10: Population Projections" (September 28, 1960), box 9, folder 4 "Planning Report: 30.10: Population Projections, 9/28/60," SW6, RG 77, NARA; "Water Plan Draws Stiff Protest Here," *Abilene Reporter-News*, July 18, 1966, www.newspaperarchive.com; "West Texas Water Plans Surveyed," *Big Spring Daily Herald*, June 15, 1977, www.newspaperarchive.com; Katharyn Duff, "Population Guesses Draw Council's Fire," *Abilene Reporter-News*, July 15, 1966, www. newspaperarchive.com; "Five Dams on Brazos are Vital to Texas Progress," *Waco News-Tribune*, July 17, 1956, www.newspaperarchive.com; "TWQB studies problems," *Belton Journal*, September 1, 1977, www.newspaperarchive.com; "Brazos Water Quality Planning Study Stated," *Hearne Democrat*, August 4, 1977, www.newspaperarchive.com; "Population Continues Upward Trend," *Brazosport Facts*, April 30, 1961, www.newspaperarchive.com.

8.   "L. Jackson Report Shows: City Outgrows Newest Projects," *Brazosport Facts*, September 20, 1956, www.newspaperarchive.com; "Population Continues Upward Trend."

9.   Thadis W. Box and Gerald W. Thomas, "Ecology and the use of Water Resources," ca. 1970, box 986, no. 31, WATER INC, TTU-SWC.

10.   Riley Dunlap and Angela Mertig, *American Environmentalism: The U.S. Environmental Movement, 1970–1990* (New York: Taylor & Francis, 1992); Andrew G. Kirk, *Counterculture Green: The Whole Earth Catalog and American Environmentalism* (Lawrence: University of Kansas Press, 2007).

11.   Donald Worster, *Nature's Economy: A History of Ecological Ideas* (New York: Cambridge University Press, 1994), 343–44.

12.   Spencer Rich, "Damming the Dam Builders' Cash Flow," *Washington Post*, January 3, 1972, www.newspaperarchive.com; Robert Gottlieb, *Forcing the Spring: The Transformation of the American Environmental Movement* (Washington, D.C.: Island Press, 1993); Philip Shabecoff, *A Fierce Green Fire: The American Environmental Movement* (New York: Hill & Wang, 1993); Box and Thomas, "Ecology and the use of Water Resources."

13.   Texas Water Development Board (hereinafter TWDB), "About the Texas Water Development Board," TWDB, http://www.twdb.state.tx.us/about.

14.   Charles D. Curran, "Resolving Conflicts Apparent to the U.S. Study Commission–Texas" (lecture, Sixth Annual Water for Texas Conference, College Station, TX, September 9, 1960), box 1, folder 7, SW6, RG 77, NARA.

15.   "Sunny Skies Dry Texas Moisture," *Paris News*, September 29, 1955, www.newspaperarchive.com; "Frontier Therapy at Hot Wells," *Del Rio News-Herald*, April 15, 1988, www.newspaperarchive.com; "Flood Threat Rises in Plains, Midwest," *Pacific Stars and Stripes*, July 29, 1962, www. newspaperarchive.com; "Weather," *Bakersfield Californian*, July 28, 1962, www.newspaperarchive.com; "Flood Crest Said Reached: Brazos River Flood Threats Eased Considerably," *Cuero Record*, September 27, 1955, www. newspaperarchive.com; "Mild Cool Front Moves into Texas; Watch Hurricane," *Corsicana Daily Sun*, September 29, 1955, www.newspaperarchive.com; "Texas Cities Erect Levees against Water," *Walla Walla Union-Bulletin*, April 30, 1957,

www.newspaperarchive.com; "BRA Schedules Meet Here Wednesday 8 PM," *Hearne Democrat*, July 24, 1964, www.newspaperarchive.com; "Brazos River Flood Crest Due Friday," *Brookshire Times*, May 20, 1965, www. newspaperarchive.com; "Brazos Waters Flood Farmland," *El Paso Herald-Post*, May 22, 1965, www.newspaperarchive.com; "Major Flood Threat Grips Eastern Texas," *Blytheville Courier*, April 30, 1957, www.newspaperarchive.com; "Floods, Storms Lash at Texas," *Billings Gazette*, April 25, 1957, www. newspaperarchive.com; "Texas Floodwaters Sweep on toward Cities Still Felled by Earlier Blows," *Independent Record*, May 5, 1957, www.newspaperarchive. com; "Tornado-Hit Texas is Waterlogged," *Independent Record*, April 23, 1957, www.newspaperarchive.com; "New Floods Hit Towns in Texas," *Corpus Christi Times*, September 29, 1955, www.newspaperarchive.com; "Texas Flood Loss Soars," *Hutchinson News*, May 8, 1957, www.newspaperarchive.com.

16. "New Floods Hit Towns in Texas," *Ruston Daily*, May 3, 1957, www. newspaperarchive.com; "Brazos River nears Flood Stage at East Columbia," *Brazosport Facts*, April 29, 1966, www.newspaperarchive.com; "River Up, Overflow at East Columbia Seen," *Brazosport Facts*, May 20, 1965, www. newspaperarchive.com; "Violent Weather Easing but Floods Pose Threat," *Mexia Daily News*, April 30, 1957, www.newspaperarchive.com; "Flood Perils Shift to South Texas," *El Paso Herald-Post*, April 30, 1957, www. newspaperarchive.com; "Texas Flood Loss Soars."

17. "Texas Flood Death Toll Rises," *Journal Courier*, August 6, 1978, www.newspaperarchive.com.

18. "Flood Crest Begins Moving Through Palo Pinto County," *Odessa American*, August 9, 1976, www.newspaperarchive.com.

19. Frank Carey, "Tired of Screwball Weather? You Can Blame the 'Air Dip,'" *Big Spring Daily Herald*, May 26, 1957, www.newspaperarchive.com; Rita Carlson, "Drought Could Hurt Galveston County," *Galveston Daily News*, January 8, 1989, www.newspaperarchive.com; "Flood Ends Drought in Texas with Rainfall Deluging Cities," *Daily Chronicle*, July 19, 1957, www. newspaperarchive.com; "Drought Areas Staggered by April Rains," *Independent Record*, May 5, 1957, www.newspaperarchive.com.

20. "Salt Water Invades Brazos after Dry Season," *Brazosport Facts*, January 20, 1989, www.newspaperarchive.com.

21. Ibid.

22. "Crops Being Wiped Out by Raging Texas Floods," *Waterloo Daily Courier*, April 30, 1957, www.newspaperarchive.com.

23. Erin Hanafy, "Keeping River on the Riverfront," *Waco Tribune-Herald*, July 23, 1997, Lake Brazos Vertical File (hereinafter LAKE BRAZOS), Texas Collection, Baylor University (Waco, TX) (hereinafter TXBU).

24. "Facts about the Study Commission, December 15, 1959," 1959, box 1, folder 3, SW6, RG 77, NARA.

25. U.S. Study Commission–Texas, news release, October 9, 1961, box 3, folder 2, SW6, RG 77, NARA.

26. "Facts about the Study commission, December 15, 1959."

27. Curran, "Resolving Conflicts."

28. "Facts about the Study Commission, December 15, 1959."

29. Ibid. (quotation); U.S. Study Commission–Texas, news release, October 9, 1961.

30. "Facts about the Study Commission, December 15, 1959."

31. "Running Water 700 Miles Uphill!: . . . to West Texas," *Houston Post*, December 3, 1967, box 462, folder 6, S 653.1, MAHON PAPERS, TTU-SWC.

32. G. H. Nelson (lecture, Texas Water Development Board, June 17, 1966), box 465, folder 13, S 653.1, MAHON PAPERS, TTU-SWC; Curran, "Resolving Conflicts."

33. Lieutenant General F. J. Clarke (lecture, Lubbock, February 17, 1970).

34. G. H. Nelson (lecture, Texas Water Development Board, June 17, 1966).

35. "A Note of Urgency," *Big Spring Daily Herald*, December 17, 1968, www.newspaperarchive.com.

36. George Mahon to Honorable Richard C. White, April 17, 1975, box 465, folder 29, MAHON PAPERS, TTU-SWC; George Mahon to Russell Thompson, July 24, 1972, box 488, folder 1, S 653.1, MAHON PAPERS, TTU-SWC; Office of Governor Preston Smith, message to the Legislature, February 16, 1971, box 462, folder 3, S 653.1, MAHON PAPERS, TTU-SWC; George Mahon to Raymond C. Turnbull, February 7, 1972, box 462, folder 1, S 653.1, MAHON PAPERS, TTU-SWC; Untitled notes, July 14, 1967, box 465, folder 37, S 653.1, MAHON PAPERS, TTU-SWC; George Mahon to Honorable Bill Clayton, October 30, 1969, box 465, folder 35, S 653.1, MAHON PAPERS, TTU-SWC; Keith, notation RE: Water Import Study to Mr. Mahon, February 24, 1971, box 488, folder 3, S 653.1, MAHON PAPERS, TTU-SWC; *West Texas–Eastern New Mexico Import Project* (December 1971), box 488, folder 1, S 653.1, MAHON PAPERS, TTU-SWC.

37. Duane Howell, "Harmony Needed on Water Issue," *Lubbock Avalanche Journal*, December 12, 1968, box 462, folder 5, S 653.1, MAHON PAPERS, TTU-SWC.

38. George Mahon to Beeman Fisher, February 22, 1971, box 462, folder 3, S 653.1, MAHON PAPERS, TTU-SWC; George Mahon to Russell Thompson, July 24, 1972.

39. G. H. Nelson (lecture, Texas Water Development Board, June 17, 1966).

40. "Running Water 700 Miles Uphill!: . . . to West Texas."

41. Gene Wilhelm, "West Texas–Eastern New Mexico Water Import Study" (speech, ca. 1971), box 462, folder 3, S 653.1, MAHON PAPERS, TTU-SWC.

42. "Running Water 700 Miles Uphill!: . . . to West Texas."

43. Leslie E. Mack, "Operation Southwest: Crises and Opportunities," box 838, folder 17, WATER INC, TTU-SWC.

44. Bernard Goss to B. H. Carpenter, September 28, 1971, box 838, folder 17, WATER INC, TTU-SWC.

45. Ibid.

46. A. S. Fuqua to Honorable George Mahon, February 10, 1968, box 462, folder 6, MAHON PAPERS, TTU-SWC; George Mahon to C. P. Lawrence,

May 24, 1968, box 462, folder 6, S 653.1, MAHON PAPERS, TTU-SWC.

47. John Moore, "Water Importation Project is Pushed," *Amarillo Globe-Times*, December 14, 1967, www.newspaperarchive.com.

48. Arleigh Laycock to Representative George Mahon, November 23, 1971, box 462, folder 1, S 653.1, MAHON PAPERS, TTU-SWC; George Mahon to O. B. Ratliff, August 5, 1968, box 462, folder 6, S 653.1, MAHON PAPERS, TTU-SWC; George Mahon to C.P. Lawrence, May 24, 1968.

49. Raymond Turnbull to George Mahon, January 28, 1972, box 465, folder 35, S 653.1, MAHON PAPERS, TTU-SWC; George Mahon to Raymond C. Turnbull, February 7, 1972.

50. Raymond Turnbull to George Mahon, January 28, 1972, box 465, folder 35, S 653.1, MAHON PAPERS, TTU-SWC.

51. Raymond Turnbull to George Mahon, January 28, 1972.

52. "Water Plan Sponsor Said Paid $125,000 in Farm Support," *Corpus Christi Times*, November 15, 1970, www.newspaperarchive.com; "Water Board Maps Plans for Populous Houston Area," *Victoria Advocate*, July 6, 1966, www.newspaperarchive.com; "Public Hearings to Air 54-Year Water Plans," *Abilene Reporter-News*, July 6, 1966, www.newspaperarchive.com; Johnson, "Water Plan Opposition Comes from East, West"; "A Note of Urgency."

53. Moore, "Water Importation Project."

54. Lee Jones, "Water Plan Proposes $10 Billion Package: System of Giant Canals Foreseen," *Big Spring Daily Herald*, December 17, 1968, www.newspaperarchive.com.

55. "Plan at a Glance," *Big Spring Daily Herald*, December 17, 1968, www.newspaperarchive.com; "Main Features of State Water Plan," *Corpus Christi Times*, December 17, 1968, www.newspaperarchive.com.

56. Moore, "Water Importation Project"; Johnson, "Water Plan Opposition Comes from East, West."

57. "East Texas Water Source," *Corpus Christi Times*, December 17, 1968, www.newspaperarchive.com; "West Texas to Get Huge Supply."

58. "Added Water to be Needed by 1985, Planners Report," *Abilene Reporter-News*, December 17, 1968, www.newspaperarchive.com.

59. Loretta Fulton, "Water Supply Said the Major Problem," *Abilene Reporter-News*, June 9, 1973, www.newspaperarchive.com; "A Note of Urgency"; "Water Plan Proposes $10 Billion Package: System of Giant Canals Foreseen."

60. "West Texas to Get Huge Supply," *Corpus Christi Times*, December 17, 1968, www.newspaperarchive.com.

61. Ibid.

62. G. H. Nelson (lecture, Texas Water Development Board, June 17, 1966).

63. George Mahon to Honorable Richard C. White, April 17, 1975.

64. George Mahon to Raymond C. Turnbull, February 7, 1972.

65. "A Note of Urgency."

66. Charles Curran to Austin Hancock, January 25, 1961, box 2, folder 3, SW6, RG 77, NARA.

67. "Water Board Hears Threat of Lawsuit," *Abilene Reporter-News*, July 18, 1966, www.newspaperarchive.com.

68. "A Note of Urgency."

69. "West Texas to Get Huge Supply."

70. "East Texas Water Source."

71. Johnson, "Water Plan Opposition Comes from East, West."

72. "West Texas Not in Trans System," *Abilene Reporter-News*, July 3, 1966, www.newspaperarchive.com; Johnson, "Water Plan Opposition Comes from East, West."

73. "Water Board Hears Threat of Lawsuit."

74. Katharyn Duff, "West Texas Written Off in Water Plan?," *Abilene Reporter-News*, July 3, 1966, www.newspaperarchive.com; Johnson, "Water Plan Opposition Comes from East, West."

75. "West Texas to Get Huge Supply."

76. Memphis and Shelby County Port Commission, petition, January 17, 1968, box 462, folder 7, S 653.1, MAHON PAPERS, TTU-SWC; Gene Wilhelm to Keith, January 31, 1968, box 462, folder 7, S 653.1, MAHON PAPERS, TTU-SWC; Joseph Hanover to Congressman Joe L. Evins, January 17, 1968, box 462, folder 7, S 653.1, MAHON PAPERS, TTU-SWC.

77. Keith, notation re: Water Import Study to Mr. Mahon, February 24, 1971.

78. "Water Plan May Undergo Changes Before Finalization," *Abilene Reporter-News*, July 3, 1966, www.newspaperarchive.com.

79. Duff, "West Texas Written Off in Water Plan?"

80. Duff, "Population Guesses Draw Council's Fire."

81. "Dry Times Ahead for West Texas," *Abilene Reporter-News*, June 12, 1977, www.newspaperarchive.com.

82. "Water Board Hears Threat of Lawsuit."

83. Duff, "West Texas Written Off in Water Plan?"; "Lubbock Politician Blasts Water Plans," box 465, folder 13, S 653.1, MAHON PAPERS, TTU-SWC.

84. "$3.7 Billion Dollar Plan Gets Cautious Compliments," *Denton Record-Chronicle*, July 20, 1966, www.newspaperarchive.com.

85. William Whipple to Maj. Gen. F. M. Albrecht, February 11, 1959, box 15, folder 5, SW6, RG 77, NARA.

86. Hon. John Carroll, "Vast Southwest Water Plan Recommended by U.S. Experts" (lecture, July 2, 1960), box 1, folder 6, SW6, RG 77, NARA.

87. Ibid.

88. Letter to Congressman Frank Ikard, August 20, 1957, box 459, folder 12, S 653.1, MAHON PAPERS, TTU-SWC.

Chapter Seven

1. John Graves, *Goodbye to a River: A Narrative* (New York: Knopf, 1960).

2. "High Plains Water Management Study, Texas," in Jim Casey to Honorable George Mahon, July 31, 1973, box 465, folder 31, S 653.1, George H. Mahon: An Inventory of His Papers, 1887–1986 and undated

(hereinafter MAHON PAPERS), Southwest Collection, Texas Tech University (Lubbock) (hereinafter TTU-SWC).

3.   "During the Brazos Flood," *Marshfield Times*, September 15, 1899, www.newspaperarchive.com; "During the Brazos Flood," *Postville Review*, September 15, 1899, www.newspaperarchive.com.

4.   "Report Score Dead in Dallas Floods; Hundreds Homeless," *Janesville Daily Gazette*, December 4, 1913, www.newspaperarchive.com; "Return of Life Savers," *Galveston Daily News*, July 11, 1899, www.newspaperarchive. com; William Creager to H. A. Montgomery, August 8, 1936, box 6, folder 5, FW17—"Subject Files Relating to the Construction of Possum Kingdom Dam, 1936–1937" (hereinafter FW17), Record Group 77—Records of the Army Corps of Engineers, Southwest Division (hereinafter RG 77), National Archives and Records Administration (Fort Worth, TX) (hereinafter NARA); H. A. Montgomery to W. H. McAlpine, October 17, 1936, box 1, folder 3, FW17, RG 77, NARA; Record Card, Engineer Department, U.S. Army, Subject: Possum Kingdom Dam, Mineral Wells, Texas, October 2, 1936, box 1, folder 2 "Poage Bill" (hereinafter FOLDER 2), FW17, RG 77, NARA; Inspector Crotty to John C. Kramer, May 29, 1909, box 4, folder 400, E.FW18—"Records of the Dallas Engineer Office" (hereinafter E.FW18), RG 77, NARA; F. P. Blums to S. M Wilcox, December 13, 1913, box 4, folder 400, E.FW18, RG 77, NARA; "[Flood in Waco, Texas]" to Louise Buchanan in Waco, Texas, Postcard Collection (hereinafter POSTCARD), Texas Collection, Baylor University (Waco, TX) (hereinafter TXBU); George S. Conner to his "darling baby face," October 1, 1936, box 2D208, folder 7 "George S. Conner Personal Materials: Correspondence—J. O. A. Conner typescripts," George S. and Jeffie O. A. Conner Papers, TXBU; "Thrown in Brazos Flood as Bridge Gives Away—Checking up Toll of Texas Tragedy," *Beatrice Daily Sun*, May 17, 1922, www. newspaperarchive.com; "Frio, Guadalupe Block Highways, Brazos Flattens Out," *San Antonio Express*, September 30, 1936, www.newspaperarchive.com; "The Floods in Texas," *News*, July 7, 1899, www.newspaperarchive.com; "Flood's Passage Through Delta is Proceeding Slowly," *Denton Record-Chronicle*, December 11, 1913, www.newspaperarchive.com; "Crest of Brazos Flood in Waller; 20 more Drown," *Denton Record-Chronicle*, December 8, 1913, www.newspaperarchive.com; "Fatal Cloudbursts," *Lebanon Daily News*, April 28, 1900, www.newspaperarchive.com; "Plans for Relief," *San Antonio Daily Express*, July 11, 1899, www.newspaperarchive.com; "Over Hundred Bodies Recovered in Texas," *Winnipeg Free Press*, September 13, 1921, www. newspaperarchive.com; "Brazos Crest Passing Slowly," *Corsicana Daily Sun*, December 11, 1913, www.newspaperarchive.com.

5.   [W. R.] Poage et al., *Senate Concurrent Resolution No. 38* (April 15, 1935), box 1423, folder 22 "Brazos River 1927–1934," POAGE; John Washington Lockhart, "Boating on the Brazos: First Trip of the 'Mustang' to Washington—A Regular Packet Line Afterward—The Terrible Overflow of 1842—Interesting Reminiscences," *Galveston Daily News*, February 12, 1893, in John Washington Lockhart, *Sixty years on the Brazos: The Life and Letters of Dr. John Washington Lockhart, 1824–1900* (Ann Arbor, MI: Argonaut Press, 1930), 82; Frank Carey, "Tired of Screwball Weather? You Can Blame

the 'Air Dip,'" *Big Spring Daily Herald*, May 26, 1957, www.
newspaperarchive.com; Rita Carlson, "Drought Could Hurt Galveston
County," *Galveston Daily News*, January 8, 1989, www.newspaperarchive.
com; "Flood Ends Drought in Texas with Rainfall Deluging Cities," *Daily
Chronicle*, July 19, 1957, www.newspaperarchive.com; "Drought Areas
Staggered by April Rains," *Independent Record*, May 5, 1957, www.
newspaperarchive.com; William Warren Rogers, ed., "'I am Tired Writeing'":
A Georgia Farmer Reports on Texas in 1871," *Southwestern Historical
Quarterly* (hereinafter *SHQ*) 87, no. 2 (October 1983): 187; William Pool,
"Westward I Go Free: The Memoirs of William E. Cureton, Texas
Frontiersman," *SHQ* 81, no. 2 (October 1977): 172; Henry J. Caufield to
Watson Caufield, September 25, 1860, box 2B384, folder 2 "Correspondence,
1858–1861, 1871–1872, 1888" (hereinafter FOLDER 1858), Caufield Family
Papers (hereinafter CAUFIELD), TXBU; "News," *Sheboygan Journal*,
August 6, 1857, www.newspaperarchive.com; "Later from Texas," *New York
Daily Times*, April 14, 1853, www.newspaperarchive.com; Henry J. Caufield
to Watson Caufield, July 8, 1855, box 2B384, folder 1 "Correspondence,
1847–1857" (hereinafter FOLDER 1847), CAUFIELD, TXBU; Henry J.
Caufield to Lizzie Caufield, December 8, 1855, box 2B384, FOLDER 1847,
CAUFIELD, TXBU; Mary Jane Caufield to Watson Caufield, July 29, 1859,
box 2B384, FOLDER 1858, CAUFIELD, TXBU; M. J. Caufield to Watson
Caufield, July 17, 1855, box 2B384, FOLDER 1847, CAUFIELD, TXBU; Wat
Caufield to his father, June 29, 1857, box 2B384, FOLDER 1847, CAUFIELD,
TXBU; Henry J. Caufield to Wat Caufield, April 25, 1859, box 2B384, FOLDER
1858, CAUFIELD, TXBU; Henry J. Caufield to Watson Caufield, July 15,
1859, box 2B384, FOLDER 1858, CAUFIELD, TXBU; R. Hedspeth to Adaline
Earle, November 1, 1884, box 2B332, folder 5 "Personal Papers:
Correspondence, 1874–1885," Graves-Earle Family Papers, 1848–1963 (hereinafter GRAVES), TXBU; Isaac Parks to Caroline Crittenden, December 23,
1862, box 2B13, folder 2 "Correspondence, 1858–1877" (hereinafter
FOLDER 1877), Isaac Parks Papers (hereinafter PARKS), TXBU; "Diary of
Isaac Parks," September 1, 1861–June 9, 1877, box 2B13, folder 1 "Diary,
1861–1877," PARKS, TXBU; Letter to "cousin," March 4, 1888, box 2B332,
folder 6 "Personal Papers: Correspondence, 1886–1891" (hereinafter FOLDER
1886), GRAVES, TXBU; Isaac Parks to John Crittenden, January 6, 1858,
box 2B13, FOLDER 1877, PARKS, TXBU; Josephine Parks to Isaac Parks,
September 24, 1876, box 2B13, FOLDER 1877," PARKS, TXBU; L. S. Ross to
Victor Rose, September 23, 1880, box 2B383, folder 3 "Correspondence,
1870–March 1881," Ross Family Papers, TXBU; U. Bet, "Waco
Correspondence," *Galveston Daily News*, August 18, 1874, www.
newspaperarchive.com; Lockhart, "Boating on the Brazos," 82.
    6.   U. Bet., "Waco Correspondence"; Lockhart, "Boating on the Brazos,"
82; "News"; "Later from Texas"; Henry J. Caufield to Watson Caufield, July 8,
1855; Henry J. Caufield to Lizzie Caufield, December 8, 1855; Mary Jane
Caufield to Watson Caufield, July 29, 1859; M. J. Caufield to Watson Caufield,
July 17, 1855; Wat Caufield to his father, June 29, 1857; Henry J. Caufield to
Wat Caufield, April 25, 1859; Henry J. Caufield to Watson Caufield, July 15,

1859; R. Hedspeth to Adaline Earle, November 1, 1884; "Diary of Isaac Parks"; Letter to "cousin," March 4, 1888; Isaac Parks to John Crittenden, January 6, 1858; Isaac Parks to Caroline Crittenden, December 23, 1862; Josephine Parks to Isaac Parks, September 24, 1876; L. S. Ross to Victor Rose, September 23, 1880.

7.   W. R. Poage to Lawson Rivers, July 27, 1955, box 466, folder 2, POAGE; Lawson Rivers to W. R. Poage, July 22, 1955, box 466, folder 2, POAGE; W. R. Poage to Loyan H. Walker, May 21, 1955, box 466, folder 2, POAGE; Loyan H. Walker to W. R. Poage, May 17, 1955, box 466, folder 2, POAGE; W. R. Poage to Loyan H. Walker, April 20, 1955, box 466, folder 2, POAGE; Loyan H. Walker to W.R. Poage, April 18, 1955, box 466, folder 2, POAGE; W. R. Poage to V. H. Diersing, May 12, 1955, box 466, folder 2, POAGE; V. H. Diersing to W. R. Poage, May 11, 1955, box 466, folder 2, POAGE; W. R. Poage to K. Kendrick, May 16, 1955, box 466, folder 2, POAGE; K. Kendrick to Honorable W. R. Poage, May 12, 1955, box 466, folder 2, POAGE; W. R. Poage to A. N. Wells, May 16, 1955, box 466, folder 2, POAGE.

8.   United States Senate, *S. 2092: A bill to control flood waters of the Brazos River and its tributaries in the State of Texas, to aid and improve agriculture and industrial development within said river basin, and for other purposes. 74th Congress, 1st session* (Washington, D.C., Government Printing Office, March 12, 1935).

9.   W. R. Poage to Marshall Croft, June 22, 1959.

10.   Army Corps of Engineers (hereinafter ACOE), "Memorandum Report on the Economic Justification from a Flood-Control Standpoint of the 13-Dam Brazos River Valley Project" (January 25, 1937), box 6, folder 9, FW17, RG 77, NARA.

11.   This list does not include small-scale municipal projects, such as the low-water dams in Abilene and Waco.

12.   "The Resources and Products of Texas," *Galveston Daily News*, May 4, 1906, www.newspaperarchive.com.

13.   "Brazos River in Spotlight Again on Two Counts," *Waco News-Tribune*, May 22, 1956, www.newspaperarchive.com.

14.   New organizations—such as Friends of the Brazos—emerged to save the river from ecological crisis, and these groups brought an environmental consciousness to the opposition that had, in one form or another, always protested Brazos improvement.

15.   E. J. Kyle to Hon. Bob Poage, March 29, 1938, box 1426, folder 46, POAGE.

16.   Wendell Phillips Dodge to the Honorable George H. Mahon, May 15, 1946, box 459, folder 4, S 653.1, MAHON PAPERS, TTU-SWC.

17.   "Ambitious but Expensive," *Denton Record-Chronicle*, August 2, 1937, www.newspaperarchive.com.

18.   Ibid.

19.   Earle Walker, "Haskell-Knox, Stonewall, Throckmorton, Dams Planned on Brazos River in Decades," *Abilene Reporter-News*, January 30, 1946, www.newspaperarchive.com; "Eastland Rock to be Used for Big Brazos Dam," *Abilene Reporter-News*, July 9, 1948, www.newspaperarchive.com;

Larry Deister, "Harnessing Wild Texas Rivers Big Task Supervised by District Engineers Here," *Galveston Daily News*, November 13, 1949, www.newspaperarchive.com; J. A. Paschal to Mr. President, January 5, 1854, box 76, folder 76.11, MS 17, Andrew Forest Muir Papers (hereinafter MUIR), Woodson Research Center, Rice University (Houston, TX) (hereinafter WRC); Brazos River and Valley Improvement Ass'n, *Permanent organization formed at Bryan, Texas, October 12–13, 1915, for the prevention of overflows and promotion of navigation* (Waco, TX: L. S. Henry, 1915), 25; Earl F. Woodward, "Internal Improvements in Texas in the Early 1850's," *SHQ* 76, no. 2 (October 1972); Colonel C. S. Riche to E. R. Hatten, August 14, 1913, box 5, folder 400, E.FW18, RG 77, NARA.

20. "Waco Tenders its Support," *Galveston Daily News*, September 1, 1906, www.newspaperarchive.com; Marion Travis, "Lake Brazos Dam Nearing Completion," *Waco Tribune-Herald* (hereinafter *WTH*), May 27, 1970, Lake Brazos Vertical File (hereinafter LAKE BRAZOS), TXBU; Marion Travis, "Lake Brazos Takes Shape," *WTH*, August 23, 1970, LAKE BRAZOS, TXBU; Erin Hanafy, "Keeping River on the Riverfront," *WTH*, July 23, 1997, LAKE BRAZOS, TXBU; J. B. Smith, "A New Era for the Old Brazos," *WTH*, October 9, 2004, LAKE BRAZOS, TXBU; "Our Low Water Dam Is Worth the Trouble," *WTH*, June 28, 1981, LAKE BRAZOS, TXBU; Helen Havelka, "Water Level Falls, Postpones Races," *WTH*, August 23, 1981, LAKE BRAZOS, TXBU; Mike Copeland, "Down the Drain: Dam Malfunction Lowers Brazos 3 Times in Week," *WTH*, August 25, 1981, LAKE BRAZOS, TXBU; Mike Copeland, "Brazos Low-Water Dam to Stay Down for Repairs: Low-Bid Dam Idea Now a Costly Reality," *WTH*, December 31, 1982, LAKE BRAZOS, TXBU; "Lake Brazos Dam Becomes a Big Joke," *WTH*, January 1, 1983, LAKE BRAZOS, TXBU; Mike Copeland, "$3 Million Needed to Fix Low-Water Dam," *WTH*, January 19, 1984, LAKE BRAZOS, TXBU; "Low Water Dam Needs Top Priority," *WTH*, March 22, 1984, LAKE BRAZOS, TXBU; "Waco Files Suit against Low-Water Dam Designers," *WTH*, January 15, 1985, LAKE BRAZOS, TXBU; Mike Copeland, "Dam Repair Leaves Races Up a Creek," *WTH*, May 17, 1985, LAKE BRAZOS, TXBU; Lin Mills, "Problem with Dam Lowers Lake Brazos," *WTH*, July 13, 1986, LAKE BRAZOS, TXBU; Mike Copeland, "Waco Planning More Repairs on Brazos Dam," *WTH*, February 20, 1987, LAKE BRAZOS, TXBU; Denise Parkinson, "Gate a July 4th Waterloo for Troubled Lake Brazos Dam," *WTH*, July 3, 1987, LAKE BRAZOS, TXBU; Denise Parkinson, "Gate Still Down on Brazos Dam," *WTH*, July 8, 1987, LAKE BRAZOS, TXBU; Mike Copeland, "Low-Water Dam Still Plaguing Waco Officials," *WTH*, July 9, 1987, LAKE BRAZOS, TXBU; Mike Copeland, "City Workers Brave Stifling Heat to Repair Dam's Hydraulic Tubing," *WTH*, July 25, 1987, LAKE BRAZOS, TXBU; Mike Copeland, "Brazos Dam Gate Dropped for repairs," *WTH*, September 10, 1987, LAKE BRAZOS, TXBU; Elizabeth Simpson, "The Dam: Troubled Decades," *WTH*, September 27, 1987, LAKE BRAZOS, TXBU; Mike Copeland, "Same Song, 2nd Verse for Lake Brazos Dam," *WTH*, December 23, 1987, LAKE BRAZOS, TXBU; Mike Copeland, "Dam Didn't Work from 1st Raising, Witness Testifies," *WTH*, June 16, 1988, LAKE

BRAZOS, TXBU; Mike Copeland, "Erosion Threatened Dam by 1983, Engineer Says," *WTH*, June 18, 1988, LAKE BRAZOS, TXBU; Mike Copeland, "Waco Wins Brazos Dam Lawsuit [against Design Firm]," *WTH*, June 25, 1988, LAKE BRAZOS, TXBU; Erin Hanafy, "Plans Rolling on River," *WTH*, June 25, 1997, LAKE BRAZOS, TXBU; Jodi Wetuski, "Lake Brazos to Be Left Low, Dry for Dam Work," *WTH*, May 21, 1998, LAKE BRAZOS, TXBU; J. B. Smith, "Restoring Lake to Old Stature," *WTH*, February 24, 1998, LAKE BRAZOS, TXBU; J. B. Smith, "'Lake Brazos' Low Blow," *WTH*, February 16, 2001, LAKE BRAZOS, TXBU; J. B. Smith, "Dam Failure Attributed to River Debris," *WTH*, March 15, 2001, LAKE BRAZOS, TXBU; Herschberger, *WTH*, March 17, 2001, LAKE BRAZOS, TXBU; John Young, "What Else We Found: Lowered Brazos and, Yikes, Dug Up a Lore More than Mud," *WTH*, January 18, 2004, LAKE BRAZOS, TXBU; J. B. Smith, "Waco Considers Local Projects for Brazos Dam," *WTH*, September 30, 2000, LAKE BRAZOS, TXBU; "Debris at the gates: Malfunction, Uncertainty Justify Retirement of Low-Water Dam," *WTH*, March 17, 2001, LAKE BRAZOS, TXBU; J. B. Smith, "Council May Pass on Brazos Proposals: Contractors' Bids for Low-Water Dam Higher than Budgeted," *WTH*, September 6, 2005, LAKE BRAZOS, TXBU; "High Water, Debris once again Damage Waco Low-Later Dam," *WTH*, November 26, 2004, LAKE BRAZOS, TXBU; Henry Beckham, "Waco Honored for Community Achievement: Hard Work Rewarded as City Joins Ranks of Texas' Most Beautiful Locales," *WTH*, October 17, 1976, LAKE BRAZOS, TXBU; "Beer Garden Planned for Lake Brazos Site," *WTH*, November 24, 1977, LAKE BRAZOS, TXBU; John Allen, "River of Dreams," *WTH*, October 9, 2004, LAKE BRAZOS, TXBU; Emily Ingram, "A River (Finally) Runs Through It," *WTH*, April 20, 2006, LAKE BRAZOS, TXBU; David Doerr, "City Officials Dedicate New Dam," *WTH*, November 14, 2007, LAKE BRAZOS, TXBU; Larry Groth, "Vision of Lake Brazos Dam Historic," *WTH*, January 8, 2006, LAKE BRAZOS, TXBU.

21. "Lake, not Mud Puddle," *WTH*, January 16, 2004, LAKE BRAZOS, TXBU.

22. "Velasco Project," *Galveston Daily News*, August 10, 1904, www.newspaperarchive.com.

23. W. R. Poage to H. S. Hilburn, July 9, 1957, box 639, file 3, POAGE.

24. Brookshire State Bank, advertisement, 1913, in *Brookshire Times*, December 12, 1913, www.newspaperarchive.com.

25. Mike Shannon, "Brazos Finally to be Navigable: Dream of Past Generations Realized," *WTH*, March 13, 1971," Lake Brazos Dam, Lake Brazos Vertical File, TXBU.

Bibliography

Archival Collections

John Adriance Papers, 1832–1903, Dolph Briscoe Center for American History, University of Texas at Austin.

Edward McCrea Ainsworth Papers. Texas Collection, Baylor University (Waco, TX).

Army Corps of Engineers. "Examination and Survey Files, 1908–1948" (G6), Records of the Army Corps of Engineers. Southwest Division (RG 77). National Archives and Records Administration—Southwest Division (Fort Worth, TX).

———. "Navigable Waterway Files, 1931–1962" (G5). Records of the Army Corps of Engineers. Southwest Division (RG 77). National Archives and Records Administration—Southwest Division (Fort Worth, TX).

———. "Records of the Dallas Engineer Office" (E.FW18). Records of the Army Corps of Engineers. Southwest Division (RG 77). National Archives and Records Administration—Southwest Division (Fort Worth, TX).

———. "Subject Files Relating to the Construction of Possum Kingdom Dam, 1936–1937" (FW17). Records of the Army Corps of Engineers. Southwest Division (RG 77). National Archives and Records Administration—Southwest Division (Fort Worth, TX).

George Barnard Papers. Texas Collection, Baylor University (Waco, TX).

John Campbell Personal Papers, 1820–1906. Woodson Research Center, Fondren Library, Rice University (Houston, TX).

Caufield Family Papers. Texas Collection, Baylor University (Waco, TX).

Basil Clemons Photograph Collection. Special Collections, University of Texas at Arlington.

George S. and Jeffie O. A. Conner Papers. Texas Collection, Baylor University (Waco, TX).

Eberstadt Collection. Dolph Briscoe Center for American History, University of Texas at Austin.

Fort Worth Star-Telegram Collection. Special Collections, University of Texas at Arlington.

Fort Worth Star-Telegram Photographs. Special Collections, University of Texas at Arlington.

Geography and Map Division. Library of Congress (Washington, D.C.)
Graves-Earle Family Papers. Texas Collection, Baylor University (Waco, TX).
Groce Family Correspondence. Woodson Research Center, Fondren Library,
    Rice University (Houston, TX).
A Guide to the Texas Composers Collection, 1836–1968. Dolph Briscoe Center
    for American History, University of Texas at Austin.
Hamman Papers. Woodson Research Center, Fondren Library, Rice University
    (Houston, TX).
William Ransom Hogan Papers, 1934–1946. Special Collections, University of
    Texas at Arlington.
Sam Houston Papers. Woodson Research Center, Rice University (Houston, TX).
John A. Hulen Papers. Southwest Collection, Texas Tech University (Lubbock).
Paintings of Don Hutson. Brazoria County Historical Museum (Angleton,
    TX).
Irion Family Papers 1825–1929, bulk 1826–1874. Special Collections,
    University of Texas at Arlington.
Kendall Family Papers, Special Collections, University of Texas at Arlington.
Lake Brazos Vertical File, Texas Collection, Baylor University (Waco, TX).
Mirabeau B. Lamar Travel Journal. Woodson Research Center, Fondren
    Library, Rice University (Houston, TX).
Samuel Maas Papers, 1824–1900, bulk 1834–1837. Special Collections,
    University of Texas at Arlington.
George H. Mahon: An Inventory of His Papers, 1887–1986 and undated.
    Southwest Collection, Texas Tech University (Lubbock).
Map Collection, Perry-Castañeda Library, University of Texas at Austin. http://
    www.beg.utexas.edu/UTopia/images/pagesizemaps/vegetation.pdf.
Map Collection. Texas Collection, Baylor University (Waco, TX).
Microfilm Collection, Amon Carter Museum (Fort Worth, TX).
Microfilm Collection. Special Collections, University of Texas at Arlington.
Andrew Forest Muir Papers. Woodson Research Center, Fondren Library, Rice
    University (Houston, TX).
National Resources Conservation Service. "Drouth Committee Report."
    Records of the Natural Resources Conservation Service (RG 114).
    National Archives and Records Administration—Southwest Division
    (Fort Worth, TX).
Isaac Parks Papers. Texas Collection, Baylor University (Waco, TX).
C. R. Perry Diary, Special Collections. University of Texas at Arlington.
James F. Perry Papers, Dolph Briscoe Center for American History, University
    of Texas at Austin.
Photograph Collection. Texas Collection, Baylor University (Waco, TX).
Photograph Collection. Texas Prison Museum (Huntsville, TX)
W. R. Poage Papers, Poage Legislative Library (Waco, TX).
Port Sullivan Vertical File. Texas Collection, Baylor University (Waco, TX).
Postcard Collection. Texas Collection, Baylor University (Waco, TX).
Robinson, Thomas B. *Thomas B. Robinson Diary (1865–1866)*, GA47, Thomas
    Robinson Diary, Special Collections, University of Texas at Arlington.
Ross Family Papers. Texas Collection, Baylor University (Waco, TX).

Records of Joseph Draper Sayers. Texas Office of the Governor, Archives and Information Services Division, Texas State Library and Archives Commission (Austin).

Texas Cotton Palace Papers. Texas Collection, Baylor University (Waco, TX).

Thomson Family of Texas Papers, 1832–1898, Woodson Research Center, Rice University (Houston, TX).

Topographic Map Collection. Texas Collection, Baylor University (Waco, TX).

Transcripts from Santa Cruz de Queretero, 1750–1767. Spanish Missions in Texas and California, 1691–1825, Dolph Briscoe Center for American History, University of Texas at Austin.

Translation of Samuel Bangs' legal petitions regarding his Texas land grant, 1830–1834, 1840. Special Collections, University of Texas at Arlington.

"U.S. Commission Study—Texas, 1958–1960" (SW6). Records of the Natural Resources Conservation Service. National Archives and Records Administration—Southwest Division (Fort Worth, TX).

Vandale (Earl) Collection. Dolph Briscoe Center for American History, University of Texas at Austin.

Waco Village Papers, Texas Collection, Baylor University (Waco, TX).

J. Russell Wait Port of Houston Papers. Woodson Research Center, Fondren Library, Rice University (Houston, TX).

Water, Inc., Papers [unlisted, uncatalogued collection]. Southwest Collection, Texas Tech University (Lubbock).

Samuel May Williams Papers. Galveston and Texas History Center, Rosenberg Library.

William Physick Zuber Papers. Special Collections, University of Texas at Arlington.

Maps

Arrowsmith, John. *Map of Texas, compiled from surveys recorded in the Land Office of Texas, and other official surveys.* London: John Arrowsmith, 1841.

Bureau of Economic Geology, University of Texas at Austin. *Vegetation/Cover Types of Texas.* Austin: University of Texas, 2000.

Giraud, Louis. *Velasco, the first & only deep water port on the coast of Texas: the commercial hope of the Trans-Mississippi by Louis Giraud.* St. Louis, MO: n.p., ca. 1892. Map Annex, Special Collections, University of Texas at Arlington.

Hergesheimer, E. *Map showing the distribution of the slave population of the southern states of the United States. Compiled from the census of 1860.* Washington, D.C.: Henry S. Graham, 1861. Geography and Map Division, Library of Congress.

Map of Texas Showing Major Vegetative Regions. In *The Mammals of Texas,* edited by William B. Davis and David J. Schmidly. Austin: University of Texas Press, 2004.

Mitchell, Samuel Augustus, and James H. Young. *A New Map of Texas, with the Contiguous American and Mexican States.* Philadelphia, PA: S. A. Mitchell, 1836.

Olney, Jesse. *Map of Texas to Illustrate Olney's School Geography.* In *Map of the United States, Canada, Texas & Parts of Mexico to Illustrate Olney's School Geography,* edited by David Robinson and Jesse Olney. New York: Pratt, Woodford, 1844.

Roessler, A. R. *Map No. 59: Texas.* Washington, D.C.: Engineer's Office, Department of the Gulf, 1865. Map Annex, Special Collections, University of Texas at Arlington.

Society for the Diffusion of Useful Knowledge. *Central America II. Including Texas, California, and the Northern States of Mexico.* London: Charles Knight, 1842. Map Annex, Special Collections, University of Texas at Arlington.

Primary Sources

Annual Report of the United States Life-Saving Service for the Fiscal Year Ending June 30, 1900. Washington, D.C.: Government Printing Office, 1901.

Baker, De Witt Clinton, ed. *A Texas Scrap-Book: Made Up of the History, Biography, and Miscellany of Texas and its People.* New York: A. S. Barnes, 1875.

Barker, Eugene, ed. *The Austin Papers.* Washington, D.C.: Government Printing Office, 1924–1928.

Barnes, Agnes Warren. *Waco, Texas: A Postcard Journey.* Mount Pleasant, SC: Arcadia Publishing, 1999.

Baughman James B. "Letters from the Texas Coast, 1875." *Southwestern Historical Quarterly* 69, no. 4 (April 1966): 499–515.

Bolton, Herbert. *Athanase de Mézières and the Louisiana-Texas frontier, 1768–1780: documents pub. for the first time, from the original Spanish and French manuscripts, chiefly in the archives of Mexico and Spain; tr. into English.* Cleveland, OH: Arthur H. Clark, 1914.

Bray, William L. "Distribution and Adaptation of the Vegetation of Texas." *Bulletin of the University of Texas* 82 (1906): 1–108.

———. "The Ecological Relations of the Vegetation of Western Texas." *Botanical Gazette* 32, no. 3 (September 1901): 195–217.

Brazos River and Valley Improvement Ass'n. *Permanent organization formed at Bryan, Texas, October 12–13, 1915, for the prevention of overflows and promotion of navigation. Proceedings of the meeting, with statistical data from various authorities. Executive committee: W. W. Seley, president . . . [et al.] . . . Executive headquarters: Waco, Texas.* Waco: L. S. Henry, 1915.

Brazos River Channel and Dock Company. *Facts with Reference to the Brazos River Enterprise and the "New South."* New York: John A. Lowell, 1890.

Breeden, James, ed. *A Long Ride in Texas: The Explorations of John Leonard Riddell*. College Station: Texas A&M University Press, 1994.

Brewer, John Mason. *Dog Ghosts*. Austin: University of Texas Press, 1958.

———. *The Word on the Brazos*. Austin: University of Texas Press, 1953.

Brister, Louis E., and Eduard Harkort. "The Journal of Col. Eduard Harkort, Captain of Engineers, Texas Army, February 8–July 17, 1836." *Southwestern Historical Quarterly* 102, no. 3 (January 1999): 344–79.

Brown, Henry John. *History of Texas from 1685 to 1892*. St. Louis, MO: L. E. Daniell, 1893.

Bryant, W. N. *All about Texas Boiled Down for 25 Cents, As It Was, As It Is! And As It Will Be!* Dallas, TX: W. N. Bryant, 1879.

Buckley, Eleanor Claire. "The Aguayo Expedition into Texas and Louisiana, 1719–1722." *Southwestern Historical Quarterly* 15, no. 1 (July 1911): 1–65.

Burke, J. *Burke's Texas almanac and immigrant's handbook for 1883, with which is incorporated Hanford's Texas state register*. Houston, TX: J. Burke, 1883.

Christensen, Paul. *West of the American Dream: An Encounter with Texas*. College Station: Texas A&M Press, 2001.

Clemmons, Caroline. *Brazos Bride*. CreateSpace Independent Publishing Platform, 2012.

Congressional serial set, Issue 6205. Washington, D.C.: Government Printing Office, 1912.

Cunningham, Debbie, ed., "Notes and Documents: The Domingo Ramon Diary of the 1716 Expedition into the Province of the Tejas Indians: An Annotated Translation." *Southwestern Historical Quarterly* 110, no. 1 (July 2006): 39–67.

Cutter, Charles. *Cutter's Guide to the City of Waco, Texas*. Waco: n.p., 1894.

Davis, Mollie Evelyn Moore. *Under the Man-Fig*. New York: Houghton, Mifflin, 1895.

de Cordova, Jacob. *The Texas Immigrant and Traveller's Guide Book*. Austin, TX: De Cordova and Frazier, 1856.

de Mier y Teran, Manuel. *Texas by Teran: The Diary Kept by General Manuel de Mier y Teran on His 1828 Inspection of Texas*, edited by Jack Jackson. Austin: University of Texas Press, 2000.

Dewees, W. B. *Letters from an Early Settler of Texas*. Louisville, KY: Morton & Griswold, 1852.

Dobie, J. Frank. *Southwestern Lore*. Hatsboro, PA: Folklore Associates, 1931.

Documentary Series 7, Letters and Memorials of Fray Mariano de Los Dolores y Viana, 1737–1762. San Antonio, TX: Old Spanish Missions Historical Research Library, 1985.

Dodd, David G. *The Complete Annotated Grateful Dead Lyrics: The Collected Lyrics of Robert Hunter and John Barlow*. New York: Simon and Schuster, 2005.

Filísola, Vicente. *Memorias para la historia de la guerra de Tejas*. Vol. 2. Mexico City: Imprenta de Ignacio Cumplido, 1848–1849.

Fisk. *A Visit to Texas: being the journal of a traveller through those parts most interesting to American settlers. With descriptions of scenery, habits, &c. &c.* New York: Goodrich & Wiley, 1834.

Flores, Dan, and Amy Winton. *Canyon Visions: Photographs and Pastels of the Texas Plains.* Lubbock: Texas Tech University Press, 1989.

Foster, L. L. *Forgotten Texas Census: First Annual Report of the Agricultural Bureau of the Department of Agriculture, Insurance, Statistics, and History, 1887–1888.* Austin: Texas State Historical Association, 2001.

Foster, William C., ed. *The La Salle Expedition to Texas: The Journal of Henri Joutel, 1684–1687.* Translated by Johanna S. Warren. Austin: Texas State Historical Commission, 1998.

Furber, George C. *The Twelve Months Volunteer.* Cincinnati, OH: U. P. James, 1857. http://scholarship.rice.edu/jsp/xml/1911/27093/1/aa00376.tei.html.

Galbreath, Lester. *Campfire Tales: True Stories from the Western Frontier.* Houston, TX: Bright Sky Press, 2005.

Gallatin, Albert. *Report of the secretary of the Treasury, on the subject of public roads and canals: made in pursuance of a resolution of Senate, of March 2d, 1807.* n.p.: W.A. Davis, 1807.

Gioia, Ted. *Work Songs.* Durham, NC: Duke University Press, 2006.

Grant, Amy. *Mosaic: Pieces of My Life So Far.* New York: Flying Dolphin Press, 2007.

Gray, William Fairfax. *From Virginia to Texas, 1835.* Houston, TX: Gray, Dillaye, 1835–1837.

Gregg, Josiah. *Commerce of the prairies, or, the journal of a Santa Fé trader: during eight expeditions across the great western prairies, and a residence of nearly nine years in northern Mexico.* Philadelphia, PA: J. W. Moore, 1849.

Habig, Fr. Marion A. *Spanish Texas Pilgrimage: The Old Franciscan Missions and Other Spanish Settlements of Texas, 1632–1821.* Chicago, IL: Franciscan Herald Press, 1990.

Hancock, Robert. *Narrative of Robert Hancock Hunter, 1813–1902: From his arrival in Texas, 1822, through the Battle of San Jacinto, 1836.* Austin, TX: Cook, 1936.

Hector, E. Roy. *Brazos River Marauders.* Bloomington, IN: iUniverse Inc., 2007.

———. *Escape from Hell's Corner.* Bloomington, IN: iUniverse, 2003.

Hill, Robert T. "Classification and Origin of the Chief Geographic Features of the Texas Region." *American Geologist* 5 (January 1890): 9–29.

———. "Geography and Geology of the Black and Grand Prairies, Texas." In *Twenty-First Annual Report of the United States Geological Survey to the Secretary of the Interior, 1899–1900,* edited by Charles D. Walcott. Washington, D.C.: Government Printing Office, 1901.

———. "On the Occurrence of Artesian and Other Underground Waters in Texas, Eastern New Mexico and Indian Territory, West of the 97th Meridian." *The American Naturalist* 26, no. 311 (November 1892): 935–36.

Hill, Thomas Edie. *Hill's reference guide for land seekers, travelers, schools, tourists, emigrants and general readers: including description and outline maps, with new method of quick-finding location, in each state of any city or village of 200 population and more . . . with location and 1910 population of 23,664.* Chicago, IL: Hill Standard Book Company, 1912.

Holley, Mary Austin. *Letters of an Early American Traveler, Mary Austin Holley, Her Life and Her Works, 1784–1846.* Dallas, TX: Southwest Press, 1933.

———. *Texas. Observations, historical, geographical and descriptive: in a series of letters, written during a visit to Austin's colony, with a view of a permanent settlement in that country, in the autumn of 1831.* Baltimore, MD: Armstrong & Plaskitt, 1833.

Howard, Robert Ervin, and Rusty Burke. *The End of the Trail: Western Stories.* Lincoln: University of Nebraska Press, 2005.

Johnson, Francis White, Eugene Campbell Barker, and Ernest William Winkler. *A History of Texas and Texans.* Chicago, IL: American Historical Society, 1914.

"Journal of Stephen F. Austin on His First Trip to Texas." *Southwestern Historical Quarterly* 7, no. 4 (1904): 286–307.

Kendall, George Wilkins. *Narrative of the Texan Santa Fe Expedition, comprising a description of a tour through Texas, and across the great Southwestern prairies, the Camanche and Cayuga hunting-grounds, with an account of the sufferings from want of food, losses from hostile Indians, and final capture of the Texans and their march, as prisoners, to the City of Mexico.* London: Wily & Putnam, 1844.

Kennedy, William. *The Rise, Progress, and Prospects of the Republic of Texas.* Vol. 1. London : R. Hastings, 1841.

King, C. Richard, ed. *Victorian Lady on the Texas Frontier: The Journal of Anne Raney Coleman.* New York: W. Foulsham, 1972.

King, Edward. *Texas: 1874: An Eyewitness Account of Conditions in Post-Reconstruction Texas.* Houston, TX: Cordovan Press, 1974.

King, Judge Rufus Y. "Indian Attack upon the Gregg Family in 1841." In *Papers concerning Robertson's Colony in Texas, October 15, 1835, through January 14, 1836.* Vol 12. Edited by Malcolm McLean. Arlington: University of Texas at Arlington Press, 1985.

League of Nations. *Rapport du Comité consultatif: Report of the Advisory Committee.* London: Harrison & Sons, 1856.

League of Women Voters, Freeport Texas. *Study of Brazos River Harbor Navigation District.* n.p.: n.p., ca. 1960.

Lincecum, Gideon. *Gideon Lincecum's Sword: Civil War Letters from the Texas Home Front.* Denton, TX: University of North Texas Press, 2001.

Lipscomb, Mance. *I Say Me for a Parable: The Oral Autobiography of Mance Lipscomb, Texas Songster.* Cambridge, MA: Da Capo Press, 1995.

Lockhart, John Washington. *Sixty Years on the Brazos: The Life and Letters of Dr. John Washington Lockhart, 1824–1900.* Ann Arbor, MI: Argonaut Press, 1930.

Lomax, Alan. *American Ballads and Folk Songs.* New York: Macmillan, 1934.
———. *Folk Song U.S.A.: The 111 Best American ballads.* New York: Duell, Sloan & Pearce, 1947.
———. *The Land Where the Blues Began.* New York: Pantheon Books, 1993.
Mackenzie, Ranald S. *Ranald S. Mackenzie's Official Correspondence Relating to Texas, 1873–1879.* Lubbock: West Texas Museum Association, 1968.
Marcy, Randolph Barnes. *Thirty Years of Army Life on the Border.* New York: Harper and Brothers, 1866.
Mauldin, Rex L. *My Stream of Consciousness, the Brazos River.* Edited by Letha L. Mauldin and Thelma Lemons. n.p.: Rex Mauldin, 2004.
McCarthy, Cormac. *Blood Meridian, or, The Evening Redness in the West.* New York: Random House, 1985.
McDonald, Walter. *Rafting the Brazos.* Denton: University of North Texas Press, 1989.
McLean, Malcolm, ed. *Papers concerning Robertson's Colony in Texas, October 15, 1835, through January 14, 1836.* Vol. 12. Arlington: University of Texas at Arlington Press, 1985.
McMurtry, Larry. *Buffalo Girls: A Novel.* New York: Simon and Schuster, 1990.
———. *Comanche Moon: A Novel.* New York: Simon and Schuster, 1993.
———. *Dead Man's Walk: A Novel.* New York: Simon and Schuster, 1995.
———. *Folly and Glory.* The Berrybender Narratives no. 4. New York: Simon and Schuster, 2001.
———. *Horseman, Pass By.* New York: Penguin, 1961.
———. *Lonesome Dove: A Novel.* New York: Simon and Schuster, 1985.
Meinecke, Tom. *Arms of God: From Prussia to Texas to Death in the Brazos River.* Bloomington, ID: Author House, 2010.
Meinzer, Wyman, and Walter McDonald. *Great Lonely Places of the Texas Plains.* Lubbock: Texas Tech University Press, 2001.
Meline, James F. *Two thousand miles on horseback, Santa Fe and Back: A summer tour through Kansas, Nebraska, Colorado, and New Mexico, in the Year 1866.* New York: Hurd and Houghton, 1867.
Memoranda and official correspondence relating to the Republic of Texas, its history and annexation. New York: D. Appleton, 1859.
A Memorial and biographical history of McLennan, Falls, Bell and Coryell Counties, Texas: containing a history of this important section of the great state of Texas, from the earliest period of its occupancy to the present time, together with glimpses of its future prospects; also biographical mention of many of the pioneers and prominent citizens of the present time, and full-page portraits of some of the most eminent men of this section. Chicago, IL: Lewis, 1893.
Mirabeau B. Lamar Travel Journal. Houston, TX: Woodson Research Center, Fondren Library, Rice University.
Moore, A. W. "A Reconnaissance in Texas in 1846." *Southwestern Historical Quarterly* 30, no. 4 (April 1927): 252–71.
Mullen, Alan. *The Man Who Adores the Negro: Race and American Folklore.* Champaign: University of Illinois Press, 2003.

Muir, Andrew Forest. "Railroad Enterprise in Texas, 1836–1841." *Southwestern Historical Quarterly* 47, no. 4 (April 1944): 339–70.

———. *Texas in 1837: An Anonymous, Contemporary Narrative.* Austin: University of Texas Press, 1958.

New Orleans and Texas Navigation Company and Mexican Gulf Railway Company. *An act to incorporate the New Orleans and Texas Navigation Company, and to incorporate the Mexican Gulf Railway Company.* New Orleans, LA: Jerome Bayon, 1837.

Owens, William A. *Tell Me a Story, Sing Me a Song: A Texas Chronicle.* Austin: University of Texas Press, 1983.

Parer, William B., ed. *Notes taken during the expedition commanded by Capt. R. B. Marcy, U.S.A. through unexplored Texas, in the summer and fall of 1854.* New York: Hayes and Zell, 1856.

Parker, Amos Andrew. *Trip to the West and Texas: comprising a journey of eight thousand miles, through New-York, Michigan, Illinois, Missouri, Louisiana and Texas, in the autumn and winter of 1834–5. Interspersed with anecdotes, incidents and observations.* New York: White and Fisher, 1835.

Payne, C. W. *The Brazos River of Texas: freight tonnage survey of Waco and Territory Tributary also commercial statistics and economic results of the improvement to commercial navigation.* Waco, TX: City Commission, 1916.

Pichardo, Jose Antonio. *Pichardo's treatise on the limits of Louisiana and Texas: an argumentative historical treatise with reference to the verification of the true limits of the provinces of Louisiana and Texas.* Vol. 1. Austin: University of Texas Press, 1931.

Pike, Albert. *Gen. Albert Pike's Poems with Introductory Sketch.* Little Rock, AK: A. W. Allsopp, 1900.

Pike, Zebulon M. *Exploratory travels through the western territories of North America, comprising a voyage from St. Louis, on the Mississippi to the source of that river and a journey through the interior of Louisiana and the North-eastern Provinces of Spain, performed in the years 1805, 1806, 1907, by order of the government of the United States.* London: Longman, 1811.

Plummer, Rachel. *Narrative of the capture and subsequent sufferings of Mrs. Rachel Plummer during a captivity of twenty-one months among the Comanche Indians.* Waco, TX: Texan Press, 1968.

Poage, W. R. *Oral Memoirs of William Robert "Bob" Poage.* Waco, TX: Baylor University Institute for Oral History.

Pool, William. "Westward I Go Free: The Memoirs of William E. Cureton, Texas Frontiersman." *Southwestern Historical Quarterly* 81, no. 2 (Oct., 1977): 155–90.

Pope, S. H. *Geyser City Record: A Texas Journal Devoted to Agriculture, Mechanical and Realty Development, Waco, Texas, May 25, 1890.* Waco, TX: Press of the News Printing, 1890.

Redford, Polly. *Raccoons and Eagles: Two Views of American Wildlife.* New York: Dutton, 1965.

Reid, Captain Mayne. *The Boy Hunters; or, Adventures in Search of a White Buffalo*. Boston, MA: Ticknor and Fields, 1853

———. *The Death Shot: A Romance of Forest and Prairie*. London: Chapman and Hall, 1873.

———. *The Man-Eaters and Other Odd People: A Popular Description of Singular Races of Man*. New York: Routledge, 1860.

Robson, Lucia St. Clair. *Ride the Wind*. New York: Ballantine, 1985.

Roemer, Ferdinand. *Texas: With Particular Reference to German Immigrant and the Physical Appearance of the Country*. Austin, TX: German-Texas Heritage Society, 1935.

Rogers, William Warren, ed. "'I am Tired Writeing'": A Georgia Farmer Reports on Texas in 1871." *Southwestern Historical Quarterly* 87, no. 2 (October 1983): 183–88.

Sheriff, Jack. *Brazos Guns*. Yorkshire, UK: Dales Large Print Books, 1998.

Smithwick, Noah. *The Evolution of a State, or Recollections of Old Texas Days*. Austin, TX: Gammel, 2000.

Southern Commercial Convention. *Proceedings of the Southern Commercial Convention*. n.p.: n.p., 1871.

South Western Immigration Company. *Texas: Her resources and capabilities: Being a description of the state of Texas and the inducements she offers to those seeking homes in a new country*. New York: E. D. Slater, 1881.

Sowell, Andrew Jackson. *Early Settlers and Indian Fighters of Southwest Texas*. Chicago, IL: A. C. Jones, 1900.

Stiff, Colonel Edward. *The Texas emigrant: Being a narration of the adventures of the author in Texas, and a description of the soil, climate, productions, minerals, towns, bays, harbors, rivers, institutions, and manners and customs of the inhabitants of that country; together with the principal incidents of fifteen years Revolution in Mexico*. Cincinnati, OH: George Conclin, 1840. Reprint, Waco: Texian Press, 1968.

Texas Almanac and State Industrial Guide. Dallas, TX: Belo, 1857.

Texas Almanac and State Industrial Guide Volume 1904. Galveston, TX: Belo, 1904.

Texas Almanac and State Industrial Guide Volume 1910. Galveston, TX: Belo, 1910.

Texas Water Development Board. *Report—Texas Water Development Board*. Austin: Texas Water Development Board, 1972.

Tharp, Benjamin. *The Vegetation of Texas*. Houston, TX: Anson Jones Press, 1939.

Thompson, Stith. *Round the Levee*. Austin: Texas Folkloric Society, 1916.

Thrall, Homer S. *A pictorial history of Texas, from the earliest visits of European adventurers, to A.D. 1879: embracing the periods of missions, colonization, the revolution, the republic and the state, also a topographical description of the country . . . together with its Indian tribes and their wars, and biographical sketches of hundreds of its leading historical and topical notes, and descriptions of the public institutions of the state . . . also, a list of the counties, with historical and topical notes.* New York: N. D. Thompson Publishing, 1885.

Trans-Mississippi Commercial Congress. *Official Proceedings of the Seventeenth Session of the Trans-Mississippi Commercial Congress: Held at Kansas City.* Kansas City, MO: Union Bank Note, 1906.

United States Army Corps of Engineers. *A Historical summary giving the scope of previous projects for the improvement of certain rivers and harbors.* Washington, D.C.: Government Printing Office, 1915.

———. *Annual Report of Chief of Engineers on Improvement of Rivers and Harbors in the Mineral Wells, Texas, District.* Washington, D.C.: Government Printing Office, 1938.

———. *Report of the Chief of Engineers.* Washington, D.C.: Government Printing Office, 1875.

———. *Report of the Chief of Engineers U.S. Army.* Washington, D.C.: Government Printing Office, 1897.

———. *Report of the Chief of Engineers U.S. Army.* Washington, D.C.: Government Printing Office, 1901.

———. *Report of the Chief of Engineers U.S. Army, Part 1.* Washington, D.C.: Government Printing Office, 1910.

———. *Review of Reports on Freeport Harbor, Texas.* Galveston, TX: ACOE, Galveston District, ca. 1970.

United States Census. Report on cotton production in the United States: also embracing agricultural and physico-geographical description of the several cotton states and of California. Washington, D.C.: Government Printing Office, 1880.

———. *Reports on the statistics of agriculture in the United States: agriculture by irrigation in the western part of the United States, and statistics of fisheries in the United States at the eleventh census; 1890.* Washington, D.C.: Government Printing Office, 1890.

United States Congressional Serial Set, Issue 3105. Washington, D.C.: Government Printing Office, 1893.

United States Congressional Serial Set, Issue 3200. Washington, D.C.: Government Printing Office, 1895.

United States Department of War. *Annual Reports.* Washington, D.C.: Government Printing Office, 1910.

———. *Annual Reports of the Secretary of War.* Washington, D.C.: Government Printing Office, 1907.

———. *Annual Reports of the Secretary of War.* Vol. 2. Washington, D.C.: Government Printing Office, 1910.

———. *Letter from the Secretary of War, transmitting, with a letter from the chief of engineers, report of examination of channel between Brazos River and Galveston Bay, Texas.* House of Representatives, 54th Congress, 2nd session, Document 89. Washington, D.C.: Government Printing Office, December 14, 1896.

————. *Letter from the Secretary of War, transmitting with letter of the chief of engineers, United States congressional serial set, issue 3105.* Washington, D.C.: Government Printing Office, 1893.

United States House of Representatives, *H.R. 6198: A bill to control flood waters of the Brazos River and its tributaries in the State of Texas to aid and improve agriculture and industrial development within said river basin, and for other purposes.* Washington, D.C.: Government Printing Office, February 28, 1935.

United States Senate. "Statement of Marshall H. D. W. Smith Jr., Assistant Engineer of the Texas and Pacific Railway." In United States Senate, Committee on Irrigation and Reclamation of Arid Lands. *Report on the Special Committee of the United States Senate on the Irrigation and Reclamation of Arid Lands.* Washington, D.C.: Government Printing Office, 1890.

————. *S. 2092: A bill to control flood waters of the Brazos River and its tributaries in the State of Texas, to aid and improve agriculture and industrial development within said river basin, and for other purposes.* 74th Congress, 1st session. Washington, D.C.: Government Printing Office, March 12, 1935.

United States Senate Committee on Commerce. *Hearings before a Subcommittee of the Committee on Commerce.* Washington, D.C.: Government Printing Office, 1930.

————. *Report on the river and harbor [appropriation] bill [1916] (H.R. 20189).* Washington, D.C.: Government Printing Office, 1915.

U.S. Engineers Office. *Report on Survey of Brazos River and Tributaries, Texas: Oyster Creek, Texas, Jones Creek, Texas.* Vol. 1. Galveston, TX: U.S. engineers Office, 1947.

Van Dyke, Henry. "Texas: A Democratic Ode, Part 1: Wild Bees." *Poetry Journal* 1, no. 4 (1913): 153–56.

Waco Business Men's Club, Committee of Brazos River Improvement. *The Improvement of the Brazos River, Texas, from Waco to Its Mouth to the Secretary of War.* Waco, TX: n.p., 1905.

Watson, William. *Adventures of a Blockade Runner, Or, Trade in Time of War.* London: T. F. Unwin, 1892.

Whilldin, M. *A Description of Western Texas.* Galveston, TX: Galveston, Harrisburg & San Antonio Railway Company, 1876.

Whipple, Amiel Weeks. *Diary of a journey from the Mississippi to the coasts of the Pacific with a United States government expedition.* Vol 1. London: Longman, Brown, Green, Longmans & Roberts, 1858.

Whitney, Milton. *Field Operations of the Bureau of Soils Volume 12.* Washington, D.C.: Bureau of Soils, 1912.

Wilson, Steve. *The Spider Rock Treasure: A Texas Mystery of Lost Spanish Gold.* Austin, TX: Eakin Press, 2004.

Zesch, Scott. *The Captured: A True Story of Abduction by Indians on the Texas Frontier.* New York: Macmillan, 2005.

Secondary Sources

Adams, John. *Damming the Colorado: The Rise of the Lower Colorado River Authority, 1933–1939*. College Station: Texas A&M University Press, 1990.

Ajilvsgi, Geyata. *Wildflowers of Texas*. Fredericksburg, TX: Shearer Publishing, 2003.

Anfinson, John O. *The River We Have Wrought: A History of the Upper Mississippi*. Minneapolis: University of Minnesota Press, 2005.

Anderson, Benedict. *Imagined Communities: Reflections on the Origin and Spread of Nationalism*. New York: Norton Company, 2006.

Aton, James, and Robert McPherson. *River Flowing from the Sunrise: An Environmental History of the Lower San Juan*. Logan: Utah State University Press, 2000.

Barber, Katrine. *Death of Celilo Falls*. Seattle: University of Washington Press, 2005.

Barr, Juliana. *Peace Came in the Form of a Woman: Indians and Spaniards in the Texas Borderlands*. Chapel Hill: University of North Carolina Press, 2007.

Barry, John M. *Rising Tide: The Great Mississippi Flood of 1927 and How It Changed America*. New York: Simon and Schuster, 1990.

Bernstein, Peter L. *Wedding of the Waters: The Erie Canal and the Making of a Great Nation*. New York: Norton, 2006.

Billington, David, and D. C. Jackson. *Big Dams of the New Deal Era: A Confluence of Engineering and Politics*. Norman: University of Oklahoma Press, 2006.

Billington, David, D. C. Jackson, and Martin Melosi. *The History of Large Federal Dams: Planning, Design, and Construction in the Era of Big Dams*. Washington, D.C.: Government Printing Office, 2005.

Bird, Peter. "Formation of the Rocky Mountains, Western United States: A Continuum Computer Model." *Science* 239, no. 4847 (March 1988): 1501–1507.

Bolton, Herbert E. *Texas in the Middle Eighteenth Century: Studies in Spanish Colonial History and Administration*. Berkeley: University of California Press, 1915.

Bradford, Thomas G. *Texas*. New York: Weeks, Jordan, 1838.

Brand, John P. "Cretaceous of Llano Estacado." *Report of Investigations— No. 20*. Austin: Bureau of Economic Geology, University of Texas, November 1953.

Brooks, James. "Served Well by Plunder: *La Gran Ladronería* and Producers of History Astride the Río Grande." *American Quarterly* 52, no. 1 (March 2000): 23–58.

Busch, John Laurence. *Steam Coffin: Captain Moses Rogers and The Steamship* Savannah *Break the Barrier*. New Canaan, CT: Hodos Historia, 2010.

Butler, Anne M. *Gendered Justice in the American West: Women Prisoners in Men's Penitentiaries*. Champaign: University of Illinois Press, 1999.

Caran, S. Christopher, and Robert Baumgardner Jr. "Quarternary stratigraphy and paleoenvironments of the Texas Rolling Plains." *Geological Society of America Bulletin* 102 (June 1990): 768–85.

Carrells, Peter. *Uphill against Water: The Great Dakota Water War.* Omaha: University of Nebraska Press, 1999.

Clayton, Lawrence. *Benjamin Capps and the South Plains: A Literary Relationship.* Denton: University of North Texas Press, 1990.

———. *Historic Ranches of Texas.* Austin: University of Texas Press, 1993.

Clayton, Lawrence, and Sonja Irwin Clayton. *Cowboys: Ranch Life along the Clear Fork of the Brazos River.* Austin, TX: Eakin Press, 1997.

Clayton, Lawrence, Jim Hoy, and Jerald Underwood. *Vaqueros, Cowboys, and Buckaroos.* Austin: University of Texas Press, 2001.

Curlee, Abigail. "History of a Texas Slave Plantation 1831–1863." *Southwestern Historical Quarterly* 26, no. 2 (October 1922): 79–127.

Dalquest, Walter W., and Norman V. Horner. *Mammals of North-Central Texas.* Wichita Falls, TX: Midwestern State University Press, 1984.

Dase, Amy E. *Hell-Hole on the Brazos: A Historic Resources Study of Central State Farm, Fort Bend County, Texas.* Technical Report Number 70. Austin, TX: Prewitt and Associates, September 2004.

Davis, William B., and David J. Schmidly. *The Mammals of Texas.* Austin: University of Texas Press, 2004.

deBuys, William. *Salt Dreams: Land and Water in Low-Down California.* Albuquerque: University of New Mexico Press, 1999.

Dering, J. Phil, and J. Bryan Mason, eds. *Prehistoric and Historic Occupation in Central Brazos County, Texas, Archaeological Investigations of Two City Parks: Veterans Park and Athletic Complex and Lick Creek Park, College Station, Texas.* College Station: Texas A&M University Press, 2001.

Derrida, Jacques. "Cogito and the History of Madness." In *Writing and Difference*, translated by Alan Bass. New York: Routledge, 1978.

Dobie, J. Frank. *The Longhorns.* Boston, MA: Little, Brown, 1941.

Dunlap, Riley, and Angela Mertig. *American Environmentalism: The U.S. Environmental Movement, 1970–1990.* New York: Taylor & Francis, 1992.

Ehrlich, Paul. *The Population Bomb.* New York: Ballantine, 1968.

Fiege, Mark. *Irrigated Eden: The Making of an Agricultural Landscape in the American West.* Seattle: University of Washington Press, 1999.

Finley, Robert J., and Thomas C. Gustavson. "Lineament Analysis Based on Landsat Imagery, Texas Panhandle." *Bureau of Economic Geology Circular* 81, no. 5 (1981).

Flores, Dan. *Caprock Canyonlands: Journeys into the Heart of the Southern Plains.* Austin: University of Texas Press, 1990.

Foley, Neil. *The White Scourge: Mexicans, Blacks, and Poor Whites in Texas Cotton Culture.* Berkley: University of California Press, 1997.

Fornell, Earl Wesley. *The Galveston Era: The Texas Crescent on the Eve of Secession.* Austin: University of Texas Press, 2009.

Foster, William C. *Historic Native Peoples of Texas.* Austin: University of Texas Press, 2008.

Fradkin, Philip. *A River No More: the Colorado River and the West.* New York: Knopf, 1981.

Francaviglia, Richard. *Cast Iron Forest.* Austin: University of Texas Press, 1998.

Frye, J. C., H. D. Glass, A. B. Leonard, and D. D. Coleman. "Caliche and Clay Mineral Zonation of Ogallala Formation, Central-Eastern New Mexico." *New Mexico Bureau of Geology & Mineral Resource Circular* 144 (1974).

Gottlieb, Robert. *Forcing the Spring: The Transformation of the American Environmental Movement.* Washington, D.C.: Island Press, 1993.

Gramsci, Antonio. *Prison Notebooks.* Vol. 1. New York: Columbia University Press, 2010.

Graves, John. *Goodbye to a River: A Narrative.* New York: Knopf, 1960.

Hall, G. Emlen. *High and Dry: The Texas–New Mexico Struggle for the Pecos River.* Albuquerque: University of New Mexico Press, 2002.

Hayward, O. T., P. N. Dolliver, D. L. Amsbury, and J. C. Yelderman. *A Field Guide to the Grand Prairie of Texas: Land, History, Culture.* Waco, TX: Baylor University, 1992.

Hofstadter, Richard. *The Age of Reform: From Bryan to FDR.* New York: Vintage Books, 1955.

Horgan, Paul. *Great River: The Rio Grande in North American History.* Middleton, CT: Wesleyan University Press, 1991.

Hudson, Kathleen. *Women in Texas Music: Stories and Songs.* Austin: University of Texas Press, 2007.

Jackson, Bruce. *Wake Up Dead Man: Afro-American Worksongs from Texas Prisons.* Cambridge, MA: Harvard University Press, 1972.

Jackson, Donald. *Voyages of the Steamboat* Yellow Stone. New York: Tickner and Fields, 1985.

Jones, Manford Eugene. *A History of Cotton Culture along the Middle Brazos River.* Master's thesis, University of New Mexico, 1939.

Jordan, Terry. "Evaluation of Vegetation in Frontier Texas." *Southwestern Historical Quarterly* 76, no. 3 (January 1973): 233–54.

Judd, Sharon. "Prehistoric Cultural Resources in the Central Llano Estacado and Western Rolling Plains of Texas." Master's thesis, Texas Tech University, 1977.

Kelley, Sean. "Blackbirders and *Bozales:* African-Born Slaves on the Lower Brazos River of Texas in the Nineteenth Century." *Civil War History* 54, no. 4 (December 2008): 406–23.

Kibler, Karl, and Tim Gibbs. "Archeological survey of 61 acres along the Bosque River, Waco, McLennan County, Texas." *Technical Reports 69.* Austin, TX: Prewitt, Cultural Resources Services, 2004.

Kimmel, Jim. *Exploring the Brazos River: From Beginning to End.* College Station: Texas A&M Press, 2011.

Kirk, Andrew G. *Counterculture Green: The Whole Earth Catalog and American Environmentalism.* Lawrence: University of Kansas Press, 2007.

Lang, William, and Robert Carriker, eds. *Great River of the West: Essays on the Columbia River.* Seattle: University of Washington Press, 1999.

Leach, Edward Dale. "Maximum probable flood on the Brazos River in the City of Waco." Master's thesis, Baylor University, 1978.

Littlefield, Douglas. *Conflict on the Rio Grande: Water and the Law, 1879–1939*. Norman: University of Oklahoma Press, 2009.

Mancini, Matthew. *One Dies, Get Another: Convict Leasing in the American South, 1866–1928*. Columbia: University of South Carolina Press, 1996.

McGreevy, Patrick Vincent. *Stairway to Empire: Lockport, The Erie Canal, and the Shaping of America*. New York: SUNY Press, 2009.

Meyers, Allan D. "Brazos Canal: Early Intracoastal Navigation in Texas." *Southwestern Historical Quarterly* 103, no. 2 (October, 1999): 174–89.

Morris, John Miller. *El Llano Estacado: Exploration and Imagination on the High Plains of Texas and New Mexico, 1536–1860*. Austin: Texas State Historical Association, 1997.

Nagle, J. C. "Irrigation in Texas." *USDA Bulletin* 222. Washington, D.C.: Government Printing Office, 1910.

Norkunas, Martha. "Narratives of Resistance and the Consequences of Resistance." *Journal of Folklore Research* 41, no. 2/3 (2004): 105–23.

Perkinson, Robert. *Texas Tough: The Rise of America's Prison Empire*. New York: Macmillan, 2010.

Phelan, Richard, and Jim Bones. *Texas Wild: The Land, Plans, and Animals of the Lone Star State*. New York: Dutton, 1976.

Phillips, Fred. *Reining in the Rio Grande: People, Land, and Water*. Albuquerque: University of New Mexico Press, 2011.

Pisani, Donald J. *From the Family Farm to Agribusinss: The Irrigation Crusade in California and the West, 1850–1931*. Berkeley: University of California Press, 1984.

Poage, Bob. *McLennan County before 1980*. Waco: Texian Press, 1981.

Prikryl, Daniel J., and Jack Johnson. *Waco Lake, McLennan County, Texas: An Inventory and Assessment of Cultural Resources*. Austin, TX: Prewitt and Associates, 1985.

Puryear, Pamela, and Nath Winfield. *Sandbars and Sternwheelers: Steam Navigation on the Brazos*. College Station: Texas A&M Press, 1976.

Rathjen, Frederick W. *The Texas Panhandle Frontier*. Lubbock: Texas Tech University Press, 1998.

Reisner, Marc. *Cadillac Desert: The American West and Its Disappearing Water*. New York: Penguin, 1993.

Rhoads, Edward J. M. "The Chinese in Texas." *Southwestern Historical Quarterly* 81, no. 1 (July 1977): 1–36.

Ruesink, Lou Ellen. "Taming the Brazos." *Texas Water Resources Institute* 3, no. 6 (August 1977). http://twri.tamu.edu/newsletters/texaswaterresources/twr-v3n6.pdf.

Sale, Kirkpatrick. *The Fire of His Genius: Robert Fulton and the American Dream*. New York: Simon and Schuster, 2002.

Schmidly, David J. *Texas Mammals East of the Balcones Fault Zone*. College Station: Texas A&M University Press, 1983.

Schneiders, Robert Kelly. *Big Sky Rivers: The Yellowstone and Upper Missouri.* Lawrence: University of Kansas Press, 2003.

——. *Unruly River: Two Centuries of Change Along the Missouri.* Lawrence: University of Kansas Press, 1999.

Shabecoff, Philip. *A Fierce Green Fire: The American Environmental Movement.* New York: Hill & Wang, 1993.

Shagena, Jack L. *Who Really Invented the Steamboat?: Fulton's Clermont Coup; A History of the Steamboat Contributions of William Henry, James Rumsey, John Fitch, Oliver Evans, Nathan Read, Samuel Morey, Robert Fulton, John Stevens, and Others.* Amherst, NY: Humanity Books, 2004.

Sharpless, Rebecca. *Fertile Ground, Narrow Choices: Women on Texas Cotton Farms, 1900–1940.* Chapel Hill: University of North Carolina Press, 1999.

Shaw, Ronald E. *Canals for a Nation: The Canal Era in the United States, 1790–1860.* Lexington: University Press of Kentucky, 1993.

——. *Erie Water West: A History of the Erie Canal, 1792–1854.* Lexington: University Press of Kentucky, 1990.

Sheriff, Carol. *The Artificial River: The Erie Canal and the Paradox of Progress, 1817–1862.* New York: Macmillan, 1997.

Stahl, Carmine A., and Ria McElvaney. *Trees of Texas: An Easy Guide to Leaf Identification.* College Station: Texas A&M University Press, 2003.

Stine, Jeffrey. *Mixing the Waters: Environment, Politics, and the Building of the Tennessee-Tombigbee Waterway.* Akron, OH: University of Akron Press, 1993.

Stribling, Johnnie E. *Twixt the Brazos and the Navasot: A Study of the Early History of Selected Communities in Northeast Brazos County, Texas, 1830–1900's.* N.p.: n.p., 1978.

Teisch, Jessica. *Engineering Nature: Water, Development, and the Global Spread of American Environmental Expertise.* Chapel Hill, University of North Carolina Press, 2011.

Templin, E. H. *Soil Survey: McLennan County, Texas.* Washington, D.C.: U.S. Government Printing Office, 1958.

Texas Department of Transportation. "Gulf Intracoastal Waterway— Legislative Report for 2003–2004." ftp.txdot.gov/pub/txdot-info/tpp/giww/giww04.pdf.

Thoms, Alston V., and John L. Montgomery. *The Archeological Resources of the Brazos River Basin: A Summary Statement.* Lubbock: Department of Anthropology, Texas Tech University, 1977.

Thoms, Alston, V., J. Bryan Mason, Stephanie K. Judjahn, and Scott A. Minchak. "Native American Land Use in the Yegua Creek Basin and Vicinity: Ethnohistoric and Archeological Records," In *Yegua Creek Archaeological Project: Survey Results from Lake Somerville State Parks and Trailway, East-Central Texas,* edited by A. V. Thoms, 35–48. College Station: Texas A&M University Press, 2004.

Trimble, Donald E. "The Geologic Story of the Great Plains: A nontechnical description of the origin and evolution of the landscape of the Great

Plains." In *Geological Survey Bulletin 1493*. Washington, D.C.: Government Printing Office, 1980. http://library.ndsu.edu/exhibits/text/greatplains/text.html.

Tuan, Yi-Fu. *Space and Place: The Perspective of Experience*. Minneapolis: University of Minnesota Press, 2001.

———. *Topophilia: A Study of Environmental Perception, Attitudes, and Values*. New York: Columbia University Press, 1974.

Tyrell, Ian. *True Gardens of the Gods: Californian-Australian Environmental Reform, 1860–1930*. Berkeley: University of California Press, 1999.

Ulrich, Roberta. *Empty Nets: Indians, Dams, and the Columbia River*. Corvallis: Oregon State University Press, 1999.

Valenza, Janet. *Taking the Waters in Texas: Springs, Spas, and Fountains of Youth*. Austin: University of Texas Press, 2000.

Vines, Robert A. *Trees of East Texas*. Austin: University of Texas Press, 1977.

———. *Trees of North Texas*. Austin: University of Texas Press, 1982.

Walker, Donald R. *Penology for Profit: A History of the Texas Prison System, 1867–1912*. College Station: Texas A&M University Press, 1988.

Wallace, Patricia Ward. *Waco: Texas Crossroads*. Woodland Hills, CA: Windsor Publications, 1983.

Ward, Evan. *Border Oasis: Water and the Political Ecology of the Colorado River Delta, 1940–1975*. Tucson: University of Arizona Press, 2003.

Webb, Walter Prescott. *The Great Plains*. Lincoln: University of Nebraska Press, 1931.

———. *The Texas Rangers: A Century of Frontier Defense*. New York: Houghton Mifflin, 1935.

West, Elliott. *The Contested Plains: Indians, Goldseekers, and the Rush to Colorado*. Lawrence: University Press of Kansas, 1998.

West Texas Geological Society. *Cenozoic Geology of the Llano Estacado and Rio Grande Valley, Guide Book Field Trip No. 2*. Amarillo: West Texas Geological Society, November 1949.

White, Richard. *It's Your Misfortune and None of My Own: A New History of the American West*. Norman: University of Oklahoma Press, 1993.

———. *The Organic Machine: The Remaking of the Columbia River*. New York: Macmillan, 1996.

Willoughby, Lynn. *Flowing Through Time: A History of the Lower Chattahoochee River*. Tuscaloosa: University of Alabama Press, 1999.

Wilson, John A. "Tertiary Shorelines, Texas Coastal Plain." *Palaeogeography, Palaeoclimatology, Paleoecology* 5, no. 1 (July 1968): 135–40.

Wolfe, Charles K. *The Life and Legend of Leadbelly*. Cambridge, MA: Da Capo Press, 1999.

Woods, Terry K. *Ohio's Grand Canal: A Brief History of the Ohio and Erie Canal*. Kent, OH: Kent State University Press, 2008.

Woodward, Earl F. "Internal Improvements in Texas in the Early 1850's." *Southwestern Historical Quarterly* 76, no. 2 (October 1972): 161–82.

Worster, Donald. *Nature's Economy: A History of Ecological Ideas.* New York: Cambridge University Press, 1994.

———. *Rivers of Empire: Water, Aridity, and the Growth of the American West.* New York: Oxford University Press, 1992.

Index

Page numbers in italic text indicate illustrations.